African Womanhood in Colonial Kenya

1900–50

EASTERN AFRICAN STUDIES

Revealing Prophets
Edited by DAVID M. ANDERSON & DOUGLAS H. JOHNSON

East African Expressions of Christianity
Edited by THOMAS SPEAR & ISARIA N. KIMAMBO

The Poor Are Not Us
Edited by DAVID M. ANDERSON & VIGDIS BROCH-DUE

Potent Brews
JUSTIN WILLIS

Swahili Origins
JAMES DE VERE ALLEN

Being Maasai
Edited by THOMAS SPEAR & RICHARD WALLER

Jua Kali Kenya
KENNETH KING

Control & Crisis in Colonial Kenya
BRUCE BERMAN

Unhappy Valley
Book One: State & Class
Book Two: Violence & Ethnicity
BRUCE BERMAN & JOHN LONSDALE

Mau Mau from Below
GREET KERSHAW

The Mau Mau War in Perspective
FRANK FUREDI

Squatters & the Roots of Mau Mau 1905–63
TABITHA KANOGO

Economic & Social Origins of Mau Mau 1945–53
DAVID W. THROUP

Multi-Party Politics in Kenya
DAVID W. THROUP & CHARLES HORNSBY

Empire State-Building
JOANNA LEWIS

Decolonization & Independence in Kenya 1940–93
Edited by B.A. OGOT & WILLIAM R. OCHIENG'

Eroding the Commons
DAVID ANDERSON

Penetration & Protest in Tanzania
ISARIA N. KIMAMBO

Custodians of the Land
Edited by GREGORY MADDOX, JAMES L. GIBLIN & ISARIA N. KIMAMBO

Education in the Development of Tanzania 1919–1990
LENE BUCHERT

The Second Economy in Tanzania
T.L. MALIYAMKONO & M.S.D. BAGACHWA

Ecology Control & Economic Development in East African History
HELGE KJEKSHUS

Siaya
DAVID WILLIAM COHEN & E.S. ATIENO ODHIAMBO

Uganda Now • Changing Uganda Developing Uganda • From Chaos to Order Religion & Politics in East Africa
Edited by HOLGER BERNT HANSEN & MICHAEL TWADDLE

Kakungulu & the Creation of Uganda 1868–1928
MICHAEL TWADDLE

Controlling Anger
SUZETTE HEALD

Kampala Women Getting By
SANDRA WALLMAN

Political Power in Pre-Colonial Buganda
RICHARD J. REID

Alice Lakwena & the Holy Spirits
HEIKE BEHREND

Slaves, Spices & Ivory in Zanzibar
ABDUL SHERIFF

Zanzibar Under Colonial Rule
Edited by ABDUL SHERIFF & ED FERGUSON

The History & Conservation of Zanzibar Stone Town
Edited by ABDUL SHERIFF

Pastimes & Politics
LAURA FAIR

Ethnicity & Conflict in the Horn of Africa
Edited by KATSUYOSHI FUKUI & JOHN MARKAKIS

Conflict, Age & Power in North East Africa
Edited by EISEI KURIMOTO & SIMON SIMONSE

Property Rights & Political Development in Ethiopia & Eritrea
SANDRA FULLERTON JOIREMAN

Revolution & Religion in Ethiopia
ØYVIND M. EIDE

Brothers at War
Tekeste Negash & KJETIL TRONVOLL

From Guerrillas to Government
DAVID POOL

Mau Mau & Nationhood
Edited by E.S. ATIENO ODHIAMBO & JOHN LONSDALE

A History of Modern Ethiopia, 1855–1991
Second edition
BAHRU ZEWDE

Pioneers of Change in Ethiopia
BAHRU ZEWDE

Remapping Ethiopia
Edited by W. JAMES, D. DONHAM, E. KURIMOTO & A. TRIULZI

Southern Marches of Imperial Ethiopia
Edited by DONALD L. DONHAM & WENDY JAMES

A Modern History of the Somali
Fourth edition
I.M. LEWIS

Islands of Intensive Agriculture in East Africa
Edited by MATS WIDGREN & JOHN E.G. SUTTON

Leaf of Allah
EZEKIEL GEBISSA

Dhows & the Colonial Economy of Zanzibar 1860–1970
ERIK GILBERT

African Womanhood in Colonial Kenya
TABITHA KANOGO

*In Search of a Nation**
Edited by GREGORY H. MADDOX & JAMES L. GIBLIN

*A History of the Excluded**
JAMES L. GIBLIN

*Crisis & Decline in Bunyoro**
SHANE DOYLE

*African Underclass**
ANDREW BURTON

* forthcoming

African Womanhood in Colonial Kenya
1900–50

TABITHA KANOGO
Associate Professor of History
University of California at Berkeley

James Currey
OXFORD
EAEP
NAIROBI
Ohio University Press
ATHENS

James Currey Ltd
73 Botley Road
Oxford
OX2 0BS

East African Educational Publishers
PO Box 45314
Nairobi

Ohio University Press
19 Circle Drive, The Ridges
Athens, Ohio 45701

First published 2005

2 3 4 5 6 11 10 09 08 07

British Library Cataloguing in Publication Data

Kanogo, Tabitha

African womanhood in colonial Kenya, 1900-50 . - (Eastern African studies)
1. Women - Kenya - Social conditions - 20th century 2. Women - legal status, laws, etc. - Kenya - History - 2oth century
3. Indigenous peoples - Great Britain - Colonies 4. Kenya - Social conditions - 20th century
I. Title
305.4'2'096762'09041

ISBN 978-0-85255-446-3 (James Currey Cloth)
978-0-85255-445-6 (James Currey Paper)

Library of Congress Cataloging-in-Publication Data available on request

ISBN 978-0-8214-1567-2 (Ohio University Press Cloth)
978-0-8214-1568-9 (Ohio University Press Paper)

Typeset in 10/11 pt Baskerville
by Longhouse Publishing Services, Cumbria, UK
Printed and bound in Malaysia

Contents

Acknowledgments vi
Abbreviations viii
Glossary ix
Map x
Photographs xi

Introduction 1

1
'Capax Doli'?
Debating the Legal Status of African Women 15

2
Sexuality in Culture & Law 42

3
Becoming Kavirondo
Clitoridectomy, Ethnicity & Womanhood 73

4
Debating Dowry
'A Daughter is Like a Bank' 104

5
Legislating Marriage 129

6
The Medicalization & Regulation of Maternity 164

7
Girls are Frogs
Girls, Missions & Education 197

Conclusion 239

Appendix: Dowries 247
Bibliography 252
Index 261

Acknowledgements

I have incurred many debts in the process of writing this book. Its preparation would have been impossible without the financial support from different sources at the University of California, Berkeley. Seed money from the Department of History and a grant from the Committee on Research enabled me to carry out field and archival research in Kenya. Funds from the Shepard Grant at the History Department paid for the transcription of the Kikuyu oral interview tapes. I am grateful for this support.

Eric Aseka, Nici Nelson, and Muigai wa Gachanja read various chapters of earlier drafts and made many constructive suggestions. Nadine Tanio and Raj Arunachalam each read the entire manuscript and offered invaluable comments. My students in the last four years have helped me clarify my thoughts and ideas on various issues discussed in the book. I am very grateful to each and every one of you.

I have benefited from the assistance of many more people. Durba Ghosh and Sydney Johnson were ingenious research assistants in the summer of 1996. Julia O'Byrne helped with the index. Professor Eric Aseka, Duncan Kang'ethe, Murunga, and Njeri Karuru helped to conduct field interviews and transcribe some of the tapes at different points of this project. It is intended to deposit copies of the tapes at the Department of History, Kenyatta University. Peter Munano Kagucia doggedly but cheerfully transcribed all the Kikuyu tapes. Gail Abbey and B. D. Howard helped with the preparation of the bibliography.

Staff at the following libraries and archives were very courteous: the Kenya National Archives, Kenyatta University, University of Nairobi, Institute for Development Studies Library, Nairobi, the Rhodes House and Queen Elizabeth House Libraries in Oxford. At QEH, Gill Short offered a good balance of professional help and friendship.

I am most indebted to all those women and men who graciously gave of their time and knowledge during long interview sessions. They provided data without which this book would not have been written. I am humbled by their generosity of spirit, hospitality, and commitment to the education of inquisitive researchers and future generations. I hope this book has captured some of their knowledge, insight and wisdom. I take full responsibility for inadequacies of the text.

I wish to thank faculty at the Department of History, University of California, Berkeley, for their continued support since I joined the department. Working with and among them continues to be very inspiring. They are wonderful colleagues. In particular I wish to thank the late Robert Brentano for his warm encouragement throughout the preparation of this work. Professor Paula Fass has been a great source of inspiration.

I would have been totally lost without patient and vital help from Gail Phillips and Nadine Ghammache. Deciphering baffling computer glitches, Gail and Nadine have rendered unfailing support. I am also grateful to Bud Bynnack.

Many friends in diverse corners of the globe have made the long gestation of this book an enriching experience. In particular I wish to thank Jan and Emma Kolaas, Celia Nyamweru, Ciarunji Chesaina, Teresia Hinga, Valerie Kibera, Margaret Anaminyi, Njambi Kahahu, Peter Kimball, Njeri Komo, Kwamboka Okare, and Inez Sutton for unfailing support and good humour. Professor Dick Herr and his wife Valerie have been very kind hosts on numerous occasions. To all of you, *asante sana*, thank you very much.

Alone, in a category of his own, is James Currey who has waited patiently as every deadline for the submission of this manuscript lapsed and a new one was set. Thank you for your personal commitment to African scholarship, especially Eastern African Studies. I hope this book will in a small way add to our understanding of Kenya. Monica McCormick of the University of California Press joined James Currey in facilitating the completion of this work. I appreciate your support.

Last but not least, I wish to acknowledge the great support that my family has continued to give me. I owe my mother Mary Wanjiku Kanogo Gichomo, my sisters Njoki, Wanjiru, Wairimu, Wangare, Wangui, Njeri, Phyllis, Wambui, and my brother Wanjohi more than words can express. This book is written for them, and in memory of three wonderful people, my father, James Kanogo Gichomo, Jane Awinja Anaminyi Nandwa and Beth Wambui Nduati.

Berkeley, California

List of Abbreviations

Afr.	Africa
AG	Attorney General
AIM	African Inland Mission
CMS	Church Missionary Society
CENT	Central Province
CNC	Chief Native Commissioner
CP	Central Province
CSM	Church of Scotland Mission
DC	District Commissioner
DO	District Officer
EAS	*East African Standard* (newspaper)
FH	Fort Hall (Murang'a)
KBU	Kiambu/Kyambu
KCA	Kikuyu Central Association
KNA	Kenya National Archives
KPP	Kikuyu Progressive Party
Lab.	Department of Labour
LNC	Local Native Council
NKU	Nakuru
NN	North Nyanza
NZA	Nyanza
NYI	Nyeri
Mss	Manuscript
PCEA	Presbyterian Church of East Africa
PC	Provincial Commissioner
RH	Rhodes House Library, Oxford, England.
RVP	Rift Valley Province
SDA	Seventh Day Adventist Church

Glossary

baraza	public meeting
boma	homestead
bure	useless, free
dukas	shops
elmoran	a circumcised unmarried man of the junior warrior grade
gakuo	dress, in its diminutive form
icakamuyu	divorcee among the Kikuyu
irua	circumcision ritual
kayama ya tembo	a measure of traditional beer
kipkondit	a Kipsigis man who inherits a widow
kirigu	an uncircumcised Kikuyu girl
litiri	burial hut for an unmarried woman (spinster)
meko	bride abduction among the Luo
misheni	mission, mission adherents
motiri	an initiate's sponsor
mukene	an unmarried but circumcised young woman among the Meru
mukoma ndi	a loose, unmarried and pregnant woman
muruithia	the circumcisor
omukoko	divorcee among the Wanga
pai-ke	free public or private sexual liaisons established by widowed Kipsigis women
pim	elderly Luo woman entrusted with the rearing of children and adolescents
shenzi	uncouth
shuka	an unstitched piece of cloth
sufuria	aluminium sauce pans
thaka	an unmarried circumcised young man among the Meru
wali	islamic leader
watu wa mungu	literally people of God; religious sect

Kenya: Administrative regions

Based on a map from W. R. Ochieng' & R.M. Maxon (eds) *An Economic History of Kenya*. Nairobi: East African Educational Publishers, 1992, p. viii

All photographs in this section reproduced with the kind permission of the Kenya National Archive (ARA/7/1 Church of Scotland Mission Reports from 1922 to 1959)

Kairo, a Christian wife, married to a Christian, holding a baby. (Chogoria, 1922–27)

Women at a market. They have brought beans, maize, potatoes, etc. to sell. (Chogoria, 1930)

Kanja, a leper, is lingering near the Chogoria Mission/ Hospital in hope of seeing her two children whom she had been persuaded to entrust to the mission to protect them from catching leprosy. (Chogoria, 1930).

Two girl boarders holding a board calling for prayer for £400 for the construction of a dormitory for girls on this plot. (Chogoria, 1936)

Hospital staff, all Christians (left to right) two clothes washers, Jakubu the cook, Jemima and Damari of the maternity ward, Jusufu, Mariko, Justo, all dressers in charge of wards, Jackson the dispenser, Henry a dresser, and Jason. (Chogoria, 1936)

Teacher trainee girls. Instructor Miss Hood is at the back. (Chogoria, 1937)

Women's Bible Class on Sunday morning before the service. (Chogoria, 1937)

Judith and Johnstone are seen here after their wedding. Judith stood out against and ultimately broke down her father's opposition to her marriage uninitiated. (Chogoria, 1939)

Mrs Grieve is seen with her senior class in domestic science at practice cooking 'under African conditions'. (Chogoria, 1946)

New Girls' Boarding School. (Chogoria, 1950)

Miss Ruth Arthur, the first woman in Kenya to attain the 'T2' teaching qualification. Seen here in girl guides uniform, she represented the Girl Guides of all Kenya at the Girl Guide Rally at Adelboden in Switzerland in summer 1951. (Chogoria, 1951)

Wedding of a hospital nurse to a teacher. (Chogoria, 1951)

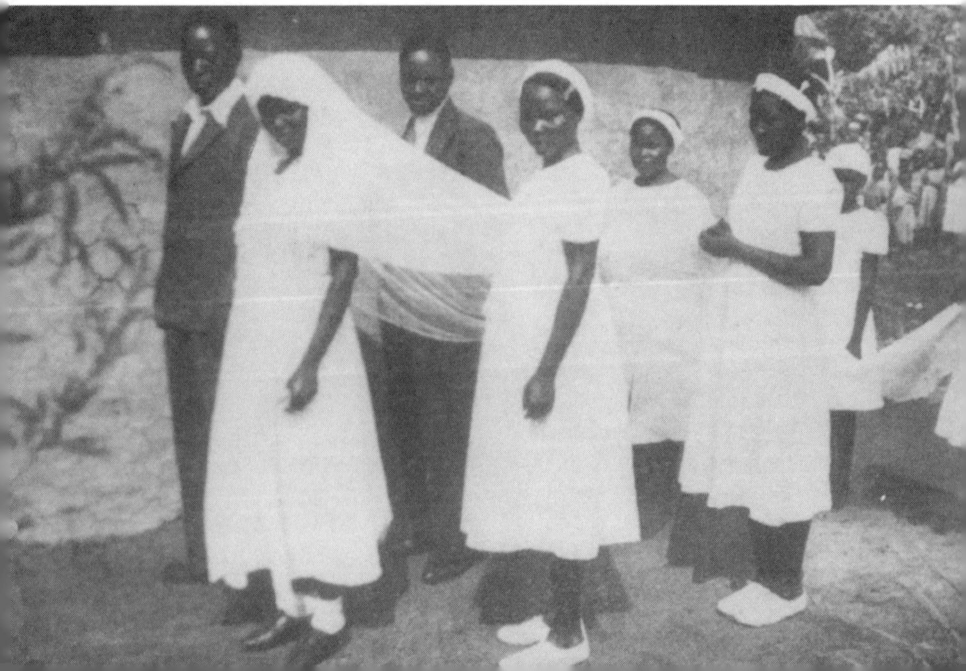

Introduction

> The Kikuyu [women] were remarkably adept at creating place for themselves in the colonial enterprise.
> David P. Sandgren, *Christianity and the Kikuyu* [1]

> In those days, it was customary for a widow to dance on a husband's graveyard. If the woman had had any relationships outside wedlock, she did not survive this dance. This belief made women to be very careful.
> Aggrey Ham Wanzetse, 27 January, 1997[2]

This book explores the history of African womanhood in colonial Kenya. By focussing on key sociocultural institutions and practices around which the lives of women were organized, and on the protracted debates that surrounded these institutions and practices during the colonial period, it investigates the nature of indigenous, mission, and colonial control of African women. The pertinent institutions and practices include the legal and cultural status of women, clitoridectomy, dowry, marriage, maternity and motherhood, and formal education. By following the effects of the all-pervasive ideological shifts that colonialism produced in the lives of women, the study investigates the diverse ways in which a woman's personhood was enhanced, diminished, or placed in ambiguous predicaments by the consequences, intended and unintended, of colonial rule as administered by both the colonizers and the colonized. The study thus tries to historicize the reworkings of women's lives under colonial rule. The transformations that resulted from these reworkings involved the negotiation and redefinition of the meaning of individual liberties and of women's agency, along with the reconceptualization of kinship relations and of community.

These changes resulted in – and often resulted from – increased mobility for Kenyan women, who were enabled to cross physical, cultural, economic, social, and psychological frontiers that had been closed to them prior to colonial rule. The conclusion to which the experiences of women in colonial Kenya points again and again is that for these women, the exercise of individual agency, whether it was newly acquired or repeatedly thwarted, depended in large measure on the unleashing of forces over which no one involved had control. Over and over, women found opportunities to act amid the conflicting policies, unintended consequences, and inconsistent compromises that characterized colonial rule. In diverse ways, individuals thus were both shaped and empowered to redefine themselves by the confluence of a host of new dynamics. Even as colonial administrators, indigenous patriarchal authorities, and missionaries sought increased control over the central elements of Kenyan women's lives, the colonial situation gave latitude to the individual in an unprecedented manner. While most of the processes disrupting the old precolonial order were seen as unavoidable contingencies of the colonial process, responses to these changes were tension-ridden, gendered, and fissured.

More often than not, travel and modernity were deemed responsible for women's unacceptable abandonment of 'traditional' obligations, roles, and spaces. Amid rapid changes, appropriate gender spaces, roles, and identities for women were reformulated, a process that women themselves tried to control. In diverse situations, women adopted negotiated solutions, outrightly violated conventional norms, or adopted novel responses to intractable problems.

Tensions often arose from the perceived loss of control by both the indigenous societies and colonizing agencies over girls and women's morality, sexuality, physical and socioeconomic mobility. Thus, concerns over clitoridectomy, dowry, some aspects of maternity, and the attainment of formal education were all debated in the context of women as threatened social capital. These debates emphasized the centrality of women in the crafting of marital, kinship, and ethnic cohesiveness and the ways in which modernity was rapidly eroding notions of social order. The interface between gender, ethnicity, customary law, and modernity was very conflicted. Forces of historical change during the colonial period thus precipitated a rethinking of the status and role of women within society. A variety of competing visions of women contended throughout the colonial period. 'Womanhood' thus became a battleground where issues of modernization, tradition, change, and personal independence were fought.

These issues included pervasive contestations over gendered notions of conformity, respectability, morality, citizenship, cultural identity, and social order. Ultimately, what emerged was a multiplicity of constructions and reworkings of gender roles and identities among African women in a period during which such roles and identities became deeply fractured and fluid. In particular, women's constructions of self as they accessed new normative and spatial options in colonial Kenya became important markers of women's agency. In what follows, the life histories of individual women give voice and immediacy to these experiences.

The territory that came to be known as Kenya became a British Protectorate in 1895. In 1920 the region was declared a colony, a status it retained till December 12, 1963 when Kenya regained its independence from Britain. Despite its brief duration, colonialism resulted in a massive transformation of the social, economic, and political livelihoods of societies therein. Conquest was violent and once established, the colonial regime was sustained by coercion.[3] From a predominantly precapitalist economy of numerous independent pastoralists, cultivators, and mixed farmers, the region was transformed into a racially stratified white settler colony where large settler plantations operated alongside peasant holdings.

Land alienation for white settlers, taxation, labour migrancy, urbanization, and missionary activities produced extensive social and economic changes. Acute inequalities along racial lines were replicated among Africans as social differentiation expanded, spurred by the commercialization of land, commodity production, and indigenous participation in other aspects of the colonial economy including the transportation sector, and waged labour. Formal education, largely provided by missionaries, became a vehicle not only for vocational training and job acquisition, but also an instrument of social mobility and cultural shift.[4] In Kenya, as in most colonial states, only men initially accessed most of these highly transformative spaces.

The juxtaposition of British common law and customary law, and the establishment of the Dual Policy complicated the day-to-day lives of Africans in myriads of ways. While Africans were denied elective representation till the late 1950s, indigenous authority structures were bolstered with the introduction of Native Tribunals, and Local Native Councils, both of which were entrusted with the broad tasks of arbitration and deliberating on matters affecting Africans mostly resident in rural areas. European colonial administrators would oversee the activities of the African functionaries. Amidst all the swirling social, cultural, economic, and political changes that were taking place, these colonial instruments found it difficult to maintain social order. The movement of people and ideas created unstable situations that did not lend themselves easily to either precolonial or colonial sensibilities. Institutions like marriage, bridewealth, maternity, and motherhood were subjected to new pressures. Gender sensibilities too were transgressed. Being a woman in the highly gendered colonial spaces precipitated a plethora of conflicts, contradictions and negotiations.[5]

In some respects, the lives of African girls and women attained the substance of public spectacle, performative existences that were subject to public surveillance and sanction. The occasions were numerous. They might include a recently widowed woman having to dance on her husband's grave to prove her fidelity during her marriage to the deceased migrant labourer[6] or the physical examination of girls' genitalia by male officials at the ritual ground to ascertain adherence to minor clitoridectomy. It might also relate to the removal of an 'undocumented' and unaccompanied rural woman from a Nairobi-bound vehicle or the abduction of someone from a mission-school dining hall at Kikuyu and her removal to the White Highlands for the clitoridectomy excision. The juxtaposition of precolonial sensibilities and colonial situations created fragile attempts to maintain the status quo. Uneasy alliances emerged between various official and unofficial groups that were determined to shape the lives of African girls and women. Women and girls became wards of a host of patrons who nevertheless did not always see eye to eye regarding the roles and status of their wards within the new colonial order. Girls and women did not always conform to the designs of their patrons. The juxtaposition of precolonial sensibilities and colonial situations also emphasized both continuities from the precolonial period and the changes in women's agency, social standing, and identity during the colonial period.

The emergence of individualism among Kenyan girls and women during the colonial period was not a comfortable process. Whether it was the mission girl who refused to undergo clitoridectomy, or the unexcised Kipsigis girl who gave birth in a mission hospital, both had to negotiate alternative social networks, even as they adopted new identities. The same applied to the runaway wife, the mission student, the widow who had married under statutory law, and the mission woman whose father demanded exorbitant bride price. Seemingly liberating migrations across old boundaries engendered other drawbacks. For the majority of these women, the social cost of such normative or spatial migrations could be extensive.

For the majority of women who underwent the process, such transgression of old boundaries did not entail a complete severing of contact with their rural kinsmen and cultural sensibilities. Although straddling customary and colonial beliefs and values, adopting new religions affiliations, acquiring new skills, and employing newly available legal strategies might enable the women to manage their lives relatively better, in many situations, it remained necessary to defer to moral economies that they had ostensibly left behind. Rather than transferring their total allegiance from one authority structure to another, women undertook multiple engagements with diverse institutions and authority figures. While a woman might find support from one such source on a particular matter, it was not unusual for her to be opposed to other strategies espoused by the same locus of authority. Even as they questioned and rejected some indigenous institutions and beliefs, women might nevertheless express dismay against missions, Local Native Councils, maternity hospitals, school authorities, and matriarchs, peers, and family members. Kenyan women and girls navigated a complex social map that held many twists and turns. There was no linear progression in the life narratives of girls and women. Ultimately, therefore, what emerges is not a linear narrative regarding how 'Kenyan women', as a group, resolved any one issue, but a representation of the conflicts, contradictions, and negotiations that each situation elicited.

The actions and experiences of the colonizers were scarcely any more consistent. 'Colonialism' in Kenya was anything but monolithic. For one thing, Western values at times took a back seat to the effort to cater to indigenous sensibilities. Colonial officials did not always want to implement legislation that might antagonize elders. In the great scheme of indirect rule, in which colonial officials directly administered urban areas, while the rural areas were entrusted to several layers of indigenous authorities, including native tribunals, Local Native Councils, and Elders' Councils, the colonial administrators were heavily dependent upon the goodwill of the indigenous authorities. In the absence of established legislation, and amid attempts to formulate such legislation, colonial officials did not always give these authorities the guidance or leadership expected of them. They frequently were groping for ways to preserve order and stability while also upholding the overall furtherance of 'civilization'. They did not always have answers that would satisfy all the interested parties.

On the other hand, some colonial administrators sought to eradicate some of the norms, practices, or sanctions that the indigenous communities enforced for the maintenance of social order. While the majority of elders believed they had the basic normative and customary law necessary to deal with ordinary daily domestic and other disorders, a number of them were also inducted into a process that would reformulate some of the ground rules. The precolonial sensibilities, which the elders espoused, did not always succeed in the unfamiliar colonial terrain. Sometimes new positions were adopted or old ones reworked. Without giving in totally to the new, elders tried to enlist the help of colonial officials to control African women and girls. That in general the contenders did not always see eye to eye with regard to their perception of the legal and social status of women quite obviously compounded an already intricate situation. That did not stop the evolution of extensive cooperation between colonial administrators, missionaries, and indigenous authorities in their varied attempts and partial successes in their efforts to control colonial Kenyan women's movement across spatial, gender, legal, ideological, and sociocultural boundaries.

All these cooperating interests increasingly emphasized domesticity, the control of sexuality, and the need to stabilize the family as paradigms of constructing women in colonial Africa.[7] However, because of cultural differences, conflicts of objectives and ideologies, and resistance from the colonized, both male and female, these groups often held disparate ideas on most issues, including constructions of gender. The result, with regard to most issues affecting women, was not the simple and uniform imposition of hegemonic rules and requirements, but inconclusive contests that lingered for decades, even as women confronted conflictual situations on a daily basis. And even as the general status of girls and women was being discussed, decisions continued to be made on individual cases as they arose. Although efforts to create notions of womanhood acceptable to all interested parties lasted throughout the colonial period, these decisions did not always provide precedents. Neither were they well-informed decisions. Consequently, women had to deal with discrepant and ad hoc decisions whose inadequacies were evident as soon as they were made.

In diverse, ingenious ways, some women recognized and 'rode' the swirling currents of colonialism while others experienced constraining restrictions. Within the first decade of colonial rule, the line separating order and normal everyday life from disorder became very thin. In a rapidly changing environment where various aspects of life became negotiable, culture, and in particular customary law, became 'an arena for debates about social morality, and advancement of citizenship'.[8] Cultural roles were contested and brokered in areas of heterogeneous populations where economic opportunities attracted migrants.[9] These included mission stations, schools, urban areas or rural venues of employment, including both rural townships and European settler plantations. In the context of the opportunities and restrictions that appeared in the course of these negotiations, women, along with other parties, initiated and at times tried to manage some of these historical changes.

By investigating the interactions between the parties described, we can begin to chart the parameters of conflict, contestation, cultural migrations, and 'normalizing' legislation that depict the multiple constructs of African girls and women. Some of these conversations occurred in official, institutional settings, and this study incorporates extensive deliberations of Local Native Councils. Concern over the erosion of patriarchal authority, the constitution and significance of bridewealth, diverse marriage-related issues, clitoridectomy, and the provision of maternity services loomed large in these deliberations, which excluded female voices.[10] However, the study also incorporates wherever possible the voices of the women themselves. Oral case histories supplement the archival data to represent the diverse ways in which African women were perceived, constructed, and affected in public and private, official, and unofficial domains. They also represent women's voices reflecting on the forces that shaped their lives.

Colonial Spaces and Women Travellers

There was widespread belief that the onset of the colonial presence interrupted a sheltered, isolated, and idyllic life in the villages.[11] This 'sense of rootedness' and social well-being of communities was put in jeopardy during the colonial period. Cultural order was represented as being synonymous with spatial locatedness.

In this world, women's travel traditionally was limited largely to visiting kinsmen and friends, the majority of whom lived within a day's travel. The most frequent and adventurous travels undertaken by girls and women in precolonial Kenya were for marriage, trade, and social journeys;[12] all were carefully arranged and kin-controlled. With the advent of colonial rule, this domestic inscription of space became increasingly untenable. Cases of runaway women and girls were most disturbing to the indigenous community, especially because the women were off to places and distances heretofore unknown – colonial spaces. They included missions, docks, urban centers, settler farms, and distant rural areas that offered a whole range of new and problematic possibilities.[13] In a social fabric so tightly woven, the unraveling of this one thread, control over physical space, began a process that resulted in the loosening of the whole, while also opening up new normative spaces for women.

In colonial Kenya, travel mediated shifts in economic, social, cultural, and legal domains for most people. Labour migrancy removed thousands of workers, mostly men and sometimes whole families, from the rural African reservations to the centres of employment. Young people also travelled long distances to missionary centres where formal education, vocational training, Western medicine, and Christianity were available. These new domains held heterogeneous populations representing diverse cultural, material, and religious moralities. The emergent colonial state and its agents, too, introduced new moralities. The migrant who went to any of these centres for any length of time returned to the village a changed person. An individual's economic opportunities, patterns of consumption, attire, religion, ideals, values, and language might undergo drastic transformation.[14] Travel, even for waged employment, opened a Pandora's box. That was more so in the case of women and girls.

Consider, for example, the effect that changes in attire, enabled by travel, had on the perception of women. The District Commissioner (DC) for Central Kavirondo observed that in 1912, 'it was the exception to meet a clothed man or woman, most had not the proverbial bead and bootlace.' Then, 'From complete nudity or skins we came to the blanket, pieces of americani and dyed Indian cloth'.[15] And by 1927, the DC for Kakamega was observing that at least 50 percent of Africans in North Kavirondo wore some kind of European clothing. By 1927, 'short brightly coloured dresses [are now] worn by very many native girls and young women. The great majority wears coloured handkerchiefs as headdresses, very few wear stockings or shoes. Recently a demand for underwear of European design but a cheap[er] material has commenced. A few women in Kisumu wear high heeled shoes and stockings and occasionally hats of European design.'[16]

Clothes signified a whole range of perceptions, and transitions. According to Mzee Elijah Mbeketha, 'Elders of an earlier period thought that any woman in [Western] dresses was a prostitute. They did not differentiate between Christianity and prostitution. They did not even know that those wearing clothes might be Swahili … they might even be Swahili of upcountry origin … including Kamba who had converted to the Islamic faith.'[17] Female protégées who embraced Western Christianity, Western dresses, and education (almost always in that order), were prime candidates for the prostitute label and accusations of immorality.

Travel to urban centres in and of itself tended to label a woman as a prostitute. Rural legislators advocated the prohibition of African women from going to Nairobi to sell produce 'as it leads to prostitution and disease'.[18] It did not seem necessary to establish whether the women were guilty; they were considered so by virtue of being in an urban area unaccompanied, or without permission, from a male in a position of authority, public or private. Increasingly, women who wanted to travel needed to demonstrate that they had written or verbal permission from a range of patriarchs including fathers, husbands, guardians, chiefs, or headmen allowing them to leave their home areas. They were also required to have legitimate reasons for visiting urban areas.

As Mzee Elijah Mbeketha also pointed out, travel and Western attire tended to confuse ethnic identities previously tied to indigenous communities. 'As far as my father was concerned,' Mary Wanjiru said, 'you could not purchase a new sheet, *shuka* (unstitched cloth) and wear it in that state … .You had to hide it until such time that you had dyed it with ochre' to give it the brownish orange colour that was common to the treated skins worn by the majority of the population.[19] Mary's father believed that proper clothing reinforced Kikuyu culture. He described himself as a true Kikuyu, opposed to Christianity, education, and Western dresses. Mission girls learnt very quickly how to cope with community beliefs about dress and ethnicity. As Monica Wanjiku Wandura observed, 'After school, one would remove the school uniform and put on *shuka* so that one's Kikuyu customs did not disappear.'[20]

During the first two decades of colonial presence in Kenya, the most frequent litany of inquiries, complaints, warnings, pleas, and deliberations between indigenous authority structures, colonial administrators, missionaries, and Islamic leaders related to untoward migrations of upcountry African women and girls. These movements were not just spatial, from place to place, but migrations from traditional conceptions of the nature and role of women to new ways of being Kenyan women made possible by the exigencies of colonial rule. In some cases, women embraced tradition with renewed enthusiasm.

In his essay 'Travelling Cultures', on the issue of travelling women in the West, James Clifford notes that there too, travelling was largely a man's preoccupation. He observes that 'good travel' (heroic, educational, scientific, adventurous, ennobling,) is something men (should) do. Women are impeded from serious travel. Some of them go to distant places but as companions or as 'exceptions' – figures like Mary Kingsley, Freya Stark, or Flora Tristan.[21] The women who travelled, Clifford observes, were 'forced to conform, masquerade, or rebel discreetly within a set of normatively male definitions and experiences'. Travel was inscribed with gender, and with spatial, racial, class, cultural, and moral markers. Both travel and modernity entailed exploring and sampling new experiences.[22]

In colonial Kenya, as in Europe, migrations of the body more often than not resulted in migrations of the mind, the heart, the psyche, and of the financial and legal personhood of the individual. Travelling and travelled women acquired a sense of agency, constructed and negotiated new roles, identities, and spaces for themselves. In Kenya it was easier to legislate against certain types of physical movement than against the overall effects of ideological, cultural, moral, and legal migrations. These were demonstrably difficult to arrest and became highly contested domains of women's lives.

The dislocations that came with colonial intervention elicited contradictory responses from a wide spectrum of constituencies. Men who occupied traditional authority structures complained of difficulties in controlling women who 'abandoned' their marital or natal homes in the reservations without the permission of various members of their families. Such errant women were accused of ignoring established social obligations in the productive and reproductive spheres. Yet both the missionaries and the colonial administrators expected and demanded that the fathers of the candidates renounce their rights over their daughters, especially when parents attempted to remove them from mission stations. Both the parents and the missions claimed the right to wardship, however, a process that placed the girls in a difficult situation. The effort to 'localize' girls and women, to keep them in bounded spaces at a time of great spatial, cultural, and economic fluidity and mobility thus became a contested process. Bodies, women's bodies, became sites for control, resistance, and negotiation.

Any unsanctioned movement by women threatened the elders' control of social capital. This related to the control of women's productive and reproductive labour, female sexuality, bridewealth acquisition and distribution, domestic and societal authority structures, gender relations, and social order. More importantly, from the women's perspective, these movements questioned and began to redefine indigenous gender constructs, cultural identities, and the very foundation on which African societies were based.

Such changes also alarmed the colonizers, who perceived them as evidence of social disequilibrium. It was deemed necessary to draw boundaries that would restore and sustain a semblance of what they took to be 'normal' as much as was possible in the fluid situation that the colonial situation precipitated. Girls and women seemed to cross those boundaries with impunity as they seized their options, expanded, and at times transformed their identities and roles. In so doing, they defied a multiplicity of authority structures.

The creation of order and hierarchy was a major colonial project.[23] In this regard, Channock (1985) and Mann and Roberts (1991) have illustrated the process of the reinvention of tradition, the codification of customary law, and its operation in courts of law alongside statutory and common law.[24] In colonial Kenya, the control of women's normative and geographical mobility fell under these broad efforts to create and enforce hierarchy and order. The process involved redefinitions and reworkings of the meaning of individual liberties and of notions of home, community, lineage, marriage, work, authority, and property, among other concerns.[25] Representations of African women as perpetual legal minors, chattels, exploited beasts of burden, not too intelligent, gossiping,[26] giggling, idle, shy, vulnerable, and dependent social victims, were countered by increasing complaints about unacceptable behaviour on the part of women.[27] This behaviour included the exploration of, and encounter with difference, experimentation, expansion, lawlessness, individualism, encounter with danger, access to diverse resources, legitimation, and creative imagination made possible by women's new ability to move across boundaries that with the advent of colonialism had become permeable.

The counter-discourses of women engaged in these activities became increasingly difficult to silence. As has already been noted, this work incorporates the voices of both ordinary and elite women who recall their experiences during the contentious times of the colonial period.[28] It attempts to examine some of the narratives, interpretations, and multiplicity of voices regarding the shifting experiences of women's lives in colonial Kenya. At the same time, however, oral and archival texts are also used here to recreate the voices of others who have not had the opportunity to be heard. These are laden with hidden transcripts and silences symptomatic of hierarchies of authority and mediation. It is therefore necessarily the case that, while it is possible, via the interviews undertaken for this project to give voice to some of the women who experienced these transformations, in many instances, it has been inevitable that what happened to women, and what they had to say for themselves, has to be reconstructed from texts produced by institutions in which the voices of women were silenced. That, as any historian knows, is a frustrating process, because the evidence can provide only intimations of what these women, if they could have spoken for themselves, could have told us.

In colonial Kenya, mobility, in its various ramifications became a genderized and hegemonic process. This created gendered and hence contestable notions of conformity, identity and respectability, social order, and ultimately, womanhood. By examining a variety of case histories of such migrants, we hope to chart the shifts in cultural, social, legal, and to a limited extent, economic experiences in the lives of the women and their families. This study, then, by tracing the permeability of cultural boundaries and the fragmented mask of gender in colonial Kenya, ultimately traces the development of women's consciousness in a setting that both encouraged and discouraged it and its articulation.

Law and Culture in Kenyan Women's Lives

A wide range of overlapping and often conflicting institutions, practices, and beliefs provided limits and opportunities, boundaries and open spaces, in colonial Kenya. To examine the ways in which women's lives were affected by these changing circumstances requires frequent shifts in focus. Hence the analysis shifts from general overviews of the ways in which both law and culture defined the status of women in the colonial era, to examinations of particular aspects characteristic of how women lived and found new ways to live under these two pressures, old and new.

Chapters 1 and 2 survey the overall legal and sociocultural status of indigenous Kenyan women in the period between roughly 1900 and 1950. Chapter 1 highlights the dilemmas regarding the contractual capacity of women as a result of colonial efforts to impose formal legal definitions concerning issues affecting the identity and agency of women on top of existing customary laws and practices and religious codes. It also explores some of the ways in which women were able to exploit the cracks opened up by those efforts in order to migrate to new spaces where both legally and culturally they could enjoy benefits previously denied to them.

Chapter 2 explores the same territory from an adjacent point of view, that of society and culture. It maps out social and cultural sensibilities regarding gender relations on the eve of and during the decades following the imposition of colonial rule and demonstrates the discrepant social positioning of women. While recognizing their agency on certain issues, indigenous communities generally subsumed women under community and kinship structures, a factor which in certain respects reduced women's individual agency. By examining the moral economies and cultural assumptions underlying such processes as pawning of women, the status of sexual transgressions and immorality including rape, premarital sex and pregnancy, and wife inheritance, the chapter illustrates societal ambiguity regarding the personhood of women. This chapter thus expands the discussion of women's mobility and self-assertion, most particularly by focusing on the domain of sexuality and the control of sexual activity among young women.

Chapter 3 narrows that focus further to concentrate on a central institution that for many defined not only a woman's sexual identity, but also her ethnicity and that of her community – clitoridectomy. Efforts to criminalize or at least to regulate clitoridectomy by missionaries and colonial administrators resulted in intensive, graphic, and public discussions about the refashioning of female genitalia, transforming private anatomy into a public site for contestation, negotiation, and prescription. One result of the clitoridectomy controversy was that, despite administrative efforts to medicalize and politicize the procedure, resistance to efforts to curtail it grew. The chapter explores the role of clitoridectomy in the construction of Kenyan women's identities and the reasons underlying indigenous resistance to its abolition.

Chapter 4 explores another institution central to the construction of women's identities in colonial Kenya – dowry. In addition to the sexual and ethnic components of a woman's identity, there was an economic dimension. Because of the institution of dowry, parents viewed daughters as investments that would bring wealth to the family in the form of the livestock customarily used as dowry payments. To limit the litigation that ensued from such exchanges, the colonial administration sought to restructure dowry rates, abolish instalments in the payment of dowry, and substitute cash payments for livestock. Missionaries likewise advocated the reduction, official codification, and surveillance of dowry to safeguard mission endeavour to create Christian 'civilized' communities. Because the institution of the dowry lay at the core of a number of institutions and practices, from marriage to farming, colonial attempts to restructure in the institution impinged upon diverse cultural, religious, legal, and economic transitions that were taking place in the lives of African women, and the colony in general.

Chapter 5 refocuses more broadly on the institution of marriage. Efforts to enforce colonial conceptions of marriage were part of a more extensive programme for the social engineering of African families. For the colonial government, the civil registration and codification of diverse aspects of indigenous marriages promised to reduce the seemingly endless marriage-related litigation while securing more agreeable conditions for married women. However, indigenous patriarchs feared that the government would usurp the authority for the creation, maintenance, and dissolution of marriages from family heads. Major issues raised by colonial authorities included the perceived lack of women's consent resulting in forced marriages, conflicts about the age of maturity and the resultant child marriages, the status of widows, especially regarding leviratic marriages, and child custody. As these issues were contested, women seized or created opportunities and options that reshaped marriage, running away from unsatisfactory marital arrangements, choosing alternative partners, and marrying under contentious legal and religious arrangements. Nevertheless, as the chapter illustrates, the struggle to give women a voice while upholding patriarchal authority was a difficult undertaking.

The immediate focus of Chapter 6, the medicalization and regulation of maternity by colonial authorities and the consequent professionalization of maternity care, with its opportunities for education, leads once again to a broader prospect in Chapter 7, the effect of educational opportunities, especially those supplied by missions, on Kenyan women. Maternity was another key site at which traditional culture and modernity came into contact in colonial Kenya, sometimes resulting in conflict, or in cultural exchanges, or in opening new avenues allowing women to traverse old boundaries. Issues raised at this site included the Christianization of maternity, the imposition of Western notions of propriety and decency of dress, and the participation of women in practices with widespread cultural significance – practices that included infanticide and abortion.

It was education, however, that provided women in colonial Kenya with the greatest opportunities for physical and cultural migration from old ways of life to new ones. As Chapter 7 shows, it was also education that, as a consequence, inflicted the most widely distributed anguish over such change. The education of girls entailed a process of separation, isolation, and restructuring of individual consciousness, social rhythms, and worldviews. Deciding to pursue formal education at mission schools in colonial Kenya entailed the crossing of numerous very contentious boundaries. At mission boarding schools, girls could not learn and practise the broad spectrum of custom and law that previously had constituted the sum of knowledge. Consequently, they underwent a kind of social death, becoming 'something else' in the eyes of parents and community members left behind. Schools constituted alternative organizing categories which challenged pervasive cultural, generational and peer solidarities. The story of the education of Kenyan women exemplifies the changes both enjoyed and suffered by women in colonial Kenya.

Notes

1 Sandgren, David P., *Christianity and the Kikuyu: Religious Division and Social Conflict* (New York, 1989), 1.

2 Oral Interview, Aggrey Ham Wanzetse, 27 January, 1997

3 Bruce J. Berman, *Control and Crisis in Kenya: The Dialectic of Domination* (London, 1990).

4 See for example, Gavin Kitching, *Class and Economic Change in Kenya: The Making of an African Petite-Bourgeoisie, 1905–1970* (New Haven, 1980).

5 For the gendered nature of African colonial states see, Margot Lovett, 'Gender relations, class formation, and the colonial state in Africa' in Jane L. Parpart and Kathleen A. Staudt (eds.) *Women and the State in Africa* (Boulder, 1989), 23–46.

6 See Susan Reynolds Whyte, 'The widow's dream: sex and death in Western Kenya', in Jackson, M. and Karp, I. (eds), *Personhood and Agency: The Experience of Self and Other in African Cultures* (Washington, 1990), 95–114.

7 See, for example, H. Callaway, *Gender, Culture, and Empire: European Women in Colonial Nigeria* (London, 1987); Diana Jeater, *Marriage, Perversion, and Power: the Construction of Moral Discourse in Southern Rhodesia, 1894–1930* (Oxford and New York, 1993); Elizabeth Schmidt, *Peasants, Traders, and Wives: Shona Women in the History of Zimbabwe, 1870–1939* (Portsmouth, NH, 1992); Tabitha Kanogo, 'Colonialism and gender: depiction and control of African women', in Bianca Maria Carcangiu (ed.) *Orientalia Karalitina, Quaderni Dell' Instituto Di Studi Africani e Orientali*, Numero 2 Decembre (1993), 85–100; Tabitha Kanogo, 'Mission impact on women in colonial Kenya', in Fiona Bowie, Deborah Kirkwood and Shirley Ardener (eds), *Women and Missions: Past and Present, Anthropological and Historical Perceptions* (Providence & Oxford, 1993), 165–86; Regina Smith Oboler, *Women, Power, and Economic Change: The Nandi of Kenya* (Stanford, 1985); Luise White, *Comforts of Home: Prostitution in Colonial Nairobi* (Chicago, 1990).

8 Terence Ranger, 'The Invention of tradition revisited: the case of colonial Africa', in Bianca Maria Carcangiu (ed.), *Orientalia Karalitina*, Numero 2 Decembre (1993), 164.

9 Fredrick Cooper, *Struggle for the City: Migrant Labour, Capital, and the State in Urban Africa* (Beverly Hills, 1983) and also *On the African Waterfront: Urban Disorder and the Transformation of Work in Colonial Mombasa* (New Haven, 1987).

10 Local Native Councils (LNCs) were established in 1924 in rural districts with the mandate to collect taxes and deliberate on local issues. They were composed of appointed and elected Africans. The European District Commissioner acted as the president of LNCs and could overrule any decisions passed by the LNCs. See Carl Rosberg Jr. and John Nottingham, *The Myth of 'Mau Mau': Nationalism in Kenya* (New York, 1966), 189–90.

11 KNA/PC/CP7/1/1: Native Customs and Law, PC Nyeri to DC Meru, 28/10/1919.

12 See, for example, Claire C. Robertson, *Trouble Showed the Way: Women, Men, and Trade in the Nairobi Area, 1890–1990* (Bloomington, 1997).

13 See Anthony Clayton and Donald Savage, *Government and Labour in Kenya, 1895–1963* (London, 1974); Sharon Stichter, *Migrant Labour in Kenya: Capitalism and African Response, 1895–1975* (London, 1982); Tabitha Kanogo, *Squatters and the Roots of Mau Mau, 1905–1963* (London, 1987).

14 See for example David W. Cohen & E. S. Atieno Odhiambo, *Siaya: The Historical Anthropology of an African Landscape* (London, Nairobi & Athens OH, 1989).

15 KNA: PC/NZA.3/3/1/9 DC Central Kavirondo, Kisumu to PC Nyanza, 31 December 1927.

16 KNA: PC/NZA.3/3/1/9 DC Central Kavirondo, Kisumu to PC Nyanza, 31 December 1927.

17 Mzee Elijah Mbeketha, oral interview, Tala, Machakos, 30 July 1993.

18 KNA: PC/CENT/2/1/4 LNC Minutes, Kyambu District, 22-23 November 1928.

19 Mary Wanjiru (Nyina wa Cibira), oral interview, Limuru, 14 July 1993

20 Monicah Wanjiku Wandura, Nairobi, November 1996. *Shuka* was an unstitched piece of cloth that was wrapped under one shoulder and secured atop of the other shoulder.

21 James Clifford, 'Traveling Cultures', in L. Grossberg, C. Nelson, and P. Treichler (eds), *Cultural Studies* (New York, 1992), 105.

22 Jean Margaret Hay, 'Luo Women and Economic Change During the Colonial Period', in

Nancy J. Hafkin, Edna G. Bay (ed.), *Women in Africa: Studies in Social and Economic Change*, Stanford, CA, 1976, 87–109. See also Mildred Adhiambo Jalang'o-Ndeda, 'The Impact of male labour migration on rural women: a case study of Siaya District, c. 1984–1963' PhD. dissertation, Kenyatta University, 1991.

23 David M. Anderson and David Killingray (eds), *Policing and Decolonisation: Politics, Nationalism, and the Police, 1917–65* (Manchester; New York, 1991).

24 K. Mann and R. Roberts (eds), *Law in Colonial Africa* (London, 1991); M. Channock, *Law, Custom, and Social Order: The Colonial Experience in Malawi and Zambia* (Cambridge, 1985).

25 Kanogo, 'Colonialism and Gender', in *Orientalia Karalitina, Numero 2 Decembre* (1993), 86.

26 Micere Mugo emphasizes the importance of language, its concepts, implications, and emotive stimuli, which serve to produce negative representations of women. See Micere Mugo, 'The Role of Women in the Struggle for Freedom', in Achola Pala, Thelma Awori, Abigail Krystal (eds), *The Participation of Women in Kenya Society* (Nairobi, 1978), 210.

27 See for example KNA:MAA/2/3/16/iv, 1947, p.3 in which a colonial administrator who was exasperated with the recalcitrant behaviour of 'amazonian' women opposed to soil conservation work noted that the year 1947 'came like a lamb but went out like a lion', Cited in Kanogo, 'Colonialism and Gender', in *Orientalia Karalitina, Numero 2 Decembre* (1993), 95.

28 While acknowledging the contributions of Luise White, Jean Davison and Cora Presley, John Lonsdale underscores the general paucity of the voices of ordinary women in writings on Kenya. See B. Berman, and J. Lonsdale, *Unhappy Valley: Conflict in Kenya and Africa, Book Two: Violence and Ethnicity* (London, 1992), 320–1; Luise White, *Comforts of Home;* Cora Ann Presley, *Kikuyu Women, the Mau Mau Rebellion, and Social Change in Kenya* (Boulder, CO, 1992); Jean Davison and the Women of Mutira, *Voices From Mutira: Lives of Rural Gikuyu Women* (Boulder, CO, 1988); see also Muthoni Likimani, *Passbook Number F. 47927 Women and Mau Mau in Kenya* (London, 1985). Not an ordinary woman herself, Muthoni does represent the lives of ordinary women in this fictionalized, semi-autobiographical account of women's experiences during the Mau Mau liberation war.

One

'Capax Doli'? Debating the Legal Status of African Women

At present no native woman attains her majority; she is held to be under guardianship all her life.
John Ainsworth, Chief Native Commissioner [CNC] to I.L.O. Gower, Solicitor General, 'Legislation Re: The Status of Native Women', KNA: AG 4/2791, 12 April 1919.

[A] native woman cannot be subjected against her will to remain forever a suppressed being tied to the retrogressive customs operating amongst the tribes; she must be allowed to come of age and have an individual existence.
John Ainsworth, CNC to acting AG KNA: AG 4/2791 Status of Native Women, 22 March 1920.

[I]t will take many years yet before the native man is able to realize that a native woman has any right to choose her own course to life.
CNC to acting Attorney General, KNA: AG 4/2791 Status of Native Marriages and Native Women Leaving the Reserves, 13 April 1920.

A native woman is 'capax doli' according to the rules which apply to women of other races, or to persons of the other sex.
Attorney General [AG] to CNC, KNA: AG 4/2791 Status of Native Women, Legal Status of Native Girls, 7 September 1931.

On 31 May 1912 the Assistant District Commissioner (hereafter ADC) in charge of Kyambu district dedicated a paragraph of his monthly report to a *shauri*, problem, between two African men within his jurisdiction. A Mr. Kinwangika had complained to his employer, Mr. Lushington that 'a man called Waihotho had prevented women from going to work with him.'[2] Kinwangika was an African labour recruiter for Mr. Lushington. Kinwangika had ostensibly ordered Waihotho's wives to work for Mr. Lushington but Waihotho, who was in the process of building family huts, had refused to let his wives go. Prior to this incident the District

Commissioner (DC) had told Mr. Lushington that Kinwangika would recruit labour for him.

Earlier, in the middle of May 1912, the DC in charge of Kyambu District had received a letter from his superior regarding an unfolding controversy the likes of which would preoccupy various authorities throughout the colonial period. The Provincial Commissioner (PC) was concerned about reports of African girls supposedly held against their will by the African Inland Mission (AIM) at Matara, Kijabe. Mr L. H. Downing,[3] who was in charge of the station, denied the allegations. He also stated that some of the girls sought refuge at the mission in a bid to 'avoid marriage with persons they have a violent dislike of'. He claimed that the father of the girl in question had not been denied permission to see his daughter.[4] In his zeal to forestall further conflict or misunderstanding, the PC stated:

> I have explained [to McKendrick, the Mission Superintendent] that the government does not intend in any way to interfere with native marriage laws, under which a woman is first the property of her father and then of her husband and that the idea that a girl can dispose of herself as she wishes cannot be entertained. I have, however told him that in any case where there is a deadlock the District Commissioner will intervene and endeavour to arrange a compromise.[5]

Arranged or forced marriages were just one of the issues concerning the status of women with which the harried DC and PC had to deal. It was not easy for colonial administrators to sort out the myriad controversies surrounding the lives of women in colonial Kenya. Earlier, Downing had explained that with regard to the question of marriage, his mission was in favour of the payment of dowry, or bride price. The PC said he was 'relieved' to hear this. Had the mission taken an oppositonal stance on this issue, he believed it might have been counterproductive to the mission's programme. However, the PC noted that 'one cannot of course prevent disobedient daughters from running away into Nairobi, or to the mission stations, in fact morally it is better that if they run away they should go to the missions, especially if the mission continues to support the payment of dowry'.[6] The PC also advised the DC to encourage fathers to allow their daughters to marry their chosen suitors as long as acceptable dowry was paid to the fathers. If a father already had received dowry from another man, he was to return it. In the unfortunate event that a girl went to Nairobi and 'wandered off ' with, say, a Swahili, her father would have to return the goats and face the probability of not getting any bride price from the Swahili. The PC believed that most problems could be solved with the exercise of tact and patience on both sides. He argued that it would make the situation more manageable if Mr. McKendrick, the man in charge of the girls' mission home at Matara, did not 'take a heated view of the situation,' but looked at it 'in an unbiased manner'.[7]

In these few exchanges, the ADC was confronted with a plethora of concerns from individuals representing diverse groups that mediated the lives of African girls and women in colonial Kenya. These included parents, spouses, missionaries, colonial administrators, and perceived distractors, especially the Swahili, an urbanised Islamic coastal society. This middle-level bureaucrat consequently was forced to address issues that were to constitute the core of gender relations in colonial Kenya. Less than two decades after the establishment of colonial rule, the effect of colonial intervention on the representation and construction of African womanhood was well under way. Issues involving runaway girls and women, forced marriages, women as property, patriarchal authority, bride price, mission intrusion, and the general theme of women's unsanctioned movement all had been broached. New spaces constituted by shifts in the cultural, social, economic, educational, moral, and political domains had begun to make old gender relations tense and fragile. In the public mind, the movement of women from rural reservations to towns, settler farms, mission stations, and other unsanctioned spaces entailed multiple migrations, displacements that were normative and material as well as spatial. These movements conjured images of a host of vices to which social disorder was attributed. Existing communities, and especially the older men and women in them were not ready for the swirling wave of changes, which ushered ostensibly nontraditional practices over which elders had little or no control.

One principal way of representing the role of women in Kenyan colonial society involved their formal legal status. Women's legal capacity was exercised and delimited in formal settings such as colonial judicial courts and in informal venues such as households and villages, where the issues catalogued above, and many others, were played out. The legal status of women involved, among other things, their ability to make accusations, enter into contracts, lodge complaints, give evidence, and make a variety of other individual decisions. Under the colonial administration, however, virtually no one in authority – no one on any side of the many particular issues in which the legal status of Kenyan women was involved – could express much satisfaction with the way that women's legal status was defined.

Not all the colonial administrators were inclined to accept the perceived precolonial legal subordination of women and their consequent lack of agency. 'At present no native woman attains her majority; she is held to be under guardianship all her life,'[8] John Ainsworth, the Chief Native Commissioner (CNC) noted, and 'it will take many years yet before the native man is able to realize that a native woman has any right to choose her own course to life'.[9] Nevertheless, 'A native woman cannot be subjected against her will to remain forever a suppressed being tied to the retrogressive customs operating amongst the tribes; she must be allowed to come of age and have an individual existence'.[10]

At the same time, a variety of patriarchal kin, especially fathers and husbands, as well as some colonial administrators, sought to limit what they regarded as unacceptable behaviour on the part of girls and women. Even as certain colonial administrators advocated greater freedom and agency for girls and women, the DC quoted above noted that while some of the elders were beginning to see the futility of forcing their daughters into unwanted marriages, they 'complained of the disobedience of their wives and children in general'.[11] The women were engaged in activities to which the wider kinship took exception. Any attempts to confer legal agency on girls and women thus caused fissure in families. Some colonial officials were uncomfortable about administrative or legislative reformulation of the rights of African women. Instead, they advocated internal transformation and social evolution as the least harmful ways of achieving change. Hence, in 1919, the PC for Mombasa stated:

> I am strongly of the opinion that any attempt to extend the rights of native women would strike a severe blow at their tribal organization and be disastrous. The social evolution must come from within and not be forced on them. The right to enter into a contract by a woman should, I consider, only be recognised if the consent of the woman's lawful or customary guardian is first obtained.[12]

African men, for their part, expected colonial administrators to adhere to 'customary law' in arbitration over disputes. However, like the colonizers, those who operated this precolonial legal machinery also found themselves trying to cross treacherous terrain. Neither the forces enabling Kenyan women to realize the aspirations that some administrators held for them in the legal realm nor the forces opposing that realisation, however, were in any real sense under anyone's coherent direction. Groping for a policy on women in general and their legal status in particular during the formative, deeply fractured and fluid period from 1910 to 1930, colonial officials encountered a complex, highly mobile, and rapidly changing female population that accessed multiple legal and physical spaces. The evolution of colonial policy on the formal legal status of women reflects efforts to cope with the protean nature of what was happening in the lives of women across Kenya. For the administrators, the result was fragmented and conflicted, an indication of the rudimentary nature of colonial administration.

In redefining their lives under these conditions, women defied the notion that they represented a monolithic identity. They were becoming a social and legal mosaic. Deliberations in the colonial administration illustrate representations of the composite nature of women's social map in early colonial Kenya. This chapter examines official efforts to identify shifts in the legal conceptualization of women. More importantly, it portrays the lack of consensus among officials regarding the multiple shifts that were taking place among women and the absence of any final single identity for 'Kenyan women' as a result. Ultimately, we are left with images of a varied and restless female population and a conflicted official 'policy' towards them.

Official correspondence affords us glimpses into the attitudes, opinions, nuances, dilemmas, and misrepresentations that fed into the official and indigenous perception of women's worlds in colonial Kenya. Representing a colonial state that was perpetually reconstituting itself, the administrators did not articulate a homogenous body of thought or of moral practice. For this and other reasons, the search for a common policy on the legal status of women was dogged with complications.

'Interfering with Native Law and Custom'

Writing to the Solicitor General in April 1919, CNC John Ainsworth was concerned to find out whether it was possible to pass legislation that would allow native women to attain majority status at the age of twenty-one.[13] Ainsworth was troubled about what he perceived to be an increasing number of women whose attempts to enter the wage-labour market away from their rural bases were thwarted by a multiplicity of indigenous power structures, coinciding with an acute shortage of labour.[14] Ainsworth was hopeful that such legislation would enable women to take up jobs whenever and wherever they chose and that such women would be able to keep the proceeds of their labour. As he put it, 'Amongst the native tribes a woman never comes of age, therefore strictly speaking she is never free to please herself; with the advent of civilization this disability must disappear'.[15] There was already an increasing number of Kikuyu women who sought employment on coffee estates adjoining the African reservation in Central Province. However, Ainsworth did not expect to 'interfere with the women in the Reserve'. He was more concerned about women over twenty-one years of age who had already left the reserves. This group represented an increasing minority, which, though not completely independent of male control, had crossed the threshold of customary law and was operating on a new and ill-defined frontier.

In raising questions about the restrictions on an African woman's ability to 'please herself', Ainsworth was treading on uncharted ground. Colonial administrators, indigenous authorities, and the women involved all had to find ways to deal with new conditions created by the colonial intervention. For the women and for the authorities, both indigenous and colonial, a major condition was the unprecedented mobility in physical space, across the boundaries previously drawn by customary law and social prohibitions.

Maintaining a workable balance between controlled modernization and social stability became a dilemma for colonial administrators. For some, stability implied the coexistence of two mutually exclusive moral economies, the 'traditional' and the modern, the rural and the urban, the community and the individual. Thus, in 1920, Acting Attorney General (AG) Ivon Gower advocated a policy of official noninterference in the rural areas, the administrative domain of community elders and of customary law. For Gower, the question of women's agency, contractual capacity, and legal majority most likely would remain a matter governed by traditional values. In a resigned manner, he concluded: 'It will be some-time before the matter can be dealt with fully and I have grave doubts as to the advisability of interfering with native law and custom in a country like this'.[16]

As Ainsworth pointed out to Gower, this was a retrogressive and unrealistic policy. Burying one's head in the sand did not help the situation. Colonialism's disruptive influences could not be evaded. Ainsworth retorted: 'When you say you have grave doubts as to the advisability of interfering with Native Law and Custom in a country of this kind I am afraid I do not quite follow what you mean. The interference is already taking place and we seem powerless to prevent such interference'.[17]

Legislating Marriage

Ainsworth was not alone in focusing on the inability among both Africans and colonial administrators to deal with the rapid pace of change introduced by colonial rule. Like many others, Ainsworth depicted the changes as hallmarks of civilization in contrast to tenacious but uncivilized indigenous moralities. While he advocated legislation to enable women to respond more freely to the changes, he was optimistic that even if such legislation was not effected, change was inevitable, regardless of resistance from any quarter.

The various migrations of women were among the most salient of these changes. Administrators found themselves unable to deal with all the complaints, litigation, and general displeasure regarding them, but because women were not a homogeneous group, colonial administrators agonized over the formulation of appropriate policy. Interfering with Native Law and Custom by legislation also frequently involved issues that also displayed other aspects that were addressed differently by other legislative policies and other policy makers with their own agendas. Issues, policies, and responses overlapped and sometimes produced conflicts, inconsistencies, and gaps that women could exploit. As we shall see in Chapter 5, the same sorts of complications involving customary and colonial law that played out in the question of a woman's legal coming of age arose around the question of the legal status of marriage. Clitoridectomy as a way of coming into the marriageable state, the payment of dowry, and issues of childbearing and child custody, comprise a few of the many issues that involved the increasing physical and normative mobility of women.

Ainsworth believed that, in general, legislation had to supplant customary law if women ever were to achieve the status he believed they should have. Otherwise it would be impossible for women to navigate the troubled waters of the day. As long as they remained on the reservation, African women were said to be 'under tribal conditions', a euphemism for rigid male control enshrined in native law and custom. Ainsworth asserted that under native and customary law,

> [A] woman is practically a chattel, she never comes of age and although she is transferred from the custody of her father or guardian to some other man on payment of the so-called marriage price she still remains a chattel, so long as she remains in the Reserve she remains under tribal conditions

> which a civilized order only recognizes so long as the woman herself does not object; should she, however, leave the tribal Reserve in order to emancipate herself, it is repugnant to civilized ideas to compel her to return to her former existence.[18]

In particular, the status of married women in the reservations was perceived as an additional legal inhibition to the alleviation of women's predicament. Some colonial administrators were unclear on various levels regarding the married status. Lawrence Tooth, the Crown Counsel, wondered aloud:

> I do not know how native custom works out in practice. If a native woman leaves her Reserve, either temporarily or permanently, and earns money outside her Reserve, is it the fact that her legal guardian takes all she saves, if she is married, from her? If she be married, different considerations arise. In regard to this particular point, she is in the same position as a wife in England before 1870 was in at the Common Law.[19]

Could the same rights and privileges that had been gained by British women after a long struggle and exposure to 'civilization' be extended to African women, who were supposedly 'barely exposed to civilization'? Theoretically, it was possible to introduce legislation that would enable women to explore and participate in new colonial spaces without infringement from African men. As Tooth observed in 1919, 'there is nothing of course to prevent the legislature from repealing or modifying existing Native Law and Custom. It is reduced to a question of policy'.[20] For Tooth, there was only one relevant law: British statutory law. In comparing them to British women, Kenyan women had become part of Empire debates on the legal position of women.

The status of married women in Kenya was very complicated. Only a very small proportion of the population adopted the 1902 East African Marriage Ordinance as the basis for constructing their marriages. Many colonial administrators, on the other hand, adopted the ordinance as the defining code of marriages among Africans. Both Article 35 of the ordinance and a 1923 ruling by Justice O. J. Hamilton, which concluded that 'a native marriage is not a legal marriage if polygamous', seemed at least to recognize native unions. But the term 'marriage' was used loosely in much of the discourse about native marriages, and from the colonial point of view, Hamilton declared, 'the marriage law of the Protectorate expressly omits native union from its purview and though recognizing their existence does not deal with them as legal marriages.'[21]

According to this ruling, native marriages could exist as long as they did not seek legal recognition by state institutions and functionaries, and consequently, in marital disputes, an offended man could not seek litigation as a husband because he had no legal standing. Section 5 of Article 34/1920 of the East African Marriage Ordinance appeared to give legal recognition to marriages in accordance with native law and custom by making it an offence for anyone married under customary law to contract a Moslem marriage.[22] Although this provision made the native marriage a state of fact, recognizing it as such did not give that marriage legal standing. In this context, the Islamic law, like the East African Marriage Ordinance, adopted an exclusionary stance toward African customary marriages.

Colonial administrators who witnessed the day-to-day unfolding of African lives had varying opinions about the essence of African marriages. Despite blatant differences between the rites and ceremonies that characterized Western Christian or civil marriages and indigenous marriages, and despite legislation and judicial interpretations that denied indigenous marriages a legal standing, the field administrators were cognizant of the binding nature of such marriages. The DC for Kaloleni, for example, considered the majority of Ganzi marriages as equal to civil, Islamic and Christian marriages. Recounting the betrothal procedure of the Ganzi, he was able to vouch for women's consent: 'A asks B, B consents. B's parents visit A's taking *kayama of tembo*, a gourd of liquor, B's father calls her and asks three times if she wishes to marry A. B says three times A is my husband'.[23] This was followed by 'A' dipping into the beer and giving her father the drink. This ritual signified the betrothal, which was followed by many formalities pending the exchange of bridewealth, or payment to the bride's family household, which in 1919 was set at one bull, seven cows, or seventy goats.

The DC asserted that the betrothal was between consenting parties. More importantly, the girl or her parents and the man or his parents could object to the betrothal. As far as the DC was concerned, this gave the Miji Kenda marriage 'all the necessary formalities of a true marriage'.[24] He granted that these might differ from the English customs and ceremonies, but they were nevertheless equally elaborate and legally binding.

He also noted that there were less orthodox but equally acceptable methods of marrying among the Miji Kenda. As we shall see, the *wirani* or *kinyakani* marriage entailed what he called the 'abduction' of a bride from a dance venue – actually, an elopement – following which, to make the marriage legitimate, the man had to undertake all the rituals that normally pertained to marriage. In other words, the social customs of the day made provision for this mode of acquiring a bride. For administrators, however, the whole process represented a lack of contractual capacity on the part of a woman.

Colonial administrators dealing with the question of the married status of women and their legal status in a host of other matters, expressed intentionally and unintentionally, a sense of the 'otherness' of African women. They also showed an understanding of the complexity of the issues posed by existing laws and customs and how these affected the evolving colonial institutions and policies.

Spaces between Colonial and Customary Law

The position that CNC Ainsworth articulated about this situation was also the general colonial understanding of their predicament: that the African women were oppressed and of an inferior status to African men and that colonization would result in women's emancipation.[25] Faced with increasing requests for arbitration regarding disputes whose origins derived from supposed breaches of customary practices by women (who at times had male accomplices), colonial officials differed on how to proceed. 'Emancipation' proved to be a relative term, because even the colonial administrators who envisioned it had to negotiate the status of women within existing native and customary law.

Thus, even well-meaning colonial administrators such as John Ainsworth leaned toward a policy on the marriage of indigenous women that supported the customary laws even though at these times denied women any form of choice of partner, or even the choice not to marry. According to Ainsworth, there was no ordinance in the Protectorate that provided for what was commonly referred to as 'Marriage under Native and Customary Law'. Such contracts between Africans were referred to only by the 1902 East African Marriage Ordinance, which barred anybody who had been married under customary law from contracting another marriage under the same Ordinance unless it was with the same party they were married to under customary law. Beyond that, Ainsworth argued, the ordinance 'would appear to have travelled outside the regions of practical application in that it had not defined what native marriage is and would seem to have overlooked the fact that marriage as understood in civilized communities does not really exist among the native tribes where unlimited possession of women by men is permitted'.[26]

Ainsworth argued that under the prevailing circumstances, the loss of a wife was interpreted as loss of valuable property; thus he considered it reasonable for a man to sue for the loss of his property. Overlooking raging arguments against bridewealth, Ainsworth, among others, thus felt obliged to provide remedy for husbands whose wives had left the jurisdiction of their tribes. Administrators believed it would be unreasonable not to allow men to sue for the recovery of what they considered to be lost property.

This attitude represented a combination of a conservative colonial, paternalistic spirit, and a more liberal one, which sought an accommodating partnership with the indigenous patriarchs. Ultimately this reinforced precisely the notion that Ainsworth sought to supplant, that women were valuable assets and that unsanctioned movement on their part resulted in loss of property, an injustice to men.

In order to reach some kind of accommodation between colonial efforts to legislate the status of women and customary laws and practices, it was considered necessary to establish limits on proposals to facilitate women's movement and agency. The records of the colonial administration with respect to issues related to the legal status of women reflect an ongoing effort to steer by dead reckoning between the assumption that British law unquestionably should apply and the dictates of indigenous laws and customs often at odds with that law. How a woman fared in such a state of flux could not be determined in advance or in principle.

A decade after Ainsworth had posed the question of the legal status of African women, his successor was still seeking guidance on the issue, this time from the highest legal resource in the land, the Attorney General. And a decade after that, Ainsworth still focussed on the question of when a Kenyan woman could be said to attain the age of legal majority. The issues had not been resolved.

During this period missions served as refuges for girls and women seeking to escape from unions that were increasingly categorized as forced marriages, child marriages, or just plain bad marriages. Missionaries believed from experience that the undesirable situations that befell women could be avoided if they were allowed to attain legal majority. This would give them the right to make various life choices, including the choice of preferred marital partner at an appropriate age. It would also enable girls to embrace Christianity and formal education without interference from their kinsmen. Consequently, the missionaries were among those who advocated that the colonial government should deliberate on the legal status of African women with a view to determining an age of majority, and were in the vanguard of wrenching African girls from the hold of traditional customs.

In a letter of 28 August 1931 to Kenya's CNC, the Kenya Missionary Council sought to know whether there was an age 'at which a girl passes out of her minority'. This enquiry had been spurred by 'several most urgent cases', most probably of men seeking to remove their daughters and wives from missions to which they had fled. According to the alarmed missionary council, 'decisions by local administrative officers' seemed to 'point to a permanent minority, the native girl always being a mere chattel at the disposal of her relatives'.[27]

Although the CNC viewed the debate on the legal status of women and girls as ongoing, the AG considered the enquiry 'so vague' that he was 'at a loss how to attempt to reply'. He did not understand what the CNC meant by 'legal status', since to him the situation appeared to be self-explanatory. As far as he was concerned, 'A native woman is "*capax doli*" according to the rules which apply to women of other races, or to persons of the other sex'.[28] Referring to the ability to commit a crime or capability of criminal intent, *capax doli* described the condition of possessing sufficient intelligence and comprehension to be held criminally responsible for one's deeds.[29] In this context, it acquired new significance. To a newly-arrived AG, *capax doli* implied that all legally culpable people were equal before the law, regardless of their sex or race. That included African women. As members of a specific gender, women had no separate 'legal status' from that of men. However, this was far from the reality. It was one thing to be held legally responsible for one's mistakes, and quite another to have the legal rights to determine one's future.

By 1931, Kenyan women were accessing various legal systems depending on a wide variety of prevailing circumstances, including the geographical location of the litigant. This legal multiplicity served to complicate the situation for women and colonial administrators alike. It also afforded women avenues for exploring and defining new options. Among colonial administrators, there was still no consensus as to which legal codes applied to African women. In such a situation, women could be caught between codes and suffer the consequences, but they could also use the spaces between them to move beyond the legal, social, and cultural confines that had restricted them in the past.

As early as 1919, it had become evident that African women constituted varied social categories representing changing indigenous communities in the colonial state. In this context, Lawrence Tooth, the Crown Counsel responded to Ainsworth's question about the legal status of women, and sought clarification about the possibility of legislating Kenyan women's majority status at twenty-one:

> Is it intended that such legislation shall apply only to women who have definitely severed themselves from their tribe or to all women who have temporarily left the reserve in the tribe to which they belong lives [sic]? Then again, is such legislation to apply to single women or to include women married in accordance with Native Law and Custom? If the latter class were included, it would appear that the policy of the Married Women's Act of England is being introduced. It must be remembered that the first such act was not passed in England till the year 1870. Further, if the age of 21 is fixed upon, it cannot be doubted that there would be a large number of cases in which the point to be decided would be the age of the woman. In the absence of all birth registration certificates, this raises almost insoluble difficulties.[30]

Recognizing the heterogeneity of African women, Tooth seemed to anticipate varying legal provisions for women of different marital and residential status. In this as in other situations, where women lived became a central determining factor. Conversely, the legal status of men was not predicated on their physical location or marital status. Although colonial administrators were concerned about the economic and social effect of male migration on rural productivity and social stability, they did not seek to formulate policy on male migrancy on the basis of women's reactions to this mobility. This is not to say that colonial administrators did not react to complaints raised by wives of errant migrants.[31]

In colonial circles, it was understood that men could make independent decisions in response to the widening challenges of the colonial situation. Women's agency, on the other hand, was a matter for debate and negotiation, especially with regard to women's movement out of rural areas. More importantly, it was considered necessary to ensure that migrant women did not abdicate their productive and reproductive obligations in the rural area, which marriage had secured. By the time Tooth expressed his concern, however, that institution was in greater jeopardy than it had been before.

Ainsworth's concern about women's attainment of the age of majority reflected a questioning of the entire established social structure already confronted with a barrage of eroding forces, colonial and otherwise. For a start, the organic nature of communities revolved around households, which in turn were constructed around conjugal units. Women, especially married women, were pivotal to the establishment, subsistence, and reproduction of these units. Upon marriage, a young man established a nucleus household. The fact that such a household was potentially polygamous did not erase the significance of that first marriage, which ushered the man into an important stage of his life cycle, that of being the head of a household and therefore potentially the head of a clan. Between the two of them, a man and his first wife constituted the foundation of an organic component of the society.

Heads of households were entrusted with the task of enforcing the provisions of customary law in their households. In his proposal, Ainsworth thus was necessarily questioning the wisdom of local communities, which regulated African women's ability to participate in wage labour and in most cases prevented them from moving to areas where participating in such labour was a possibility.

By 1919, elders considered it necessary to introduce a bill 'to protect fathers and guardians of native women and to regulate contracts or unions entered into between men and women in accordance with Native Law and Custom and to recognize native rights thereunder'.[32] Elders detested and feared socially disruptive possibilities available to women who operated beyond the control of customary law and practice. It was anticipated that the prospective bill might be called 'The Native Women's Ordinance, 1919'.[33]

Linked to Ainsworth's proposal for women attaining majority at the age of twenty-one also were fundamental assumptions and questions relating to a woman's position within the household. Colonial officials tended to maintain local patriarchal values; ethnographic material on various African societies provides ample information about dynamic social institutions concerned with the maintenance of social order among women.

In indigenous households, men were ultimately responsible for any breaches of norms, and for the day-to-day oversight of their households, including the distribution and supervision of labour. Above all, the honour of the household was filtered through the actions of its various members. In the colonial reserves, the departure of a woman from the household for whatever reason raised a number of issues. Such a departure had to be authorized. Even the absence of one person from a household called for the redeployment of resources. Colonial changes led to uneasy gender and authority relationships.

Colonial policy tacked and veered among these competing cultural and legal interests, responding to particular instances without ever achieving an overall direction. Despite interest in conferring majority status on women who reached twenty-one, there were legal distinctions regarding the legal status of African women on the basis of age. Citing Criminal Case No. 85 of 1919 in the matter of the Master and Servants Ordinance No.4 of 1910, and in reference to Section 447 of the Criminal Procedure Ordinance 1913, No. 6 of 1914, the AG pointed out that unmarried girls in a reserve remained in a state of permanent minority.[34] In this case, the Supreme

Court had held that 'a native girl of 15–16 years of age, living in her reserve, could not validly contract'. The AG was not clear on how the court would rule in the case of an unmarried girl living out of the reserve 'and in a detribalised state'. He assumed this would 'depend on the custom of the tribe to which she belonged, and the degree of detribalisation as evidenced by the facts'.[35]

The Indian Majority Act also did not apply to natives.[36] As if to underscore the perplexed, ad hoc nature of policy formulation on African women, the AG stated that he was glad to express his opinion on any concrete cases and specific questions the Missionary Council might care to submit. But no opinion was concrete enough for actual situations in the lives of women. Even as the lives of women changed under pressure from diverse colonial processes, official inertia failed to institute laws that would help women negotiate these changes without patriarchal encumbrance.

Likewise, when the Kenya Missionary Council, in its campaign for the 'emancipation' of African women, pursued the possibility of 'European and Indian Women being brought under English law, and if so, whether government would favour the extension of this law to include African girls,'[37] it eventually got a response from the Acting AG, A. D. A. MacGregor, that had all the hallmarks of official confusion regarding the legal predicament of African women. MacGregor stated:

> [I] regret that I am unable from the terms thereof to appreciate what amendment of the law you propose. As you are aware Europeans and Indian women, and for that matter African women, are in very many respects amenable to English Law. If you care to let me know the respects in which your Council feels that the present legal status of women of any race could be improved I shall be glad to deal with your representations.[38]

If MacGregor's response was correct, then Ainsworth and the missionaries had been waging an unnecessary battle. Ainsworth, among others, was apprehensive about local efforts to restrict women's lives to the dictates of customary law; he saw them as futile, as trying to turn the clock back. On the other hand, to allow women to weave in and out of the various colonial spaces was a risk in itself, a risk that the colonial administrator appreciated as well as the elders who governed rural communities. Diverse economic, moral, social, and physical spaces had opened up with the establishment of colonial rule. 'Domesticity' consequently became the battle cry among both colonizers and indigenous men concerned to maintain the status quo for women.

Runaway Wives and Aggrieved Men

Marriage and other domestic arrangements had defined the lives of most women. By running away from marital homes or forging new marital arrangements, women explicitly redefined their social status and plunged rural households into disharmony. The deserted men blamed the colonial state for creating an aggravating situation, appealing to memories of a more functional past: 'Before the Europeans came if a woman ran away to the cost [sic – 'coast'] the elders complained to the Liwali and the woman was restored. Since the Europeans came the arrangement has been spoilt and the men now lose their women without redress *bure*, a total loss.'[39] But men were themselves in new arrangements of wage labour, voluntary or forced. This did not always go down well with women who were themselves trying out 'new arrangements'.

Women's voluntary labour, which concerned Ainsworth, did not factor into the concerns of another colonial official, Lambert. In the discourse of aggrieved husbands, little if anything about the many reasons why women might want to desert their marriages during the long absences of their spouses was mentioned. Women fled from their marital homes for other reasons too. For the newly married, long separations and lack of communication from husbands over long periods made the unions very fragile. Jalang'o-Ndeda's study recounts cases of newly married women who complained of loneliness as a result of their husbands' long absences at distant places of employment. Such women were prone to establish new liaisons, prompting, in return, accusations of immorality.[40] In some cases, they teamed up with returnee migrants who were on leave and who might take them to their places of work at the end of their leave.

In the absence of spouses, young brides were placed under the supervision of parents-in-law and other older members of their husbands' families. Claims of ill treatment by this wide network of custodians were frequent. Some cited physical beatings by 'difficult' relatives. Some husbands also failed to remit cash, making it difficult for their wives to meet family needs and obligations. At worst, cases of food shortages due to lack of money were not unusual.

Some men failed to provide their families with such basic necessities as shelter. The absence of male labour, combined with customary taboos regarding house construction and maintenance by women, could leave a wife without shelter and desperate. Among the Luo, only men could construct houses. Should a woman construct a house herself, she would be contravening received conventions.[41] Despite the fluidity of the colonial period and the increasing flexibility of independent Kenya, a Luo woman who dared build a house became the subject of public debate. Such an act might be commemorated in song.

Meru Ogoyo dala
Meru gangla
Olang'o K'Obilo
Min Ogoyo dala
Meru gangla
Kara meru Thuon

Your mother built a home
She's extraordinary

Olang'o K'Obilo
Your mother built a home!
She's wonderful
She's a warrior.[42]

Moving in and out of the different legal spaces that physical movement made accessible to them, some women managed to attain what amounted to temporary reprieve from bad marriages. In the meantime, women themselves remained contested terrain, with different authority systems claiming the right to define their marital options. They also suffered imputations designed both to characterize their experiences negatively and to foreclose the possibility that others would follow their example.

Depictions abound of women and girls as malleable victims (especially of urban Don Juans), in an effort to discourage female movement to urban areas. These were associated with depiction of urban spaces as a breeding grounds for vice.

Such frantic and unprecedented efforts to portray women as the custodians of culture and as adjuncts to men provided the background against which women's movement was strictly controlled. With regard to women, the individualizing power of the colonial process was denied for a long period. While mission stations sought to acknowledge and alter this fact, they were themselves responsible for creating a host of restrictions for mission girls.[43] Girls and women who went mission stations merely traded one form of social control for another.

The PC for Mombasa argued that the issue of runaway wives was among 'the greatest grievances for the Wa Nyika [Miji Kenda] federation of tibes[sic – 'tribes']', and that its redress should go a long way to improve the relations of government with these people.[44] He was particularly enraged about the court ruling, which dismissed the validity of customary marriage. To the best of his knowledge, he said, girls were party to the creation of marriages; hence the government should recognize these marriages. The differing opinions of colonial administrators over this issue were captured in his closing remarks: 'After all, the people [read 'men'] are the best judges of what they want, and there is nothing in this matter which is repugnant to equity and morality.'[45] With regard to marriage, the laws and practices in the past had worked well for Miji Kenda men. The same cannot have been true for women who periodically ran away to the coast, and even then, soon ran out of luck.

There were colonial administrators who did not see any good reason why women would desert their marriages and who did not have any problems with the unilateral enforcement of marital arrangements under customary law. However, as the complaints of aggrieved men about runaway wives in the official records attest, there also were many forces at play in colonial Kenya making it difficult for old practices to thrive. Home was becoming a variable concept. Social reproduction no longer was possible only within familiar and prescribed institutions of customary marriage or natal domiciles. The acquisition of agency and the act of choosing alternative livelihoods and homes were slow and painful processes for women. They entailed the subversion of long-standing authorities and the risk of losing one's social standing in 'society'. However, even beginning to realize that the concept of community no longer represented a monolithic, indomitable whole was a major transition. 'Community' itself was a rapidly changing concept that was beginning to accommodate diverse identities and multiple legal standings. Within the marriage institution, women were already beginning to juggle their various options. Home was no longer confined to one's natal or contemporary marital area. One's wider kinship group need not prescribe one's home. Home was a place the individual desired and appropriated. It was a state of mind that women could imagine and create, independent of wider kinship groups.

Marriage, Islam, and Women's Agency

Among the fissures through which women took advantage to reach new physical and cultural spaces was the one opened by Islam, especially its attitudes towards marriage. At the coast, for example, Miji Kenda men hoped for government intervention to return Miji Kenda wives who left their reserves 'to contract unauthorized unions under Mohammedan [sic, Islamic] law in the 10 miles coastal zone'.[46] A letter from the elders to the governor expressed the community's consternation with the state of flux:

> We the Giriama elders of government and Kambis request you to remove one thing that happens in our district and which we do not like. We do not like our women running away to Mombasa where they are converted to Mahommedanism [sic] after which we cannot get them although we go and ask them. Such an act is very heavy on us and we therefore request you Sir to return all our wives and children that have become Mahomedans [sic]. If a Mswahili comes to our District and his parents want him back we at once allow him to go back but we cannot see why they will not let ours. This we feel as an injustice and that is why we think we better submit the matter to you Sir, and out of your kindness we hope for a reply.[47]

Miji Kenda men were reluctant to take up jobs away from their homes, since they stood to lose their wives during their absence.[48] A state of insecurity pervaded the male community, 'preventing men from leaving the Native Reserves for work outside'. [49] The DC to whom this plea was addressed, R. W. Lambert, DC for Kaloleni, agreed that 'such occurrences are not likely to encourage other natives to leave their wives and families to go out to work and are unfortunate to say the best of it, coming just at a time when the government is insisting on policy throughout of voluntary labour'.[50] Having been away for several years, engaged in wage labour, perhaps as a result of conscription into the Carrier Corps during the First World War, a man 'returns to find his wife has left him for a Mohammedan at the Coast and refuses to return' ... 'Can't something be done, if not otherwise, by legislation to put right the injustice?' the DC asked, passing the issue on to his superiors.[51]

Ainsworth might have found the provisions of the proposed legislation agreeable, had it been put into effect. It provided that if a woman left the reserve to another district or area without the consent of her father, lawful guardian, or husband, 'it shall be competent for a magistrate of the 1st or 2nd class to take an order for her return.' However, if the magistrate was satisfied

> that such female has been ill treated by her father, guardian or husband or [sic] that such female being of age 21 years or over has obtained of her own wish and desire reputable employment...[or] of her own free will elects to remain outside her tribe with another man, it shall be competent for a court to make an order on the application of a husband or of the father or guardian for the restoration of the Mahari [dowry] ... [and] on compliance with such order, an original contract registered in the reserve shall be deemed null and void.[52]

In so far as the proposal anticipated reprieve for ill-treated women who were under twenty-one, it seemed to go beyond Ainsworth's vision of emancipation at that age.

For the Miji Kenda woman, Islam provided a crack in the system that could be put to good use in asserting a degree of agency.[53] The *Kadhi*, the Islamic judge, did not recognize the complaints of the Miji Kenda men According to Islamic matrimonial laws, unions among the Miji Kenda became obsolete if the women in question converted to the Islamic faith prior to or after marrying Moslems. The Moslem Kadhis therefore refused to recognize the rights of 'pagan' husbands who lost their wives to Moslem men and could not reclaim their bridewealth. To legitimate their marital migration, the women were 'hastily islamised'[54] before a Kadhi whom the colonial government recognized. The Waduruma elders appealed to the government to ensure that women already married under customary law should not be married under Islamic law.[55] The ADC for Rabai claimed that he 'had seen many cases of great hardship to pagan husbands in which they lose their wives and cannot reclaim the marriage price paid'.[56]

Despite these attitudes, access to areas where Islam was the predominant religion allowed African women to continue to explore new options, to choose alternative domestic arrangements and redefine their legal status. For example, among the Digo, one of the nine Miji Kenda tribes, women could hold property only in 'trusteeship ... on behalf of male minors'.[57] There was also a general belief among the Miji Kenda that 'no native woman can make a valid contract'.[58] Islamic law, on the other hand, was said to help pastoral Orma women avoid leviratic marriages – the sometimes compulsory marriage of a widow to a brother of her late husband – and to form unions of their own choosing. Divorce was not an option in traditional Orma society.[59] It was made possible for women who embraced the Islamic faith, and provided other appealing terms. Although 'under Islamic law there is no community of goods between husband and wife, she is absolute owner of her own property and whatever her husband settles on her as dower'.[60] A marriage was considered invalid if a husband had not paid dowry. It was alleged that this provision alone was sufficiently attractive to entice women from their native customary marriages. In any case, according to the *Sharia*, the Islamic legal code, women could own and inherit property, contrary to the practice among the Miji Kenda.

It was easy for a non-Islamic woman to contract an Islamic marriage. Such a woman was said to have left 'her heathen relatives and enter[ed] the pale of Islam'.[61] At a later stage, she might seek to subject her new alliances to rites and ceremonies practised by her natal family, a rubber stamp for a *fait accompli*. The woman, of her own accord, and in an effort to fulfill some unmet needs from her earlier marriage, would have chosen her partner and set up residence with him. Only then would the kinsmen be informed, if at all. Among other things, Islamic law did not have a fixed age at which girls were considered marriageable; rather, discretion and puberty were used to emancipate girls from the status of minors into adults. Hence, at puberty, a Muslim woman did not need the consent of her father or guardian to contract a marriage. Marriage in the Islamic world thus was becoming an institution in which the individual female could endeavour to satisfy her personal needs. This was the reason why there were literally hundreds of women who, for a variety of reasons, deserted their matrimonial homes and either entered into new domestic arrangements or lived as single women.

Missionaries and some colonial administrators openly condemned the use of puberty as a marker of marriageability. Female consent as construed among Moslems also found opposition upcountry and was the subject of indigenous surveillance and calls for government intervention. As late as 1939, Local Native Council (LNC) members in Meru wondered whether girls could be validly married by Mohammedan law without the consent of their parents. Such attempts by members of indigenous power structures to enlist the help of colonial administrators and the Islamic community in clipping the wings of the wayward women encountered half-hearted responses.

In the above instance, the response of the president of the Meru LNC raised additional issues. He observed that the marriage of a minor 'was not valid without the consent of her parents or guardians, but a girl of over 21 years was supposed to have enough sense to look after herself'.[62] In this particular case, this implied that the colonial state was supportive of the marriage of minors as long as their guardians or parents were in agreement. As we shall see in Chapter Five, this response was given amidst a raging debate about this very issue all over the colony. While colonial administrators were divided about it, mission groups were openly opposed to the marriage of minors.

The colonial government was itself disentangling local legal and social institutions in an attempt to formulate what it considered to be a civilized policy largely based on British statutory law and social sensibilities with the ultimate aim of imposing it. Hence the government could not be relied upon to provide satisfactory solutions, at least not at all times; any decision was bound to offend one party or the other.

Controlling Women's Freedom

The debate on the legal status of the African woman boiled down to the issue of control. Unable to prevent the movement of girls and women to urban areas and rural venues of employment, including both rural townships and European settler plantations, or to the refuge offered by Islam in such places as Mombasa, some parents and family members were at times forced to settle for what was regarded as the lesser of two evils, the flight of women from traditional communities to mission stations.[63] Flight to Nairobi was perceived as an obvious route to prostitution. Even then, there was a general belief that 'a native girl of ten goes to a Mission, not through any love of religion, but in order to associate with her girl friends who when they get together become undesirable, and the very mission girls become prostitutes'. [64] Missions, of course, held out the opportunity for education, but this was hardly a stabilizing option where mobility through employment prospects was helping women redefine their roles.

Whether a girl was admitted to the mission with or without her father's permission, the communities were even more surprised by a girl's refusal to leave the mission when her parents ordered her to, in order to marry at their bidding. At stake was 'whether, or in what circumstances a girl should be allowed to have a choice in the matter'.[65] Opinions included suggestions that such girls 'should be made to carry out [their] parents' wishes'.[66] The sort of compromises that were achieved can be seen in the minutes of the Kyambu meeting. While daring to 'interpret the feeling of the meeting to be that parents should not, in all cases, have the power to prevent their daughters from attending Mission Schools', chief Hezekiah Ndung'u was keen to ascertain the nature of a girl's agency. Hence his enquiry:

> 1. At what age should a girl be considered to have freedom of choice?
> 2. Should a girl be allowed to choose her own mission, or should her parent choose it for her?[67]

While upset about the girls' disobedience, the members of the Kiambu LNC rejected this 'extremist' position in 1931. According to its chairman, 'the forcing of anyone to marry against her will is a crime'.[68] The chairman was optimistic in assuming that 'it may be concluded that native public opinion as a whole has ceased to believe in it [forced marriage]'. The dilemma was how to balance the perceived benefits of girls' education and the corrupting influence of the movement it entailed.

Confronted with the possibility of prosecution for inhibiting girls' movement, the council revived the issue of an existing institution of control: clitoridectomy. 'Majority opinion seemed to favour freedom of choice for a girl shortly after she had been circumcised, or has attained that age. The majority favoured the parent rather than the girl choosing the particular mission which his daughter should attend'.[69] Such opinions, however, were not binding to anybody, since they constituted 'just a preliminary discussion', and that the chairman might consult them again.[70]

Effort to control girls and women, took many different forms. In the adjoining Fort Hall Reserve, the LNC recommended extensive restraints on unsanctioned movement by women. A 1932 LNC meeting observed that 'native women visiting townships were often led astray and they [the councillors] desired steps to be taken to prevent as far as possible native women, unaccompanied by their husbands or other male relations, from hawking and sleeping in [such places as] Nairobi and Thika Town'.[71] This kind of intensive surveillance took more immediate forms in some areas and lasted longer. In Meru, in 1947, the practice was that 'girls may not leave the District in a taxi without the written permission of their chiefs'.[72] By 1948, a resolution was already in force 'preventing Meru women from entering buses or from leaving the District without passes. Offenders against this resolution should be prosecited [sic]'.[73]

Conflicts over efforts to control women's movements were compounded by intergenerational tension. For example, the Fort Hall LNC echoed common sentiments in the country when they reported that 'cases in which youth took girls away from the Reserve without their fathers' consent are on [the] increase, and ... Kiamas [elders' councils] should be asked to impose heavier fines in such cases ... elders should be asked to impose a fine of Shs. 150 on the seducer, such fine to be divided according to native custom'.[74] Primary guilt for women's unsanctioned movement was placed on young males. Significantly, the notion of men as seducers implied a lack of initiative on the part of women who were merely portrayed as accomplices.[75] The African reservation from which the women in question travelled were represented as areas that women left only with the connivance, permission, or supervision of men.

Even in the vicinity of rural areas, a variety of spaces were considered unsuitable for women, except for specific, acceptable purposes. Thus, the Nyeri LNC resolved that 'chiefs should issue orders prohibiting women from entering the Township [Nyeri] on Sundays except for the purpose of going to church or for some legitimate reason known to the girls' parents, husband, etc'.[76]

Apart from issues of movement, existence at the frontier of legal identity could make the married status of women ambiguous in other ways, such as in controversies about the legal personhood of wives married by custom. In *Rex* v. *Toya son of Mamure*, the defendant was charged and convicted of killing his first cousin, Toya, son of Makajumbe.[77] In the appeal in 1932, Toya Mamure submitted, 'that his wife was not a competent or compellable witness' and that 'the decision of this court in *Rex* v. *Robin* (infra) is bad and should be departed from'. With regard to the admissibility of the wife's evidence, the judge concluded that the East African Court of Appeal had dealt with this issue in the case of Mwakio

Asani son of Mwanguku Criminal Appeal No. 63 of 1930. In this case, the decision given in Rex v. Amkeyo, Law Report 7, E.A.L.R. (East Africa Law Report) 14 'was followed and approved.' The ruling in this latter case provided authority stating that a wife's evidence against her husband was admissible. On this basis, Toya Mamure's appeal was dismissed. In the *Rex versus Robin* case, the magistrate had ruled that a wife's evidence was admissible if the accused to whom she was married consented.[78] What this case illustrated was not the usual contention regarding the admissibility of a spouse's evidence, but the contentious nature of the very definition of a spouse – of a wife, to be more exact.

In this case, conflicts within colonial law itself and between colonial law and customary law caused the problem. Evidence was evaluated in the context of the Indian Evidence Act, section 122. This provided that 'no person who is or has been married shall be compelled to disclose any communication made to him during marriage by any person to whom he is or has been married'.[79] But in dismissing Toya Mamure's claim that his wife could not give evidence, and in dismissing his appeal, the court referred to the precedent of *Rex* v. *Amkeyo* (1917), holding that 'the case is authority for holding that the evidence of a wife by native custom against her husband is admissible'. In the 1917 ruling, Chief Justice Hamilton was 'of the opinion that a so-called marriage by native custom of wife-purchase is not a marriage within the meaning of Article 122 of the Indian Evidence Act, and that a party to such a union cannot claim the protection granted by the section'.[80] Toya's objection to the admissibility of his wife's evidence thus was pre-empted by the fact of his customary marriage, which disqualified him from accessing the protection of the Indian Evidence Act, Article 122. According to the ruling, his wife under customary law was not his wife under colonial law. Hence she could give evidence against him. While Toya's wife, (who remained unnamed in the records), gained legal recognition, of a sort, she, like her husband, lost her marital status in the official records.

But conflicts within colonial law itself and between colonial law and customary law could be resolved in exactly the opposite way: a wife under customary law could in fact be judged a wife under colonial law. One Daudi Odong'o had been accused of committing adultery with Mulama the wife of Obedi Sangai. In Daudi Odongo's preliminary trial, the magistrate was of the opinion that 'section 497 of the Indian Penal Code [I.P.C.] did not apply to a person who was a wife only by native law and custom'.[81] Daudi Odongo thus was released 'on the ground that a woman who was married according to native law and custom is not a wife within the meaning of that word in section 497 I.P.C'. An earlier section of the Indian Penal Code, section 494, dealt with bigamy. A comprehensive reading of these two provisions, however, required that they be read in conjunction with the Marriage Ordinance of 1902. Daudi Odongo was accused of committing adultery with her. In Daudi Odongo's preliminary trial, the magistrate was of the opinion that according to the Marriage Ordinance of 1902,

> a union according to native law and custom is regarded as valid and as creating a status which prevents a further union under the Ordinance by one of the parties with a third person; and if the person married under native law and custom has a plurality of wives, section 33 of the Ordinance appears to bar the marriage of a third party under the ordinance with any of those wives.

The converse was true. Thus, the institution of native marriage was regarded as valid under Islamic law and under the Marriage Ordinance, although not (according to the magistrate) under the section of the Indian Penal Code that he cited.

On appeal, the Supreme Court interpreted the Indian Penal Code in its larger context and ruled 'that for the purpose of section 497 I.P.C., a native woman married according to native custom is a wife within the meaning of that word as used in the section. We therefore reverse the acquittal [of Daudi Odongo] and remit the case to the magistrate to enter judgement in accordance with the facts, and if he find[s] the accused guilty, pass sentence according to law'.[82] The Marriage Ordinance forbade marriage under the native law and custom to any party married under the 1902 Marriage Ordinance. Likewise, section 6 of the Islamic Marriage, Divorce, and Succession Ordinance made invalid an Islamic marriage with a third party already married under native law and custom.

Uncoordinated rulings such as these, not necessarily guided by previous rulings, or guided in different directions by the same ones, arrived at more by individual inclination, predilection, and prevailing local practice, continued to be made. The colonial government was confronted with endless dilemmas as it tried to arbitrate gender-related issues, which were constructed out of customary practices and constituted incomprehensible texts whose ethical basis was unacceptable. To some, customary laws and practices were inimical to justice. Meanwhile the notion that African women were mere chattels of males and could have no legal personhood was constantly being subverted as women took charge of their lives in various ways, including redressing their ills.

Nothing illustrates this better than the story of Leya Ogaye's threat to run away. In 1947, J. A. Gardener, the District Officer (DO) for Central Kavirondo, Kisumu wrote a letter to the Honourable Director of Public Works in Nairobi regarding a Mr. Malome Madoda, an employee of the above government agency. He observed: 'This man's wife, Leya Ogaye, who is living in the Reserve with her father is threatening to run off with another man. It appears that Malome has not been home for five years, and I shall be grateful if you could give him compassionate leave to come to settle this domestic problem'.[83] In this case, Leya had already moved back to her father's house. By threatening to elope with another man, she was about to reinterpret the limitations on her spatial movement and reconfigure her marital options. However, she would first approach the colonial system within which her husband operated.

Using New Spaces: Leya Ogaye

By moving a distance of over 250 miles to his place of employment, Malome had become part of a greater process of transformation. He had crossed many boundaries. He was, in a manner of speaking, an urbanite and a wage labourer, a representative of the societal atomization that the colonial situation had created. He had subjected himself to an alternative authority structure. Leya, on the other hand, had been situated in the Reserve, where individuals were cast in a communal mould and expected to exist as members of organic communities and kinship groups. At the Reserves, the needs of the individual were subsumed into those of the community. Or were they?

It is necessary to acknowledge the networks linking women even as various forces sought to 'localize' them. It can be assumed that Leya had already exhausted indigenous structures of conflict resolutions before turning to the DO, while reserving running away as an alternative plan if colonial authorities failed to solve her problem. The DO represented the very system that was responsible for her husband's absence in the first place. The system owed her.

On the other hand, by availing herself of the services of a colonial bureaucrat, Leya acknowledged her interconnectedness with the colonial state. Getting her voice heard within the dominant power structure enabled Leya to explore a new and alternative method of negotiating domestic disharmony. The colonial state had taken her husband away; it might also help solve any problems arising from his absence.

By initiating the conflict-resolution process and by stating that she would elope with another man should her husband not meet his responsibilities, Leya became a participant in the remaking of her future. In so far as the authority of a nonkinsman, the DO, could be invoked to salvage a marriage whose contractual basis fell outside statutory law, Leya had recognized cracks within the system and was taking full advantage of them.

A question that arises from Leya's experience is whether the alternative liaisons that resulted from the separation of families necessarily represented 'undesirable' associations or the creation of alternative and empowering spaces for women. Eloping represents metaphors of rebellion, resistance, and migration. Such relocations certainly contravened notions of respectability, stability, and order. Leya could have relocated to an urban or alternative rural area to take up a job, instead. In any of these possible locations she might also remarry. There was also the possibility of becoming self-employed.[84] An increasing number of women were willing to venture beyond traditional conventions.

Luise White's study of prostitutes in colonial Nairobi[85] illustrates how one option provided a variety of spaces for women who had diverse reasons for leaving rural Kenya. Colonial Nairobi was frontier territory. It was an irregular situation into which most men did not bring their wives. It therefore offered irregular solutions to regular needs. It was the land of the entrepreneur, both male and female. Different combinations of sex, food, companionship, accommodation, laundry, and personal hygiene services could be offered for different rates. Prostitution provided reconstituted services traditionally offered under a variety of conventional domestic arrangements. In their response to colonialism, women, not unlike men, adopted unconventional life strategies.

By confronting and in some cases transgressing the prohibitions that customarily had circumscribed their lives, or by taking advantage of the new opportunities offered by colonial rule to overcome their lack of legal agency, women were extending the possibilities of the institution of marriage. For these women, neither the authority of District Commissioners, the Wali (the Islamic legal counsel), nor of customary law was beyond challenge. All were rendered fluid and negotiable. To borrow from Terence Ranger's observation, '"customary law", so far from being a seamless whole, was in fact an arena for debates about social morality, and advancement of citizenship'.[86] The agonizing of colonial administrators as to whether to locate African women at par with British women only added another dimension to the diverse debate on African women. Through various actions of defiance, women increasingly located themselves in a variety of new spaces and slowly redefined their citizenship.

Notes

1. The term *Capax Doli* refers to capability to commit crime, or capability of criminal intent. The phrase describes the condition of one who has sufficient intelligence and comprehension to be held criminally responsible for his deeds. See Henry Campbell Black, *Black's Law Dictionary*, St. Paul, Minnesota, 6th Edition, 1990, 208. As applied by the Attorney General in 1931, the term implied that African women were equal before the law as those of European and Indian descent. See Attorney General [AG] to CNC, KNA: AG 4/2791 Status of Native Women, Legal Status of Native Girls, 7 September 1931.
2. KNA: PC/CP1/4/1 Kikuyu District Political Records, Assistant District Commissioner-In-Charge, Kyambu, 31 May 1912. Commonly known as Kiambu, 'Kyambu' was the product of European pronunciation, hence spelling of the name of this town on the outskirts of Nairobi.
3. L. H. Downing, a pioneer missionary, was the superintendent of Kijabe and the field director for African Inland Mission [AIM] in Kenya. See Sandgren, *Christianity and the Kikuyu*, 90.
4. KNA: PC/CP1/1/4/1 Kikuyu District Political Records, McKendrick's views quoted in correspondence from PC Nairobi to Assistant DC Kiambu, Girls At Matara Under McKendrick, 15 May 1912.
5. KNA: PC/CPI/4/1 PC Nairobi to Assistant DC Kiambu, 15 May 1912.
6. *Ibid.*
7. *Ibid.*
8. KNA:AG 4/2791 John Ainsworth, CNC to I.L.O. Gower, Solicitor General, 'Legislation Re: The Status of Native Women', 12 April 1919.
9. KNA:AG 42791 'Status of Native Marriages and Native Women Leaving the Reserves', CNC to acting Attorney General, 13 April 1920.

10. KNA:AG 4/2791 Status of Native Women, John Ainsworth, CNC to acting AG (Mombasa) 22 March 1920.
11. KNA: PC/CPI/4/1 Political Record Book, Kyambu, 31 May 1912, 349.
12. KNA:AG 4/2791 Status of Native Women, PC Mombasa to CNC, 'Contracts by Women', 27 June 1919.
13. KNA: AG 4/2791 John Ainsworth, CNC to I.L.O. Gower, Solicitor General, 'Legislation Re: The Status of Native Women', 12 April 1919.
14. Carl G. Rosberg Jr. & John Nottingham, *The Myth of Mau Mau*, 61.
15. KNA: AG 4/2791 John Ainsworth, CNC to acting AG PC, 'The Status of Native Women', 22 March, 1920.
16. KNA: AG 4/2791 acting AG to CNC, 'Native Women Leaving Their Reserves', 26 March 1920.
17. *Ibid.*
18. *Ibid.*
19. KNA: AG 4/2791 'Status of Native Women', Lawrence Tooth, Crown Counsel to CNC, 16 April 1919.
20. *Ibid.*
21. KNA: AG4/2790 P.A. McElwaine, Crown Counsel to Acting Senior Commissioner Mombasa, 'Re: Pagan Women Deserting and Marrying Mohammedans [Moslems]', 8 October 1923.
22. *Ibid.*
23. KNA: AG 4/2491 DC Kaloleni to PC Mombasa, 25 March 1919. *Tembo* is traditional beer.
24. *Ibid.*
25. Obuler, *Women, Power, and Economic Change*, 2–3.
26. KNA: AG 4/2791 'Status of Native Marriages and Native Women Leaving the Reserves', CNC to acting AG, 13 April 1920.
27. KNA: AG 4/2791 'Status of Native Women', H.J. Butcher, Hon. Secretary Kenya Missionary Council to CNC, Native Affairs Department, 28 August 1931.
28. KNA: AG 4/2791 'Status of Native Women', AG to CNC, 'Legal Status of Native Girls', 7 September 1931.
29. See Henry Campbell Black, *Black's Law Dictionary*, 208.
30. KNA:AG 4/2791 'Status of Native Women: Opinion.' Lawrence Tooth, Crown Counsel to CNC 15 April, 1919.
31. For example, see Jalang'o-Ndeda, *Impact of Male Labour Migration*, 1991.
32. KNA: AG 4/2791 'Status of Native Women: Legislation Re: Extract from summary of meeting at Ganzi, Coast Province between DC Kaloleni, F. M. Lamb, PC Coast Province, and Kambi 300 elders, 23 March 1919.' The deliberations of the meeting were to be conveyed to the governor.
33. *Ibid.*
34. KNA: AG 4/2791 'Status of Native Women', AG to CNC, Legal Status of Native Girls, 7 September 1931.
35. *Ibid.*
36. *Ibid.*
37. KNA: AG 4/2791 'The Status of Native Women', T. F. C. Bewes, Secretary Kenya Missionary Council to AG, 2 March 1932.
38. KNA: AG 4/2791 'The Legal Status of Native Women', AG A. D. A. MacGregor to T. F. C. Bewes, Secretary Kenya Missionary Society, 16 February 1933.
39. KNA: AG 4/2791 'Status of Native Women', R. W. Lambert, Assistant DC Kaloleni to PC Mombasa, February 1919. Quote from Giriama who Lambert believed 'could hardly be biased because his religion saves him from this particular hardship'.
40. Sometimes the women teamed up with young unmarried men living in the village. These young men 'could not afford to marry and … were all too willing to take advantage of the absence of the husbands many miles away'. Jalang'o-Ndeda, *Impact of Male Labour Migration*, 127.
41. See, for example, *Ibid.*, Appendix C, Letters on Labourers Family Affairs, 378.
42. Cohen and Atieno Odhiambo, *Siaya*, 86.

43. See Kanogo, 'Mission impact on women in colonial Kenya', in Bowie, Kirkwood & Ardener (eds), *Women and Missions*, 165–86.
44. KNA: AG 4/2791 'The Status of Native Women', PC Mombasa to CNC Nairobi, 13 March 1919.
45. *Ibid.*
46. *Ibid.*
47. KNA: AG 4/2791 Letter given to DC Kaloleni and PC Mombasa by Ganzi elders for onward transmission to the governor, 23 March 1919.
48. KNA: AG 4/2791 PC Mombasa to CNC Nyika [Miji Kenda], Marriages and Desertion of Women, 31 March 1919.
49. KNA: AG 4/2791 'Status of Native Women', CNC to AG, Native Women Leaving the Reserves, 19 April 1919.
50. KNA:AG 4/2791, 'Status of Native Women', R.W. Lambert, Assistant DC, Kaloleni to PC Mombasa, February 1919
51. *Ibid.* Under different circumstances, John Ainsworth could be very firm where he perceived mistreatment of women. He set free 'forty four pawned Maasai women purchased or captured by Kamba in 1893 and ninety-nine in 1894'. John Ainsworth, 'Kenya Reminiscences', covering 1890–1900, n.d., Rhodes House, Mss Afr. s. 380, cited in Luise White, *The Comforts of Home*, 235.
52. KNA: AG 4/2791 'Status of Native Women', Proposed Legislation, 1919.
53. KNA: AG 4/2791 R. W. Lambert, Assistant DC Kakoneni [sic: Kaloleni] to PC Mombasa, February 1919.
54. KNA: AG 4/2791 'The Status of Native Women', Assistant DC Rabai to PC Mombasa, 12 March 1919.
55. KNA: AG 4/2791 'The Status of Native Women', Assistant DC Rabai to PC Mombasa, 12 March 1919.
56. *Ibid.* The situation was compounded by a High Court ruling 'that a pagan marriage is no marriage, although a civil contract before a Registrar … [meant] that consequently no pagan can enforce tribal custom as to the payment of dowry against anyother [sic] native who may seduce his wife, unless that other is a pagan also'. KNA: AG 4/2791 'The Legal Status of Native Women', R. W. Lambert, Assistant DC Kaloleni to PC Mombasa, February 1919.
57. KNA: AG 4/2791 'Status of Native Women', PC Mombasa to CNC, 'Contracts by Women', 27 June 1919.
58. *Ibid.*
59. See Hilarie Ann Kelly, 'From Gada to Islam: The Moral Authority of Gender Relations Among the Pastoral Orma of Kenya' (Los Angeles, upublished PhD, 1992), 5.
60. KNA: AG 4/2791 'Status of Native Women: Legislation Re:' Chief Native Commissioner, 22 March 1920. This issue is discussed in greater detail in Chapter Five.
61. KNA: PC/CENT/2/1/9 LNC Meetings, Meru, Marriage of Girls Without their Parents' Consent, 7 December 1939.
62. *Ibid.*
63. For missionary activities, see for example, R. W. Strayer, *The Making of Mission Communities in East Africa: Anglicans and Africans in Colonial Kenya, 1875–1935* (London, 1978); Sandgren, *Christianity and the Kikuyu.*
64. KNA: PC/CENT/2/1/4 LNC Minutes, Kyambu District, 23 December 1931.
65. *Ibid.*
66. *Ibid.*
67. *Ibid.*
68. *Ibid.*
69. *Ibid.*
70. *Ibid.* Chairman Kyambu Local Native Council.
71. KNA: PC/CP/2/1/5 LNC Meetings, Fort Hall District, 14-15 January 1932.Fort Hall District is also referred to as Murang'a.
72. KNA: PC/CENT/2/1/9 Meru LNC Meetings, 10 December 1947.
73. KNA: PC/CE/2/1/8 President Meru LNC Meetings, 2-3 June 1948.
74. KNA: PC/CENT/2/1/8 LNC Meetings, Fort Hall District, 23-24 July 1940.

75. Colonial attribution of female agency to male prompting and instigation was also evident in the late 1940s as women protested against soil conservation work. See Tabitha Kanogo, 'Women and Environment in History', in Shanyisa Khasiani (ed.), *Groundwork: Women as Environmental Managers* (Nairobi, 1992), 15. A short-lived apolitical conceptualization of women was also evident during the Mau Mau war. See Kanogo, 'Kikuyu Women and the Politics of Protest', in Sharon Macdonald, Pat Holden & Shirley Ardener (eds), *Images of Women in Peace and War* (Oxford, 1987), 89–90. For a comprehensive analysis of women's participation in political protest and the Mau Mau war, see Presley, *Kikuyu Women.*
76. KNA: PC/CENT/2/1/8 LNC Meetings, 10–13 November 1947.
77. The details of the case were reproduced at the appeal court. See Colony and Protectorate of Kenya, Supreme Court, Law Reports of Kenya, Vol. XIV, 1932, 145-146.
78. Other cases including Rex v. Lapworthy, 22 C.A. Reports, 87; Rex v. Amkeyo (7E.A.L.R.14), 1917; East African Law Report 134, Rex v. Palmer (1913), 2 K.B. 29 also served as authority in the original ruling.
79. Quoted in Colony and Protectorate of Kenya, Report on Native Tribunals, Arthur Phillips, 1945, 292.
80. Supreme Court, Rex v. Amkeyo (7E.A.L.R.14), 1917, 82 quoted in Colony and Protectorate of Kenya, Report on Native Tribunals, Arthur Phillips, 1945.
81. Colony and Protectorate of Kenya, Supreme Court, Law Reports of Kenya, Vol. X, 1924–1926, Rex (Appellate) v. Daudi Odongo (Respondent), Criminal Appeal 25, 1926, 49.
82. *Ibid.,* 50.
83. M. A. Jalang'o Ndeda, 'The Impact of Male Labour Migration on Rural Women' (Nairobi, unpublished PhD, 1991), 378.
84. See for example, Robertson, *Trouble Showed the Way*, 164.
85. White, *Comforts of Home.*
86. Ranger, 'The invention of tradition revisited', 164.

Two

Sexuality in Culture & Law

> Nothing can 'belong to' a Kikuyu woman but what may be called her 'peculinium' viz, her two leather garments, her bracelets, earrings and necklace. If she goes off with 'illegitimate' children it merely means that they belong, not to her but to whoever happens to be her next owner, whether he is her next husband or her brother or some other guardian.[1]

The status of women is defined by more than just their formal legal standing; in any society, it is also a matter of culture, not just of law. As we have already seen, customary law and formal colonial law produced complex and varied interpretations of the status of women in colonial Kenya. At the same time, the intervention of the formal procedures of colonial law influenced the cultural status of women and allowed them to find new avenues for self-assertion and agency within the confines of custom and customary law.

On the eve of the colonial era, women were embedded in gendered constructions of power, authority, and ownership of and access to property in a manner that publicly diminished their individual agency. Their lives were cast in a host of community moulds that perpetuated unequal gender relations. Women's power and authority operated within circumscribed women's spheres. But general statements do not capture the complexity of women's' social roles in precolonial and colonial Kenya. During this period, a rich assembly of intricate social processes mediated gender and sexual relations. These were, by and large, spaces into which the colonial intervention did not reach very far. When it did, the increased geographical and cultural mobility that the colonizing process made possible did not always work to the benefit of Kenyan women.

Numerous studies have illustrated how inequitable access to and control of basic resources such as land and livestock, for example, characterized relationships between women and men. In different communities, women nevertheless did have varying degrees of control over certain categories of livestock, agricultural produce, and houses.[2] However, these studies arrive at diverse conclusions about women and property, women as property, and the social order emanating from diverse property relations.[3] Some have sought to underscore the complementarity of women and men in their productive and social activities. Tracing a complicated social map, the studies represent the duality and overlap of social processes. Some of them argue that women did not in fact occupy a subordinate position in precolonial African societies. As well as recognizing women's ownership and right to dispose of certain categories of livestock, the studies agree on women's usufructuary rights in livestock and land, which were clearly defined and well protected. In these cases, the subordination of women thus appears as a product of colonial processes.[4]

There is a general acknowledgement in some studies of women's autonomy and ability to influence diverse social processes.[5] Women's councils and age sets, for example, had limited jural authority, and women could resort to a whole range of informal actions enabling them to influence community affairs. Within the broad spectrum of possibilities, women did not always defer to male authority. Social order, even in precolonial times, was a contested process.

Other studies point towards a definite marginalization of women in the economic and social domains. Margaret Jean Hay captured the inherent vulnerability of the women: 'The women of Western Kenya – the Luo, Luyia, and Gusii, in particular – seem to have strikingly limited access to all forms of property, in comparison to many other parts of Africa. These limits generally operate to require that a woman remain in a viable marriage in order to enjoy access to agricultural land, livestock, and children.'[6]

The inheritance of immovable property by women was particularly problematic. Writing around 1947, H. E. Lambert, a colonial administrator cum ethnographer, observed that 'some Kenyan tribes have a custom by which a woman may be freed from the control of her individual guardian in special circumstances, but this does not mean that she can become the owner of immovable property.'[7] In the course of her life, a woman's guardians would include her father, husband, brothers-in-law or other male relatives, if her husband died, and, ultimately, her son, once he married.[8] Women could acquire livestock in their own right. This might take the form of marriage gifts from a father, or a woman might barter surplus produce for cattle.[9]

The multiplicity and changing nature of women's experiences demand analyses of women's legal status 'qualified and differentiated relative to [the] historical moment, social relations, the life cycle, women's subsistence roles, and various other aspects of social life'.[10] In such circumstances, the examination of individual cases can develop useful roadmaps for exploring the complexities of women's experiences. Questions regarding perceived notions of citizenship, identity, gender, kinship networks, ethnicity, control of sexuality, social capital, and women's agency arise from these cases, as we shall see below and in the following chapters.

Women's mobility and self-assertion into the domain of sexuality and the control of sexual activity among young women is a first point of enquiry. The way in which some communities dealt with marital conflicts and sexual crimes prior to and after the consolidation of colonial rule, in particular, is particularly illuminating. While these indigenous solutions persisted during the colonial period, newer approaches to similar situations illustrate both the transitions and the shifts that became necessary in colonial attempts to deal with the changing nature of women's social roles.

Colonial administrators found it difficult either to understand or to ignore prevailing indigenous sensibilities concerning cultural and customary legal practices regulating sexuality. In some cases, administrators deferred to local sensibilities while expressing their indignation. In others, colonial functionaries totally ignored local strategies for dealing with problems and instead resorted to statutory law. This was a sure way to a system full of protracted negotiations, contestations, and reformulations of strategies applied by the diverse constituencies that mediated women's lives. Women, too, responded to these changes with alternative solutions.

A variety of conflict situations involving women emerged during the transitional period, including the close of the nineteenth century and the formative colonial period, up to the mid-1920s. They demonstrate both the elision of women from the social contract, and the ways in which women nevertheless might shape it with regard to relations between the sexes. The colonial status quo was always a highly gendered, but contested situation. By juxtaposing conflict situations emanating from the precolonial period and adjudicated during the colonial period, this chapter illustrates the tensions and the tentative nature of colonial efforts to change the status of African women. The intervention of colonial officials did not necessarily spell reprieve for women. Rather, it highlighted the protracted process involved in the conceptualization of African womanhood.

Pawning, Abduction and the Status of Women

The first case to be examined skirted the question of sexuality. Some of the ambiguities arising in it, however, emanate from the undefined nature of the sexuality of pawned women. Mukuthi, a Kamba woman, was brought to public notice by an ecological disaster that ravaged Kamba territory during most of the last decade of the nineteenth century.[11] Bovine pleuropneumonia and rinderpest epidemics devastated Kamba livestock, and drought, locust invasions, and an outbreak of smallpox also hit the region. The recurrent epidemics and resulting famines throughout the 1890s, culminated in the great famine of 1899–1900.[12] Such natural calamities stretched the capacity of the male heads of households to retain control over their people. One way a household could preserve itself was by the practice of pawning some of its women, who would be sent into the custody of another ethnic group in return for the food needed to survive, thus simultaneously relieving numbers and gaining the means to feed those that remained.

Mukuthi's mother had been pawned by her Kamba kinsmen in exchange for foodstuff to the less ravaged Kikuyu during the great famine. She was initially 'bought' and married to Kahuthwa Mbui, bearing a daughter, Mukuthi. While still a child, Mukuthi and her mother were sold to Chief Njegga of Baricho, in Nyeri. Here, Mukuthi grew into a mature girl and in time got married to Chief Njegga. Together, this couple brought forth offspring, at least one who was considered too young to be separated from its mother, when a Kamba kinsman, Karuti, took Mukuthi away in a clandestine effort to redeem her some time in 1921.[13]

A woman referred to as Chief Njegga's wife provided the details of the initial transaction and subsequent abduction.[14] She was possibly the Chief's eldest wife, who had witnessed the whole saga. As the matriarch of the family and Njegga's senior wife, she would have kept watch over the women in the household and at times of crisis would have mediated with the outside authorities on behalf of her husband and the household. She also would have come to perceive Mukuthi and her child as part of her husband's household's social capital. From this point of view, as a co-wife, Mukuthi was fulfilling important productive and reproductive roles, as were other women in the household.

Marriages constructed out of pawnship arrangements were in reality political alliances that enabled a community facing economic crisis to exchange some of its human social capital to acquire sustenance for the rest of the population pending the recovery of its economy. Attempts to get pawned women back without the payment of redemption compensation consequently resulted in resistance. As early as 1902, for example, Akamba elders were seeking restitution from the Provincial Commissioner in Central Province. The conflict extended to the beginning of the early 1930s and highlighted central concerns about women during this formative colonial period.[15]

Unlike her mother, Mukuthi was born of a Kikuyu father.[16] We do not know why Mbui subsequently disposed of Mukuthi and her mother. Maybe Mbui had married Mukuthi's mother only to oblige his father, and the marriage had turned sour. It is also possible that Mukuthi's mother never quite settled down in her new domicile, always longing to go back to her kinsmen. Maybe she was melancholic and difficult to get along with. It is likewise possible that Mukuthi's father had become a small-time operator seeking to expand the capital base of his household by disposing of an unfortunate Kamba woman and her child at an opportune time. Maybe her initial purchaser was merely speculating, playing the market and trying to make some profit.

Conventional colonial wisdom held that 'alliances struck between famine victims and their buyers are regarded as any other marriage.'[17] Thus, although Mukuthi was legally defined as an offspring of the marriage of Mbui and a Mkamba woman, the nature of such marriages in indigenous culture is difficult to categorize. Even if a semblance of marriage was sealed at some stage, Mbui must have changed his mind after Mukuthi was born, because for the second time, Mukuthi's mother was sold off, this time with her infant daughter, to a local 'big man', Chief Njegga. But just what was the status of the women that Mbui had sold? Had he sold a wife and daughter, or two females of ambiguous cultural status? Was Mukuthi a Kamba, like her mother, or a Kikuyu, like her father? And was her mother the wife of Mbui, with all that entails for the nature of their sexual relations, or was she his property, with all that entails, as well, and then the property of Njegga? Was Mukuthi herself Njegga's wife, or his chattel, and what was the status of their children?

The Kikuyu community was patrilineal and patrilocal. In that situation, an offspring becomes a member of her father's clan where the mother was married to the father of the baby. The DC for Embu had explained to the Senior Commissioner for Nyeri that 'by native law the title to children descends in perpetuity', even in cases of pawnship.[18] It would seem that the disposal of a kinless woman and her female children was easy: the fact that women became members of their husbands' clans upon marriage points to their migratory identity. This possibly explained the ease with which Mukuthi and her mother were treated as property, not kin, and sold.[19]

Since both the Kamba and the Kikuyu are patriarchal, under normal circumstances, Mukuthi would derive her lineage affiliation from her father. But the circumstances were not normal. Mukuthi did not reside with her biological father, and the Kamba refused to recognize the purchase of Mukuthi and her mother by Njegga. For the Kamba, Mukuthi was a Kamba born in exile. The construction of kinship under circumstances of pawnship thus created conflict between the Kikuyu and the Kamba, who otherwise embraced similar kinship practices in general.

The DC for Chief Njegga's locality, Nyeri, advocated a civil procedure to resolve the issue. Writing to his counterpart in Kitui, Mukuthi's kinsman's home, the DC suggested that both Mukuthi and Karuti, her Kamba rescuer, be sent back to Nyeri, where the latter could make a case for the recovery of Mukuthi. In the meantime, Njegga had already made a summons against Karuti for the return of Mukuthi. The DC for Nyeri forwarded this summons to his counterpart in Kitui. The Senior Commissioner, however, was quite curt in his response: 'Claims arising out of this famine are not allowed to be heard in Ukamba and presumably are also barred in Kenya.'[20] Provincial Commissioners from Ukamba and Kenya had met and decided that no claims arising from any famine in the period before 1918 were to be considered. In this light, Karuti was judged to be in the wrong and prosecuted accordingly: Mukuthi was to be returned to Njegga. Mukuthi was thus treated as property, and as Kikuyu property, not Kamba kin.

It is not clear what type of a relationship this entailed. In deliberating Mukuthi's case, the DC for Machakos characterized it as a 'quasi-marriage'. Marriage might bring honour and social status to a pawned woman, but it might also put her in an unwelcome situation, as colonial administrators were aware. According to the DC for Machakos, 'It is in fact difficult to regard her either as a chattel or as a woman married by her own wish and consent and logically we have no right to punish any person who assisted her to exercise her own free will...we may not be very far wrong if we suspect that their position is something between a concubine and a slave.'[21]

There also might be pawned women whose lives unfolded along conventional and predictable paths, including marriage, motherhood, establishment of social networks among their marital kinsmen, and an average existence like that of most married women. Not all pawned women tried to run away. In certain ways the particularities of their lives were collapsed into wider social moulds. Mukuthi did not have an independent jural position. To the DC's understanding, this was because the status of a pawned woman was constructed within the general provisions of marriage. Under this situation, 'A Kikuyu woman whether bought by payment of bridewealth, captured in war, or rescued from starvation is held to be the property of her lord and master'. [22]

Although it was suggested that this conflict should be treated as a civil case to be heard by Second Class Magistrate, the practice was for such matters to be heard by colonial administrators who wore many hats, including the judicial. For this reason an administrator's decision in a pawnship case might displease his superiors, as happened in the case of Njegga versus Karuti. The DC Kitui had decided that the woman Mukuthi and her child should be allowed to stay in the land of her maternal relative and Njegga the claimant should receive statutory payment.[23] The Senior Commissioner was concerned that this and future cases of pawned women be subject to legal arbitration, so he intervened, rather harshly, in his letter to DC Kitui:

> I direct you, in your administrative, not your judicial capacity, to send the woman Mukuthi and the man Karuti without further delay to the office of the Baricho magistrate in order that he may decide who is entitled to the woman. As I have previously stated I regard the above case as a special one and I want you to defer action on general lines regarding other famine refugees until the Hon. C.N.C. has dealt with the matter and settled what policy should be followed.[24]

The Senior Commissioner expected his orders to be carried out 'without further demur'.

It is nonetheless significant that throughout the Mukuthi case, no reference is made to Mukuthi's desire or opinion in the matter. The practical arrangements of pawning agreements do not seem to have taken into consideration the anguish and trauma of the pawned. That she accompanied Karuti to Kamba territory is possibly the greatest indicator of Mukuthi's position in the whole affair. That Mukuthi had lived all her life in Kikuyu territory, and still accompanied a Mkamba in flight is significant. It is possible that her mother had been extremely unhappy as a pawned woman and that this fact had not escaped Mukuthi. Maybe her mother talked constantly of her wish to return to her kinsmen, a return to what she viewed as normal. In this context, Kambaland would not denote foreignness to Mukuthi. It would have represented the place where her much-desired maternal kinsmen lived, kinsmen who even after two decades had not forgotten her mother and who did all they could to get her, Mukuthi, back – the one aspect of being contested social capital that Mukuthi accepted. Whether Mukuthi opposed or welcomed the 'abduction', her opinion was not sought, according to the archive. It is impossible to say if she was a willing accomplice to Karuti's 'crime'. Even as the subject of a protracted conflict, her agency was ignored.

In this as in other instances, there was a difference of opinion among the administrators as to how the case should be handled. Although the DC for Kitui was sure that Mukuthi was Njegga's property, and he was not sure as to 'what the position under the pact is as regards small children recently born by such women to their Kikuyu owners', the DC felt that Mukuthi should not be returned to Njegga because she was 'a relic from the Big famine'. He also considered the child to be 'much too small to be separated from the mother'. His suggestion was for the DC for Nyeri to send a representative of Njegga 'to receive the statutory payment'.[25] The colonial administration's reading of local sensibilities was summarized thus: 'In native eyes, a man who takes away a woman from her husband or guardian is a thief; his offence is regarded as a crime of the same kind as, but greater in degree than the theft of a cow. The above remarks apply equally to Kikuyu women of the 1918 famine.'[26] Akamba refugee women of the 1899 famine could be redeemed for six cows equally weighted so that three represented the worth of the woman and the balance represented 'the cost of maintaining her'.[27]

Because Mukuthi had fled back to Kamba with some of her own offspring, Karuti had struck a double blow to the Njegga's Kikuyu kin group. Before colonial intervention, the purchaser of a pawned woman claimed ownership of both the woman and her progeny. According to the Acting DC for Nyeri, if a Kamba woman who was regarded the property of her husband left him to join her relations, 'the person taking her in must pay the injured husband an equivalent, [which] varies according to the number of children born by her to her husband'. The redemption of a pawned woman was said to be dependent upon her agreeing to leave her children behind, which 'they seldom do, at least until the children are married'.[28] Motherhood seemed to outweigh ethnic considerations. By this reckoning, not just Mukuthi herself, but also Mukuthi's children, the offspring of her sexual relations with Njegga, would be Njegga's property. Thus, the DC for Nyeri could declare:

> Nothing can 'belong to' a Kikuyu woman but what may be called her 'peculinium' viz, her two leather garments, her bracelets, earrings and necklace. If she goes off with 'illegitimate' children it merely means that they belong, not to her but to whoever happens to be her next owner, whether he be her next husband or her brother or some other guardian.[29]

For their part, as in the effort to deal with issues involving the formal legal status of women, administrators found it difficult to respect native habits and custom while striving to impose the 'spirit of civilized law'.[30] For example, as objects of the pawnship transaction, women might object to their purchaser's claims and try to get back to their homes. It is therefore probable that the movement of pawned women was under constant surveillance by their new custodians. Their precarious situation irked some colonial administrators, who hoped for legal solution to the problem. The DC for Machakos stated 'Our law, if the matter were ever tested in a court of justice, would probably give complete freedom to the woman and her children, unless definite marriage could be proved.'[31] On the other hand, there were concerns over the 'just claims of the purchaser', who might need official protection 'as far as equity and justice would allow', as the colonial administrators saw it. The DC for Machakos wondered whether colonial administrators could or should 'allow freedom of movement to the subjects of famine bargains.'[32]

Furthermore, the administration was concerned that settling any one case would give rise to many more, when there was not enough staff to deal with such an eventuality. At worst, it 'would close down the tax collection and registration'. In any case, a more experienced crop of Assistant District Commissioners would be required to deal with such complaints. For the DC for Embu, it seemed better to ignore all matters involving pawned women. The potential administrative and financial resources required would be formidable, and the outcomes might have unintended consequences. Should the indigenous communities know that the government did not support claims arising from pawning arrangements, subsequent famines might not elicit the reciprocal spirit that pawning did. In other words, 'possible benefactors would not think it worth their while, from a pecuniary point of view, to save the starving: and the rigours of a famine might be even more distressing than they need be.' Some of the administrators also were very conflicted as to the exact nature of the pawning arrangement. It was not clear whether the term 'sale' meant the same thing to the administrators as to the indigenous communities. The DC Machakos asserted: 'It would, I think, be repugnant both to our mode of thought and to the best of native opinion to treat the matter in this light and a bargain for the possession of [a] human being for a few bags of food in the distressing circumstances of a famine would best be described as harsh and unconscionable.'[33]

The vulnerability of pawned women is best summarized by the reflections of an emaciated, blind Nandi woman who was once pawned and who was now a prospective convert to the Christian faith. Approached by a missionary who represented himself as a harbinger of good news, the woman confessed to not having heard good news for a long time. The missionary had found her lying behind a hut in the Kapsabet area. The ensuing conversation painted a grim picture of pawnship:

> 'But how do you come to be lying here mother?' said the missionary. 'Ara, shall I not tell you how? At the time of the great famine, I was given to the Jaluo as a pledge for some sacks of grain. My people took the grains and left me with the Jaluo, saying that they would come back some time and get me again. They never came back for me. When I grew up I was married to a Jaluo and lived all the days on the Kano plains beside the lake [Victoria]. When I grew old and was no longer of any use in the garden, for I was blind as you see me now, they drove me out, because I only ate food and could not do enough work. I gradually came back to Nandi country, hoping to find my own people, but they had moved a long way to the farms. Then one day I found these women in Boma. Because they are distantly related to me, they brought me here; but they do not really want me. They put me out here in the morning and give me some food, and they take me into the house at night. My own people live a long way from here,' said the old woman. 'Well mother, I have brought you good news today.' 'Good news? No one ever tells me news.'[34]

In all likelihood, this old woman did not have children who would take care of her. Maybe she had daughters only, who were married in distant places and therefore not in a position to take in a desperate parent. Her kinlessness and ethnic otherness exacerbated her plight. Pawnship created a void of social marginality and disequilibria for its victims.

Bridewealth and Divorce

One of the many issues that arose out of pawnship controversies to vex the colonial administrators related to the question of bridewealth, or dowry: the livestock, goods, money or services customarily given by a prospective husband to his bride's family.[35] It was not unusual for a young bride to go to her husband's home before he had paid bridewealth.[36] Unless the Kamba were like the Kipsigis, for whom the delay was part of the customary timetable, a magnanimous father and impoverished young suitor might enter into an arrangement, with the elder allowing his daughter to get married prior to the payment of bridewealth. Similarly, the father of a pregnant daughter might agree to a rushed 'marriage' pending payment of bridewealth, to save face. Among the pastoral Turkana of northwestern Kenya, a bride could not be initiated into womanhood unless an acceptable amount of bridewealth had been give over.[37] The aspersion of poverty that resulted from a failure to pay undermined the man's authority as head of household and his wife's social status. However, in the wider traditional construction of womanhood, this bridewealth component became more tenuous. Poorer men no longer cared that their wives had not been inducted into womanhood,[38] especially if the wife in question was previously divorced. A similar initiation rite for brides, the *enyangi*, was performed among the Kisii. At the time of the ceremony, the last of the bridewealth livestock was delivered to the wife's home, ensuring the wife's graduation from girlhood. At the ceremony, the woman took a new name and was allowed to don iron ankle rings for the first time. More importantly, she was invested with the status of a wife.[39]

As we shall see later (in Chapters 4 and 5), marriage was part of a cultural process, rather than an institution which was created in a one-time action at a registrar's office, or in a church. In customary practice, society was concerned to maintain long-term cordial relations between the families of the spouses, so that it was expected, for example, that if a bride should die during her first childbirth, the husband would be liable for the 'unpaid balance to the extent of two cows and one bull'.[40] For the same reason, with the passage of time, the bereaved young man could recover some of his payment. He was entitled to request for a calf from his former father-in-law, offering first a gift of beer to the elder.[41]

A husband who married a pawned woman was still expected to supply bridewealth to her family, and if she escaped, he might also demand its return. In 1921, the DC for Machakos considered it reasonable for the husband in that situation to claim as much as half the current rate being paid in the husband's area.[42] At about the turn of the century, the bride price among the Akamba was fixed at three cows, two bulls, 'and value of food of all kinds to the extent of a cow'.[43] These figures might change due to adverse climatic conditions, which might result in famines and therefore reduce the bridewealth. Extended favourable weather would create bounty and therefore inflate the bridewealth.

If a newly-married woman died during the birth of her first child, it was expected that out of goodwill, the father of the girl would return one cow to his bereaved son-in-law. There was no compulsion in this action. It was obvious to the older gentleman that the young man would soon have to address the question of bridewealth payment in his next marriage. A bit of goodwill was seen to be in good taste; a 'gracious' act on the part of the girl's parents.

There were other circumstances besides escape and death in childbirth where a husband might request his bridewealth back, principally divorce. There was an established procedure by which a man could divorce his wife. If after full payment of bridewealth he found it impossible to sustain the marriage, he would follow the stipulated protocol for the recovery of his property. In the presence of his wife's relations, the man would state his grievances and 'beg' for his father-in-law to take his daughter back and return the bridewealth.[44] Treading carefully, the bridegroom did not demand his property. Any antagonistic move on his part might jeopardize his chances of a refund and therefore of a quick replacement of his spouse. At the end of the nineteenth century in Nyanza, however, such refunds would entail huge losses to the woman's family. There, before the outbreak of cattle epidemic, bridewealth among the Luo numbered between forty to sixty heads of cattle.[45]

The archive does not include women's views, if any, on this divorce procedure. The return of bridewealth 'wipe[d] out a Kikuyu customary marriage completely'.[46] But if a father was not willing to give back bridewealth to a son-in-law, a woman who contemplated divorce might have to endure a bad marriage. However, among the Luo of Nyanza, if a woman made accusations of witchcraft and impotence, she was more likely to attain a divorce. In such a situation, the right to divorce was granted regardless of subsequent courses of action with regard to bridewealth.

Under customary practices, however, a man had to wait for the remarriage of his ex-wife before he could get a refund of his bridewealth. This cannot have taken very long, otherwise the society would not have adopted it as part of a workable remedy for incompatible spouses. The procedure was predicated on the belief that divorced women would remarry quickly. Like unmarried girls, a divorced woman was subjected to moral appraisal. 'A disciplined [divorced] lady always got another man. It was rare to miss,' according to the conventional wisdom. Those who went back to live in their natal homes attained a new and less than honourable social status, that of *omukoko* and *icakamuyu* (divorcée) among the Wanga and the Kikuyu respectively. Although she was allocated land at her natal home for herself and her children (if she had kept them), the divorced woman remained a social embarrassment to her family. At death, she would be buried away from other relatives, at the periphery of the family property.[47] If the divorce resolution excluded the return of bridewealth, however, she received a better reception. 'She would be kept well because they [her family] had consumed her dowry'.[48]

Social stigma was also associated with spinsterhood. Among the Luyia, such a girl would be allocated land in her natal home where she 'built a house "outside the *boma* [homestead]". It is from there that she had her "free time" [liaisons with men]. But such a lady was not respected. Even her sisters-in-law did not like her. Some of those who did not get married and were not welcomed at their homes started working in places like bars.' Among the Wanga, when such an unmarried woman died, a '*Litiri*', or burial hut for an unmarried woman, was built 'outside the home'. [49] Even the women married into a household would have less respect for an unmarried daughter of the *boma*. Hence, girls who had gained maturity but never married, always felt unwelcome in their own homes. When they died, they were buried in the rear part of the compound, in the banana plantation. In life, as in death, an unmarried woman remained an enigma. Her respectability was massively reduced by her unmarried status.

Increasingly the proceeds of bridewealth were used to meet diverse financial needs, including school fees.[50] In general, brothers of the divorced woman were the key beneficiaries of bridewealth proceeds, especially livestock. They were also the major stake holders in the family lands, a portion of which a divorced woman would hope to access on her return to unmarried status, and which would remain hers if she did not remarry. This land would be particularly vital if the woman had growing children to support. Male children were particularly problematic because they might have to be absorbed into their maternal home and allocated land, unless their paternal kinsmen bequeathed them their inheritance.

A girl's father might not consider it necessary to take back his daughter. Rather, he might try to remedy the situation by pleading 'lack of education' on the part of his daughter and place her under instruction, promising to deliver a much-improved wife within a few days.[51] He would endeavour to have his daughter steeped in the 'traditional' sensibilities of wifedom. As well as protecting his property, that is, his livestock, the response of the girl's father reflected society's prime concern, that of safeguarding the stability of marriages and marital alliances. Unless considered adverse, domestic and sexual disputes did not result in the dissolution of marriage. More importantly, neither spouse could take any course of action on an individual basis.

The husband could still reject the re-educated wife. Ultimately, the dissolution of the union and the return of the bridewealth required that the man be not responsible for the breakup. This implies that a wife, most likely by proxy, got the chance to respond to the charges made by her husband, giving women the opportunity to mediate their lot in marriage. Later, at the beginning of colonial rule, elders would attempt to galvanize the support of the government by reinventing customary law and totally subsuming women's voices to male domination in matters of domestic discord and resolution.

A man who contemplated divorce and had children could pick one of two options. He could choose to keep the children and therefore forfeit the return of his bridewealth. Alternatively, he might opt for the return of bridewealth and its increase, thereby forfeiting all rights to his children, who would be absorbed in the clan of their maternal grandfather.[52] This would incur a heavy loss of potential members to the divorced husband's clan, for marriage and procreation were the most common ways of building social capital.

Divorce therefore was said to be rare, but not nonexistent, in marriages contracted under customary law.[53] An overly distraught wife might desert the marital home and return to her natal home, but she might not find herself welcome. However, residence with a paternal grandmother served the purpose of providing both a less fraught environment and an uninhibited forum where she could discuss her marital problems with her grandmother, something she might not want to do with her mother.[54] These discussions might include sexual matters. In the public discussions of the divorce, a husband would use idioms to express dissatisfaction in this very private domain.[55]

By custom, the right to initiate a divorce was largely limited to men. Among the Kipsigis, for example, a woman could seek divorce on one ground only: 'If her husband is neglecting his conjugal duties in favour of some other woman (to whom he is not married) to such an extent as to lessen to such a great degree the probability of her ever becoming a mother.'[56] An older brother of the woman, outraged by his brother-in-law's behaviour, was 'usually deputed to fight her husband'. The quest for divorce would follow only if the husband did not 'mend his ways'. Thus, adultery per se on the part of the man was not sufficient cause for

Kipsigis women to seek divorce. Additionally, the performance of a *katunisiet* ceremony, which was considered the most important of all the marriage ceremonies, could preempt divorce. This gave the husband 'not only complete authority over his wife, as after *katunisiet* she cannot divorce him; but also it makes him independent of his parents-in-law, as after this ceremony, they cannot force the bride to leave her husband and marry another man'.[57]

Despite such tight restrictions on women's right to seek divorce, they sought it in unprecedented numbers during the colonial period via the new legal avenues that the administration made available. They expected a fairer hearing in colonial courts than from the customary venues. In this respect, colonial sensibilities worked to the advantage of women. Of Nyanza, O. S. Knowles, the Provincial Commissioner observed in 1949:

> Normally a woman has no right under customary law to seek a divorce from her husband, but modern developments...enable a woman to plead before the indigenous elders and the formal chief's *baraza* [public village forum] for an annulment of her marriage. Usually she is told to return to her husband to give the marriage further trial. This may happen twice or thrice. Finally the *baraza* accepts her refusal to live with her husband and gives her permission to return to her father. It is, I believe, the desire of the woman in the more advanced areas to have this order of the Chief's *baraza* confirmed by a court order, which makes them institute 'divorce' proceedings before the Native Tribunals.[58]

Initially, a disgruntled wife might draw the attention of her brothers-in-law to her misgivings about their brother. Economic impropriety on the part of the husband, including wanton disposal of livestock, food crops, family land, or failure to remit cash to family was a characteristic complaint.[59] Among her kinsmen, a wife also could lodge her complaints to natal elders, who would summon the accused husband. Both parties would be given a hearing, after which the elders would arbitrate and make a ruling.[60]

Apart from resorting to conventional mediating fora, feuding couples in Wanga might try something else. 'There was some medicine cooked and given to them in order to coerce them into accepting one another.'[61] This portion did not always rekindle marital bliss. Some women preferred to ride the storm of divorce and the consequent social marginalization if they did not manage to remarry.

It was no longer enough for women that elders at a Chief's *baraza* had deliberated on a divorce plea and granted the request. They sought the protection that the formal documentation of a court order was perceived to confer. 'In their view, the matter is then on record in the court files.'[62] Women were exploiting changes initiated by the presence of the colonial legal system in order to transform and enlarge traditional spaces for initiating and discussing divorce. According to Knowles, women sought divorces in order to 'ensure freedom to remarry irrespective of the vagaries of bride price refunds by relatives, and secondarily, to ensure the custody of children sired by another man, whether or not the petitioner was legally married to the man at the time'. In this last concern, women were necessarily creating a new, nonlineal and female-centred basis for the custody of children.[63] By the 1950s, women were filing for divorces on diverse grounds, including 'physical cruelty; failure to provide necessities such as clothing, soap or a hut; impotence and childlessness; chronic alcoholism; desertion; witchcraft (usually by the mother-in-law); sexual perversion; and venereal diseases...mental cruelty and general incompatibility'.[64] Knowles's study of South Nyanza indicated that more divorce petitions were successful than otherwise. Where a petition did not succeed the first time, there was always the possibility of appeal and positive outcome.

Rape

While some women used new opportunities to redefine divorce and gain agency in marital relationships, there were other aspects of male-female conflict that were harder to change. Where divorces might create new freedoms, by being shifted from the customary, or private sphere to the colonial, public system, other aspects of sexual matters needed to be changed in order to give women a voice in this very sensitive matter.

Sexual relations were not private or personal in traditional Kenyan societies. Having intercourse affected the welfare of the families and clans of the parties doing it.[65] Sexual misconduct of all categories was perceived as a transgression against the clan members of either one or the other of the parties involved. Among the Kamba, for example, if a married woman was raped, a fine of a bull and a goat was imposed on the offender, and the animals were slaughtered and consumed by the relatives of the woman.[66] The rapist's guilt was cleared with the payment of the stipulated fines: it was the clan that was perceived to be the aggrieved party to be appeased, for the woman had no individual standing in the matter, cultural or legal. She could not be individually accused or sued for sexual crime: a male guardian who acted as the spokesperson for the victim undertook the public defence of a woman's honour as a member of the clan. Social responsibility was gendered, which, while sparing women the social anguish of culpability, also robbed them of agency. Meanwhile, their personal suffering was irrelevant.

These social representations of the rape crime treated women as social capital, to the exclusion of their individual legal personhood. If the raped woman became pregnant, the rapist would be expected to pay an additional fine of another goat. However, in the case of an unmarried girl, the rapist had a choice. He could either pay this fine or marry her. The payment of the stipulated fine was considered sufficient to exonerate the rapist of the crime and restore him to the dignity of a prospective suitor.[67] If the rapist did not marry his victim, if she became pregnant and he failed to pay the stipulated fine, and if the child died, he would be liable for another fine of one bull and two goats. If he had paid the first goat and the child died, he would have to pay one bull and one goat only. Force would be applied if the man refused to pay these fines. The payment of a higher fine for the death of the child than for the initial rape crime seems to consolidate the case for the clan's concern with social capital. Rape, unlike death, did not rob the community of social capital.

In the absence of information about the opinion of the woman in question, it could be assumed that she, too, subscribed to the group's sensibility and considered the rapist a prospective suitor. There is every possibility, however, that such women were unwilling marriage partners to men who had used force, violated their honour and personal integrity. Rape, in any cultural context, is physically an act of violence. Perhaps the shame of having been raped and a possible decrease of marriage chances made victims more amenable to marrying their rapist in a society where unmarried spinsters were extremely rare and despised.

The social diffusion of rape minimized the seriousness of the crime, vindicating the male culprits and relegating the female victims to situations of double jeopardy if they had to marry the perpetrator. The subsuming of an individual's misfortunes to lineage welfare meant that women did not get a fair representation in rape cases. Generally, marriage 'restored' the girl's honour and social identity. In effect, it was a forced marriage to the perpetrator.

It was not necessarily the loss of virginity that made rape a transgression in most of these communities. The significance of a bride's virginity differed among ethnic groups in Kenya. In some groups, including the Abakhayo, Marachi, Banyala, Samia, Bukusu, Kabras, and Tachoni subgroups of the Abaluyia, a girl's virginity was significant. On the other hand, while the Maragoli and Babukusu considered virginity a special virtue, its loss was not considered a disgrace. The virginity of a bride did not seem to be particularly important among the Kamba.[68]

Unlike single girls, who were in a transitional status until marriage, married women were social capital already realized. By paying bridewealth, a clan had invested in and appropriated the procreative and productive services of their daughter-in-law. The rape of a married woman therefore elicited a fine of one bull and one sheep – greater than the fine for the rape of a single woman. In the rape of a married woman, the honour of her husband's clan also was in jeopardy.

The traditional communalization of culpability and litigation, whereby clans were the litigants in cases of rape, was in contrast to the colonial process, which individualized litigation and responsibility. During the latter period, all efforts were made to eradicate the communal interest in the issue and to attribute personal responsibility for sex-related offences. By 1920, litigation reconfigured the punishment for rape in a manner that attempted to bring the legal personhood of the woman to the fore. In Fort Hall, where the fine for rape of a married woman was once four large sheep paid to and consumed by the *kiama*, the elders' council, the colonial government intervened so that the *kiama* received two sheep, and the balance went to the raped woman.[69] This compensation recognized the woman as the offended party and went some way towards appeasing her. The Kikuyu woman almost always sold the livestock, since it was not their custom to own it.

An unmarried girl was still not compensated. In this case, the fine of ten goats was higher than that for rape of a married woman, a possible indicator of changing notions of the comparative degree of violation, yet it was the father who received the livestock. The *kiama* received two sheep. In the eyes of colonial administrators, the rape of an unmarried girl appeared to be more grievous than that of a married woman. Surprisingly, even under colonial surveillance, the *ciama* (plural of *kiama*) did not feel obliged to mete out additional punishment to repeat offenders.

Ciama decisions regarding the rape of unmarried girls remained characterized by lingering legal ambivalence. This was most telling in cases where uncircumcised boys had consensual sex with circumcised girls. In such cases, a boy would be deemed responsible and fined three large sheep, which were divided between the *kiama* and the girl's father. If the sexual relations were against the girl's consent, then five large sheep were payable, three to the *kiama* and two to the girl's father.[70] Among the Kikuyu, circumcision for both sexes resulted in full admission to the tribe and entry into adulthood. This carried certain responsibilities and privileges.[71] That an uncircumcised boy who would belong to the lower social rank of the uninitiated could be held responsible for the crime of consensual sex with a circumcised girl, and the latter was not held culpable is both odd and poignant. It would appear that such a society viewed all males, including the uncircumcised, as more responsible than circumcised girls.

In legal parlance, the circumcised girl was not viewed as competent to stand trial. Her legal personhood was in question. While her testimony was vital, she still was not a litigant per se. Her male guardians again undertook the public defence of the girl's honour. As we already have seen, this is a question that reared its head throughout the colonial period as different colonial administrators tried to enforce the recognition of the legal personhood of African women over twenty-one years.[72]

Throughout the 1920s, 30s and 40s sexual violation of adult and juvenile females received increasing government attention. The 1930s are particularly replete with court cases on rape charges. Women could seek redress in formal courts. Additionally, communities increasingly enlisted the official sanction of the colonial state. Once people took to prosecution, the range of situations that arose was great. There were juvenile perpetrators of rape, and juvenile victims of rape.

For example, the case of Rex v. Opiri Meope and Opiri Osano hinged upon the age of the accused; the question was whether a person who was physically incapable of committing rape could be legally culpable. Brought before Judge Joseph Sheridan of the Supreme Court in Criminal Case No. 65 of 1927, Opiri Osano had been convicted of rape of a woman while Opiri Meope had been convicted as an abettor. Opiri Osano was over fourteen years of age and, more importantly, he had reached the age of puberty. In his appeal ruling, Judge Joseph Sheridan observed that Opiri Osano 'was capable physically of committing rape on the woman and that he did commit rape'. Opiri Meope, on the other hand was 'a boy from twelve to thirteen years, over twelve years on the evidence'. Although physically incapable of committing rape himself, and giving him the benefit of the doubt, Judge Sheridan concluded 'I find he assisted his companion to do so and therefore is guilty as an abettor.'[73]

Dynamics emanating from colonial changes complicated rape cases further. Ethnicity became particularly important in some cases, leading colonial courts to ascribe the obstruction of justice to ethnic partisanship, at times. In Criminal Case No.158 of 1939 one Kasemas, son of Omungi, was accused of raping an eight-year-old girl. Each of the three assessors was said to return an opinion of not guilty. The appeal judge was infuriated by this verdict and observed,

> I suspect that their opinions are based not upon the evidence they have heard but upon their inter-tribal prejudice. They are Jaluos, the accused is a Jaluo, and the complainant child is a Kikuyu. I deplore their opinions which are the result of either stupidity or perverseness.'[74]

The complainant, a child of eight, was described as a 'slight and shy little girl' who gave her evidence 'in a straightforward if timid way'. Because of her age, she was not sworn. For this reason, her statements had to be corroborated substantially to get a conviction. For the appeal, there was ample corroboration because the accused was suffering from gonorrhea at the time of the offence. More importantly, the child too had contracted gonorrhea by the seventh day after the alleged rape. A doctor Chaudri and the child's grandmother confirmed that the child had not suffered from the disease before the alleged assault. The medicalization of legal procedures expanded the repertoire of evidence although at first this did not go unchallenged. In this case, the admissibility of gonorrhea as corroborative evidence was in question. The appeal judge quoted from Taylor's Medical Jurisprudence, 8th Edition, Vol. 2, page 123:

> As a preliminary of these remarks on purulent and muco-purulent discharges, we may observe that they should not be admitted as furnishing corroborative evidence of rape, except, first, when the accused party is labouring under gonorrheal discharge; second, when the date of it appearance in a child is from the third to the eighth day after the alleged intercourse; and third, when it has been satisfactorily established that the child had not suffered any such discharge previously to the assault.[75]

Upon physical examination, there was evidence that she had been recently raped at a date approximate to when the child claimed it had happened. The accused had been at the child's home on the material day while her grandmother, who cared for the child, was away. He had an opportunity to commit the crime. The grandmother and Asha, another witness for the prosecution also claimed that when confronted, the accused had acknowledged interfering with the child and that he tried to hush the matter by giving the grandmother shs.20 and promising a further shs.50. The grandmother instead took the money to the police station and reported the case.

While the grandmother, Asha and the girl were said to give their evidence in 'an honest and straightforward manner' the accused was represented as unreliable, suggesting in a 'rambling and garrulous fashion', that somebody else had infected the little girl. His alibi was weak and his 'denial that he knew he had gonorrhea is sufficient to stamp him a liar'.

This rape case was partly the unfolding story of complex urban, labour, ethnic and gender dynamics. The trial description of the accused as a new lodger and a poor man implies that he lived with the girl's family for a fee. He was either a seasonal or long-term migrant worker. Underpaid migrant labourers who could not afford to rent independent housing became lodgers. Extensive trust was invested when taking in total strangers, especially for families with young children. As well as recreating shifts in household arrangements, this case also depicts some of the strategies that female heads of households employed to alleviate financial needs.

Allegedly threatened with beating if she spoke about her ordeal, the little girl did not confide in her grandmother until after the latter had discovered the gonorrhea. The appeal judge found that the child's infection and the attempt by the accused to hush up the matter by giving money to the grandmother was enough to convict the accused on the first count of rape. The judge considered the crime 'horrible and detestable' befitting a severe sentence. A sentence of 5 years imprisonment with hard labour and 'twenty strokes of the whip' was imposed.[76]

Curative Rape

Increasingly, rape cases were referred to and tried by protectorate courts, where the violation of single girls resulted in more severe sentences, a probable indication of emergent gender equity in the legal sphere. Colonial sensibilities tended toward the reworking of social hierarchies to the advantage of women and at the expense of men, but they came into conflict with major and deeply ingrained cultural practices, even in this seemingly uncontroversial area. Among some clans among the Kipsigis, for example, on the eve of their initiation, boys were expected to rape a woman as a way of foisting their youthful uncleanliness on to her. This was part of a wider perception that rape could be curative, particularly for venereal disease in men. In essence, women, the supposed source of vice, could also bestow health. J. G. Peristiany observed, 'when they [the Kipsigis] feel the first signs of syphilis, they will immediately think of rape as a potential panacea.'[77] This practice found parallel among other communities in the colony.

On 27 July 1920, the DC for Nyeri reported rumours among the Kikuyu under his jurisdiction regarding Swahili claims that venereal diseases could be cured if one had sex with an uninfected female from an ethnic group other than his own.[78] Notions of cleanliness and potency were not necessarily linked to virginity, so that the woman did not have to be a virgin for the cure to be effective. Given the unscientific basis of the practice, it seems safe to assume that multiple rapes might be considered necessary as the afflicted males worked on the assumption that at least one of their attacks would be successful.

This pseudoscientific knowledge was gender-specific in its origin, content, objective, and target. Circulating among men – mostly migrant workers – the rumour did not anticipate the possible infection of women in the course of the curative rape. It represented women as passive participants. There did not seem to be any moral judgement about this category of rape. Disease, gender, ethnicity, sexuality, and health became momentarily linked in the popular imagination among infected men. Significantly, the colonial administrators did not deliberate on the predicament of healthy African women whose well-being was in jeopardy, any more than the indigenous men who acted on the rumour. It was a male-centered business.

The Kikuyu first noticed reports of sexually transmitted diseases in 1901. The severity and novelty of this condition is evidenced by the fact that the contemporary age grade during that year was named after the disease, *Gatego*. Only girls were circumcised in this year.[79] Before 1920, North Kavirondo seems to have generated the most comprehensive inventory of sexually transmitted diseases. In 1913, there were 2820 medical cases, of which 34 were syphilis and 4 were gonorrhea. In 1914, syphilis had increased to 43 cases, gonorrhea to 14; in 1915, 40 and 18 cases respectively. By 1916, more people were seeking Western medical services: 3,630 recorded medical cases of all categories. This was quite an increase from the 2833 cases recorded in 1915.[80]

It is possible that mandatory medical examination for World War I service unearthed more cases of sexually transmitted diseases. By 1916 North Kavirondo recorded 21 syphilis and 6 gonorrhoea cases, half as many as those recorded the previous year. In the course of routine check-ups prior to enlistment for military service in 1917, Western medicine doubled the figures: 49 cases of syphilis and 10 of gonorrhoea. Even so, the authorities believed that these figures were not an indicator of the extent of the malaise since '[The] majority with whatever disease never attend hospital even if living near station.'[81] At the end of the second decade of colonial presence in this area, sexually transmitted diseases were a large proportion of the reported medical cases. Of a total of the 1431 medical cases attended to at the hospital, 68 were for syphilis and 18 for gonorrhoea.[82]

Although these figures are not disaggregated by gender there were possibly more female casualties, since some of the infected males were polygamous, not to mention the consequences of their customary extra-marital and premarital liaisons. The picture, however, is not that simple. Wives of migrant labourers were increasingly being accused of extra-marital liaisons. How this factored into the spread of the sexually transmitted diseases, if at all, is not clear. The men who suffered from venereal diseases were more often than not at least one-time migrant workers. Their infection might result in sterility.[83] In Maragoli, venereal diseases came to be referred as *urukuzu rwa avakali*, women's diseases, after World War I. Here, conventional wisdom had it that men contracted the diseases from women.[84]

Just when disease was being medicalized, its ethnicitization and genderization created an additional layer of discourse on African women. Literature from diverse cultures associating women with ritual uncleanliness abounds.[85] This is largely related to menstruation and childbirth. In the context of the rumour, notions of cleanliness were not necessarily linked to virginity, so that the woman need not be a virgin for the cure to be effective. The implication points to desperate searches for quick cures, hence the rapes.

The rumour about the curative effects of rape was a product of the dynamics of urban areas, at once the source of vice and virtue, fortune and misfortune. Increased mobility for women, as well as men, did not always have positive effects. Because of the requirement that the rape victim be from a different ethnic group, these rapes would take place away from the perpetrator's home base, perhaps in a coastal town or an inland urban area. Centres of heterogeneous populations were popular haunts for infected men. Increase in mobility and the growth of such urban centres in the middle of reservations possibly gave more credence to the rumour.

A close look at the ethnic and racial composition of the population of Kitui town in 1912 reveals its gradual complexity. The figures given exclude the native Kambas living within the township area.[86]

Table 2.1 Kitui in 1912

Ethnicity	Adult males	Adult females	Children
Europeans	3	0	0
Goanese	4	1	4
Indians	38	1	2
Swahili	9	1	0
Arabs	9	0	0
Wanyamwezi	30	4	4
Other natives	8	15	12
Islamicised women living with Swahilis	0	35	37

Source: KNA:PC/CP.1/2/1 Kitui District Part I. Akamba Laws and Custom, p.469.

In the official, colonial mind, the thirty-five Islamicised women constituted a distinct category apart from other social groups. To Africans, these women had become foreigners. Such de-ethnicised women would be good subjects for infected men who subscribed to the curative rape rumour.

Victims could also include European children. Regardless of people's racial or cultural background, children commonly represent innocence and purity. In this desperate situation, that included medical purity. The acting District Commissioner for Meru claimed personal knowledge of the abuse of female European children in Nairobi by Africans who had venereal infections.[87] And although the DC for Fort Hall stated that no actual cases or attempts of rape of white children by Africans had been brought to his notice, he did point out that in the past, in the absence of the Assistant Superintendent of Police on safari, cases had been reported to the Commissioner of Police.[88] Whether adult or juvenile, Europeans were as far removed from any indigenous ethnic group as possible, and their children were more vulnerable as possible victims of rape. But the fact that some sufferers of venereal disease chose female European children, the least accessible of juveniles, reveals the multiple perceptions of the European as the other. Possibly the rape of European children symbolized attempts not only to procure a cure, but also to defy colonial domination and depict the vulnerability of the colonial administrators and their families. In these assaults, race, gender, disease, and colonialism were juxtaposed.

By contrast, the innocence of African children in sexual matters was not presumed. Although the DC for Fort Hall noted that 'no notice is taken of [sexual] relations between uncircumcised boys and uncircumcised girls',[89] it was implicit that sexual activity among this group was presumed. In this context, the DC for Nyeri observed that 'there [was] no indication that children [in Nyeri] suffered' from the belief that coitus with noninfected women could cure venereal disease.[90] It seems preposterous for the administrator even to imagine that juveniles might be privy to the idea, but there did seem to be fear that some male children were infected and that they, too, might rape women in search of a cure.

It is possible to read a conflation of ethnicity and gender into this unscientific 'therapy'. If a society could redeem its health by violating women of a different ethnic group, maybe there was dignity in the act. However, that the rumour did not allude to a cure for infected women could be interpreted as an indication of male guilt for the spread of sexually transmitted diseases. Men possibly considered themselves responsible for the vice and needed women to get them out of the predicament. At any rate, curative rape in the informal domain of rumour, was a powerful effort to counter the ravages of possibly the most prevalent of colonial diseases.

'Illicit' Sex and Free Unions

The lines between what are regarded as legitimate sexual relations and 'illicit' sex may be drawn in different ways from culture to culture, and even then, tolerance or intolerance for what is regarded as 'illicit' may vary. There are ample references in the ethnographic literature regarding the pervasiveness of permitted variations of premarital sexual relations in diverse ethnicities in precolonial and early colonial Kenya.[91] Ethnographic reports refer to intricate gradations of sexual activities. Most societies had a moral economy that was in general opposed to premarital coitus and applied an array of sanctions depending on the circumstances surrounding the illicit sex and its consequences. Opinions varied regarding the sexual morality of African societies at the dawn of colonization of Kenya. Extremist views expressed by missionaries and colonial administrators painted a picture of widespread, unregulated, and widely accepted premarital sex. These representations did not delineate the various modes of sexual behaviour, and by implication, collectively pointed only to coitus, thereby blurring diverse aspects of African sexuality. While missionary and government officials bemoaned what they characterized as pervasive promiscuity, on the one hand, and lack of choice and consent for girls with regard to their marriage partners, on the other, this ethnographic data sends a different message. There was a wide range of formally sanctioned sexual behaviour.

For example, in 1910 a colonial administrator noted of the *thaka*, an unmarried man between sixteen and thirty years old among the Meru, 'during this time he is free to go with any unmarried girl he pleases, but as a rule he marries the girl with whom he has been sleeping whilst he is an *elmoran*', that is, a circumcised, but as yet unmarried young man belonging to the junior warrior grade.[92] These liaisons might take place in special accommodations for initiated males or girls. Adolescent girls from ethnic groups that did not have initiation ceremonies also slept in accommodations separate from their parents. Thus, it was up to the girl to create a satisfactory site for the rendezvous.

> The custom among the Meru is that every girl who sleeps with an elmoran must have her own hut in her village, where the elmoran comes. The girl has not got to consult her father or mother but goes with the elmoran of her choice. The girls or '*Mukene*' have a great influence over the *thaka* and formerly used to make up songs laughingly at any of the *thaka* who showed any sign of fear. They have to supply their *thaka* with food, and as a rule the latter break the soil for their shamba and cut poles and sticks for building for girls huts.[93]

There is no indication that these relationships were short-lived, frivolous affairs. It was only as a result of official and missionary Victorian prudishness that sexuality acquired an ugly face. The fact that the *thaka* married the girl he had associated with longest points toward what in today's parlance might be a combination of a long relationship and an engagement, all wrapped up in one. It was customary for the *thaka* to labour at the girl's home during his long association with her, a hitherto unexplored aspect of sexuality and possibly courtship among the Meru. It is unimaginable that a *thaka* would proceed to toil from one girl friend or lover's home to the next. It is possible that once a young man started

Table 2.2 Nyeri Register, 1913–1931. Compensation Due for Offences.

Sexual Offense	*Tetu*	*Mazira*	*Rurunga*	*Mungé and Kuchina*	*Ndia*
Adultery	2 sheep	2 sheep	1 sheep/goat	–	1 goat
Adultery and pregnancy	10 goats	2 sheep	2 goats	5 goats	2 goats
Adultery, pregnancy, and death in childbirth	33 goats	33 goats	33 goats	–	20 goats and 1 bull
Adultery and stillbirth	3 goats	3 goats	2 goats		
Rape	–	10 goats	3 goats	5 goats	3 goats
Rape and pregnancy	10 goats	3 goats	4 goats		
Rape, pregnancy, and death	30 goats and 3 fattened sheep	30 goats	30 goats	–	20 goats and 1 bull
Illicit sex	2 goats	10 goats	4 sheep	–	7 goats
Illicit sex and pregnancy	10 goats 1 fattened sheep	10 goats	13 goats	–	10 goats
Illicit sex, and death	30 goats and 3 fattened sheep	33 goats	33 goats	–	3 cows and 1 ram

Source: KNA: DC/NYI/6/1 Register: Nyeri 1913–1931: Compensation Due for Offences.[94]

to offer his services to any one particular home, that was the society's way of recognizing premarital commitment. In the event these premarital sexual relations resulted in pregnancy but not marriage, the twin problems of an illegitimate child and an unwed mother could result. When they did, the line between acceptable consensual sexual relations and relations recognized as illicit had been crossed. Even then, the transgressions cannot really be said to have been 'criminalized', in the same sense as European law.[95] Among the Kamba, for example, both of these circumstances could be remedied with a single fine of a goat, which gave the child legitimacy and acceptance into the clan of the pregnant girl's father. The same fine also removed the feeling of repugnancy surrounding unwed motherhood.[96] If the man paid a further fine in the form of the usual bridewealth, he could claim the deflowered maiden as his wife and the child, as his own. In some cases, however, the life of an unwed mother might be irredeemable if, for example, she was perceived as having been morally loose. Among the Kikuyu of Kirinyaga District, such a woman would be referred to as *mukoma ndi*, a loose, unmarried, and pregnant woman.[97] Among the Abaluyia, she might never get married, but she could become a concubine.[98] There was no equivalent sanction against local Don Juans.

On record were a variety of sexual crimes and the stipulated fines.

The conflict created in cases of 'illicit' sexual activity once again was seen as primarily between the men within the clans of the protagonists. The compensation specified by the fines was designed to eliminate the feud between families or clans involved. Among the Akamba, where adultery with another man's wife resulted in fine of one bull and one goat, for example, both animals were slaughtered and eaten by all in the husband's clan in the vicinity – the offended party. Here, there was the general understanding that adultery was 'not a very serious crime provided the culprit pa[id] the customary fine'.[99] While some of the anthropological monographs fail to point to any guilt on the part of the female partner in adultery cases, among the Kipsigis, adultery by a woman was a legitimate basis for a husband to demand divorce. Women were held culpable for sexual improprieties, especially if these were compounded by desertion.[100] Wives could not accuse husbands of adultery, however, and Peristiany observes that a husband's fidelity to his wives was not pledged.[101] In most societies, a man's guilt in an adultery case, as in a rape case, was cleared with the payment of the stipulated fines. These crimes did not break marriages. Even when the line between the legal and the illicit was transgressed, both the consequences and the parties involved were different from those under European and colonial law.

One of most contested aspects of women's lives during the colonial period related to the guardianship of widows, their children, and the property of a deceased husband. Different ethnic groups invested diverse male relations of the deceased with varying responsibilities for these. Chief among these was leviratic marriage, commonly referred to as 'wife inheritance', in which a brother or other member of the family became the widow's new husband. [102]

In a polygamous homestead among the Akamba, for example, the eldest widow was entrusted to the elder brother or any elder in the clan of the deceased. As the 'mother' of the entire household of the deceased, she was not allowed to leave the village of her late husband. No additional bridewealth was paid for her. Children of the deceased belonged to the clan, and hence the clan did not have to engage in double expenditure to obtain what was already secured. If any of the widows remarried outside their deceased husband's family, they lost the guardianship of the children, limited as it was under the patriarchal system. Even where the women remarried within their prior marital clan, they only retained what amounted to very secondary rights over their children. Younger Akamba widows would be married to the sons of their co-wives.

Among the Kipsigis, it was the unmarried men who were given priority in the remarriage of widows. These included the brothers of the deceased and the sons of his paternal uncles.[103] Akamba sons could subsequently marry off their inherited wives. The disposal of the widows would result in the inheritance of the property of the deceased. Among the Tiriki, the remarriage of a widow did not confer her new husband with access to the property of the deceased. There, wife inheritance was looked at 'not as ... increasing the family and estate of a deceased clan brother; rather it is viewed as a way of caring for the widow and children of the deceased and of helping the clan to grow through the fullest utilization of the widow's childbearing capacity.' The conforming male was accorded the status of *pater* and *genitor* of the children he bore with the inherited wife.[104] More commonly, children born of such circumstances were clearly identified with the deceased, and not the *levir*. Among the Kipsigis, a young unmarried man who inherited a widow could claim fatherhood only after he got married to another woman. Hence the role of a *kipkondit* (a man with an inherited widow) among the unmarried men of the Kipsigis cannot have been an enviable one.[105]

However, even before the imposition of colonial rule, it was not unusual in some communities for a widow to object to leviratic marriage and to establish private or even public liaisons. These free unions, called *pai-ke* among the Kipsigis, became more common during the colonial period.[106] Some widows, especially those who had married under Christian and civil codes, were particularly opposed to wife inheritance and some employed the spaces opened up by these colonial interventions to establish unions more to their own liking. The colonial period thus provided new grounds for contesting leviratic marriages and establishing liaisons based on choice.

The chapter has illustrated the nature of female dissension and the ensuing contestations over the control of female sexuality and agency. The lived experiences of women mirrored societal attempts to comprehend and partake of the changes. The next chapter examines ways in which impassioned discourses around clitoridectomy helped redefine womanhood for all caught in the controversy.

Notes

1. KNA: DC/NYI/3/10 Native Affairs: Return of Akamba Women from Kenya 1921-23, DC Nyeri to Senior Commissioner Nyeri, 7 April 1922.
2. For example, see Oboler, *Women, Power and Economic Change*, 238–55; Patricia Stamp, 'Kikuyu Women Self-Help Groups: Toward an Understanding of the Relationship Between Sex-Gender Systems and Modes of Production in Africa', in Robertson & Berger, *Women and Class in Africa* (London, 1986), 35; Fiona Mackenzie, 'Gender and Land Rights in Murang'a District, Kenya', *Journal of Peasant Studies* (Vol. 17, No. 4, July 1990), 609–43; Fiona Mackenzie, 'Without a Woman There is no Land: Marriage and Land rights in Smallholder Agriculture, Kenya', in *Resources for Feminist Research* (Vol. 19, No. 3–4, 1990), 68–74; Carolyn Martin Shaw, *Colonial Inscriptions:*

Race, Sex, and Class in Kenya (Minneapolis, 1995); Robertson, *Trouble Showed the Way*, 158–60; Jomo Kenyatta, *Facing Mount Kenya: The Tribal Life of the Gikuyu* (New York, 1965), 11–12, 108, 171–2; Harold K. Schneider, *Livestock and Equality in East Africa: The Economic Basis for Social Structure* (Bloomington, 1979), 9–10, 221–30; Melissa Llewelyn-Davies, 'Women, Warriors and Patriarchs', in S. Ortner & H. Whitehead, *Sexual Meanings* (Cambridge, 1981), 330.

3. For example, see Bonnie Kettel, 'The Commoditization of Women in Tugen (Kenya) Social Organization', in Robertson & Berger (eds), *Women and Class in Africa*, 47–61; Dorthe von Bulow, *Reconsidering Female Subordination: Kipsigis Women in Kenya* (Copenhagen, 1991); Fr. C. Cagnolo, *The Akikuyu, their Customs, Traditions and Folklore* (Nyeri, Kenya, 1933), 29ff; Jean Margaret Hay, 'Women as Owners, Occupants and Managers of Property in Colonial Western Kenya', in Jean Margaret Hay & Marcia Wright (eds), *African Women and the Law: Historical Perspectives* (Boston, 1982), 110–23; Jean Margaret Hay, 'Luo women and economic change during the colonial period', in Nancy J. Hafkin & Edna G. Bay (eds), *Women in Africa: Studies in Social and Economic Change* (Stanford, 1976), 87–109. See also, Simeon H. Ominde, *The Luo Girl: from Infancy to Marriage* (London, 1952); Paul Mboya, *Luo: Kitgi gi Timbegi* (Nairobi, 1967); Gunter Wagner, *The Bantu of Western Kenya: With Special Reference to the Vugusu and Logoli*, Vols. I and II (London, 1970). For a lucid exposition on Kikuyu women, see Jeanne Fisher, *The Anatomy of Kikuyu Domesticity and Husbandry* (Cambridge, 1955); Robert A. LeVine & Barbara B. LeVine, *Nyansongo: A Gusii Community in Kenya* (New York, 1966); Alan Jacobs, 'The traditional political organization of the pastoral Maasai' (Oxford, 1965). To the question to what extent a woman (widow) could be said to own a hut, the Kyambu LNC established that the woman only held the hut in custody until her eldest son got married at which point he would become his mother's guardian. Till then, the widow could only sell the house with the consent of her immediate guardian, a brother to her deceased husband. The proceeds of such a sale were to be held by the guardian and turned over to the woman's son once he was of age. See KNA: PC/CENT/2/1/4 LNC Minutes, Kyambu District, 17 June 1930.
4. For example, see von Bulow *Reconsidering Female Subordination* 1991; Greet Kershaw, *Mau Mau From Below* (Oxford, 1997), 24ff; Jane I. Guyer, 'Household and community in African studies', *African Studies Review*, Vol. 24, (1981), 87–137.
5. Carolyn M. Clark, 'Land and food, women and power, in nineteenth century Kikuyu', *Africa*, Vol. 50, No. 4 (1980), 357–69; Henrietta L. Moore, *Space, Text and Gender: An Anthropological Study of the Marakwet of Kenya* (Cambridge, 1986), 64–71; Robertson, *Women and Class*, 27–37; H. E. Lambert, *Kikuyu Social and Political Institutions* (London, 1956), 95–100.
6. Hay, 'Women as owners', 112. The colonial situation is said to have exacerbated the said dependency. See Sharon Stichter, 'Women and the labour force in Kenya 1895-1964', *Rural Africana*, Vol. 29 (1975); Achola Pala, 'Daughters of the Lakes and Rivers: Colonization and the Land Rights of Luo women', in Mona Etienne & Eleanor Leacock (eds), *Women and Colonization: Anthropological Perspectives* (New York, 1980), 186–213. In some polygamous marriages wives held the livestock given as bridewealth for their daughters. This would be used as bridewealth for the wives' sons. See, for example the case of the Maragoli in Wagner, *The Bantu*, 51–52.
7. KNA: PC/NZA/2/1/183 Native Laws and Customs: S/F.ADM.42/10/36A Natal Code of Native Law, Memorandum prepared by H. E. Lambert Esq. OBE. In unusual circumstances including physical disability and resultant unmarriageability, or lack of male siblings, a Kikuyu woman might inherit land. See Kershaw, *Mau Mau*, 59–60.
8. KNA: PC/CENT/2/1/4 LNC Minutes, Kyambu District, 17 June 1930.
9. Oboler, *Women, Power*, 243–44.
10. Corinne A. Kratz, *Affecting Performance: Meaning, Movement, and Experience in Okiek Women's Initiation* (Washington, 1994), 45.
11. KNA: DC/NYI/3/10 Native Affairs: Return of Akamba Women from Kenya 1921-1923, DC Kitui to Assistant DC Baricho-Nyeri, undated but note indicates it was a response to an earlier letter of 17 July 1921.

12. These famines ravaged Kamba, Maasai and Kikuyu, and Embu territories and resulted in considerable pawning of women and children during the worst moments of the ecological crises. See for example, Charles H. Ambler, *Kenyan Communities in the Age of Imperialism: The Central Region in the Late Nineteenth Century* (New Haven, 1988), 96–7; Robert, R. Tignor, *The Colonial Transformation of Kenya: The Kamba, Kikuyu, and Maasai from 1900 to 1939* (Princeton, 1976), 16, 313; J. F. Munro, *Colonial Rule and the Kamba: Social Change in the Highlands, 1889–1939* (Oxford 1975), 38–39, 47–48; Richard Meinertzhagen, *Kenya Diary, 1902–1906* (Edinburgh, 1957), 291.
13. KNA: DC/NYI/3/10 Native Affairs: Return of Akamba Women from Kenya 1921–1923, DC Kitui to Assistant DC Baricho-Nyeri, undated but note indicates it was a response to an earlier letter of 17 July 1921. Compared to males, women, especially girls were more likely to be pawned. See Claire Robertson & Martin A. Klein, 'Women's importance in African slave systems', in Claire C. Robertson & Martin A. Klein (eds), *Women and Slavery in Africa* (Portsmouth, 1997), 11.
14. KNA: DC/NYI/3/10 DC Nyeri-Baricho to DC Kitui, 20 August 1921. Although Chief Njegga's wife implies that Mukuthi had come with her mother as an infant, this possibly refers to their transfer to Njegga's household from Kahuthwa Mbui whose father had purchased Mukutha's mother from her Kamba relatives.
15. KNA: DC/NYI3/6 Native Affairs: Return of Akamba from Kenya, 1921–1932.
16. KNA: DC/NYI/3/10 Senior Commissioner to DC Nyeri, 12 September 1921.
17. KNA: DC/NYI/3/10 DC Nyeri to Senior Commissioner Nyeri, 7 April 1922.
18. KNA: DC/NYI/3/10 Native Affairs: Return of Akamba Women from Kenya 1921-1923, DC Embu to Senior Commissioner Nyeri, 18 November 1921.
19. For example, see Cagnolo, *The Akikuyu*, 29, 287.
20. KNA: DC/NYI/3/10 Senior Commissioner to DC Nyeri, 12 September 1921. Here, the usage of the term Kenya referred to what came to be known as Central Province.
21. *Ibid.* In his ethnographic work Kenyatta has denied the practice of forced marriage. See Kenyatta, 171.
22. KNA: DC/NYI/3/10 Native Affairs: Return of Akamba Women from Kenya 1921–23, DC Nyeri to Senior Commissioner Nyeri, 7 April 1922.
23. KNA: DC/NYI/3/10 Native Affairs: Return of Akamba Women from Kenya 1921–1923, DC Kitui to Assistant DC Baricho-Nyeri, undated but note indicates it was a response to an earlier letter of 17 July 1921.
24. KNA: DC/NYI/3/10 Native Affairs: Return of Akamba Women from Kenya 1921–1923, Senior Commissioner to DC Kitui, 1 December 1921.
25. KNA: DC/NYI/3/10 Native Affairs: Return of Akamba Women From Kenya 1921–1923, DC Kitui to Assistant DC Baricho-Nyeri, undated but note indicates it was a response to an earlier letter of 17 July 1921. DC Nyeri responded to above on 20 August 1921.
26. *Ibid.*
27. *Ibid.*
28. KNA: DC/NYI/3/10 Native Affairs: Return of Akamba Women from Kenya 1921-1923, Acting DC Nyeri to PC Kenya, 4 November 1921.
29. KNA:DC/NYI/3/10 DC Nyeri to Senior Commissioner Nyeri, 7 April 1922. In a passing remark the DC observed that legitimacy or illegitimacy had little or no meaning with regard to Kikuyu children.
30. KNA: DC/NYI/3/10 Native Affairs: Return of Akamba Women from Kenya 1921-1923, DC Machakos to Senior Commissioner Nairobi, 7 November 1921.
31. *Ibid.*
32. *Ibid.*
33. *Ibid.*
34. Stuart M. Bryson, *Light in Darkness: The Story of the Nandi Bible* (London, 1959), 16. The good news was not about being reunited with her long lost kinsmen. It was the Christian gospel.
35. Also referred to as bridewealth or dowry, this refers to the transfer of livestock, services, goods, or money from a prospective husband and his kin to the bride's family. This was in exchange for a woman's productive and reproductive services.

The payment of bridewealth gives the union a legitimate standing in the community and affords the husband and his kin specified rights and obligations regarding the wife and children. Bridewealth and marriage bind two kinship groups on other reciprocal levels. For example, see Njeru Enos Hudson Nthia, 'The Farming Herders: Irrigation, Reciprocity and Marriage Among the Turkana Pastoralists of North-Western Kenya', Ph.D. dissertation, University of California, Santa Barbara, 1984.

36. Among the Kipsigis, for example, the payment might not happen for as long as three or more years after the bride had moved to her husband's home. See J. G. Peristiany, *The Social Institutions of the Kipsigis* (London, 1939), 65.
37. Nthia, 'The Farming Herders', 72–3.
38. *Ibid.*, 100.
39. Phillip U. Mayer, 'Privileged obstruction of marriage rites among the Gusii', *Africa*, Vol. 20, 1950, 114–15.
40. This was the case among the Akamba. See KNA:PC/CP.1/2/1 Kitui District Part I. Akamba Laws and Custom, 49.
41. *Ibid.*
42. KNA: DC/NYI/3/10 Native Affairs: Return of Akamba Women from Kenya 1921-1923, DC Machakos to Senior Commissioner Nairobi, 7 November 1921.
43. KNA: PC/CP.1/2/1 Kitui District, Part I. Akamba Laws and Custom, 49.
44. *Ibid.*, 51.
45. A. B. C. Ocholla-Ayayo, 'Female Migration and Wealth Dissipation Among the Patrilineal Exogamous Communities in Kenya: With Special Reference to the Luo of Nyanza Province', unpublished paper read at the Nyanza Province Cultural Festival Seminar, Kisumu, 19-21 Dec. 1985, 8. See also Harry H. Johnston, 'The Uganda Protectorate', in *Geographical Survey*, Vol. I (1902), 71. Should animals given as bridewealth die, and for some reason a wife runs away, the Kamba husband was not entitled to a refund. The hides and the meat for each of the dead animals, however, were given to the man. If the meat could not be given to him, two goats were added to the skins. KNA: PC/CP.1/2/1 Kitui District, Part I. Akamba Laws and Custom, 87. Reference was made to civil case No. 7, 1910 (Assistant DC's court).
46. See Eugene Cotran, *Casebook on Kenya Customary Law* (Nairobi, 1987), 191 and 149–52.
47. Eliud Amatika Elichina, oral interview, Ebukambuli, Kakamega, February 1997.
48. Beth Njambi, oral interview, Limuru, 14 July 1993.
49. The *boma* would comprise an extended family: a man, his wives and children, grown sons, and their wives and children. It was common to have three generations of male heads of households. Eliud Amatika Elichina, oral interview, Ebukambuli, Kakamega, February 1997.
50. Wycliffe Etindi, oral interview, Ebulakayi, Kakamega, 11 January 1997.
51. KNA: PC/CP.1/2/1 Kitui District, Part I. Akamba Laws and Custom, 52.
52. KNA: PC/CP.1/2/1 Kitui District Part I. Akamba Laws and Custom, 52–3. The same practice was in operation among the Kikuyu, Kisii, and Luyia. See Cotran, *Casebook on Kenya Customary Law*, 151–5. Informants gave contradictory views about the fate of children of divorced families. Esther Njeri Mugunyi stated that 'a Kikuyu [woman] would never leave her children behind.... But there are children who would return to their father after their mother had taken them away. In the end, a woman who had gone back to her home would have some of her children while the others would be at their father's home. The children at their father's home will ultimately make you go back to your husband. It is difficult for a Kikuyu to abandon [throw away] children ... we were very concerned about our blood [progeny].' Esther Njeri Mugunyi, oral interview, Limuru, 20 July 1993. Beth Njambi, on the other hand, stated that a Kikuyu woman left her children behind voluntarily upon divorce. The divorcee's rationale was captured thus: 'I came here with two feet, two hands, and two eyes. And I will leave with these six attributes. I do not wish to impose a burden upon myself. I will not take the extra burden. She cannot, will not, take children. Neither would children of those days follow their mother.' Beth Njambi, oral interview, Limuru, 14 July 1993.
53. Mary Wanjiru observed that she had only witnessed one divorce. Mary Wanjiru

(Nyina wa Cibira), Limuru Kwa Mbira, oral interview, 14 July 1993.

54. Beth Njambi, oral interview, Limuru, 14 July 1993.
55. Esther Njeri Mugunyi, oral interview, Limuru, 20 July 1993.
56. Peristiany, *The Social Institutions*, 88.
57. *Ibid.*, 67. The ceremony was an expensive undertaking, which most husbands delayed for a number of years. Anyone marrying a woman for whom *katunisiet* had been performed would, like the previous husband, have to go through all the marriage ceremonies collectively referred to as *ratet.* See Peristiany, 56–64.
58. O. S. Knowles, 'Some Modern Adaptations of Customary Law in the Settlement of Matrimonial Disputes in the Luo, Kisii and Kuria Tribes in South Nyanza', *Journal of African Administration,* 8, 1 (1956), 11. Maasai customary law was said to lack provision for divorce in cases where the woman had a child. Hence the return of bridewealth was not an option in such a case. See Colony and Protectorate of Kenya, Report on Native Tribunals, Arthur Phillips, Crown Counsel, 1945, 142.
59. Mzee Elijah, oral interview, Tala, Machakos, 30 July 1993.
60. Hamisi Makapia Wanga, oral interview, Ebumanyi, Mumias, 21 January 1997.
61. Rajab Ngashira, oral interview, Ebumanyi, Mumias, 22 January 1997.
62. Knowles, 'Some Modern Adaptations', 11.
63. In her discussion of *malaya* prostitutes in colonial Nairobi, Luise White argues that as heads of households, these prostitutes established new lineages. See White, *The Comforts of Home*, 120.
64. Of the one hundred divorces examined by Knowles in South Nyanza in 1954 all but three had been filed by women. See Knowles, *Some Modern Adaptations*, 12.
65. KNA: PC/CP.1/2/1 Kitui District, Part I. Akamba Laws and Custom, 55. See also Diana Jeater, *Marriage, Perversion, and Power*, 37.
66. Sometimes the crime of rape has been appended to the initial sexual experience of a 'reluctant' bride who screamed her way to her husband's home and to the matrimonial bed. See Catherine Coquery-Vidrovitch, *African Women: A Modern History* (Boulder, CO, 1997), 203. The phenomenon of the 'reluctant' bride is covered in chapter 5.
67. KNA: PC/CP.1/2/1 Kitui District, Part I. Akamba Laws and Custom, 55.
68. See Francis-Xavier S. Kyewalyanga, *Marriage Customs in East Africa* (Freiburg, 1977), 66–68. For the Kipsigis, virgins occupied special places at initiation dances. See Peristiany, *The Social Institutions*, 51.
69. KNA: PC/CP/7/1/2 DC Fort Hall to acting PC Nyeri, 26 June 1920.
70. *Ibid.*
71. Kenyatta, *Facing Mount Kenya*, chapter six.
72. Although the colonial legal machinery was concerned about the plight of juveniles in the criminal justice system, gender does not seem to have been a significant determinant of how litigation was conducted. In dealing with cases of deviant child sexuality, age, rather than gender, was of the essence in colonial courts. It overrode any social constructions of sexuality and legal culpability. See, for example, Colony and Protectorate of Kenya, Supreme Court, Law Reports of Kenya, Vol. XI, 1927–1928, 90. See also Rex v. Solu Tutu, (1934) 1 East African Court of Appeal 183 Rex v. Ramazani (1936) 39; Rex v. Cherop A. Kinei and another 3 East African Court of Appeal, 124; Rex v. Opet (1936) 3. East African Court of Appeal, 122.
73. Colony and Protectorate of Kenya, Supreme Court, Law Reports of Kenya, Vol. XI, 1927–1928, 90. See also Rex v. Solu Tutu, (1934) 1 East African Court of Appeal 183 Rex v. Ramazani (1936) 39; Rex v. Cherop A. Kinei and another 3 East African Court of Appeal, 124; Rex v. Opet (1936) 3. East African Court of Appeal, 122.
74. Colony and Protectorate of Kenya, Supreme Court, Law Reports of Kenya, Vol. XIX, Part 1-1940, Criminal Case No. 158 of 1939.
75. *Ibid.*
76. Colony and Protectorate of Kenya, Supreme Court, Law Reports of Kenya, Vol. XVI, Part I, 1934, 107.
77. Peristiany, *The Social Institutions*, 20. Peristiany reported that in colonial times some Kipsigis had been accused of trying to rape European children in an effort to rid themselves of disease.

78. KNA: PC/CP7/1/2 Native Rape Cases, DC Nyeri to acting PC Nyeri, 27 July 1920. In a more contemporary (1999) version of somewhat similar argumentation, the paucity of medical knowledge and the creation of quack remedies threaten the lives of large populations. Discussing the Aids (acquired immune deficiency syndrome), which has killed thousands of Kenyans and ostensibly left two million people infected, local leaders in Central Province were concerned to create a grassroots strategy to combat the pandemic. During the deliberations it was asserted that 'The high incidence of HIV/Aids among teenage girls in Western Province is being exacerbated by the belief among older infected men that having sex with teenagers can cure their infection. Thus, 'An HIV/Aids symposium in the [Central] province yesterday heard that older men from age 35 and above were luring students and teenage girls into unprotected sex after learning that they were infected with either sexually transmitted diseases or HIV. The symposium was told that the main contributors to the escalating cases of child defilement in the province were being caused by the same kind of men.' See *Daily Nation*, 26 July 1999.
79. KNA: CP/1/1/4/1 Kikuyu District Political Record Books, 1901.
80. KNA: DC/NN/1/1 North Kavirondo Annual Report 1917, 18.
81. *Ibid.* On venereal diseases in colonial Kenya see, for example, Marc Dawson, 'The 1920s Anti-Yaws Campaigns and Colonial Medical Policy in Kenya', in *International Journal of African Historical Studies*, Vol. 3 No.3 (1987), 417–35.
82. KNA:DC/NN/1/2, North Kavirondo Annual Report, 1918–1919.
83. Kenda Mutongi refers to the grief of Maragoli women whose migrant sons had contracted venereal diseases and thus became sterile. See Kenda Beatrice Mutongi, 'Generations of Grief and Grievances: A History of Widows and Widowhood in Maragoli, Western Kenya, 1900 to the Present.' (Virginia, 1996), p.33.
84. *Ibid,* p.50.
85. See for example, Ian Q Orchardson. *The Kipsigis.* (Nairobi, 1961), 34–44; A.C. Hollis. *The Nandi: Their Language and Folklore* (Oxford, 1909), 91–2. New initiates were also considered unclean among the Nandi and Kipsigis.
86. Like other emergent towns, Kitui was characterized by great gender imbalance.
87. KNA:PC/CP/CP7/1/2 Ag. DC Meru to PC Nyeri, n.d.
88. KNA:PC/CP/CP7/1/2 DC Fort Hall to acting PC Nyeri, 26 June 1920
89. *Ibid*
90. KNA/PC/CP7/1/2 DC Nyeri to acting PC Nyeri, 27 July 1920.
91. For example, see Cohen & Atieno Odhiambo, *Siaya*, 93. See *ibid.*, 96–9 for the consequences of unregulated pre-marital sex; Peristiany, *The Social Institutions*, 49–55; Kenyatta, *Facing Mount Kenya*, 148–56; Wagner, *The Bantu*, 397; Hannah Kinoti, 'Aspects of Kikuyu traditional morality', PhD dissertation (Nairobi, 1983).
92. KNA: PC/CP/1/9/1 Meru Political Record Book 1910, 7.
93. *Ibid.*
94. In June 1942 Councillor Fransesco proposed and the Nyeri council approved 'That all tribunals in the District be directed that the customary payment for causing pregnancy in Nyeri district be 1 bull, and 2 Rams, 10 goats and shs.10/='. See KNA: PC/CENT2/1/10 Minutes of Nyeri African District Council, 17 June 1942.
95. It is possible that by engaging in 'illicit' sex, youths were challenging established moral norms regarding sexuality. Possibly the younger generation was sending a message to the effect that there was need to change established notions of social order, forcing their families into accepting forbidden marital unions. In other words, what was perceived as social deviancy on the part of young women and men could have been subterfuge and an outlet for frustration among the youth. Breaching sexual codes and becoming pregnant was one alternative for a girl who had her heart set on a candidate abhorred by her family. That the situation had to be criminalized before the option for regularizing the union was offered is the paradox that embraces the ambiguity of the moral and legal cultures of various ethnicities.
96. KNA: PC/CP.1/2/1 Kitui District, Part I. Akamba Laws and Custom, 56–57.
97. Jean Davison, *Voices from Mutira: Lives of Rural Gikuyu Women* (Boulder, CO, 1989), 123.
98. Wagner, *The Bantu*, 396.

99. KNA: PC/CP.1/2/1 Kitui District, Part I. Akamba Laws and Customs, 53.
100. Peristiany, *The Social Institutions*, 88.
101. *Ibid.* 84. Wives, however, might get very annoyed if a husband sustained his liaison with any one particular lover.
102. In leviratic marriage the woman continued to reside in her marital home, 'and if still of childbearing age, to bear children [for her deceased husband]'. See for example, Oboler, 129.
103. Peristiany, *The Social Institutions*, 83.
104. Walter H. Sangree, *Age, Prayer and Politics in Tiriki, Kenya* (New York, 1966), 25.
105. See Peristiany, *The Social Institutions*, 83.
106. *Ibid.*

Three

Becoming Kavirondo

Clitoridectomy, Ethnicity & Womanhood

> I was abducted in the morning on our way from chapel to the dining hall to eat porridge. I was taken to the Rift Valley [for circumcision]. What could be worse than being delivered in handcuffs to your father and in the company of a policeman, Sarah asked.[1]
> Sara Sarai , Kinoo December 1993.

> Europeans [were] trying to depopulate the land by preventing circumcision of women so that the land may be taken over by Europeans. [2]
> Watu wa Mungu, 1934.

> [The] repudiation of female circumcision involved detribalization....if his sons [or daughters] repudiated tribal law he would have neither sons nor grandsons and the family inheritance had been squandered for the procreation of an alien tribe.'[3]
> Mwimbi, Muthambi and Chuka elders, 1929.

> The self-detribalised sons could have no rights to clan land and had better be provided with plots on Mission land. Fathers naturally wished their sons to inherit but no father dare be so disloyal to the tribe as to allow a 'Kavirondo' to inherit from him.[4]
> Mwimbi, Muthambi, and Chuka Elders, 1929.

One of the central cultural institutions in the indigenous constructions of gender and identity in precolonial and colonial Kenya was the practice of clitoridectomy, or female circumcision. This entailed the excision of the clitoris and in some cases the labia minora and part of labia majora as part of a rite of passage among diverse ethnic groups, including the Kikuyu, Embu, and Meru. During the late 1920s and early 1930s, clitoridectomy was the cause of a major controversy in Kenya, one that captured national and international attention. Basically, what the missions, the colonial government and other detractors referred to as 'circmcision' clearly overlooked the more complex process of initiation, which both precedes and follows the surgery. This is the essence of the Kikuyu *irua*, for which the English translation, 'circumcision', simply does not capture the process.

The deep fissures and tensions created during this period have outlived the colonial era and continue to reverberate in independent Kenya. Clitoridectomy remains an international political and social issue today.[5] For the historian, however, the surgery at the centre of the controversy is the least significant aspect of the ritual; it is the cultural function as a whole that is of interest. The female body becomes iconic, and its reconstruction represents a normalizing process. In precolonial and colonial Kenya, the rite delineated right from wrong, purity from impurity, insiders from outsiders. It is thus culturally determined, and is linked to many societal issues. The connections between clitoridectomy, ethnic identity, gender, reproduction, land claims, morality, sexuality, patriarchal and state authority and religion therefore provide a rich arena in which to examine multifaceted struggles over Kenyan womanhood. These issues were passionately debated by parents, elders, missionaries, political parties, colonial officials, and medical practitioners during the 'circumcision controversy' in the late 1920s and early 1930s. In response to a changing colonial political climate at this time, the female body was placed at the centre of the refashioning of modern Kikuyu, Embu, and Meru societies. Thus, the female body, or more specifically, its genitalia (at times graphically illustrated in intact and excised forms), increasingly became a site for contestation, negotiation, and prescription involving a wide range of issues that were raised by the encounter of indigenous culture with modernity.

The controversy over clitoridectomy involved diverse struggles over the control of women, their agency, and their sexuality. The varieties of women's responses represented contradictory positions inspired by new notions of self-determination. Unlike any other conflict in colonial Kenya, the clitoridectomy issue provided a broad forum for women of diverse persuasions to exhibit their anger, resilience, and willingness to break with protocol – with customary expectations, but also with those imposed by the colonisers – in order to chose their own options. As we shall see, the spaces for female agency that were opened by the colonial intervention were used by women in unexpected ways.

At the height of the controversy, Kikuyu, Embu and Meru men and women who supported the missionary campaign against clitoridectomy risked social death. They would become '*Kavirondo*', the other. In colonial parlance Kavirondo referred to the Luo, a nilotic population that inhabited the Lake Victoria region.[6] This group did not practice clitoridectomy, or circumcise their men. For circumcising groups, the uncircumcised represented the aberrant, outsider, nonconformist, and an unknown quantity to be kept at a distance. The Kavirondo were both spatially and ideologically removed from the rural homes of the Kikuyu, Embu and Meru. The abolition of clitoridectomy threatened to blur the boundary between these different groups that did not share in each other's culture. In this respect, the emergent uncircumcised, and/or uncircumcising *Misheni* (missionized) group was considered different or inferior by Kikuyu, Embu and Meru people. They were not *karing'a*, pure. The ritual affirmed an individual's ethnicity and their ties to family and land.

The clitoridectomy controversy placed women in a pivotal position in the colonial process. It also revealed the vulnerability of the colonial process. As the controversy unfolded, it once again became evident that women's identities formed a mosaic of diverse social categories, not a single, monotone picture. It was not easy for the state to contain all these categories at all times. Like the colonial state itself, the lives of women were unfolding in diverse and at times conflicting directions.

Agnes Wairimu Hinga

The case of Agnes Wairimu clearly illustrates the dilemmas inherent in efforts to control individuals determined to direct their lives according to multiple realities. One early morning in 1926, Agnes Wairimu, a baptized Christian, accompanied her mother on a family errand that brought them in the path of a group of girls in a circumcision procession.[7] Agnes soon recognized some of her peers and friends in the group. She probably knew that some of these girls had been preparing for the initiation.

Suddenly, Agnes felt an urge to join the procession.[8] The group would have been headed for the river, where they would not only wash away their childish ways, but where the chilly morning water would numb them in preparation for the operation.[9] Agnes had already violated many tenets of the ritual, however, and once the group arrived at the ritual ground, her infiltration of the ceremony was discovered. Unlike the other candidates, Agnes did not have a *motiiri*, an official sponsor, a woman who would secure the initiate in a steady position in readiness for the surgery. But Agnes was determined to get circumcised. She took her position on the ground and awaited the *muruithia*, the surgeon, who enquired whose candidate she was. A woman stepped forward on the spur of the moment, adorned Agnes with the ceremonial bead necklace, and assumed the role of a sponsor. This woman had not anticipated the awkward situation, so it can be assumed that she recognized Agnes and stepped in to save the situation.[10]

Soon after Agnes got home, following the surgery, it became clear that all was not well. In her version of the story, related to this writer, Agnes indicated that at some earlier date, her brother, who was affiliated with a Protestant church, had sarcastically asked her whether she intended to get circumcised. In response, Agnes merely blew her nose. Agnes explained that the gesture was an indication of her disgust with her brother's audacity to enquire about a decision that she considered was her own to make.

But that is not the only version of what happened. A second, told to a family member, revealed that Agnes's maternal uncle was surprised to learn that his sister's daughter had been circumcised without his permission. Like her brother, her uncle stood in a position of power with regard to Agnes and could expect to have a say in the matter: custom required that a prospective initiate actively seek the permission of her maternal uncles.[11] Even more incensed was her uncle's wife, who would have played the important role of *motiiri*. In this version, Agnes's uncle did not wish to discuss the issue with all present, and it was he who blew his nose when somebody tried to enquire about what had just transpired, signifying that his disgust was beyond words.

In both narratives, generational, gender, and conventional social codes had been breached, and boundaries, both customary and newly-erected in Kenyan society, had been transgressed. Agnes had defied the efforts of both parties that, from different vantage points, were trying to control her transition to womanhood, and had compromised the integrity of her family and its conceptualization of the rite. For family members who supported the ritual, protocol had been violated. For her Christian brother, the ritual was taboo. As the two versions of the story reveal, the family had come to regard the ritual in contradictory ways. So in effect had Agnes. She may have been a Christian, but she wanted to be with her friends. Her determination to conform to tradition and secure her social standing among her peers came not only at the expense of family allegiances, but required personal defiance of the tenets of her new faith.

The fracture within Agnes's family between her Christian brother, who opposed circumcision, and her maternal uncle and aunt, with their concerns for traditional proprieties, was not the only division. Despite her tender age, Agnes was not spared the agonies of gender, religious, cultural, and colonial conflicts that affected not just her own family, but the indigenous societies in general. For getting circumcised, Agnes was suspended by the church authorities from her Protestant school. But colonial interventions meant that Agnes had other options – and other sources of conflict within her family. She recalled, 'there was tension and conflict between my two brothers with each wanting me to go a school affiliated to their denomination.' Thus, 'When I was suspended, I had a brother who loved me very much and was a Catholic. My other brother was a Protestant and a teacher. He was *kirore*, a community of people opposed to female circumcision. This group would threaten to *kung'ea*, behead, those in support of the rite. Even though he was my brother, we would run away whenever we saw him.'[12] Consequently, she recalled, 'After my suspension from the Protestant school, my Catholic brother suggested I go to a Catholic school.'

Beginning 1929 and continuing into the following year, Protestant missions demanded loyalty pledges whereby church followers denounced clitoridectomy. The requirement initially included teachers, preachers and other mission employees. Those who supported the missions' position were referred to as *kirore*, thumbprint. Illiterate supporters of the church imprinted their thumbprints as a sign of their loyalty. Those who opposed the missions' position were referred to as *aregi*, denoting their refusal, *kurega*. The latter group, which comprised the majority of church members, left the church en masse, establishing independent churches and schools.[13]

Agnes's suspension affected her social life. She soon found herself isolated from other Protestant church members, a situation that she was expected to endure until her suspension was lifted.[14] Agnes observed, 'Even if you went to the church to which you belonged, once you got out of the church, nobody would talk to you... they would not greet you [till the suspension period was over].... Neither could you go back to school before the suspension was over.' This might last for six months.[15] Despite longing for reunion with those who now shunned her, she said, 'I was forced to go to the Catholic school. A lot of force was used. I preferred to go to the Protestant school.'[16] Protestant missions had criminalized clitoridectomy: it 'figure[d] in the records with sexual offences and addiction to alcohol as the three areas in which the Church's standards were most contravened.'[17]

Protestant opposition to the operation was evident as early as 1906, when, the Church of Scotland Mission was concerned about the medical repercussions of clitoridectomy. In 1916, it began to forbid church members from participating in the rite. At a 1922 meeting of the Alliance of Protestant Churches, missionaries were exhorted to discourage the practice among their members. This opposition created a hostile rhetoric that represented the rite as primitive, brutal, and a mutilation of the female body. The Protestant bodies involved in the campaign included the Church Missionary Society, African Inland Mission, Gospel Missionary Society, and the Church of Scotland Mission, this last being the driving force.[18] Female circumcision was the missionary *pièce de résistance.*[19]

Clitoridectomy was posited as being incompatible with Christianity. For the indigenous population the campaign called for a rejection of an important cultural practice, and an uncritical adoption of Western culture under the guise of Christianity. In 1929, the Protestant missions adopted an uncompromising stance and called for the total repudiation of the practice by their followers and employees. Unwillingness to do this would result in the loss of jobs, excommunication, and expulsion of their children from mission schools. The fallout was great. For example, the Church of Scotland Mission lost up to ninety per cent of its membership immediately after its demand for the repudiation. Dissenters established many independent schools and churches, free from missionary control, and which took on teachers and catechumens who lost their jobs.

While many denominations such as the Church of Scotland Mission at Kikuyu, Tumutumu, and Chogoria condemned the rite, others, including the Methodist and Catholic Churches were more conciliatory.[20] Agnes was lucky. She was able to take advantage of the denominational conflicts that divided colonial missionaries. As she observed, 'The Catholic Church did not oppose circumcision. It would even arrange for the circumcision of poor children under its care. This happened to a lady friend of mine.'[21] The Catholic Church believed that circumcision was a social event that defined the initiate's position in their ethnic group and did not have any effect on matters of faith or morality.[22] Her one Catholic brother ensured that Agnes's education did not suffer; her family was already divided by the time Agnes was old enough to understand. She recalled that they had 'started off as Protestants. I only became a Catholic after circumcision and the subsequent suspension.'[23] Although she did not explain how her brother had come to be a Catholic, it was not unusual for individuals and parents 'to appease the missionaries by professing the Christian faith' in order to get their children admitted into mission schools.[24] A prospective pupil could apply the same strategy on his or her own behalf. The possibilities and pressures introduced by colonial interventions thus could result in a variety of outcomes.

For some, responding to these possibilities and pressures entailed temporary membership in the mission church. For others, it might develop into permanent adherence, as was the case for Agnes. The DC for Meru was of the opinion that if the mission wanted to continue keeping Meru youth in their stations for vocational training and religious instruction, it should enter into a formal agreement with the parents in the presence of a magistrate before their children entered. More importantly, the DC believed that mission work should not interfere with the circumcision custom. After all, 'the desires and opinions of the tribe [had] also to be sought.'[25] Likewise, other missions including the African Inland Mission at Kijabe, sponsored a less comprehensive ritual that excluded all other components except surgery.[26] But what would the identity of a circumcised Christian Kenyan woman like Agnes be? And what would be the identity of a woman who had resisted or had not chosen circumcision?

Clitoridectomy and Identity

Agnes's story is indicative of the changing dimensions of the social, ritual, and public lives of women in colonial communities. The succession of irregular events on the day of her circumcision mirrored the fragmented nature of *irua* by 1926. As well as revealing the fluid nature of the ritual, Agnes's action provides a context for investigating what the contravention of the ritual in general entailed for the individual and the community at large. Agnes' lone and spontaneous action interrupted a process that had been preceded by massive preparations and instruction on the part of all the other candidates desiring to become members of the Ndege 'A' age group. The ritual was a protracted social function whose preceding festivities involved neighbours, members of the extended family, and friends.[27] In Kenya, clitoridectomy was practiced among Kikuyu, Embu, Meru, Elgeyo, Nandi, Kipsigis, Okiek, and Terik communities, among others. It was a communal rite that defined an individual's niche in the sociosexual order and was deeply embedded in the social, religious, educational, and political institutions of participating groups.[28] The surgery was largely perceived as an external symbol, a validation or permanent marker of a much more intrinsic and pervasive ontological process. It underlay the construction of ethnic identity and social organization. It created cohesion among peers, defined individual rights and obligations, and represented the initiate's transition from childhood to adulthood. Behind this culminating act, the most important preparation was the instruction that prospective initiates received regarding the socio-cultural and historical sensibilities of their ethnicity. Induction could not take place without both instruction and the subsequent surgery. The protracted preparatory period was also characterized by feasting and dancing, as was the period immediately after the surgery. However, *irua*, the circumcision ritual, was an institution capable of change in the face of conflict. Jomo Kenyatta's representation of a carefully orchestrated public ritual in *Facing Mount Kenya: The Tribal Life of the Gikuyu* elides the differences present in colonial indigenous society and effaces its capacity for spontaneity in reworking the ritual in response to the new situation.[29] The ritual certainly changed under the pressures of colonial interventions, not least in response to efforts to mitigate or abolish the practice. In some places, opposition became more extreme.

In the colonial period, two versions of clitoridectomy were practised. The less extensive surgery, which involved the partial removal of the clitoris, was the more widely performed. The less common, extreme form, which involved the removal of the clitoris, labia minora, and part of labia majora, was a recent introduction. It was associated with the Fort Hall and Nyeri Reserves and was said to have been unknown in Kiambu 'until the missionaries attempted to enforce abolition of female circumcision in 1929'.[30]

Agnes's case illustrates other, more subtle ways in which the ritual underwent changes in the wake of the colonial interventions. The ability of a single adolescent to subvert the protocol and substance of an institution heretofore represented as corporately constructed and executed along a predictable standardized format is instructive on various levels. Agnes had not undergone the instructional preparations that would normally precede the surgery. She had missed the normative instruction and test. She also had missed the advantage of the special diet for the duration of two weeks. The diet ostensibly countered loss of blood after surgery and ensured the rapid healing of the wound. She failed to participate in the *koraria Murungu* ceremony that invoked the protection and guidance of the ancestral god. In the next ceremony, *korathima ciana*, a senior elder who held the senior office in the ceremonial council blessed all the prospective initiates. She also had missed out on the great ceremonial dance, *matuumo*, and the *mogumo* ceremony at which the candidates were inducted into 'all the necessary rules and regulations governing social relationship between men and women.'[31] Agnes would have to negotiate womanhood without the advantage of first-hand instruction. One of the final ceremonies before surgery included the *kuuna mogumo*, the breaking of the ceremonial mugumo tree, at which the initiates, both boys and girls, took the tribal oath, *muuma wa anake*, administered by the elders of the ceremonial council. Agnes had missed this ceremony, too.

The surgery symbolized a person's membership in the Kikuyu ethnic group. It also created solidarity among members of the same age grade. How much subversion was too much? What would get one ostracized? What was sufficient to get one initiated? What did it mean, or entail, to become Meru, Embu, Kikuyu, or Nandi in colonial Kenya? How might one fail to become one of these and become something else, something different? That Agnes was still allowed to undergo the surgery despite missing all these ceremonies is worth further examination.

The crafting of ethnic identity was a complex process that unfolded in diverse arenas and at different times.[32] By all accounts, Agnes and her family had embraced other beliefs, in addition to the customary ones, beliefs that cut across and disrupted ethnic identities and that were themselves riven and disrupted. Why was it nevertheless permissible for the community to allow Agnes to undergo the operation?

Social and Ethnic Death: The Feminization of Ethnicity

The answers to all these questions are to be found in the social status of clitoridectomy. Female circumcision has lent itself to multiple readings. Cultural, ethnic, nationalist, imperialist, feminist, and religious imaginings have addressed the practice.[33] It has been attributed to efforts to control women's productive and reproductive activities while also contributing to making of Kikuyu male and ethnic identities.[34] John Lonsdale states, 'the first Kikuyu approach to initiation … was Freudian.'[35] The excision of the clitoris, it was claimed, would remove sexual symmetry, establish a gender divide, and facilitate procreation. Its omission would divert Kikuyu fecundity to other ethnicities. Some writers, such as Susan Pedersen, have lamented the lack of attention to the medical and sexual effects of the operation on women, while the focus has tended to remain on the imperial and policy ramification of clitoridectomy.[36]

As much as all of these readings solicit the attention of anyone trying to understand the significance of clitoridectomy in colonial Kenya, it is worth asking why someone like Agnes would embrace clitoridectomy. But asking that very question obscures another that might come closer to the heart of the issue for Kenyan women in her situation. We might begin by asking, instead, why she would have resisted the influences that sought to dissuade her from the practice.

The controversy surrounding clitoridectomy came to the boil in 1929, when the Protestant missionaries tried to have the practice abolished by the colonial government. The ramifications behind the effort to abolish clitoridectomy, however, were more intricate than the government, missionaries, or mission adherents could have imagined.

For the indigenous population, support for the abolition of the rite entailed social death. Women were represented as the nucleus and symbol of nationhood, so that for the Mwimbi, Muthambi, and Chuka elders from Embu, the 'repudiation of female circumcision involved detribalization'.[37] Meru elders declared:

> tribal privileges could only be accorded to members of the tribe; no uncircumcised person could be a member of the tribe and no person who refused to allow his children to be members of the tribe could be granted tribal privileges since he had failed in his main duty to his tribe, which was to support its integrity and maintain its strength by bringing up his children to become members of it.[38]

The controversy surrounding the operation thus threatened the ethnic basis of communities. Educated people who had to repudiate circumcision in order to access education in mission-controlled schools were no longer considered members of their respective ethnic groups. Included in that category were women who had refused to get circumcised and all who had denounced the rite and embraced Christianity.

So in choosing circumcision and rejecting efforts to dissuade her from it, Agnes was taking sides and choosing to affirm a central part of her identity. Elders observed that the mission rule would 'divide each tribe into two, the educated being no longer Mwimbi, Muthambi or Chuka but merely '*Misheni*', since in order to get education a young man or woman must repudiate [female] circumcision and ipso facto, a woman must repudiate her elders, her clan, and her tribe.'[39] Detribalization could also result from marrying an uninitiated girl. The woman, her husband, and their progeny would all be shorn of their ethnic identity.

Because the mission decision to implement the ultimatum against circumcision was sudden, parents felt that their young children had not been given an opportunity to confer with them and with clan elders over the matter. The ultimatum had come 'as a thunder from the blue'. The Kikuyu had not anticipated the forced separation of tradition and Christianity, preferring to retain their cultural practices, maintain their relationship with the churches, and send their girls to school. Suddenly, parents and students had to choose between the beliefs of their elders and education.[40] Likewise, adults in mission-related employment had to repudiate the custom or relinquish their jobs. While adults could make informed decisions, the elders felt that schoolchildren should have been allowed to 'grow up to such an age as to understand fully the implications [of either choice]'.[41] By her action, Agnes was simultaneously transgressing against this belief in community-based judgement on the one hand, and on the other, the very colonial forces that were undermining the authority of the community and the hegemony of its elders.

For their part, the elders envisaged a total breakdown of social ties with anybody who denounced clitoridectomy. Thus, if daughters repudiated the operation, even after they got married, fathers 'could naturally have no more to do with their daughters and sons-in-law'. Fathers thus jeopardized their chances of obtaining bridewealth for their daughters. Wishing to limit contact with his '*misheni*' in-laws, a father might demand that his daughter's bridewealth be paid in total, in contrast to common practice whereby dowry was paid over a long period. Such a father rarely got the bridewealth, because his young sons-in-law did not have the necessary property, and also forfeited the wider social relations that marriage alliances created between in-laws.

Clitoridectomy represented conformity, belonging, and respectability for the mothers of initiates too. For this reason, a daughter who resisted the operation jeopardized her mother's social status and ability to operate in society. For example, among the Chuka and Mwimbi, where girls were circumcised after puberty, 'a woman whose daughter has been circumcised cannot cohabit with her husband again.'[42] This was a major marker of her sexuality, a transition in her life cycle. The spatial separation from her husband was an event openly observable by the community. Any delay in this transition would reflect negatively on her and impute improper sexual conduct to her.

There was a price to be paid by all associated with women who repudiated circumcision. In many respects, mission supporters themselves became alienated from the rest of their families. Friendships would fall out and patterns of mutual social and material reciprocity would be broken. For example, an unmarried mission man might not get the traditional material help from kinsmen for the payment of dowry. In helping a son establish his own homestead, an elder was investing for his own old-age social security. He would expect social and at times material help from his son, daughter(s)-in-law, and grandchildren. The connectivity of a wide network of people was at stake. The prospect of losing the opportunity to continue to be a father and to become a father-in-law and a grandfather became a real threat to the corporate nature of social organization. Other members of the extended family would experience parallel losses.

The cohesion of the communities caught in the clitoridectomy controversy was particularly threatened with regard to land, which formed the basis of the people's spirituality, as well as of their economic and social livelihood. It was their raison d'être. The bond it represented was in jeopardy.[43] By 1934, the *Watu wa Mungu* religious sect even believed that 'Europeans [were] trying to depopulate the land by preventing circumcision of women so that the land may be taken over by Europeans.'[44] In the minds of the members of indigenous communities, direct links existed between clitoridectomy, marriageability, procreation, ethnic perpetuation and purity, and control of the key economic asset, land. Women were the connective tissue in this whole process. As even the DC for Embu recognized, 'Land [is] in the hands of the *Muhiriga* [clan] and would not be owned in any sense by people of another tribe. The self-detribalised sons could have no rights to clan land and had better be provided with plots on Mission land. Fathers naturally wished their sons to inherit but no father dare be so disloyal to the tribe as to allow a "Kavirondo" to inherit from him.'[45]

Disinheritance of the new '*misheni* Kavirondo' tribe was the only way to distinguish the difference between the culturally pure and the other. Thus, it was said that 'if his sons [or daughters] repudiated tribal law [a man] would have neither sons nor grandsons and the family inheritance had been squandered for the procreation of an alien tribe.'[46] By rejecting clitoridectomy, however, the uncircumcised girl was rendered unacceptable even among those who did not excise. The highly emotive contemporary *Muthirigu* song stated:

> There is not a single place
> God for them [*Iregu* (sic) - uncircumcised girls]
> For if they go to the West [Kisumu]
> Their teeth will
> Be taken off.[47]

The song combined anti-mission, anti-government, and land-related grievances with pro-clitoridectomy sentiments among the Kikuyu. The latter were evoked through extreme abuse of uncircumcised girls, who were represented as being socially immature, incontinent, smelly, and unmarriageable, since they were considered sterile.[48]

In as much as joining a mission group and adopting its position on clitoridectomy were voluntary actions, the element of self-expulsion from one's ethnic group puzzled the community. In certain instances, the naiveté, ignorance, and tender age of some of the repudiators was held responsible for their action. These factors angered the elders greatly.[49] They were convinced that missions had taken advantage of protégés' youth, blackmailing them into repudiating clitoridectomy without full knowledge of the social implications.

Choosing clitoridectomy in the colonial context, as alien as that choice may have seemed to the colonizers and may still seem in the light of modernity, was thus a way of choosing an identity, of becoming Meru, Embu, Kikuyu, or Nandi, not Kavirondo. As Mary Wambui observed, 'you would yourself be very keen to get circumcised. If you did not [get excised], your peers would leave you behind. Whom would you associate with?'[50] It may therefore be of little surprise that, given the ways in which opposition to clitoridectomy threatened one of the bases of ethnic identity, the traditional community was willing to accept women who chose to be circumcised even though they violated some of the protocol associated with the ritual. To choose otherwise was indeed an opportunity to become something else. However, despite the enticement of education and employment that lured people to the Protestant missions, the penalty of becoming Kavirondo, the other, could well outweigh the benefits. Social and ethnic death was imminent.

The clitoridectomy controversy underscored the fluid nature of social institutions as a result of the introduction of colonialism and Christianity. Amid the resulting complex of fissures and fusions within indigenous communities, the assertion by Embu elders that mission influence had resulted in the split into two ethnicities, Embu and 'Kavirondo', is actually overly simplistic. As the case of Agnes Wairimu illustrates, the anti- and pro-clitoridectomy factions still shared a whole range of cultural, physical, material, and social spaces, and crossing between the two positions could be done on a moment's notice.

The majority of mission adherents resided in the villages. As kin, they were parties to a host of social relations. In mission, government, and other employment, mission followers delivered services and goods to all and sundry in the community. These included health services, educational instruction, and administrative intervention. This did not minimize the tensions; rather, it reiterated the complexities of the period. It defied exclusive categorization of the emergent groups. In their roles as daughters, wives, and mothers, women found themselves occupying positions straddling the old and the new; the boundaries were permeable, but crossing them was fraught with distress for all involved.[51] Self-identity and womanhood in their various forms, including acceptance in one's natal family, peer group, becoming a wife, daughter-in-law, sister-in-law, mother, mother-in-law, grandparent, or member of women's councils, were all at stake, whichever choice a woman made.

Medicalizing and Politicizing *Irua*

In 1929, the Protestant missions finally sought to make their opposition to clitoridectomy official, and hoped that this would become government policy. As we shall see, the actual response of the colonial government was extremely fragmented, as it was in almost all other matters. The government did, however, seek to abolish the extreme form of the operation.[52] The ultimate desire was its total abolition and its substitution with a form of moral instruction at puberty that would act as a rite of passage.

In 1926, the Native Affairs Department appealed to all Senior Commissioners to make all efforts 'to mitigate the brutality that attend[ed] the rite of female circumcision'. The District Commissioners had the responsibility to prevail on LNCs in their areas 'to adopt the milder form of the practice (that is to say simple clitoridectomy) in the areas wherein the more exaggerated forms have been introduced'.[53] Even attempts to enforce the legislation prohibiting the more extreme operation created unprecedented conflict. As it developed, the indigenous ritual was translated into Western medical terms and simultaneously transformed into an issue within the arena created by colonial political institutions, including the political parties that arose under colonial rule. Legislation and politicization both took place in medical terms that were supplied by the colonizers, not the colonized.

The Embu LNC was among the first to legislate against any form of operation that removed more than the clitoris. This stipulation was the core of an Embu LNC bye-law ratified by the Governor-in-Council.[54] The Meru LNC insisted that only authorized persons perform the operation. As will become evident, the introduction of public supervision necessitated further intrusion into female sexuality and elicited strong opposition from various quarters, since it simultaneously violated the gender roles inscribed in the *irua* ritual and the Victorian sense of propriety in sexual matters among the colonial authorities. To ensure that only the milder form of the operation was performed, the council demanded that 'no incision of greater extent or depth than is necessary for the removal of the clitoris' be done. Parents or guardians authorizing more than one operation on the same woman would be considered guilty of an offence punishable under the Native Authority Amendment Ordinance of 1924.[55]

The government did not adopt a strong-arm approach to eliminating clitoridectomy in general, convinced that gradual persuasion and education would convince communities to give up the practice. Government authorities were doubtful about the wisdom of direct LNC administrative action, and preferred 'indirect propaganda and influence of administrative officers to individual natives'. Not only missionaries and educators, but also medical authorities fell into this mediating category. District Commissioners were to consult with Local Native Councils and persuade them to enforce the milder surgery in their regions. As the Chief Native Commissioner cautioned: 'The subject is one that requires utmost tact in discussion. If the impression is given that the government intends to prohibit an ancient custom we shall meet with sullen and resentful opposition.' At the same time, efforts to respect indigenous values and practices kept clashing with Western 'scientific' notions – chief among them the enthusiasm for eugenics, the scientific management of reproduction. Thus, the CNC continued, 'it must be made clear that there is no idea of total prohibition but merely a desire in the interest of humanity, native eugenics, and increase of population to revert to the milder form of the operation, which is indeed in keeping with ancient tribal usage.'[56]

In the colonial context, where the authorities associated themselves with the introduction of civilization in the effort to raise Africans to a higher social level, clitoridectomy was said to hamper the breeding or evolution of Africans into stronger populations. Excised women were said to give birth to weaker children. This was thought to be worse in the case of children whose mothers had undergone the more severe form of excision. This pseudoscientific logic was strongly articulated in the official campaign against the operation. Arguments against the rite emphasized negative effects resulting from the extensive scarring, while clitoridectomy was said to be associated with infant and maternal deaths, difficult childbirth, mutilation, reduced fecundity, immorality, and barbarity. Critics of the rite alleged that the firstborn of circumcised women were predominantly stillborn. The assertion that first-born children of circumcised women did not survive might have been a useful tool, if backed with facts, to illustrate the adverse impact of the operation on the population of the affected communities. There was, however, no medical or other evidence to support this assertion. That the scars resulting from the operation might make childbirth difficult was a medical fact indeed. To conclude that the operation would affect the genetic characteristics of the population, however, was to make a major pseudoscientific leap.

In linking procreation with colonial projects of social engineering, women were represented as spokes in the grand wheel of change crafted by the colonial power. While in some contexts women were portrayed as the last group to embrace change initiated by the colonial state, at other times, they were said to be more progressive than men. In the clitoridectomy controversy, however, the onus on women was both social and biological: only they could facilitate the evolution of a stronger race by returning to the milder form of the operation. However, women in communities that did not practice female circumcision were not credited with raising strong populations.

Women were represented alternately as both villains and victims of the ritual. Officials mistakenly mapped the roles of villains and victims over clear generational differences, hoping that these could be exploited to ensure that clitoridectomy was stopped and quickly forgotten. For example, in 1929, the Kerio Province Senior Commissioner observed that if the few old women who were performing the operation against government orders were put to jail, 'the practice would cease'.[57] Portrayed as the villains in the controversy, the old women were said to insist on the operation, 'jeering and vituperating' at girls opposed to circumcision. Old women ostensibly pressured the youth, both male and female, into believing that the ceremony was essential. On the other hand, girls were said to be particularly impressionable victims, receiving information about circumcision at a time in their lives when motherhood loomed large on their minds.

In either case, colonial administrators believed that in general, women were largely responsible for the persistence of clitoridectomy. The DC for Embu stated that 'the stumbling block to complete eradication was the women but the men of the tribe must be sufficiently virile to overcome women's objection to the removal of this disgrace.'[58] Likewise, missionaries believed that women exacerbated the crisis. They argued that 'women in tribal society were much more conservative than men in their attitudes to social change' and that 'there is plenty of evidence to suggest that Kikuyu women, when united on a public issue, easily resort to direct action without regard to the consequences.'[59] In an unusual construction of power and authority, indigenous men were portrayed in a subordinate role.

The tendency to cast the clitoridectomy controversy in eugenic terms was part of a wider medicalization of the issue. Among medical practitioners, there was general concern about the perceived lack of vital medical knowledge among local communities relating to the link between female circumcision and difficult and at times tragic cases of childbirth. The Medical Officer-in-Charge of Native Civil Hospital Nairobi, Dr. Braimbridge, echoed official frustration in the matter. He noted that 'it was the Government's wish to help and teach the natives in all directions of medical science, but that they are obstructed by native customs which are aptly responsible for the fact that infant mortality among the Kikuyu is four times greater than in England.'[60] It is doubtful if the colonial government had a clear picture about infant mortality rates among the Kikuyu by 1926, and the implication that the lower infant mortality rate in England was due to the uncircumcised nature of English mothers was questionable.

Medicalization made possible new ideas regarding the sculpting of women's genitalia as the campaign to protect the clitoris continued. In 1931, the Medical Officer in Kerugoya wrote to the acting PC in Kikuyu suggesting that if the operation were modified further to consist of the removal or slitting of the prepuce only, the fold of skin surrounding the clitoris, this would avoid any interference with the clitoris itself.[61] The call was for the substitution of excising the glans clitoridis for excising the entire clitoris. There was fear on the part of colonial medical personnel that such medical knowledge might be beyond Africans' comprehension. This exasperation was clearly articulated by the Fort Hall Medical Officer: 'I am of the opinion that the removal of the glans clitoris only would be a great improvement on either of the above operations but fail to see how this can be understood by natives.'[62] Indeed, even with regard to the minor operation, the administration doubted 'if the operators could, with the usual instrument, have removed the clitoris with less cutting of the other parts.'[63]

The actual problem was not Africans' unfamiliarity with women's anatomy. The DC for Embu confirmed that he had had no difficulty in explaining the meaning of 'glans clitoridis' to Africans. 'As a rule, the native appears to be much more familiar with the structure of the parts than does the average European.'[64] Right there was the dilemma of the African communities – their reluctance to adopt reforms imposed by authorities that did not recognize their indigenous knowledge or respect their cultural practices. With the medicalization of the debate, the resculpturing of the female genitalia was getting more and more technical and exasperating for all those immersed in it. 'In my opinion,' said the DC for Embu, 'we have gone as far as can be expected for some years, except that possibly some of the psychological harm entailed might be reduced by a reduction of the age at which circumcisions are performed. I am carefully sounding Native opinion on this point at present.'[65]

Even as the colonial government continued to 'educate native opinion' regarding its position on the operation, doctors focused on the minor details of the operations, distinguishing the acceptable from the unacceptable. This was a work in progress, and the dimensions of acceptable changed as discussions progressed. No more than one operation on the same initiate was allowed;[66] apparently a parent or guardian might insist that the operation was insufficient, calling for additional work.[67] This would most likely involve requests for the extreme form of the operation.

The medicalization of the discussion also required fine distinctions about female anatomy, which could lead to endless argument in which experts had to determine whether they were dealing with a case of minor or major surgery.[68] For some experts, the minor operation entailed no more than the removal of the glands of the clitoris. However, the removal of the glands of the clitoris without the removal of the clitoris was thought to be 'an operation requiring far more skill than the Kikuyu operators possess[ed]'.[69] If an operator removed more than the glands, they were likely to be accused of performing the major operation. This ostensibly opened a legal loophole whereby the accused 'has only to plead that her intention was to do only the minor operation, but that she had not the necessary skill and in error did more. In most cases this defence could not be rebutted, and she would have to be acquitted on the criminal charge.'[70]

Seen in medical terms, not cultural ones, the major operation was increasingly defined as 'maiming' or 'mutilation'. The Director of Medical Services described maiming as 'the operation of female circumcision which involves the removal of the labia majora, labia minora or any of them'.[71] As the PC for Central Province informed the Chief Native Commissioner, that definition made '99 per cent of female circumcision operations as practiced among the Kikuyu tribes illegal'.[72] Other officials perceived the operation as an act of self-mutilation, since it was 'committed at the request or with the consent or at any rate without the opposition of that person'.[73] Because self-mutilation was usually not the target of the legislation, this raised an important, but unpursued issue – the possible prosecution of voluntary initiates. But the PC mused that the operation was probably no more harmful to women's health than 'the practice of wearing tight-laced stays'.

From the medical perspective taken by some colonial administrators, the fact that indigenous people associated clitoridectomy with traditional gender roles, including marriage and childbearing, and accepted it enthusiastically was evidence of the working of the savage mind. This conviction seemed to call for and justify official intervention: 'We must take as our justification only the patent fact that in this regard we have greater knowledge than is possessed by the people and that we cannot allow stupidity, prejudice, cruelty, or superstition to sway us in our desire to prevent untold suffering upon the women both during the performance of the rites and the subsequent and consequent birth pangs.'[74] The clitoridectomy controversy thus provided ample room for official privileging of Western knowledge and served to legitimate the colonial project.

The medicalization of the clitoridectomy controversy also played directly into the way that the issue was cast in the political arena, where the legitimacy of the colonial project was itself the principal issue. Indigenous, 'progressive', pro-colonial apologists espoused the pseudo-scientific condemnations of clitoridectomy. In this, as in other contexts, the operation became a site for articulating a vision of ethnic identity, but it was a vision that differed essentially from that held by those who retained the sense of community defined by ritual processes such as the *irua*. Women's sexuality thus became a key building block in the alternative construction of ethnic community proposed by these political groups. The female body, nevertheless remained an icon for the control and embellishing of ethnic markers.

In September 1929, the Secretary of the Kikuyu Progressive Party (KPP) wrote to the editor of the *East Africa Standard* condemning what he termed 'an old barbarous, evil custom'. He asked the government 'that this custom which kills the first children of Kikuyu girls and the Kikuyu nation, be ended altogether like the English government ended the Hindu custom of burning widows with their husbands' bodies'.[75] The use of a parallel from colonial India introduced a less often articulated argument, that of the patriarchal subordination and exploitation of women, into the clitoridectomy controversy. The KPP posited clitoridectomy as an objectionable remnant of obnoxious customs, the bulk of which had already been discarded. According to the KPP, the piercing of ears and the filing of teeth were among some of the indignities to which women were previously subjected. In the past, too, the strangling of first-born twin children and the exposing of children to death alongside their dead mothers were said to be customs once thought important, but already abandoned. The KPP credited Christianity and colonialism for the abandonment of such practices, while the British were portrayed as the panacea for all the problems confronting African women. Echoing a metaphor that missionaries used repeatedly, the KPP asserted that the welfare of women is a good measure of a nation's 'civilization'. Thus, the KPP adopted the discourse of colonialist eugenics, asserting that 'we of the Progressive Party hate all customs which bind the Kikuyu and prevent them knowing the true religion, and going forward in civilization and becoming a strong people, able to receive their inheritance of mind and body.'[76] In this vein, women were represented as the pivotal vehicles for the spread of civilization:

> We see that the beginning of civilization is in honouring women, because the strength and power of a people is from its women. The nations

> which belittle women, we, know, that they do not go forward, but go back, and we know that the British government makes women equal to men, and does not belittle women like the African people....We of the progressive Kikuyu Party see that the women of Africa are not respected, and their voice is not listened to.[77]

Sounding prophetic and ahead of its time, the KPP condemned the marginalization and silencing of women and attested to women's voices. It also located the predicament of Kenyan women in a global context while representing Britain as the only power that could salvage the situation. Ironically, to achieve these ends, the KPP created an image of a marooned female population robbed of any agency in the circumcision controversy and caught in a cycle of pain and death. This belied data from various quarters depicting female opposition to the operation, on the one hand, and their participation in the operation against mounting opposition from family and church, on the other.

The KPP was pitted against the Kikuyu Central Association (KCA), which became the standard bearer for clitoridectomy, adopting a hard-line and increasingly nationalistic politics. The KCA emerged in 1924 as a political organization among the Kikuyu in Central Province, and in diaspora in urban areas and the White Highlands. While the KPP was articulating the signs of things to come and their imagined community was choreographed in the context of colonial intervention, the KCA was determined to recover lost cultural ground and minimize colonial and missionary intrusion. Women were caught in the middle, a contested icon of possible future community in the wake of colonial interventions.

As the standard bearer for clitoridectomy, the KCA equated the perpetuation of the custom with continued well-being of Kikuyu nationhood. The KCA did not envisage or tolerate calls for transforming this custom at all. On their part, colonial administrators were determined to overlook KCA support for the rite, convinced that the KCA would continue to disgrace itself and 'cover itself in ridicule'. Missionaries believed otherwise. Dr. John W. Arthur was convinced that 'If it had not been for this Association and its attitudes to female circumcision, the question would by this time, have been within reasonable hope of abolition.'[78] In Fort Hall, where the KCA was strongest, there were no refuges for uncircumcised girls at the Church of Scotland Missions at Kahuhia and Weithaga. From the KCA's perspective, the continual dissemination of medical information to the communities was simply a form of propaganda. Their opposition was effective enough to frustrate some colonial administrators.

The government's efforts to supervise and legislate a culturally constructed practice created resistance, which at times, colonial administrators failed to see. Thus, when in 1930 the Fort Hall DC stated that 'Last year female operators were *all* given a lesson in minor clitoridectomy by Dr. Miller',[79] he overlooked operators who might not be registered with the government. This category did not attend the (re)training session and was probably practising the banned major operation.

Fragmented Colonial Policies and Local Resistance

Amid all the condemnations and conflict, the government adopted a very cautious approach to the controversy. Administrators on the spot were forced to weigh their options carefully as tempers began to run high and the issue became increasingly politicized. For example, the Senior Commissioner for Kikuyu, one of the most divided regions, advised the Colonial Secretary that the government policy regarding clitoridectomy should be one of 'masterly inactivity'.[80] This did not in any way entail government capitulation or inability to flex it muscles. The Senior Commissioner was suggesting that it would be impolitic and untimely for the government to adopt draconian and summary legislation against the custom, although it could have done so had it wished. In the thirty years prior to the eruption of the controversy, the government had given moral support to the custom. A sudden change of opinion or an attempt to legislate against it, he thought, would most likely lead to 'friction and bloodshed.' The government was afraid a hard-line policy would alienate its African supporters or drive them into the KCA fold. Formed against the backdrop of these concerns, colonial policy was consequently characterized by confusion and compromise

Given the effort to limit clitoridectomy to the minor version of the operation, there were concerns about the age at which girls underwent the procedure. What the policy was or should be was unclear. Missionaries complained that girls nine to ten years of age were being circumcised with the consent of their parents. The DC for Kiambu wondered whether under the existing laws any crime was being committed and whether he should be prosecuting operators involved in such cases.[81] There was no law on the matter. The response of the Senior Commissioner for Nyeri, from whom the DC Kiambu was seeking guidance, indicated the government's indecision about the matter. On whether any crime was being committed in operating on girls below the age of twelve, the Commissioner said 'Most emphatically no: probably over 80% of the girls are circumcised under 12 years of age'[82] (the age at which the consent of the girl was required).[83] In 1929, the Kiambu LNC decided that girls would be circumcised before the onset of menstruation.[84] This ruling was touted as a possible remedy to the problem of pregnancy before circumcision: if a girl became pregnant before marriage but after circumcision, there was no long-term disgrace involved, and after the necessary rites her child was considered an asset in her father's lineage.

Some saw infant circumcision as a possible solution to the whole problem – a compromise that might satisfy everyone, from those who held medical or cultural objections to adult clitoridectomy to those who defended it as an essential cultural rite. Despite their hard-line stance, even the missions were not averse to exploring this as a possible solution to the impasse. R. W. Lambert argued for the change in eugenic terms, claiming that the operation on infants would eliminate 'particularly the stultifying effect on the intelligence which results from an operation of the sexual parts of an adolescent'.[85] He hoped the missions would agree to early-infancy circumcision, involving the removal of the prepuce and a portion of the glans only, as a significant shift away from the major operation. He was also was hopeful that the mission would agree to the replacement of the series of rituals, *mambura*, associated with the operation, which the missions found very offensive and obscene, with 'moral' instruction at the age of puberty. Because the girls would be circumcised at infancy, the instruction would have to be delayed. Lambert's assertion that mission adoption of these provisions for the daughters of Christians would have the girls 'recognized by all classes in the district as fully initiated', also presumed the acquiescence of pro-circumcision elders. The switch to infant circumcision was a drastic departure from common practice, and Lambert failed or refused to recognize the inseparability of the physical surgery and the socio-religious teachings that preceded the operation. A temporal separation of the intertwined components of the rite threatened to destroy its very essence. Consequently, the future of Lambert's proposal looked dim.

As we have seen before with regard to other issues, colonial administrators adopted policies toward clitoridectomy that were fragmented and ineffective at satisfying the demands of any of the participants. Cognizant of regional differences, the government advised that 'the steps to be taken in each area must largely be left to the man on the spot.'[86]

The regional differences in the colonial administration's response to the controversy were most evident in the Rift Valley. Here, its 'masterly inactivity' was so thoroughly practised that by 1931, no charges whatsoever had been brought under the Penal Code or under the LNC resolutions in this region in connection with the operation. This state of 'ignorant bliss' was attributed to the fact that the people in the Elgeyo Marakwet district, for example, were 'as yet fully uneducated and extremely conservative [so that] it must be years before they will begin to view favourably the abolition of a custom to which the victims have never objected and of which the results have not been demonstrably evil.'[87] Here (where the milder form of the rite was practised), the local administration observed that the women in the area would be 'the first to resent any interference with this ceremony'. Dubbed 'backward', Elgeyo Marakwet was as yet unevangelized. Although the government viewed the practice of female circumcision with disfavour, it was convinced that 'it will only go with education',[88] and missionaries were largely responsible for the provision of formal education during the first three decades of the twentieth century.

Elsewhere, the government was more active, far from consistent, although consistently ineffective. By 1928 a number of LNCs had passed resolutions 'either forbidding female circumcision entirely or its more extreme form'.[89] The role adopted by Native Tribunals in the conflict was in complete contradiction to their traditional role. Previously meant to police and ensure conformity to cultural practices, the councils were now being asked to prosecute those observing one of the most important of them. The councils were transformed into colonial instruments, and the government was anxious to find out what effect, if any, their resolutions were having on the practice. One way of establishing the trend was to find out if the Native Tribunals had undertaken any prosecutions as a result of the resolutions.

Many DCs had very little report that was positive. The Embu district, in the forefront of the campaign, displayed wide regional differences, but resistance to its anti-clitoridectomy resolution was restricted to the Chuka and Wimbe regions. In 1926, there were only five prosecutions by the Elders' Councils, the *ciama*, resulting in five convictions, with fines of 85 shillings each. In 1927, fifteen prosecutions resulted in thirteen convictions, with fines of 80 shillings each. But in 1928, there were just five prosecutions which resulted in five convictions, with fines of 100 shillings each.[90] The Chuka region was said to be 'extremely conservative and backward', needing much more propaganda before real progress against clitoridectomy could be achieved.

The LNCs were not at all compliant with the colonial administrators, so that other DCs had nothing positive to report, at all. This was especially the case in areas such as South Nyeri, whose LNC had decided as early as 1925 not to introduce any changes in the circumcision of girls. In 1928, a dejected DC stated that the 'ultra conservative attitude is typical of the tribe [Kikuyu] and I do not think that there is much chance of any changed opinion when the matter is debated'.[91] He was of the view that the most effective way to control the practice was to enforce the registration of authorized practitioners. This had already been done in Kitui among the Kamba people, and by 1926, a by-law had been approved by the Governor in council demanding the registration of all female operators in Embu.

In Fort Hall District, the President of the LNC encountered what was close to unanimous opposition to the alteration or abolition of female circumcision. Adopting what he presumed to be a matter-of-fact approach, he informed the full council that modern medical opinion considered female circumcision harmful. With the exception of two mission members, all the councillors strongly opposed any interference with the practice, 'stating that it would meet the greatest disapproval from the people'.[92] While no resolution was passed, the President appealed to the LNC to ensure that no girl was forced if she or her parents objected to the operation. The Elgeyo and Marakwet Native Councils declared that they did not wish to interfere 'in any way as they did not consider the form of female circumcision [practised in their regions] to be undesirable or nocuous'.[93]

By the end of 1929, however, all LNCs except Nyeri had passed a resolution banning the severe form of clitoridectomy. At the same time, a 150-shilling fine or two months imprisonment for default had been introduced.[94] Local administrators felt that this punishment was insufficient; further, the minimum clause attached to the penalty was said to tie magistrates' hands with regard to discretionary sentences. Some colonial administrators considered entrusting the LNCs with the task of policing the adoption of the minor operation as inadequate. One asserted that any British government worth its name should enact an immediate law prohibiting female circumcision, 'except that performed by a qualified medical practitioner'. The Commissioner in question also considered existing penalties to be insufficient and suggested greater punishments for breach of the recommended law.[95]

Sentences imposed also differed from area to area and elicited strong criticism from different viewpoints. When in April 1929 the Kiambu Local Native Council fined two women 30 shillings each for performing the major operation, the local community was enraged, while Dr. Arthur, of the Church if Scotland Mission wrote to the *East African Standard* to protest at what he considered to be too light a sentence.[96]

By these resolutions, in an unprecedented manner, female operators were made accountable to male colonial functionaries in the practice of their trade. For example, in May 1927, five operators were brought before the Fort Hall LNC, and the Embu LNC circumcision rules were read to them. Attempts to instruct the operators publicly supplemented earlier requests that these rules be interpreted into the local language so that the whole community understood them.[97] But the registration of female operators did not ensure that they would perform only the minor operation. Some continued to practise the major form. In 1929 in Nyeri, one such convicted operator even pleaded ignorance of the government's regulation.[98] Those it most affected treated the registration campaign itself with disdain. At the beginning of 1929, none of the five registered licensees at Fort Hall had collected their licenses. They did not need official validation to proceed with their practice, nor did clients request to see the imposed certification.

The administration was still keen to ensure conformity with the modified operation. To do that, periodic inspection of the work of the operators was necessary. This opened a whole new Pandora's box of issues. It revealed the ineffectiveness of the government campaign and also transgressed established cultural and gender roles among both the indigenous colonial functionaries and those they sought to administer.

One such inspection in Kimani wa Njama's location in Fort Hall revealed that the operator 'had in no way abated the severity of the operation'.[99] In April 1929, the DC for Fort Hall reported: 'I sent a representative to witness a ceremony that took place yesterday, and he assures me that the operation was carried out exactly in the same way as formerly, and that when he remonstrated with the operator, both she and the girls on whom the operation was being performed resented any interference therewith.'[100]

Noncompliance was only one of the problems. While both administrators and indigenous authorities considered it an unpleasant task, 'it was the duty of chiefs to witness the operations, and to prosecute offenders when necessary.'[101] According to custom, this male gaze was taboo. As John Mbuthia, a member of the Murang'a LNC stated in 1929, 'no man could be expected to witness an operation of this nature.'[102] In a reflection of changing times, Chief Muriranja of Fort Hall said that he took 'a personal interest in the operations performed in his locations',[103] but this did not mean he inspected the initiates for infractions of the by-law. One might ask how the authorities verified the exact form of operation when it involved such private and personal parts of the female anatomy.

This issue of surveillance raised the question of the limits of enforcing control. Consider, for example, what happened when a male representative, possibly an elder, undertook the (unenviable?) task of verifying the nature of operation at a Fort Hall ritual ground. Many questions regarding the execution of this task come to mind. How close to the operator and the initiates did the male inspector get in order to execute his mission successfully? How did he actually get to verify the nature and extent of the operation? Did he examine the wound of the initiate, or did he ask to see and examine the flesh that was excised before he could determine whether the minor or major operation was being performed? Under normal circumstances, where was the excised flesh put? Was it easily available for all and sundry to examine, assuming this is one of the methods applied by the male gazer? It remains possible that he examined both the initiate and the excised flesh.

Whichever way it was done, the level of intrusion and invasion was of the most intimate nature. It is not clear at what point the gazer raised an objection about the performance of the major version of the operation, furthermore. Was it after the operation of the first candidate, the second, third, or at the end of the ritual? Assuming he arrived at the scene before the beginning of the ritual and made it known that he was in attendance, if the operator proceeded to perform the major version, it clearly was an indication of the contempt with which government intervention was held. What, if anything, could he do about it?

In addition to these difficulties, there were places where the resolutions against the major version of clitoridectomy did not apply, for they were enforceable only in Native Reserves. Parts of Kiambu District, which were adjoined to settler farms and forest reserves, for example, did not have to conform to the provisions of the resolution, although some of the settler farmers were keen to join in the anti-clitoridectomy campaign.[104] These areas provided a safe haven for parents determined that their daughters should undergo the major operation. Similarly, girls who sought the operation, but whose parents were opposed either to the major operation or to any operation at all, could run away to the settler farms or forest reserves, where they could have the operation as they preferred it. As in issues involving the legal status of women in general, spatial movement played a part in the opportunities for self-definition and agency that arose during this controversy.

In many places, any transition from the extreme operation to the modified minor one was a major leap, and indigenous communities resisted it. In South Nyeri, three years after the eruption of the circumcision controversy in 1929 there was no noticeable change in attitude. The majority of the population still practised the extreme form of the operation, and the LNC refused to adopt the modified form.

Among the youth, however, there were those who repudiated circumcision. In their effort to escape hostility and possible forced operation, they sought refuge in mission stations in the region, but the safety provided by missions was not always adequate. At the beginning of 1932, the DC for Nyeri reported two successful prosecutions for the forced circumcision of girls at mission schools.[105] These prosecutions created a major stir in Southern Nyeri. Elders and chiefs went to the DC's office 'to protest against the imprisonment of any Kikuyu for following an ancient custom of theirs which is still closely connected with their tribal life and religion'.

The possibility of adopting infant circumcision also raised the question of the girl candidate's ability to exercise her own agency in the matter. An infant girl could not make the choice between accepting or refusing to participate in the operation. The DC's response to this concern was a clear indication of how quickly administrators could abandon a concern that no longer seemed expedient in the pursuit of new and supposedly more workable ideas. Although forced clitoridectomy had been a central aspect of the controversy, the DC dismissed the question, representing it as an insignificant matter: 'The fact is, however, that the girls represent a very conservative element in the tribe and any repudiation of initiation rarely, if ever, comes from them. I know of no instance in this District where an uncircumcised girl has even pretended to repudiate it. The suggested condition would not, of course prevent parents from repudiating circumcision on behalf of their daughters.' [106] Yet conservatism was in itself an act of resistance and resilience.

To the medical professional, preference for infant circumcision was purely pragmatic. Scar tissue occurring so early does not grow at a greater rate than the rest of the body. This, as well as the fact that such a scar has a greater length of time within which to get absorbed and to lose a great deal of its inelasticity, made it a practical alternative to adult circumcision. Later scarring was said to interfere with childbirth, among other things. This was especially important because under the prevailing practice, girls got married shortly after circumcision. According to Dr. E. W.C. Jobson, the Medical Officer Kerugoya, and others in his profession, scarring was at its worst exactly when the girls got married. Jobson and his kind believed that if circumcision was done at infancy, girls' tissues 'would have a considerable number of years to regain something of their elasticity'.[107]

By 1931, the Embu LNC was supportive of circumcision at infancy. This practice was said to be in operation among the Taita and Akamba people in the coastal and eastern parts of Kenya, respectively. The question of abolishing female circumcision had not arisen in these areas, illustrating the regional nature of the conflict. Mwimbi men who married Kamba women did not consider it necessary to demand further initiation ceremonies for their brides. The offspring of such unions were perceived as full members of the Mwimbi tribe, a fact used to validate the acceptability and appropriateness of the Ukamba practice for the Mwimbi. Clitoridectomy as a precursor to womanhood took diverse paths.

In 1926, Chief Kinyanjui summarized the absurdity of colonial and mission audacity in the circumcision controversy by stating that 'the customs of the British and Kikuyu are different and the Kikuyu were not prepared to alter theirs.'[108] A spokesman for the great majority of his people, Kinyanjui reiterated a message that had been articulated in many ways: that the imposition of colonial rule did not give colonial administrators and missionaries unlimited authority over every aspect of the lives of the colonized. Colonial social engineering would be challenged where it threatened the very essence of a people's moral and social fibre.

Kinyanjui's retort summed up what we have seen repeatedly in this controversy – that Western sensibilities did not command an unqualified allegiance from the local community. In this particular case, even Western medicine and science did not override African culture and reproductive knowledge. Six months after Kinyanjui's statement, the Kiambu LNC did adopt the modified operation that required the removal of the clitoris only, to be performed once only on initiates by authorized surgeons. Violators of these provisions were to be prosecuted under the Native Authorities Amendment Ordinance. While conceding to some changes, Kiambu along with other regions had not thereby engaged in the wholesale abandonment of their customs. Out of a colonial and mission barrage, they had salvaged some respectability and control over an important aspect of their lives.

By the late 1940s, the whole controversy had not died down completely, and its significance in the definition of womanhood and ethnicity lingered throughout the colonial period. It became a text in cultural nationalism and was linked to the outbreak of Mau Mau, the liberation war that rocked the colony between 1952 and 1956. The Kikuyu, Embu and Meru ethnic groups constituted the majority of its supporters.[109] As Mau Mau was waning, a resurgence of the controversy erupted among the Meru. Here, the banning of clitoridectomy in April 1956 by the *Njuri Ncheke*, Elders' Council, came about thirty years after the Meru LNC had ruled against the excision of girls against their consent. In the period from 1956 to 1959, 'over 2,400 girls, men, and women were charged in African Courts with defying the *Njuri*'s order. Interviews suggest that thousands of others who defied the ban paid fines to local *Njuri* councils and headmen.'[110]

In threatening to circumcise themselves, these young girls once again used the culturally available practice of ritual convention to challenge gender, generational, and colonial authority. The clitoridectomy controversy illustrates how women constituted the connective tissue in the construction and maintenance of ethnicity. At stake was the girls' ability to make the transition to womanhood, a status that would allow them to fulfil a host of social and economic obligations, assume responsibilities as well as acquire certain privileges. However, transition to womanhood could only take place if the girl underwent clitoridectomy. Attaining the status of womanhood ensured that the initiate became a full member of the ethnicity. As well as procreation, a married woman was entrusted with economic production in her marital home. The abandonment of clitoridectomy put these services and resources in jeopardy. Social purity, integrity, and fecundity, marriage, motherhood, kinship, circulation and accumulation of bridewealth, and statehood and civilization were all said to hang in the balance. All these issues revolved around the refashioning of female genitalia. The transition from girlhood to womanhood in some communities thus brought the colonial project to a crossroads. As we have seen, in many ways, it brought the policies of that project to a standstill.

Notes

1. Sara Sarai, oral interview, Kinoo, December 1993. Sara's age group was the first *Ndege*,1926, named after the aeroplane.
2. KNA:PC/CP/8/7/3 DC Embu to PC Central Nyeri, 20 October, 1934.
3. KNA: PC/CP/8/1/1 DC Embu to Senior Commissioner Nyeri, 15 October 1929, Summary of *baraza* at M'Ncheru on 10 October 1929 attended by, among others, elders from Mwimbi, Muthambi and Chuka in response to Dr. Arthur's memorandum on circumcision, and his action in Chogoria Mission and out-schools. *Barazas* were open-air public meetings at which indigenous and other colonial officials addressed communities, communicated and discussed important issues especially government policies. The DC was also in attendance.
4. *Ibid.*
5. For an account of metropolitan high politics on clitoridectomy in Britain see Susan Pedersen, 'National bodies, unspeakable acts: the sexual politics of colonial policy-making', *Journal of Modern History*, 63 (1991), 647–80.
6. The term Kavirondo was already in use as early as 1898. See E. S. Atieno Odhiambo, 'A world view for the Nilotes? The Luo concept of Piny', in E. S. Atieno Odhiambo (ed.), *African Historians and African Voices* (Basel, 2001), 57.
7. Although various ethnic groups in Kenya use the term circumcision to describe the genital surgery of boys and girls, clitoridectomy is the appropriate term with regard to girls. In this chapter clitoridectomy and female circumcision are used interchangeably to reflect indigenous, colonial, and scholarly sensibilities.
8. Agnes Wairimu Hinga, oral interview, Ndumberi, Kiambu, 18 July 1993.
9. Kenyatta, *Facing Mount Kenya*, 138.
10. Jean Davison records an incident of a girl who joined the prospective initiates at the ritual ground and was excised without the support of a *motiiri*. See Davison, *Voices from Mutira*, 148.
11. Davison, *Voices from Mutira*, 96.
12. Agnes Wairimu Hinga, oral interview, Ndumberi, Kiambu, 18 July 1993.
13. See for example, Sangree, *Age, Prayer and Politics*, 87–95; Joseph B. Ndungu, 'Gituamba and the Kikuyu independency in church and school', in Brian G. McIntosh (ed.), *Ngano* (Nairobi, 1969); Frederick Burkewood Welbourn, *East African Rebels* (London, 1961).

14. Agnes Wairimu Hinga, oral interview, Ndumberi, Kiambu, 18 July 1993.
15. *Ibid.*
16. *Ibid.* Among the Protestant denominations, the Church of Scotland Mission (CMS), the African Inland Mission (AIM), and the Gospel Missionary Society were strongly opposed to clitoridectomy. The Roman Catholic Church and the Protestant Church Missionary Society (CMS) did not support the above group. See Rosberg & Nottingham, *The myth of 'Mau Mau'*, 121.
17. KNA: PC/CP/2/1/5/ LNC Meetings, Fort Hall District, 22 May 1927. See Macpherson, *The Presbyterian Church in Kenya*, 106. For the histories of the two main mission groups and their involvement in the clitoridectomy controversy in Kenya, see Strayer, *The Making of Mission Communities* and Sandgren, *Christianity and the Kikuyu*, on the African Inland Mission.
18. For a detailed account of the origins and development of the controversy see Kenyatta, *Facing Mount Kenya*, 125–48; Rosberg & Nottingham, *The Myth of Mau Mau*, 105 35. See also Jocelyn Murray, 'The Kikuyu female circumcision controversy with special reference to the Church Missionary Society's "sphere of influence"' (Los Angeles, 1974); Sandgren, *Christianity and the Kikuyu*, 71–2.
19. KNA:PC/CENTRAL/2/1/11 Part III Meru – Disintegration and Reintegration in the Meru Tribe. H.E. Lambert DC Meru, 9 January 1940.
20. *Ibid*, 112. See also John Nthamburi Zablon, 'A history of the Methodist Church in Kenya, 1862–1967', unpublished PhD. (Claremont, 1981), 139. While Protestant missionaries were the major body championing the eradication of clitoridectomy, they had not always adopted an abolitionist stance. For example, as early as 1919, Reverend R. T. Worthington of the United Methodist Church in Meru had written to the local DC stating that 'some Africans wished to undergo the ceremony under Christian influence'. KNA: PC/CP7/1/1 Native Customs and Law: Circumcision, Rev. R. T. Worthington, United Methodist Church, Meru to DC Meru, 24 September 1919. The mission was offering a much-sanitized form of clitoridectomy, which excluded all sorts of rituals, which the mission considered immoral. European doctors at some mission hospitals were already performing the surgery. KNA: PC/CP7/1/1 Native Customs and Law: Circumcision, PC Nyeri to DC Meru, 28 October 1919.
21. Agnes Wairimu Hinga, oral interview, Ndumberi, Kiambu, 18 July 1993.
22. Welbourn, *East African Rebels*, 137.
23. Agnes Wairimu Hinga, oral interview, Ndumberi, Kiambu, 18 July 1993.
24. M.H. Kovar, 'The Kikuyu Independent Schools Movement: Interaction of Politics and Education in Kenya', unpublished PhD (Los Angeles, 1970), 98.
25. KNA: PC/CP77/1/1 Native Customs and Law: Circumcision, DC Meru to PC Nyeri, Circumcision of Mission Boys and Girls, 26 September 1919.
26. Sandgren, *Christianity and the Kikuyu*, 74. Other missions embroiled in the controversy included the Church of Scotland Mission, the Church Missionary Society and the Gospel Mission Society.
27. Kenyatta, *Facing Mount Kenya*, 130–7. See Chapter 6 for a discussion of the initiation process among the Kikuyu. See also William Scoresby and Katherine Pease Routledge, *With a Prehistoric People: The Akikuyu of British East Africa* (London, 1910); Cagnolo, *The Akikuyu.*
28. For a most comprehensive analysis of the complexities of the initiation in a specific community see Kratz, *Affecting Performance.*
29. Kenyatta, *Facing Mount Kenya*, 125–48 recreates *irua*, which constituted the rituals, and the actual circumcision of the initiates.
30. Kovar, 'Kikuyu Independent Schools Movement', 124. The process of infibulation, the fastening together the labia majora of girls to prevent intercourse was not practised in the regions discussed in this chapter.
31. Kenyatta, *Facing Mount Kenya*, 136.
32. J. Lonsdale, 'When did the Gusii (and any other group) become a Tribe?' in K. Janmohamed & W. Ochieng (eds), *Kenya Historical Review*, 5 (1977), 123–33; J. Lonsdale, 'The moral economy of Mau Mau', in Berman & Lonsdale, *Unhappy Valley*, 2: 265–504.

33. Claire Robertson, 'Grassroots in Kenya: Women, Genital Mutilation and Collective Action, 1920–1990', *Signs*, 21/3 (1996), 615–42; Davison, *Voices From Mutira;* Moore, *Space, Text and Gender*, 57–60, 172–76; Shaw, *Colonial Inscriptions*; Pedersen, *'National Bodies'*, 647–80; L. S. B. Leakey, 'The Kikuyu Problem of the Initiation of Girls', *Journal of the Royal Anthropological Institute*, 90 (1931), 277–85; Lambert, *Kikuyu Social and Political Institutions*.
34. Robertson, *Trouble Showed the Way*, 95.
35. Berman & Lonsdale, *Unhappy Valley*, 389.
36. Pedersen, *op. cit.*
37. KNA: PC/CP/8/1/1 DC Embu to Senior Commissioner Nyeri, 15 October 1929, Summary of *baraza* at M'Ncheru on 10 October 1929.
38. KNA: PC/CP/8/1/1 DC Embu to Senior Commissioner Nyeri, 15 October 1929, Summary of *baraza* at M'Ncheru on 10 October 1929.
39. *Ibid.*
40. For a deeper understanding of the impact of this missionary stance see Kamuyu-wa-Kangethe, 'The role of the Agikuyu religion and culture in the development of the Karing'a Religio-Political Movement, 1900–1950 with particular reference to the Agikuyu concept of God and the rite of initiation', unpublished PhD thesis (Nairobi, 1981).
41. KNA: PC/CP/8/1/1 DC Embu to Senior Commissioner Nyeri, 15 October 1929.
42. See Lynn M. Thomas, 'Imperial Concerns and 'Women's Affairs': State efforts to regulate clitoridectomy and eradicate abortion in Meru, Kenya, c.1910–1950' in *Journal of African History*, 39 (1998), 121.
43. Ultimately, the clitoridectomy controversy did not merely become 'entangled' with the protest over alienated Kikuyu lands. Rather, it was at the core of the continuing construction of regional ethnicities, their territoriality, and cultural framework.
44. KNA: PC/CP/8/7/3 Political Unrest, DC Embu to PC Central Nyeri, 20 October 1934.
45. KNA: PC/CP/8/1/1 DC Embu to Senior Commissioner Nyeri, 15 October 1929, Summary of *baraza* at M'Ncheru on 10 October 1929. The DC admonished the chiefs and elders to do all in their power to advocate for the adoption of the simple operation. He was unsympathetic to the elders' views 'so long as the major operation was allowed to be practised even sporadically in their tribes.' Similarly, Kikuyu men who married uncircumcised girls were threatened with disinheritance. See Kenyatta, 127–8.

The suggestion that members of the new social category, the Kavirondo *misheni*, should be settled on mission land was not done graciously. The lands that missions owned had been granted to them by communities that had hoped for education and medical services in return. The Mission had broken faith with the tribes by refusing them education and a properly staffed hospital. KNA: PC/CP/8/1/1 DC Embu to Senior Commissioner Nyeri, 4 October 1929. Missions were also accused of acquiring more land than was deemed necessary for their goals. Some of the missions were involved in the cultivation of coffee. Kenya Land Commission: Evidence and Memorandum, Vol. 1, HMS, 1934, Memorandum of Kikuyu Central Association, Fort Hall Branch, 121.

46. KNA: PC/CP/8/1/1 DC Embu to Senior Commissioner Nyeri, 15 October 1929, Summary of *baraza* at M'Ncheru on 10 October 1929
47. Sandgren, *Christianity and the Kikuyu*, 180. The removal of some lower teeth was a common rite of passage among some ethnic groups in the 'Kavirondo' cluster.
48. *Ibid.*, 90–5.
49. KNA: PC/CP/8/1/1 DC Embu to Senior Commissioner Nyeri, 4 October 1929.
50. Mary Wambui, oral interview, Nairobi, November 1996.
51. For a most informative examination of constructions of ethnic identities see Thomas T. Spear and Richard Waller (eds), *Being Maasai: Ethnicity & Identity in East Africa* (Athens, 1993); Mukhisa Kituyi, *Becoming Kenyans: Socio-Economic Transformation of the Pastoral Maasai* (Nairobi, 1990).
52. There was an assumed fraternity of all European opinion in support of the suppression of the practice. KNA: PC/RVP.6B/1/5/1 A.T. Watkins, PC RVP to Honourable

CNC, Nairobi, 28 November 1929. The wives of European settlers joined the debate through their umbrella organization, the East African Women's League. In 1931, they condemned the operation and proceeded to 'ask the government information on what steps are being taken to suppress the brutal custom of circumcision of native girls, and also urge the government to do all in its power to protect those girls who wish to break away from tribal custom'. KNA: DC/FH/3/4 PCEA: CSM 'Memorandum on Female Circumcision, 1931' quoted in Kovar, *The Independent Schools*, 128.

53. KNA: PC/RVP.6B/1/5/1 CNC Native Affairs Department to all Senior Commissioners, 23 August 1926.
54. KNA: PC/CP.4/1/1 Kikuyu Province Annual Report, 1926, 17.
55. KNA: PC/RVP.6B/1/5/1 CNC NAD to all Senior Commissioners, 23 August 1926.
56. *Ibid.*
57. KNA: PC/RVP.6B/1/5/1 Senior Commissioner's Office, Kerio Province, Eldama Ravine to CNC 23 September 1929.
58. KNA:PC/CP.8/1/1 DC Embu 15 October 1929.
59. Macpherson, *The Presbyterian Church in East Africa*, 105.
60. KNA: PC/CENT/2/1/4 Native Council Minutes, Kyambu [*sic*, Kiambu] District, 9 February 1926.
61. KNA: PC/CP/8/1/1 Medical Officer Kerugoya to acting PC Kikuyu, 20 June 1931.
62. *Ibid.*
63. *Ibid.*
64. KNA: PC/CP/8/1/1 DC Embu to acting PC Nyeri, 7 July 1931.
65. KNA:PC/CP/8/1/1 DC Embu to Acting PC Nyeri, 7 July 1931.
66. KNA: PC/CP/8/1/1 PC Nyeri to CNC, 23 June 1931.
67. Teresia Hinga, personal communication, 18 July 1997.
68. As greater and more intricate details were gathered about actual operations, legislation against violators was refined to cover every possible detail. But refinement brought with it inconsistencies. By 1929, the Standard Resolution 1 clause 6 stipulated that the infliction of bigger incisions than the permitted would incur a one-month jail sentence and 50-shilling fine. That provision, however, was in conflict with the Native Authority Ordinance 26(2) 7. Cap. 130 which provided for fines of up to 150 shillings with no imprisonment for the same offence. This penalty discrepancy did not augur well in the attempt to pass a strong and common message to all involved. In an attempt to standardize the law and implement a much stiffer punishment, the Attorney General called for an amendment of the less harsh Native Authority Ordinance. This way, breaches of the standard resolution would be punished while enforcing imprisonment for not less than three months, not more than six months, and a fine not more than 200 shillings and not less than 100 shillings for inflicting the major operation on an initiate.
69. KNA: PC/CP/8/1/1 DC Kiambu to Honourable Senior Commissioner Nyeri, 6 March 1930.
70. KNA: PC/CP/8/1/1 DC Fort Hall to PC Nyeri, 4 March 1930.
71. KNA:PC/CP/8/1/1 CNC to PC Nyeri, 9 September 1930.
72. KNA: PC/CP/8/1/1 PC Nyeri to CNC, 9 October 1930.
73. KNA: PC/RVP.6B/1/5/1 PC RVP to Honourable CNC, Nairobi, and 28 November 1929.
74. KNA:PC/RVP.6B/1/5/1 Senior Commissioner Kerio Province, Eldama Ravine to CNC 25 September 1929, re: Female Circumcision Circular No. 64 of 16 September 1929.
75. KNA: PC/CP/8/1/1 Secretary Kikuyu Progressive Party to the Editor, East African Standard, 7 September 1929 cc to CNC, Senior Commissioner Nyeri, and DC Nyeri.
76. *Ibid.*
77. *Ibid.*
78. KNA: PC/CP/8/1/1 Memorandum on the Circumcision of Kikuyu Native Girls by John W. Arthur, M.D., Member of Executive Council Representing Native Interests, 27 August 1929. This memorandum was sent to the CNC who copied the same to all PC's and DC's expecting responses from PC's especially on sections 7 and 8 which

dealt with the amendment of existing legislation, synchronization penalties, possibly making them more stiff, and provision of protection for those against the operation.

79. KNA: PC/CP/8/1/1 DC Fort Hall to PC Nyeri, 4 March 1930.
80. KNA: PC/CP/8/1/1 Senior Commissioner Kikuyu Province to Colonial Secretary, 12 October 1929.
81. KNA: PC/CP/8/1/1 DC Kiambu to Senior Commissioner Nyeri, 17 March 1930.
82. KNA: PC/CP/8/1/1 Senior Commissioner Kikuyu to DC Kiambu, 22 March 1930.
83. It is not clear how missionaries arrived at twelve as the age of consent. Unlike other issues regarding women and girls' affairs, the question of the age of consent for female circumcision was never debated. While cases of forced circumcision were numerous, where the age of the girls was mentioned, it was in the more oblique reference to 'adult' girls whom the government would protect from being circumcised against their will. KNA: PC/CP/8/1/1 DC Fort Hall to PC Nyeri, 4 March 1930. At what age girls were considered adult is also not clear.
84. KNA: PC/CENT/2/1/4 Native Council Minutes, Kyambu District, 20–21 February 1929. Minute 6 of 1929 nullified Resolution 14 of 1927.
85. KNA: PC/CP/8/1/1 DC Embu to Ag. PC Nyeri, n.d. Placed between July 1931and January 1932.
86. KNA: PC/RVP.6B/1/5/1 CNC Native Affairs Department, Nairobi, to all PCs, Re: Female Circumcision, 4 May 1931. Despite this accommodating message, the CNC reminded the PCs that penalties reported under the Penal Code and Embu Council Resolution No. 3 of 1926 or any other resolution adopted would be expected at the end of 1931.
87. KNA: PC/RVP.6B/1/5/1 DC Elgeyo Marakwet to PC Eldoret, Female Circumcision, 23 January 1932. This area had had little or no contact with missionaries at the time this was written.
88. KNA: PC/RVP.6B/1/5/1 PC Nzoia to CNC Nairobi, Female Circumcision, 5 February 1932.
89. KNA: PC/CP/8/1/1 Office of Senior Commissioner Kikuyu to all PCs ccs to DCs, 18 December 1928.
90. KNA:PC/CP/8/1/1 Dc Embu to Senior Commissioner Nyeri, 27 December 1928.
91. KNA: PC/CP/8/1/1 DC South Nyeri to Senior Commissioner Nyeri, 21 December 1928.
92. KNA: PC/CP/2/1/5 Native Council Meetings, Fort Hall District, 17–18 July 1925.
93. KNA: PC/RVP.6B/1/5/1 acting DC Elgeyo Marakwet to Senior Commissioner Kerio Province, Eldama Ravine, and 8 December 1926.
94. KNA: CP/PC/8/1/1 DC Kiambu to the Senior Commissioner Nyeri, 16 October 1929.
95. KNA: PC/RVP.6B/1/5/1 Senior Commissioner Kerio Province Eldama Ravine to CNC, 25 September 1929. For a first offender, he suggested not less than one year or more than two years of imprisonment and not less than a 1,000 shilling fine. A second offender would get not less than two and not more than three years imprisonment and a fine of not less than 2,000 shillings. A third conviction warranted not less than four and not more than six years imprisonment and a fine of not less than 5,000 shillings.
96. Had these penalties been adopted, they would have been extremely stiff in comparison to existing guidelines.
97. East African Standard, 10 August 1929, cited in Kovar, *The Independent Schools*, 127.
98. KNA: PC/CP/2/1/5 Native Council Meetings, Fort Hall District, 27 May 1927. The need was expressed for the translation of the resolutions into the local Kikuyu language to 'be read at the Provincial *Baraza* so that there can be no doubt in the minds of anyone as to what has been passed and that the South Nyeri Local Native Council be invited to come into line.'
99. KNA: PC/CP/8/1/1 acting CNC Native Affairs Department to PC Nyeri, 1 May 1929.
100. KNA:PC/CP/8/1/1 DC Fort Hall to PC Nyeri, 4 January 1929.
101. KNA: PC/CP/2/1/5 Native Council Meetings, Fort Hall, Clitoridectomy, 20–21 February 1929.

102. KNA: PC/CP/2/1/5 Native Council Meetings, Fort Hall, Clitoridectomy, 20–21 February 1929.
103. *Ibid.*
104. See Kanogo, *Squatters*, 77–8..
105. In March 1930 a pupil thirteen or fourteen years old at Tumutumu Boarding School run by the Church Missionary Society was forced by her father to be circumcised against her wish. The father was sentenced to fourteen days' imprisonment, while the operator had to pay a fine of 70 shillings. KNA: PC/CP/8/1/1 DC Nyeri to PC Kikuyu, 27 January 1932. Later in the year, in October 1931 another student of the same age at Tumutumu Mission was 'forcibly circumcised by her mother on October 8th while on a visit to her home'. This time the girl's mother, the operator, five other women, and one man who assisted in forcibly carrying out the operation were prosecuted and convicted at Nyeri. The mother and the operator got three months of imprisonment and hard labour. Each of the remaining six people accused of abetting the offenders received six weeks imprisonment with hard labour. KNA: PC/CP/8/1/1 DC South Nyeri to PC Kikuyu, 27 January 1932.
106. KNA: PC/CP/8/1/1 DC Embu to acting PC Nyeri, n.d. Placed between July 1931–January 1932.
107. *Ibid.*
108. KNA: PC/CENT/2/1/4 Native Council Minutes, Kyambu, 9 February 1926.
109. Rosberg & Nottingham, chapter 4; John Spencer, *The Kenya African Union* (London, 1985), 71–96; Tignor, *The Colonial Transformation of Kenya*, 235–50.
110. Lynn M. Thomas, ''Ngaitana (I Will Circumcise Myself)': The Gender and Generational Politics of the 1956 Ban on Clitoridectomy in Meru, Kenya', *Gender and History*, 8 (1996), 338.

Four

Debating Dowry
'A Daughter is Like a Bank'

> Girls never got married without the payment of dowry. Every man had to pay dowry. There was no alternative. If one did not pay dowry, which was the marriage certificate, the wife could not be counted as his.[1]
> Isaac Were Osundwa, Kakamega, 23 January 1997.

> A cow is of more consequence than a wife; though a daughter is a valuable possession, as she will one day, when she is married, bring in more cattle for her father.[2]
> G.W.B. Huntingford, 1929

> A daughter is like a bank and it is only a right that her father should be able to draw on her from time to time.[3]
> John Mbuthia, Fort Hall District Native Council Meetings, 27 May 1927

> The girls though disliking marriage with ancients do like being paid for.[4]
> Senior Commissioner Kisumu to CNC Nairobi, 6 September 1927.

> A mission/educated girl would accept a marriage proposal from a poor man who could not pay dowry. Her father would *kurura ta mbaki,* become as bitter as snuff, become very furious.[5]
> Mary Wanjiru 14 July 1993.

> All the boys are saving up to buy wives; the only married one so far is the cook. He bought a wife the other day: she was dreadfully expensive, costing six cows, and he only got her at that price after long days of haggling with his prospective father-in-law. He is paying for her on the installment system, but no doubt finds consolation in the thought that his bride has the reputation of an excellent worker.[6]
> Etta Close, *A Woman Alone in Kenya, Uganda and the Belgian Congo,* 1924, 7.

Among cultural institutions that affected the lives of women during the colonial era, one of the most widely debated and litigated was dowry. The debates were most vigorous and numerous during the interwar period. Commonly referred to as bridewealth or brideprice, dowry traditionally entailed the delivery of livestock by a suitor to the father of his prospective bride in exchange for the woman's reproductive and productive labour.[7] The payment of bridewealth established an alliance between two families or clans, compensated the bride's family for loss of labour, and assured them of the bridegroom's family's goodwill towards the bride.[8] Bridewealth also defined the relations and obligations between young people and elders.[9] More importantly, the institution of bridewealth created protracted relations between two families that outlived the marriage itself and that had the potential of generating a host of conflict situations. Deliberations about bridewealth therefore unfolded around different life stages of girls and women.

Argument over dowry payments represented struggles over the control of marriage and women's positions in families. The tension reflected shifts in social, economic, gender, and moral relations in a rapidly changing colonial situation. Generational authority and power struggles between elders, youth, and missions over access to and control over new forms of resources and conceptualizations of marriage were played out around the institution of dowry, and thus illuminate another aspect of the shifting nature of women's identity. The question of women's agency and its frustration are recurring themes in these conflicts. Dowry-related debates opened new spaces for women to inhabit and broke down old barriers, creating new options for marriage arrangements, in particular. The deliberations of Local Native Councils, missionaries, colonial administrators, and communities at large as they sought to streamline and codify dowry reveal diverse conceptualizations of women and their multiple roles in the dowry conundrum. Women were both vilified and vindicated. They were represented simultaneously as victims and as contending parties in the dowry debates. Indigenous households sought to domesticate cultural change by creating new dowry conventions. In the process, girls and women continued to be contested terrain. The colonial administration's efforts at public codification of dowry were problematic and ineffective, just as they were with regard to other contested issues.

Extensive colonial archives including official, missionary, and Local Native Council records and other contemporary writings of the period overwhelmingly used the term 'dowry' to refer to the institution of bridewealth. Today, Kenyans continue to use the term 'dowry' to refer to bridewealth. In anthropological terminology and common practice, 'dowry' refers to the property that a woman brings to a marriage. Bridewealth, on the other hand related to goods and services that a bridegroom and his kinsmen transferred to the family of the bride. In this chapter, I use the term dowry instead of bridewealth to illustrate the ways in which colonizers appropriated and lent meaning to indigenous situations, irrespective of spatial and temporal divides. The dowry debate was in many ways about inscribing colonial sensibilities on a central aspect of marriage customs in colonial Kenya.

During the colonial period, efforts to restructure the institution of dowry included attempts to limit dowry rates, the abolition of instalments in the payment of dowry, and to substitute cash for livestock. These were attempts to simplify the burdens of colonial rule.[10] Here, as with other issues we have examined, colonial administrators hoped that the registration of dowry amounts agreed upon and what was paid would pre-empt litigation. Part of the effort to do so involved efforts to impose a statute of limitation to deter endless litigation on antiquated dowry debts. The overlapping and merging of legal systems, traditional and colonial, once again complicated the situation, especially with regard to concerns over women as property and exchange value.

During the colonial period, conflicts over dowry revolved around two major concerns. The first represented women as the interstices between the customary and the statutory legal systems. The second, which flowed from the first, sought to disentangle the social from the individual conception of women by separating their roles as daughters, wives, and property, on the one hand, from their position as legal agents, on the other.

Negotiation and mutual concession were important in dowry talks.[11] The calculation of dowry involved diverse issues, including notions of beauty, industry, the desirability of a bride's family connections, and the socio-economic background of the couple. In the case of wealthy suitors, it was not unusual to provide all the livestock agreed upon at one go. Dowry could also be paid in instalments after marriage.[12] Some girls opted for marriage into polygamous situations if the homesteads were wealthy.[13] Claims of standardized dowry 'for everyone' at an earlier period are not unusual. A woman who got married in 1900 in Maragoli in Western Kenya stated that *uvukwi*, dowry, was three cows and ten to twelve *tsimbago*, traditional hoes.[14] Earlier, *uvukwi* took the form of fighting knives. Clearly, with time, dowry changed in its composition and in the amount paid, mode of negotiation, and timeframe for payment.[15] With the advent of colonial rule, however, and particularly at the urging of Christian missionaries, efforts were made to limit dowry, and even to eliminate it entirely, portraying it as 'uncivilized'.

Limiting Dowry

Colonial officials believed that limiting dowry would prevent a host of problems. Any attempt to legislate on issues that had been the purview of customary institutions, however, raised strong objection from local communities. For example, in 1928, Kiambu chiefs Koinange and Kinyanjui argued that such limitations would be 'contrary to the inherent principle of dowry payment',[16] the drawn-out pattern of dowry disbursement related to different life stages of a woman. Marriage, seen as an alliance between two clans, was a process that unfolded in stages, with a host of accompanying rituals. Dowry was the key component of this process and could not be transacted all at once. For this reason, the Kiambu LNC postponed any decision on the limitation question while they sought the opinion of the tribe.

Native Tribunals increasingly dealt with more and more cases of contested dowry payments. Litigants were always male. If they disagreed with the ruling of the tribunals and decided to enter into civil appeals, then a completely different legal machinery was introduced; the following case affords us glimpses into the archaeology of social, economic, and legal dynamics that might haunt a woman even as she strove to get into an acceptable marital union.

The case emanated from the decision of the 3rd Class Subordinate Court at Kyambu, which was an appeal from the decision of a Native Tribunal in a suit over dowry balance. The suit related to the marriage of the respondent's father to the appellant's sister. While the appeal at the Supreme Court was lodged in 1927, the actual transaction had taken place about 1899 or 1900 when both parties to the litigation were 'at most small children'. Once the appeal was lodged the court had to deal with it as if it was an original case subject to the procedure applicable to suits. This included the Indian Limitation Act, 1877. Under the Kenya Order-in-Council 1921, Article 7, the court had the authority to exercise discretion in regarding the application of the law of limitation. It was under these circumstances that the following case came to court. Sir J.W. Barth, the Chief Justice, heard the suit, C.A. 9/1927 that was between Waiharo wa Kingate (Appellant, and original Defendant) and Kamwete wa Nginyi (Respondent, and original Plaintiff)

> The respondent's allegation is that his father paid sixty-five goats and five rams for the appellant's sister. She returned to her father and twenty goats were returned to the respondent's father. She subsequently returned to the respondent's father.
>
> The great famine (1899–1900) separated them once more and it is alleged that the woman went off with a Mkamba who paid, the appellant alleged before me, 100 goats for her. In evidence the respondent said 120 goats as the price given. The respondent brought a suit before the Native Tribunal for the return of the balance of the marriage price paid by his father. The suit was brought in the Native Tribunal last year.
>
> The Native Tribunal awarded him thirty goats and that has been upheld on appeal by the Assistant District Commissioner.... [who] held that there was no law of limitation among the native's cases. It is a fact that no specific of limitation has been applied to Native Tribunals, and in my view it is highly desirable that there be some check on hearing suits based on events which happened, in some cases, before the advent of the government.[17]

The judge ruled for the appellant and observed that 'to allow a suit in a cause of action arising at least some twenty-seven years ago would be to inflict injustice. The respondent's father apparently took no steps to enforce the rights on which his son is now relying.'[18] Seemingly unaware of the storm that was building around her, the woman in question had left her first husband once, got back to him, and was separated for a second time during the 1899–1900 famine. Given her earlier separation from her first husband, the woman's father, and possibly the woman too, seem to have preferred an alternative, and certainly more lucrative marital arrangement. Although the woman was not an active party to the resultant dowry problem, she was certainly an important part of the wrangling.

For the younger male generation, the payment of dowry in instalments during the colonial period had become equally important, but for different reasons. Wage employment had afforded young men some degree of independence from the elders.[19] They could raise money with which to buy livestock for the payment of dowry. In any case, the increased commercialization of life also meant the individualization of responsibilities. By the 1920s, young men could no longer depend on the clan to pay dowry for them. With increased financial demands, it was not always possible for a young man to come up with all the money necessary for the purchase of sufficient livestock to pay dowry. For the same reason that the opportunity to make their dowry payments in instalments was a welcome option, many young men also favoured the limitation of dowry.[20]

By the 1920s, complaints about exorbitant dowry demands by the fathers of prospective brides were common. According to open *barazas*, public meetings or hearings held in Kisii in 1926 to discuss the issue, some of the young men, unable to pay the price, were said to have resorted to stock theft, which was on the increase. Immediate and drastic action was considered necessary.[21] 'It was very hard for a young man who was unable to meet the expenses expected at a girl's home. Others took the girl by force even as they looked for the expenses [dowry] gradually,'[22] and some, 'before the dowry was fully paid ... might take the girl by force.'[23] In what was in reality elopement, culpability was placed on men, who were considered guilty of enticing their suitors into 'marriages' before the dowry transaction was complete or at a stage acceptable to the girl's parents. Consequently, at the end of May 1926, at one of these *barazas*, chief Nzungu stated that 'after due deliberation the majority of Kisii were in favour of making a compulsory marriage rate of three heads of cattle.'[24] Because the introduction of the limited rate would be ineffective unless punitive sanctions were appended to the resolution, Chief Nzungu suggested that the Local Tribunals be allowed to fine anyone who either paid or asked for more.

1926 was not the first time a dowry rate had been introduced in Kisii. An earlier attempt failed when people did not abide by its provisions. Amidst general agreement about the introduction of the rate, some elders 'were not enthusiastic, probably because they had daughters for sale'. Had the measure been implemented, an optimistic Hodge, the acting DC for Kisii concluded, '[Y]oung men would be able to get married instead of seducing another [sic] men's wives as they do now and further stock thefts would decrease in number as the main incentives to the same would have been abolished.'[25]

Nevertheless, by 1927, no LNC had enacted such legislation, and it was still not clear what the position of the LNCs was over the question of limiting dowries. Sentiments expressed at public meetings did not always find support among members of the LNCs. It is difficult to gauge the extent of opposition to the contemporary dowry rates or the exact numbers of livestock involved in dowries. What is clear is that there was a whole range of opinions which tended both to conform to, yet in some ways to defy, gender, generational, institutional, and hierarchical divides. One Senior Commissioner spoke of ' a feeling among a number of natives that the marriage price is going up and should be reduced'.[26] While his junior, the DC, agreed that 'there is no doubt that the natives as a whole are extremely desirous that the government should endeavour to investigate the matter and come to some arrangement whereby the marriage price of girls can be definitely limited', he also noted that 'the measure of course is unpopular with the wazee [elders] as a whole who have marriageable daughters to get rid of who keep on putting up the price.' [27] Oguta Ongoro observed that 'the comparatively young men on the LNC might favour limitation, but that the men with girls to dispose of would never agree. It had been tried over and over again and had completely failed.'[28]

This implies there was an absolute generational divide over the issue, with the elders opposing limitation out of self-interest and men of marriageable age supporting it for equally selfish reasons. However, there is no general indication that all the young members of the LNCs were supportive of the suggested changes. In the case of the Kakamega LNC, a unanimous resolution (54 to nil) opposing the introduction of dowry limitation was the very first resolution passed in 1925, as soon as the LNC was established. The DC despaired of achieving any changes from the North Kavirondo LNC, whose Resolution No. 1 of 1925 required: 'That no law be made standardizing dowries, as it is a matter for each bride's parents and not a concern of government.'[29]

The LNCs that finally passed resolutions in favor of limitation were in essence asking 'the government [to] come to some arrangement whereby the marriage price of girls can be definitely limited'. The final word about their deliberations, decisions, and recommendations, however, lay with the higher colonial authorities. Such was the reality of the colonial situation.[30] The LNCs could only come up with resolutions, which the government had to approve before they were applied.

Mission Protégées and Dowry

In addition to the position of the Local Native Councils, there was a missionary point of view on the question of legislating dowry limitations, and in large measure it drove colonial efforts to restructure the institution of dowry and the institution of marriage in general. E. A. Beavon, a missionary at the Nyang'ori Mission who became a major advocate of dowry limitation, argued that Kisii Christians found themselves in a very unpleasant and peculiar predicament. The Christian Marriage Ordinance required that both man and woman accept the Christian faith before they could have a Christian marriage. The mission had about one thousand students, most of them young men eager to get married. There were, however, only a few dozen mission girls. Understandably, the young men 'hesitate to marry girls who have never lived at a mission because such easily tire of the restraints which the Christian religion imposes'.[31] Therein lay the problem: the gross shortage of prospective mission brides.[32] Beavon and the young men asserted that 'mission girls, and their parents put up the price accordingly'. Five to ten heads of cattle was the common brideprice around 1926. If a young man failed to pay that much, the girl was 'dragged away from the mission and forced to marry a raw native' who would pay the required sum.[33] So, inflated dowries seemed to threaten the missions' ability to retain their female students.

The missions had to tread a narrow line here, however. Although Beavon was looking for administrative intervention to stop fathers from demanding exorbitant dowries for their daughters, he warned that the policy had to be carried out 'without embittering possible fathers and mothers-in-law against mission people [mission students as potential husbands] thus making it still more difficult for them to find wives'.[34] At times, missions actually supplemented the dowry offered by a poor mission follower, hoping this would draw the support of elders who were reluctant to marry their daughters to mission adherents. This in turn was said to inflate dowries.[35]

The same problem threatened the status of the missions' male students. Beavon perceived the resistance to dowry limitations as an anti-Christian strategy by Kisii elders, and he claimed that mission adherents were expected to 'pay an excessive price for their wives or give up religion'. He was also troubled about situations where, having paid a higher dowry than was stipulated, only a fraction of the dowry was returned to the mission boy should the marriage fail. He feared that this would encourage the extortionate practice of fathers marrying their daughters to mission boys, calling the girls home, and returning only part of the dowry each time. Beavon reported cases of young mission men who were afraid to marry mission girls,

> lest the old men should order the girls home for their private profit after the marriage had taken place; what is to stop grasping old men saying to their daughters: 'skip along and get married to such and such a mission boy; you needn't stay with him for more than three months. When the three months are up, you come back to us. Your hubby will sue me for ten cattle he will get 3, and the rest will be sheer profit for your old dad!' When a man has waited for thirty or forty years for a wife, and he finds he can't get one for less than 8 or 10 cattle, what is he to do? If in desperation at last he pays the price demanded, it seems to me he is less to blame than the hard-fisted parent who is merely out to make money is.[36]

In painting this scenario, Beavon represented mission girls as willing accomplices to their fathers' greedy antics.

As early as 1912, a colonial administrator expressed fears about a father's perpetual hold on a daughter even after she was married. His authority was said to emanate from custom. Writing on the Akamba in 1912, C. Ndundas noted 'the latter [father] never seems to lose his hold of the woman and is entitled at any time to take her back without special reason provided he returns the dowry paid and all presents given.'[37] At a *baraza* of all the chiefs in Kitui District, the chiefs denied the allegations stating that once a father had married his daughter off and received the stipulated dowry, '[he] had no authority to take his daughter back and sell her to another woman.' Beavon and the mission boys believed otherwise. Perhaps there was a regional variation on the matter.

All the same, men who paid excessive dowry could not sue for more than the stipulated amount because the government believed this would serve as a deterrent, and 'only very few [young men] would be foolish enough to pay the enhanced price after a few failed to get the full refund'.[38] But in reality it meant that old men might exploit the predicament of mission boys. The government hoped that this would not be the case. As the DC for Kisii observed, 'This may seem hard on the boy but the whole idea is to try and make marriage more feasible for a man with only a few head of cattle.'[39] Young people who were determined to get married considered it much easier to pay the going price rather than await the implementation of an official policy amid all the controversies and indecision on the question of dowry limitation.

What was at stake was not necessarily the delay of a mission boy's marriage, or even the fact that he might have to pay exorbitant bridewealth. Rather, the missionaries stood to lose ground in their effort to bring Christianity and 'civilization' to Kenya should mission boys enter into marital liaisons with non-mission girls. This seemed to be an imminent reality. As Beavon observed, 'Half of our adherents are saying there is nothing for it but for them to turn '"*shenzies*" [uncivilized]'.[40] And Beavon complained to the government that it forced the *shenzi*-ization of African Christian males by supporting the elders 'in their contention that unmarried girls should not be allowed to attend mission schools.... This being so, the majority of our young men if they get married at all must marry girls who have not the slightest conception what Christianity means and who have never worn other clothing than greased skins.'[41] In their effort to nurture Christian communities, part of mission strategy was to encourage mission men and women to marry among themselves to create a nucleus of 'civilized' families that would be in the vanguard of social change. Hence, claims of forceful affiancing of and marriage among catechumens were not unknown.[42] In this regard, mission women were perceived by the colonizers as strategic assets for the fashioning of new communities. This sentiment provides an interesting contrast to the clitoridectomy debate wherein uncircumcised mission girls were instrumental to the emergence of the despised *misheni Kavirondo* 'other'.

But mission women were not docile participants in this process. Some of the earliest female mission adherents included girls and women escaping from forced and or unhappy marriages.[43] In such cases, female agency preceded the enabling legal instrument of the colonial period.[44] As we have seen, the requirement that Christians marry Christians put very high premium on the dowry of mission girls, and this gave their families and the girls themselves a certain amount of leverage in dealing with husbands before and after marriage. Any association with missions, whether it was two weeks of formal education, training for baptism, or being a reader in the mission schools, could be used to increase a girl's marriage price. Mission men who married mission girls were also said to be convinced that they could not keep their wives 'unless they [continued to] placate their father-in-law with additions to the marriage price every year'.[45] As we have seen, the elders' acceptance of dowry in instalments was said to perpetuate blackmail situations whereby girls would run to their natal families if more dowry was not forthcoming and return to their husbands only after the latter had paid the required cattle. Although it is not clear to what extent, if at all, mission girls exercised such freedom, to the Seventh Day Adventist Mission, this was 'an incentive to lawlessness and immorality, and a menace to the sanctity of the marriage relation'.[46] Missions expected their protégées to conform to emerging church conventions regarding marriage. The possibilities for women to assert their agency under these conditions, however, were not so easily constrained by the missions' expectations.

At any rate, colonial administrators did not accept Beavon's version of malleable girls who succumbed to their fathers' designs of marrying them off to different men for profit.[47] Beavon's portrait of the marital woes of mission boys not only demonized mission girls, but also failed to reflect the dilemmas that both the girls and men faced. There were penalties associated with breach of various provisions of Christian marriages. Thus, once married under the Christian rite, neither the woman nor the man could get married to someone else 'without becoming liable to five years rigorous imprisonment under section 51 of the Marriage Law chapter 167'.[48] In the case of a woman contravening the marriage ordinance, while she served a possible five years, her second husband would be prosecuted for abetting. Should she decide to live with someone else without getting married, she would be guilty of abetment, while her partner would be guilty of adultery. The girls were thus represented as not just possessed of wills of their own, but as positively wilful. In 1926, the Senior Commissioner Nyanza observed, 'it is very rarely that a native woman does anything she does not want to do. Most of the complaints are that a woman refuses to go to the husband chosen for her because she wants to marry someone else and I have always said that no woman can be forced to live with a man against her will.'[49]

Reality lay somewhere in between. Some women were forced into unwanted marriages. That some of these would be mission girls married off to other suitors after initial marriages to mission boys is not inconceivable. The numbers might not be as high as Beavon intimated. Some of the earliest female mission adherents included girls and women escaping from forced and or unhappy marriages.[50]

Women married under the E. A. Marriage ordinance could seek divorce if their husbands reverted to 'paganism' and married another wife or wives, while the first marriage was still subsisting. In such cases, if the first wife left and the man could not get his brideprice back, colonial administrators hoped that this would serve as a warning to others contemplating such action. In the Catholic Church, such a syncretic practice resulted in expulsion from the church. Christian marriages cannot have been doing well.[51] Polygamy and Christianity were strange bedfellows.

For Christian men who committed bigamy there was also the additional problem regarding the dowry paid for the second wife. The DC Central Kavirondo wondered what the legal position of such men would be after their release from prison. He wondered whether they '[had] a valid claim for the refund of *mahari*, dowry.' It was anticipated that such questions would arise in his district in the future.[52] In other ways, the persistence of bigamy was indicative of women's conflicted response to mission and colonial efforts to regulate marriage. While a small but increasing minority objected to bigamy, some women considered such colonial regulation an unnecessary encumbrance.

Daughters as Investments

In refashioning marriage for their protégées, the missions ultimately usurped the role of parents and the wider kinship groups. Some communities argued that missionaries were taking over all aspects of the marriage of mission protégées. As a result, parents felt that they were being 'denied their inalienable right to decide the amount of dowry for their daughter[s] or for daughter[s]-in-law.'[53] Missionaries were accused of both overlooking and interfering with the dowry system. For the majority of people, the role of dowry as the signifier of marriage transcended arguments about quantities, quality (cash or livestock), and mission teachings on the institution. The payment of dowry made a marriage legitimate. Isaac Were Osundwa captured this conceptualization succinctly in stating that 'girls never got married without the payment of dowry. Every man had to pay dowry. There was no alternative. If one did not pay dowry, which was the marriage certificate, the wife could not be counted as his.'[54] In some cases missions advocated for the total abolition of dowry.

It was not uncommon for some mission girls to oppose the payment of dowry prior to their marriage, reflecting missionary efforts to limit or even abolish dowries. If a mission-educated girl accepted a marriage proposal from a poor man who could not pay dowry, her father would *kurura ta mbaki*, 'become as bitter as snuff' and furious.[55] This willingness, indeed audacity, to contract marriages in spite of family opposition was indicative of newly-found agency among mission girls. But so essential was the payment of dowry to the customary conception of the institution of marriage that a prospective father-in-law might refuse to accept a 'free' daughter-in-law in the case of a mission woman whose Christian family was opposed to the payment of dowry. As Rose Otolo observed about marriage between two Christian families, 'My brother's wife was supposed to be given away [married] dowry-free, but my father said he did not want a prostitute.'[56] Her father, though a Christian, insisted on the payment of dowry for his daughter-in-law.

In this context, the term 'prostitute' could have several meanings. In some quarters of society, the mission stations were looked upon as breeding centres for prostitution.[57] There was a general belief that mission girls who had abandoned a variety of indigenous cultural practices were unmarriageable.[58] In some places, Christian girls fetched a much-reduced dowry, because they had lost a lot of their cultural lustre at the missions. As for the parents, 'They would lose a lot of wealth because the girl would be looked upon as prostitutes because they had gone to the mission.'[59] However, Rose Otolo's father was not referring to any of these possibilities. Rather, he was seeking to affirm the construction of marriage as he knew it; without the exchange of bridewealth it was aberrant. He would pay dowry for his daughter-in-law. Although he was a mission adherent, this elder continued to conceptualize marriage in the context of exchange of dowry. As Agnes Wairimu Hinga put it, underscoring the centrality of dowry among the Kikuyu, an elder with daughters lived, along with his clansmen, 'to drink his daughters' beer and to receive dowry'.[60]

Part of the reason that dowry was such an entrenched cultural institution was economic. As unmarried girls represented potential capital,'once one had a daughter, she would fetch cows in the form of bridewealth.'[61] Discussing what he termed 'curious facts' about the Nandi of the Rift Valley in 1929, G. W. Huntingford, a colonial officer and ethnographer who wrote extensively on them, observed that 'A cow is of more consequence than a wife; though a daughter is a valuable possession, as she will one day, when she is married, bring in more cattle for her father.'[62]

Consequently, the attempts to limit bridewealth by missionaries and colonial administrators not only interfered with the central role of parents and kinsmen in the institution of marriage, but also struck at the heart of their economic existence. In this vein, it was said, nostalgically, 'In the olden days, old men liked cattle. Once a daughter qualified for such cattle as bridewealth, there was no need for educating them.'[63] This was the plight of Keran Akoto, a trained Homecraft teacher who got married in 1947. For her, life took a sudden turn: 'because my parents were interested in getting cows, they spoilt my plans. I had wanted to join secondary school and even if possible pursue much higher education.'[64] She estimated that the dowry paid for her and her contemporaries in Kakamega constituted four to five cows and 200 shillings.

In the central part of Kenya, in Fort Hall, where there was no support for dowry limitation, a girl was perceived as an investment whose dividends could be gleaned periodically. Hence, in 1927, John Mbuthia, a LNC member, opined, 'A daughter is like a bank and it is only a right that her father should be able to draw on her from time to time.'[65] The Kikuyu metaphor of a bank did not sit well with the Meru LNC, which was opposed to the monetarization of a cultural institution. By 1949, the Meru LNC looked at the marital practices of the Kikuyu as a ship gone wild. The Meru council unanimously agreed that, 'the Kikuyu habit of marriage to the highest bidder, and the cash sale of girls was forbidden by Meru customs.'[66] The council also affirmed that there would be no compulsion on girls to marry men who were not of their choice.

The financial worth of a girl was ostensibly enhanced by other factors including industry among other factors. Writing in 1924, a British female traveller who confessed to being curious about the 'price' of native girls in what she called the 'matrimonial market' expressed a qualified variation of the same observation. While in Kenya, she understood that among the Kikuyu, fair-complexioned daughters fetched 'a better bride price' than their darker sisters. Thus, 'A native with several 'fair' daughters is considered to be a most fortunate man and to possess a sort of walking bank balance on which he can draw at any time to his great advantage.'[67]

The economic aspect of dowry was particularly clear if livestock paid in dowry died. In 1943, the Nyeri LNC concurred with Chief Ndamayu that 'it is better that any loss incurred be borne by a young bridegroom rather than an elderly father who may have no other source of income than his one daughter.'[68] Colonial administrators found such reasoning in bad taste. To this end, the president of the Fort Hall Native Council observed that the Kiambu Native Council had passed a resolution absolving a prospective bridegroom of any responsibility if the animal or animals in question died after he had paid the dowry in full. It did not matter whether the girl had been handed over or not. This was a financial matter.

There was evidence that pointed at girls being part of what was perceived as a 'dowry extortion ring' in which daughters would collude with their parents to demand large amounts of livestock for dowry. It is not clear what the girl's motive for participating in such a plot would be, but there is documentation of girls using their sexuality to intervene in salvaging their parents' waning economic conditions. Here, acts of prostitution were linked to women's attempts to replenish family livestock,[69] which would save family from economic disaster and poverty.

A wealthy man could hold out for a wealthy suitor for his daughter, for a more generous suitor might also be a much wealthier husband. He might even be an older man – not exactly the girl's idea of a suitor, but one who might match her father's demands and thereby possibly inflate the girl's social worth. Or she might opt for an older but wealthier man who had higher social status in the community. Hence, one colonial administrator wrote, '[the] girls though disliking marriage with ancients do like being paid for.'[70] It is not unreasonable to assume that a girl would prefer to get married into a wealthy family. Her own certainly would be concerned that she married well. In any case, wealthy families tended to marry among themselves,[71] a sign of class formation.

The economic and financial elements of dowry placed heavy demands on young men, particularly on those whose own economic standing had become dependent on changes wrought by colonial interventions. Two and a half decades after the introduction of colonial rule, young men had become a permanent and vital component of the economy. Among those who were employed, the majority were migrant labourers in distant places living away from their homes. Even if they could save enough money, the task of purchasing livestock for dowry was time-consuming and often difficult to coordinate. In some cases, livestock had to be moved long distances if the prospective couple came from different neighbourhoods. Amid the difficulties caused by livestock quarantines, fluctuating livestock prices, the physical distances between places of origin and final destination of livestock and the fact that time was of the essence for working men, accumulating and paying a dowry could be a major feat.

For some colonial officials, this emphasis on economic matters in the institution of dowry so tainted the marriage institution that the latter's legitimacy was called to question. Chief Justice Sir Robert Hamilton argued that a woman was not a free contracting agent, 'but is regarded rather as a chattel, for the purchase of which a bargain is entered into between the intending husband and the father or nearest male relative of the woman.'[72] This, Hamilton argued, created an ambiguous category of women who 'are commonly spoken of, for want of a more precise term, as "wives" and as "married women".'[73] For Hamilton, this native custom did not 'approximate in any way to the legal idea of a marriage'.[74]

The Statute of Limitations

> [A] girl's family should be able to sue for dowry even two generations later and cases for debt should not be refused on grounds of antiquity if there were witnesses able to prove the debt.[75]

Because indigenous communities regarded dowry, and indeed marriage itself, as part of an on-going process that involved not just a husband and wife, but their respective families and clans, the issue of dowry limitation involved more than the problems caused by exorbitant demands, the possibility of extortion, the relation of customary practices to Christianizing efforts, and the economic importance of dowry. Litigation arising out of the payment of dowry in installments could arise in 'cases being filed by grand and great grand children of the contracting parties, in many cases [it being] quite impossible to obtain any evidence'.[76] The litigation was for some unpaid portion of the original dowry agreed upon. A lot of these cases went back to the 1899 famine, when future dowry payments were promised in the hope they could be made during better times. This situation was aggravating not only to the surviving relations of men who were held in debt over dowry, but also to the indigenous and colonial authorities who had to sort out such issues. Where there was no surviving witness to the original transactions, or where such witnesses were not willing to come forward, the situation was even more difficult to unravel.

At the root of the problem was an implied unreliability of verbal agreements about dowry between the families of the marrying couples. To colonial officials, orality did not measure up to the supposed infallibility of the written word. They expected written documents to be used as the primary source of evidence in disputes, supplemented by witness accounts, with the witnesses themselves validated by having inscribed themselves in the marriage register.[77] Recording and codifying thus would be substituted for memory and goodwill in long-term dowry disputes.

Colonial administrators were ill-equipped to determine what action to take with regard to the statute of limitation in such civil cases. For example, in Central Province, all such cases were heard and decided by Native Tribunals. Often, the cases called for the support of the colonial officer in charge of the district. Where some of the cases being deliberated revolved around matters that antedated the introduction of colonial rule, the officers tended to differ as to how to proceed. There were questions as to whether such cases should even be brought before the Native Tribunal. The PC for Central Province was particularly unsympathetic to the protracted nature of litigation regarding unpaid dowries, lamenting that:

> The practice in vogue among the Kikuyu, and presumably among other native tribes, of deferred payments in regard to marriage 'dowries' and the endless intricacies relating to the sale of livestock, with the return of certain of the progeny of the original animal to the vendor, do not make for a rapid system of purchase and exchange, and consequently the bringing of a case before the elders may with perfect propriety according to native idea be postponed literally for years. When therefore an arbitrary time limit is imposed there results some hardship and discontent.[78]

Evidence in such old cases was characterized as 'usually heresy'. Opponents of these situations considered it unfair that in the native sensibility, it seemed right for a defendant to be forced to pay a plaintiff an exorbitant number of livestock over some 'ancient' dowry situation.

One aspect of the problem, from the colonial point of view, revolved around the modus operandi of Native Tribunals that presided over dowry cases. Traditionally, elders who attended Elders' Councils' deliberations only sporadically got to partake of the slaughtered livestock 'fees', while leaving others to do the work, while those left to do the work, otherwise unsupervised, could be bribed. Thus, 'when only 3 or 4 men are present this is the opportunity for malpractice; if 60 are present the finding is almost always invariably sound and just.' By 1915, colonial administrators in Nyeri district exercised closer supervision to ensure that elders were not bribed. Here, all decisions made by elders were recognized only after they had been communicated to colonial officers by a representative group of elders. To ensure regular attendance by the elders, fees were paid in cash, as opposed to livestock, and divided at intervals among elders who had been regular at the council deliberations.

Some elders and colonial administrators consequently were anxious to set a limit of time beyond which litigation over deferred dowry payments would be considered illegal. But for the reasons we have seen – the cultural and economic centrality of dowry-based marriage in indigenous society – there were good arguments for resisting the limitation of dowry payments.[79] While colonial officials represented the local legal space as overly litigious, disorganized, and open to opportunistic and unreasonable litigants, customary arrangements seem to have been established that addressed a number of those issues that preoccupied colonial administrators. Among the Meru, for example, there was the custom of 'tying a heifer under a tree for hyenas to take in liquidation of a bride price debt when there was no living representative left of the maternal family.'[80] Here, litigation over dowry did not persist endlessly. Although the Native Marriages Registration bill suggested the codification of the amount of dowry agreed upon and actually paid, and because the suggested legislation did not provide a mechanism of subsequent entries for future payments, the legislation did not eliminate the potential for future contestation regarding dowry amounts. Thus, once again, colonial policy came into conflict with indigenous assumptions that were fundamentally different from those of the colonizers about the nature of marriage as an on-going institution with major social and economic dimensions.

Modernity and Dowry: Monetarization

Efforts by colonial administrators and missionaries to rework the nature of marriage via regulating the dowry in Kenya inadvertently created shifts away from the kinship as a basis for the institution of marriage, pushed it into the public, official arena and entrenched it even further in the commercial realm. This was part of the price paid for the introduction of modernity in colonial Kenya. These ongoing negotiations reflected the changing socio-economic conditions in the colony. More general processes thus prompted the reworkings of dowry in individual families. More importantly, they were reflective of shifts in the lives of women who effected the refashioning of socio-cultural spaces.

One consequence was that women began leaving bad marriages in large numbers. Undeterred by the financial burden that befell their natal families as a result of their actions, these women exercised their agency by returning to their natal homes, entering new marital arrangements, or establishing independent households in urban areas. The refund of dowry when marriages had broken down became the most litigated aspect of marriage during the colonial period. It is not clear whether there was an increase in litigation or that the litigation was over-reported during the period, but the increased ability of women to act for themselves outside the restraints imposed by dowry transactions is evident.[81] What they did as they crossed borders previously impermeable to women had ripple effects throughout their families and communities.

For example, Serah Mukabi (nee Kang'ethe) went to the Thogoto mission station, in Kikuyu, without her father's permission, possibly in the late 1930s. Here, her upper ears were sewn up.[82] Ear piercing of the upper and lower lobes was a preliminary rite of passage from childhood to pubescence among the Kikuyu, Embu, Meru, and Kirinyaga, among other groups. The rite did not grant the initiate the status of adulthood, which only came with circumcision. The sewing up of the ears of girls who entered mission stations was part of the refashioning of the bodies of mission protégées, as if erasing the marks of tradition.[83]

Lambert, a colonial administrator, found the missionary opposition to ear piercing laughable. While missionaries considered the act as 'a wilful damage to the body, which is the temple of the Holy Ghost', Lambert wondered why the 'fashionable ladies of London [had] not been excommunicated for having their ears pierced for earrings'. Apparently, missions charged two shillings a piece to saw up the ears of their protegées 'for the Restoration of the temple'. Government hospitals offered the service for free.[84]

Serah's father, Kangethe, was infuriated by the mission's reversal of an age-old practice. In lieu of ear piercing, Kangethe instituted an additional fee as a component of dowry in his household. The extra fee was referred to as 'Mburi cia matu ma Serah', goats for Serah's (sewn) ears. Hence the subversion of a customary practice was worked into the dowry structure within the Kang'ethe household so that men who married daughters, grand-daughters, and all subsequent female offspring of Kangethe had to pay an extra fee as a fine or compensation for Serah's sewn ears.[85] Instituted in the 1940s, this practice is still in existence in the extended Kang'ethe household over fifty years later. Such were the accommodations instituted in the name of modernity. In addition, Kang'ethe no longer required his daughters to conform to customary ear piercing and allowed any of his daughters who so wished to pursue formal education. In a rather circuitous way, Serah's quest for education had resulted in a permanent transformation of central values and practices in her natal family.

An important consequence of colonization was the monetarization of dowry. This was facilitated by the trend toward a cash-for-labour economy. From the colonial point of view, this looked like a rationalization of an unendurably messy situation, as well as a way to avoid litigation and generally make administration of the colony easier. Dowry animals naturally changed hands in the course of marriages and other transactions. While this was a normal enough procedure, it resulted in complications not encountered in a cash economy. In North Kavirondo, the administrators blamed lack of economic development on the centrality of livestock in bridewealth and for the constant and endless wrangling that ensued when anyone in the daisy chain of transactions through which an animal passed insisted on having the exact same animal returned to him after a transaction failed. One litigation might have a snowball effect, destabilizing innumerable marriages that had included the disputed animal in their dowry payment. The following text illustrates the dilemma.

North Maragoli
December 12, 1927

District Commissioner,
Kakamega
After greetings.

Regarding the cattle of Imbiru Kabaragi. With one head of cattle he married a woman of Chief Mnubis location from a man named Kigade Arule. He in turn paid a debt with this animal to one Cherovale; wo [sic] then married a woman with it, from one Ngeri-all people of Chief Mnubi.

Now one of my people, one Amulega, has bought the animal for 144/= from Ngeri. As this cow calved twice, there are now three head. This last man of mine has married a woman with these three cattle; and now this man of chief Mnubis has come to sue Amalega for his cattle. So I lay the matter before you. I am much perturbed by the affair, so Adorwa and Amulega bring their case before you.

I am

Chief Odanga.[86]

In trying to get the LNCs to ensure that all transactions were dealt with on monetary basis, the DC hoped men would 'sue for a given sum of money and not for the particular animal or its offspring'. By 1929, the transition from animal to cash transactions had been broached. Likewise, at the end of its deliberations, the Committee on Native Marriage and Divorce, which met in Nairobi early in 1928, recommended, 'in all marriage transactions the cash value of stock should be fixed by law'.[87] In 1937, the South Nyeri LNC made a resolution applicable to all marriages under Native Law and Custom requiring that 'all dowry payments shall be registered on a cash valuation and if stock is included by agreement in any dowry payment it shall be shown in the register as cash at its value as agreed upon between the parties and shall be treated as a cash payment in subsequent suits or proceedings before native tribunals.'[88] Greet Kershaw observes that among the Kikuyu, 'Until the end of the First World War 90–100 percent of the bridewealth was expected in goats; by 1925 it had dropped to 30–40 percent. By 1935 only 10–20 percent could be offered in goats, but receivers might ask for cash only, apart from the ceremonial goats.'[89]

The monetarization[90] of bridewealth did not augur well for young men, however. In spite of regional and temporal differences, it would have taken a working man several years to accumulate adequate cash to purchase the adequate livestock for bridewealth during the colonial period.[91] Moreover, with monetarization, dowry was removed from the realm of family bonds and was individualized. Previously, it was customary for the bridegroom's father to provide livestock for bridewealth. With the introduction of cash as a component of bridewealth, few parents except the very wealthy could pay for their sons. As the cash component of bridewealth became larger, parents' contribution continued to drop. In the end, among the Kikuyu for example, the parents paid only 'the ceremonial goats, which would be eaten as a token of the new alliance'.[92] This individualization of dowry gradually erased the communal basis of the institution and widened the generation gap between elders and young suitors. This necessarily embroiled young brides in family conflicts that might continue throughout the duration of the marriage.

Given the effect that the monetarization of dowry and the isolation of young men as suitors had on traditional customs and communities, neither opposition to the practice nor the terms in which it was couched are surprising. By 1945, the Meru LNC declared it was 'horrified' at the idea of brideprice being paid in cash. Representing cash as a symbol of sale, chief M'Angaine stated that 'in Meru, cash could never replace bride price in stock. Meru girls could never be considered as articles for sale in shops.'[93] The use of cash for the payment of brideprice was said to reduce the whole institution of marriage to a financial transaction in which daughters were sold, whereas the payment of brideprice in livestock resulted in the 'cementing of friendship between the two families … and was built upon reciprocity and friendship'. In this respect, the council pointed out the fact that the said livestock was divided between the two families. This latter fact possibly referred to subsequent rites which required the bride's family to give their in-laws specified livestock. The council was unanimous in concluding that 'the whole object of brideprice was to ensure the mutual friendship of both families and that frequently marriages took place without payment of brideprice in full beforehand. This outstanding debt merely strengthened the ties between the two families.'[94] As far as the LNC was concerned, 'A cash debt brings trouble, and the end of good fellowship; whereas from time immemorial a stock debt in Meru brought increased obligations and thereby a strengthening of bonds and friendship.'[95]

Among the Kikuyu, too, the payment of bridewealth was never finalized.[96] In Meru, there were isolated occasions when cash had changed hands during preliminary preparations, including the purchase of food and drinks. It was not unusual for such monies to fall into the wrong hands, resulting in embezzlement. In such cases, tradition would be invoked and the guilty party would be ostracised from his clan, a rather harsh sentence. Clearly, such money was not part of the dowry payment and could not be claimed in any dowry-related suit.

Although H. E. Lambert, the DC for Meru, was a keen student of indigenous practices and at times a great defender of them, he believed that the emphasis on communal and reciprocal bonds in institutions such as the dowry was to blame for women's restricted lives. For Lambert, only individualism would free women from 'the irksome restraints of reciprocalism' and that where 'communal responsibility was still recognized, a "Black Slave Trade" in women would persist'.[97] Although endeavouring to promote the growth of individualism in Kenyan societies, Lambert ironically found himself in agreement with those conservative indigenous voices who lamented the monetarization of dowry, concluding that 'if a girl can be "bought" outright, with whatever currency, reciprocity is no longer her protection and she soon assumes the status of a bit of goods in the shop window or a "lot" (probably a bad lot) in the auction room.'[98]

Such ironies were a frequent product of the dynamics shaping gender and economic relations in colonial Kenya.

As late as May 1948 the Nyeri African District Council resolved that the area under its jurisdiction would continue with the old procedure of dowry payment. This was in reference to the dual use of livestock and cash for the payment of dowry.[99] Earlier, in a 1943 meeting, this practice was deemed to be 'an accepted native custom'.[100] Tradition was not static: it could be reinvented. In 1948 the Nyeri council had broached the subject of the high price of dowry, but recommended that the matter be left as it was. This was a great disappointment to the president of the council because he considered it a very important problem which should not be overlooked. Clearly it was a not an issue that could be resolved quickly.

Even in widowhood, as in marriage, women's independence was closely tied to concerns with dowry, which kept them tied to either their marital homes or with new spouses.[101] The notion of women as capital overshadowed efforts to give them agency in both domains. A male from one of these two domains would be held responsible for refunding the dowry to the clan of the deceased man if the widow refused to be inherited by a kinsman of the deceased. In January 1928, for example, the President of the Fort Hall LNC sought to find out from the councillors whether upon becoming a widow, a Christian woman should return to her father, who would, in turn, be asked to refund her dowry in full. Or, should her husband's brother inherit her, even if he were a pagan? In the mind of the LNC, there was no option for the woman to lead an independent life. In response, a councillor, Chief Reuben, stated, 'We must keep to the old custom, or we shall have endless trouble. The husband's brother must inherit the woman and her children. If [s]he won't let him try and get children by her, then he can sell her to another Mission boy.'[102] If, however, the widow chose to marry again, a councillor, Paulo Getundu, suggested that the second husband should pay dowry to the deceased husband's heir. Yet in the 1990s, and possibly earlier, a widow might refund to her in-laws dowry paid for her, including a few animals to redeem her children from the in-laws, and thus gain an independent existence.[103]

Men who decided to keep the children from failed marriages could not reclaim dowry. Rather, they were required to pay any outstanding balance at the same time as they took custody of the children.[104] A man also forfeited his dowry if he walked out of a marriage.[105] Where an estranged woman kept the children, the ex-husband was entitled to a refund of his dowry. This, however, was subject to his ex-wife remarrying. Dowry from the new husband was used to reimburse the first husband. This procedure, which precluded timely reimbursement, did not always sit well with some of the ex-husbands; they might adopt menacing behavior forcing the woman's father to refund the dowry even before his daughter had remarried.[106]

Although as late as 1945 the crown counsel reported that Maasai customary law made no provision for divorce or dowry refund where a woman had born a child, when divorce ensued, the amount of livestock refund involved was very considerable. Thus, in a Loita Civil Case No. 5

of 1941, a claim was made for 'the return of 300 head of cattle, sheep ... and six donkeys'.[107] Apart from social disruption, economic stakes in dowry litigation could be extremely high. The decision by a woman to leave a marriage could make an immense dent in family resources or create excessive indebtedness. It could also enable her to determine her future, including her marital options.

Conclusion

As elders resisted the pressure to limit dowry, their daughters were represented as accomplices to their fathers' design to inflate the brideprice. The reality was not so simple. Despite this, litigation continued. The most common causes for litigation included the taking of girls for wives 'without going through the formality of asking her parents or arranging about dowry', 'the propensity to take somebody else's wife', and the 'extreme disinclination to refund dowry when a marriage is dissolved'.[108] In all the three categories, women along with men were openly violating conventional protocol for contracting marriages. But this was a protocol that was changing rapidly, as were other institutions in the society.

In the case of women, it is very probable that they were getting married not only against the wishes of their families, but out of personal choice. In North Kavirondo defiance on the part of the women was said to be the result of 'the sale of girls to the highest bidder, generally an oldish man'. In such instances the girls 'naturally gravitate(d) to a younger partner'.[109] The dowry situation had a gendered, generational, financial, and religious twist to it: all the trappings of colonial modernity were present.

Notes

1. Isaac Were Osundwa, oral interview, Lubinu, Kakamega, 23 January 1997.
2. G.W.B. Huntingford, 'The tribes of Kenya: some curious facts about the Nandi people', *The East African Standard*, January (1929), 53.
3. KNA: PC/CP/2/1/5 LNC Meetings, Fort Hall District, 27 May 1927.
4. KNA: PC/NZA.3/28/4/1 Senior Commissioner Kisumu to CNC Nairobi, 6 September 1927.
5. Mary Wanjiru [nyina wa Cibira], oral interview, Limuru, 14 July 1993.
6. Etta Close, *A Woman Alone in Kenya, Uganda and the Belgian Congo* (Sydney, 1924), 7. The bridegroom in question was a Kikuyu cook. For another account depicting a European gaze of, and intervention in a 'long argument ... [and] prolonged negotiations' about bride price, see W. Robert Foran, *A Cuckoo in Kenya: The Reminiscences of a Pioneer Officer in British East Africa* (London, 1936), 215–17.
7. Gavin Kitching, *Class and Economic Change in Kenya*, 200–7; Kershaw, *Mau Mau from Below*, 24.
8. Orchardson, *The Kipsigis*, 80–81.
9. David Parkin and David Nyamwaya (eds), *Transformations of African Marriage* (Manchester, 1987), 9; John L. Comaroff, *The Meaning of Marriage Payments* (New York, 1980).

10. In certain cases, the official call for the codification of dowry also was linked to the problem of girl/child pledging. The argument ran that the provision for the payment of dowry in instalment allowed parents to pledge their infant daughters as potential wives to men from whom parents continued to receive installments of livestock and other items as the girl grew. At the heart of the objection to this procedure was the possibility that neither the girl nor the man would have affection for each other when it was time to marry. The question of whether there was affection and consent, particularly on the part of the girl, influenced official intervention in native marital issues. In situations where such arrangements did not work, dowry might have to be refunded. The very practice of child pledging and the dowry problems it created resulted in a protracted campaign for its abolition.
11. Liza Nyambura Mwangi, oral interview, Nairobi, November 1996.
12. Monicah Wanjiku Wandura, oral interview, Nairobi, November 1993.
13. Monicah Wanjiku Wandura, oral interview, Nairobi, November 1996.
14. Judith Abunzwa, *Women's Voices, Women's Power: Dialogues of Resistance From East Africa* (Peterborough, Ont., 1997), 103.
15. *Ibid.*, 103–11.
16. KNA: PC/CENT/2/1/4 LNC Meetings, Kyambu District, 22-23 November 1928.
17. Colony and Protectorate of Kenya, Supreme Court, Law Reports of Kenya, Vol. XI, 1927-1928, 67–8.
18. *Ibid.*, 68.
19. Arthur Phillips (ed.), *Survey of African Marriage and Family Life* (London, 1953), xvii. Even then, the young man was not fully independent of the moral hold of his kinsfolk.
20. For a case study of changes in mode of payment, number of livestock, and the monetarization of bridewealth among the Iteso between 1907 and 1980, see Nobuhiro Nagashima, 'Aspects of change in bridewealth among the Iteso', in Parkin & Nyamwaya, *Transformations of African Marriage*, 183–97.
21. See KNA: PC/NZA.3/28/4/1 DC Central Kavirondo to Senior Commissioner Nyanza, 5 August 1927.
22. Susana Aseka, oral interview, Ebukambuli, Kakamega, February 1997.
23. Aggrey Ham Wanzetse, oral interview, Wanga, Kakamega, 24 January 1997.
24. KNA: PC/NZA.3/28/4/1 DC South Kavirondo to Senior Commissioner Nyanza, 31 May 1926. Limits on dowry rates had been introduced in Kisii prior to 1926. An earlier attempt was thwarted by peoples' failure to abide by its provisions.
25. KNA: PC/NZA.3/28/4/1 DC Central Kavirondo to Senior Commissioner Nyanza, 5 August 1927.
26. KNA: PC/NZA.3/28/4/1 Senior Commissioner Kisumu to DC Kisumu, Central Kavirondo, Marriage Price, 18 July 1927.
27. KNA: PC/NZA.3/28/4/1 DC Central Kavirondo to Senior Commissioner Nyanza, 5 August 1927.
28. *Ibid.*
28. Cited in KNA: PC/NZA.3/28/4/1 DC Kakamega to PC Kisumu, Marriage Price, 29 September 1927.
29. In 1926, the DC for Kavirondo was of the opinion that the idea of fixing bridewealth would be unacceptable to the elders. A prominent missionary, E. A. Beavon's suggestion that any excess cattle paid by a bridegroom should be seized by the government, sold and the proceeds credited to the government's general revenue would be tantamount to punishing the groom for a situation that was not of his own making. A more positive alternative would be to credit the LNC so that the income was not lost to the community. KNA: PC/RVP.3/28/4/1 Native Marriages and Divorces, DC Kavirondo to Senior Commissioner Nyanza, 30 September 1926. This way, also, the LNC would be persuaded to continue the campaign to curb excessive bridewealth. At a later stage, Beavon suggested that the cash be credited to the Native Trust Fund. This way, no single individual would gain from contravening a limitation regulation. More importantly, the temptation to breach the regulation would disappear. As things stood, he believed, the greed of the old men was hindering the spread of the Christian religion. KNA: PC/NZA.3/28/4/1 Native Marriages and Divorces, SDA Mission, E. A. Beavon

to DC Kisii, Re: Marriage Price of Girls, 21 October 1926.

31. KNA/PC/NZA.3/28/4/1 Native Marriages and Divorces, Mr. Beavon to Senior Commissioner Nyanza, extract of letter dated 27 August 1926.
32. To some extent, colonial administrators blamed the predicament of mission men on the missions. The latter were said to impart a superficial education on their protégés, producing 'pride of self [rather] than pride of achievement.' The mission boys were perceived as indolent, poor upstarts. The DC Central Kavirondo believed, ' it may be difficult for such persons to obtain a wife without enduring the discomforts of manual labour and the duffing of gaudy hats, ties and socks.' KNA: PC/NZA.3/28/4/1 Native Marriages and Divorces, DC Central Nyanza to Senior Commissioner Nyanza, Re: Marriage of Young Immature Girls, Marriage of Girls to Old Men, Stabilizing of Marriage Price, 4 December 1926. Colonial officials were not overly impressed by the social deportment of mission boys.
33. KNA/PC/NZA.3/28/4/1 Native Marriages and Divorces, Mr. Beavon to Senior Commissioner Nyanza, extract of letter dated 27 August 1926.
34. *Ibid.*
35. G. Gordon, 'Our First Marriage in Kenya', *Kikuyu News*, 56, August–September 1915, 4–6; Dr. Phelp, 'Character Sketches: Jonathan and Jason', *Kikuyu News,* 86, December 1923, 1–3, both cited in White, *The Comforts of Home*, 227.
36. KNA: PC/NZA.3/28/4/1 Native Marriages and Divorces, Mr. Beavon to Senior Commissioner Nyanza, extract of letter dated 7 September 1926.
37. KNA: PC/CP.1/2/1 Kitui District, page 471 quoted from Political Record Book, Vol. II, 1912, 11.
38. KNA: PC/NZA.3/28/28/4/1 Native Marriages and Divorces, Senior Commissioner to acting DC South Kavirondo, 2 October 1926.
39. KNA: PC/NZA.3/28/4/1 DC Kisii to Senior Commissioner Nyanza, extract of letter dated 3 September 1926.
40. KNA:PC/NZA.3/28/4/1 E. A. Beavon, 17 September, 1926 .
41. KNA: PC/NZA.3/28/4/1 Native Marriages and Divorces, SDA Mission, E. A. Beavon to DC Kisii, Re: Marriage Price of Girls, 21 October 1926.
42. S. N. Bogonko, 'Christianism and Africanism at crossroads in Kenya, 1909-1940', unpublished conference paper (Kenya, 1976), 18.
43. Adrian Hastings, 'Were Women a Special Case?' in Bowie, Kirkwood, & Ardener (eds) *Women and Missions*, 114.
44. Section 19 of the Marriage Law, chapter 167, provided that if both parties to the wedding were at least twenty-one years of age, no parental consent was necessary. The majority of marriages, however, fell outside the provisions of this law.
45. KNA: PC/NZA.3/28/4/1 Native Marriages and Divorces, Mr. Beavon to DC Kavirondo, extract of letter dated 17 September 1926.
46. KNA: PC/NZA.3/28/4/1 Native Marriages and Divorces, SDA Mission, E. A. Beavon to DC Kisii, Re: Marriage Price of Girls, 21 October 1926.
47. See KNA: PC/NZA.3/28/4/1 Native Marriages and Divorces, Senior Commissioner to acting DC South Kavirondo, 2 October 1926.
48. *Ibid.*
49. *Ibid.*
50. Adrian Hastings, 'Were Women a Special Case?', 114.
51. KNA: PC/CENT/2/1/4 LNC Meetings, Kyambu District, 24 November 1925.
52. KNA: PC/NZA.3/28/4/1 Native Marriages and Dowries, DC Central Kavirondo to PC Nyanza, 6 January 1928.
53. Bogonko, 'Christianism and Africanism', 18.
54. Isaac Were Osundwa, oral interview, Lubinu, Kakamega, 23 January 1997.
55. Mary Wanjiru [nyina wa Cibira], oral interview, Limuru, 14 July 1993.
56. Rose Otoolo, oral interview, Nairobi, 17 July 1993.
57. Bogonko, 'Christianism and Africanism'.
58. See Sandgren, *Christianity and the Kikuyu*, and Strayer, *The Making of Mission Communities*. In particular, see Sandgren, 175–82 for various versions of the Muthirigu song, which among other things expressed the disdain with which uncircumcised girls/women, were held.

59. Beth Njambi, oral interview, Limuru, 14 July 1993.
60. Agnes Wairimu Hinga, oral interview, Ndumberi, Kiambu, 18 July 1993.
61. Isaac Were Osundwa, oral interview, Lubinu, Kakamega, 23 January 1997.
62. G. W. B. Huntingford, 'The tribes of Kenya: some curious facts about the Nandi people', *The East African Standard*, January 1929, 53.
63. Rajab Ngashira, oral interview, Ebumanyi, Kakamega, 22 January 1997.
64. Keran Akoto, oral interview, Keveye, Kakamega, 26 February 1997.
65. KNA: PC/CP/2/1/5 LNC Meetings, Fort Hall District, 27 May 1927. Fort Hall District was also referred to as Murang'a.
66. KNA: PC/CENT/2/1/9 LNC Meetings, Meru, 6–8 December 1949.
67. Etta Close, *A Woman Alone*, 24. Citing examples from China and Japan, the writer was perplexed that 'a fair complexion should be so universally admired'.
68. KNA: PC/CP/2/1/5 LNC Meetings, Fort Hall District, 27 May 1927.
69. White, *The Comforts of Home*, pp. 29–50.
70. KNA: PC/NZA.3/28/4/1 Senior Commissioner Kisumu to CNC Nairobi, 6 September 1927.
71. Wagner, *The Changing Family*, 392.
72. Supreme Court 1917 R. v. Amkeyo (7 E.A.L.R.14) quoted in Colony and Protectorate of Kenya, Report on Native Tribunals, Arthur Phillips, 1945, 292.
73. *Ibid.*
74. *Ibid.*
75. KNA:PC/CENT/2/1/9 Meru Local Native Council Meetings, M'Imathiu, 22 February 1938.
76. KNA: PC/CENT/2/1/4 LNC Meetings, Kyambu District, Dowry Limitation Suits, 25-26 April 1929.
77. In 1937, the President of the Fort Hall LNC argued that the registration of marriages would be ineffective unless the exact amount of brideprice settled on was noted in the register. While members of the Superior Tribunal asserted that 'the amount of marriage price was always definitely fixed before the marriage ceremony', the councillors disagreed. Confusion emanated from the practice of periodic gifts and slaughter of livestock 'when the children of the marriage were circumcised, and gifts in stock were made from time to time to the father or guardian of the bride. It was quite impossible for anyone to anticipate how many goats would be required for such purposes.' Evidently, these future and ongoing eventualities did not preclude the fixing of a definite price at the time of marriage. After some discussions the councillors did agree to this conclusion and, led by Chief Michuki, eleven councillors consented to the entry in the marriage register of:
    (a) The total marriage price agreed upon.
    (b) The portion already paid at the time of registration.
    (c) The balance remaining unpaid.

    In what at the time seemed like an unexplained move, five councillors led by Job Muchuchu advocated that 'only the portion already paid should be entered in the Register; no allusion should be made to the agreed price or to the unpaid balance'. It is possible that the Muchuchu faction sought to limit the extent of government surveillance and sanction of the marriage institution by advocating the withholding of statistics vital for prosecuting defaulters. Additionally, along with all the other councillors, this faction was concerned about the continued viability of those other rites constituting the marriage institution beyond brideprice and involving livestock. Although the president argued that the customary gifts would not be entered into the register because they did not constitute the original marriage agreement, this colonial fragmentation of cultural institutions did not sit well with the community. Compromises were made. So too, were efforts to salvage the familiar, the customary. In this particular case, Muchuchu and his like lost, but not without a fight. See KNA:PC/CENT/2/1/8 LNC Meetings, 19 March 1937.
78. KNA: Coast Province, Section 9, MF-2972 Reel 38, acting PC Kenya [Central] Province Nyeri to PC Seyidie [Coast] Province Mombasa, 19 March 1915.
79. In 1938, Reverend Phillipo of the Meru LNC argued that dowry and land disputes

should not be subject to limitations because the finality of the such a statute was against the spirit of the institution of marriage and dowry. This was especially so in cases where the family of the bridegroom was poor. Then '[I]t was customary for only a token payment to be made to the bride's family...leaving the balance to be paid later if and when the groom became rich.' In the case of land sales, the right of redemption was always there. These two instances were not cases of simple debt and could not be limited by the death of one party. To further clarify the situation, one Mr. Christopher reiterated that 'cases of dowry and blood money were as one for purposes of limitation'. KNA: PC/CENT/2/1/9 LNC Minutes, Meru, 22 February 1938. Resolutions passed on 19 February 1938.

80. *Ibid.*
81. Although as late as 1945 the crown counsel reported that Maasai customary law made no provision for divorce or dowry refund where a woman had borne a child, when divorce ensued, the amount of livestock refund involved was very considerable.
82. For a fuller discussion on the significance of ear piercing among Kikuyu girls, see Davison, *Voices from Mutira*, 1989.
83. Kanogo, 'Mission Impact in Colonial Kenya', 169.
84. See KNA: PC/CENTRAL/2/1/11 H. E. Lambert, DC Meru, Meru: Disintegration and Reintegration in the Meru Tribe, Part III, 9 January 1940, 26.
85. Hannah Wariara Kahanya, oral interview, Limuru, 28 July 1993. In the extended Kangethe family, the 'goats for ears' fee took different forms. In Hannah Wariara's case, her husband built a granary for her mother. An unusual twist in this transformation of the dowry institution in the Kang'ethe clan is the fact that the change was, and continues to be transmitted through both male and female siblings. In other words, marrying a girl descended from a female offspring of Kang'ethe is the same as marrying a girl descended from the male line of Kang'ethe offspring. In either case, the *mburi cia matu* fee has to be paid. The remaking of dowry thus unfolded in both official and unofficial arenas.
86. KNA: DC/NN/1/8 North Kavirondo Annual Report, 1927, 3; Chief Odanga to DC Kakamega, extract of letter dated 12 December 1927. A 1934 hand scribbling on the margin of the above report noted that: 'In 1929 it was agreed that an animal could not be followed i.e. if used in marriage again or otherwise legitimately disposed of, the original owner could not claim that identical animal even if there was no other to substitute for it.' KNA: DC/NN/1/8 North Kavirondo Annual Report, 1927, 4. In other words, the practice of ' following individual cattle through several hands would be stopped.' KNA: DC/NN.1/11 North Kavirondo Annual Report, 1930, 19. Litigants had to accept substitute animals or wait till cattle was found that would satisfy the debt. *Ibid.* This would eliminate the possibility of upsetting 'a whole chain of marriages as had happened in the past'.
87. KNA: PC/NZA.3/28/4/1 PC Kisumu to DCs Nyanza Reserves, 16 March 1928.
88. KNA: PC/CENT/2/1/6 LNC Special Meetings, Nyeri, Marriage and Dowry, 20–22 July 1937.
89. Kershaw, '*Mau Mau from Below*', 286. At a time when young men claimed that girls' fathers were inflating dowry, it is not unreasonable to assume that even in those cases where suitors preferred to pay their dowry in cash, this might be exorbitant because of inflated quotations of livestock prices. The existence of official figures might diffuse any conflict over this issue.

Like North Kavirondo, the South Nyeri LNC left the question of dowry limitation and registration of marriages contracted under Native Law and Custom unsolved in 1937. In Fort Hall, the return of original *mahari* was still an issue as late as July 1942. In 1939 caution was given by Hezekiah Gachui that 'elders should be told not to attempt to return the stock forming part of the original *mahari*, no matters [sic] how many times it had changed hands.' KNA: PC/CENT/2/1/8 LNC Meetings, Fort Hall District, 21 November 1939. Unable or unwilling to draw a hard and fast rule about the composition of dowry, Chief Nderi of the Nyeri African District council suggested in February 1943 that the following resolution be added to the agenda of the next joint Central Province LNCs' meeting: 'That this meeting records its opinion that it is now accepted native custom in Embu, Kiambu, Nyeri districts that brideprice is payable in cash as well as in stock'. KNA: PC/CENT/2/1/10 Minutes of Nyeri African District Council, 16 February 1943.

90. The inclusion of money, either in part or whole in the bridewealth transaction is blamed for the perception of wives as purchased property. See J. H. Driberg, 'The status of women among the Nilotics and Nilo-Hamitics', *Africa*, Vol. 5, 1932, 415.
91. White, *The Comforts of Home*, 36; Kershaw, *Mau Mau from Below*, 94.
92. Kershaw, *Changing Roles*, 94.
93. KNA: PC/CENT/2/1/9 LNC Meetings, Meru, 28 March 1945.
94. *Ibid.*
95. *Ibid.* Frustrated about the slow progress, the Catholic Union was concerned that there should be a periodical retirement of *baraza* elders. It is possible that some of the older members of the *barazas* perpetuated values and conventions that were impediments to the introduction of the kind of change discussed above. This related to all manner of litigation, including dowry-related cases, which required the expertise of elders. A higher turnover of *baraza* membership might break the hold that the older generation had. .See KNA: DC/NN.1/12 North Kavirondo Annual Report, Kakamega, 1931, 15.
96. Kershaw, *Changing Roles*, 24.
97. KNA: PC/CENTRAL/2/1/11 H. E. Lambert, DC Meru, Meru: Disintegration and Reintegration in the Meru Tribe, Part III, 9 January 1940.
98. *Ibid.*
99. KNA: PC/CENT/2/1/10 Minutes of Nyeri African District Council, 17-20 May 1948.
100. KNA: PC/CENT/2/1/10 Minutes of Nyeri African District Council, 16 February 1943.
101. The ambiguities of the individualization of marriage under the Marriage Act were replayed in Kenya as recently as 1987 in the S. M. Otieno burial saga, which captured national and international attention.74 The death of the prominent criminal lawyer Silvanus Melea Otieno on December 20, 1986 precipitated a five-month legal tussle between his wife Wambui and his clan, the Umira Kager, regarding who was entitled to bury the lawyer. Amid a multiplicity of issues that arose was the question of the application of customary versus statutory law with regard to death, burial, women, and marriage. Wambui was confident that since she had married Otieno under the Marriage Act, she was the next of kin to her late husband and was therefore entitled to bury him. As it turned out, Wambui was caught in a complex and protracted legal wrangle that included, but was not restricted to, conflicts about ethnicity, modernity, tradition, statehood, gender, legal plurality, and women's rights in a modern state. In ruling that the corpse would be released to the widow and buried at Nyalgunga, Otieno's and the clan's natal home, the court denied Wambui the right to bury her husband at Ngong, the couple's residence and Wambui's (and Otieno's, according to Wambui, among others) preferred burial place. Despite twenty-three years of a very close, modern, urban and cosmopolitan marriage, in widowhood, Wambui found herself subsumed under a reinvented patriarchal, clannish mould that robbed her of agency over the burial of her husband. For the 'modern' Kenyan woman, the trial was a stark reminder that agency gained under statutory law could be eroded overnight.
102. KNA: PC/CP/2/1/5 LNC Meetings, Fort Hall District, Custom re: Christian Marriage, 26 January 1928.
103. Ayako Matayo, personal communication, March 2001. Informants name has been changed to protect her identity.
104. Mzee Elijah Mbeketha, oral interview, Tala, Machakos, 30 July 1993.
105. Oral Interview, Beth Njambi, 14 July 1993, Limuru.
106. Oral Interview, Beth Njambi, Limuru 14 July 1993.
107. Colony and Protectorate of Kenya, Report on Native Tribunals, Arthur Phillips, 1945, 142.
108. KNA: DC/NN.1/7 North Kavirondo Annual Report, 1926, 5.
109. *Ibid.*

Five

Legislating Marriage

> In my opinion, the use of the word 'marriage' to describe the relationship entered into by an African man with a woman of his tribe according to tribal custom is a misnomer which has led in the past to a considerable confusion of ideas. The elements of a so-called marriage by native custom differ so materially from the ordinarily accepted idea of what constitutes a civilized form of marriage that it is difficult to compare the two.[1]
>
> Sir Robert Hamilton, Chief Justice, 1917.

The effort to rework the institution of dowry payments was part of a larger effort to restructure the institution of marriage in colonial Kenya.[2] The colonial government believed that codifying the different facets of indigenous marriages promised to secure more agreeable conditions for brides and at the same time bring to an end seemingly endless marriage-related litigation, which included not just dowry disputes, but a host of other issues, as well.

A small, but growing number of Africans were getting married according to the provisions of the 1902 East African Marriage Ordinance, which required a monogamous marriage and provided women with the right to inherit matrimonial property. Marriages contracted under this ordinance were subject to colonial surveillance. In order to rectify the various problems identified in customary marriages, especially those that affected women and girls, the government felt it was imperative to increase the number of people participating in essentially European-style marriages. This would be achieved through alternative and less obtrusive legislation requiring the official registration of various aspects of native marriages. The campaign for marriage registration that resulted, beginning in the early 1920s, was part of an effort to enforce colonial conceptions of marriage and part of a more extensive programme for the social engineering of African families, their morality, sexuality, legality, and their interaction with the colonial economy. What the government did not anticipate was the diversity of opinions that these efforts to legislate marriage produced or the changing constructions of marriage that resulted.[3] These concerns exposed the variety of women's experiences in marriage and in society at large. It also reconfigured the spaces and boundaries of women's lives, sometimes improving conditions for them, sometimes not, but always altering them.

The Registration of Pagan Marriages Ordinance defined and codified marriage in a language and within parameters provided by the colonial state to facilitate official surveillance and control of the institution. Indigenous family heads had overseen the creation, maintenance, and dissolution of marriages in the precolonial and early colonial period. Now, registered marriages would be subject to a variety of legislation that would affect their operation and dissolution. These measures included the imposition of monogamy and measures designed to allow for the consent of the woman to a marriage. It was also necessary to prevent forced and child marriages. Efforts would also be made to deal with conflicts over the legal status of widows, including curbing leviratic marriages and the imposition of legislation regarding the inheritance of property and resolving questions of child custody. All of these measures involved elements central to indigenous marriage that the colonial authorities deemed improper, and therefore all became sites of contestation as marriage underwent transformation. The debates over marriage that revolved around these elements provide insights into the changing and diverse conceptualizations of womanhood during the colonial period. Several women and girls entered the ongoing contestations and seized a variety of opportunities to redefine their lives.

Registering Marriages

Proponents of marriage registration argued that it would stabilize the married state among Africans and possibly discourage illicit unions, which were said to be common among what colonial administrators perceived to be an ever-increasing class of detribalised Africans.[4] Initially, all marriages including 'pagan', Christian, and Mohammedan marriages were slated for registration. Tribal organizations would be used in the effort to effect the registration in the rural areas. Ultimately, only marriages contracted under customary practice were targeted. Initial projections about the nature of registration were modest. Certificates would be issued naming the parents, tribe, and sub tribe of the contracting parties, along with the brideprice agreed upon and what was actually paid.

Early on, there was apprehension that the proposal for the registration of 'pagan' marriages might draw opposition not only from various quarters within the colony, but also from the metropolitan centre. Although the government in England recognized the Mohammedan Marriage Ordinance, there was anxiety about England's response to the registration of non-Christian unions. Colonial administrators hoped to ensure that registration neither encouraged nor discouraged marriage according to native law and custom. There was apprehension that discouraging customary marriages might draw opposition from the majority of Africans, while encouraging them would offend a small but increasing number of Africans entering into marriage under the auspices of Christian churches.

Initially, there was also fear that the registration of civil marriages might draw opposition from missionary societies, which were themselves busily espousing and ultimately demanding the adoption of church marriage ceremonies among their followers. Missionaries saw Christian marriages as essential to ushering Africans across the boundaries separating indigenous beliefs and practices from modern and Western values and ways of life. As we shall see, the missionaries ultimately settled for civil marriages for those of their followers who did not wish to contract their marriages under the Christian Marriage Ordinance. They viewed any arrangement that demanded monogamy as better than customary marriage.

For administrators, the challenge was how to promote two diametrically opposed objectives: to give African women a voice while upholding the authority of indigenous patriarchs. Officials aimed to redefine local institutions and imprint imperial notions of social correctness and legality. Yet as we already have seen, thanks to the mobility afforded by the colonial situation, the marriage institution was already changing. Women were making their own marital choices. The changes suggested and implemented by the colonial state were not a panacea for women's problems. In many ways, the changes illuminated both official patriarchy and imperial gender designs.

To achieve the contradictory ends of Europeanizing Kenyan marriages and preserving indigenous institutions, it was important not only that all senior administrative officers agree, but also that they popularize their recommendations regarding the registration of marriage to the various native authorities.[5] The feasibility of this project was doubtful, however. The support of native authorities was necessary if the project was to succeed.[6] At the same time, money for the administration of the project was difficult to come by in a colony whose finances were weak. From the very beginning officials also questioned the ability of native authorities to codify and monitor all aspects of the marriage institution, beginning with registration and the issuing of registration certificates, even in the remotest places.[7]

For their part, the Local Native Councils had a variety of worries about the registration proposal – not worries about their ability to administer it, but about the imposition of colonial administrative control over a central indigenous institution. Some were concerned to find out whether the registration would affect Christian marriages only, or all types of marriages. In some sections of the African community, the registration effort was blamed on the missionaries, who were accused of trying to 'Europeanize marriage practices', a factor which 'perturbed them [Africans] to the extent that they rejected mission education'.[8] Members of the Fort Hall LNC reasoned that those who had opted for marriage under the church already had made a major departure from custom, and it would not be too much more of a departure if those marriages were codified by the state. When the president of the Fort Hall LNC informed its members that the proposed registration would involve only marriages contracted under native law and custom, there was great dismay on various levels.[9] As Simon, a council member, explained: 'We are afraid because when a marriage is performed by the D.C., if the bride subsequently runs away there is all the trouble of going to Nairobi and the expenses of judges and lawyers fees in getting a divorce and it sometimes takes years to get free.'[10]

Simon's observation was an understatement of the official agenda for redesigning the African family. As a result of registration, all matters pertaining to arbitration in a marriage would be taken away from the neighbourhood Elders' Councils and kinsmen. As Simon and those like him saw it, a distant, expensive, and procrastinating official outfit would usurp their role. The onus was on individual parties to desire to 'convert that [customary] marriage by … contract[ing] a civil marriage before a Superintendent Registrar or a Registrar in the presence of 2 or more witnesses in his office with open doors between 8.30 and 4 o'clock'.[11] This government intrusion, control, and surveillance was looked upon with disapproval and resentment by a large section of the male population in the rural areas.

Given such reservations on the part of LNC members, the implementation of the registration process was uneven, at best. However, despite its reservations, the Fort Hall LNC agreed that the registration of native marriages would become compulsory throughout Fort Hall by June 1,1927. Failure to comply with the rule would render one liable to punishment. In this, as in other decisions, however, the LNC did not have either the political leverage or the power to enforce such an all-encompassing resolution.[12] The council nevertheless was relentless in its efforts to transform all customary marriages into civil institutions.

To this end, by the middle of 1936, the LNC passed a unanimous decision stipulating that 'every marriage under native law and custom shall be registered within three months of the conclusion of the ceremony in one of the registers provided for the purpose at the Native Tribunal Centre at Kiharu, Kangema, Kigumo and Kandara.'[13] Registration certificates would be supplied free of charge, one to the husband and the other to the bride's father or guardian. In other areas where the registration of marriage was discussed, the charges were reversed so that registration was to be free but copies of the certificate would be obtained for a fee.

The acquisition of marriage certificates by both parties anticipated a potentially litigious situation. It would be expedient for each party to have a copy of that most important document. Even those marriages that preceded the introduction of the registration resolution were to be registered subject to the verification of the bona fide nature of the marriage. The District Officer would do this investigative work. The annulment of any such registered marriages would call for the appearance of the couple and their original witnesses before the administrative office where the annulment would be entered in the marriage register.

Even in Fort Hall, however, reservations remained about certain aspects of registration. Thus, at the same seating where the LNC passed the marriage registration deadline, it was also resolved that the registration of births was unlucky and contrary to custom. The registration of death would be postponed as the council waited to see 'how the registration of marriages work[ed]'.[14] The Kiambu District LNC was even more cautious. Here, the registration of marriages would be voluntary and could take place only if 'both parties to the marriage [were] present together with the father or guardian of the woman'.[15] In North Kavirondo, a few chiefs had started marriage registries in their areas by 1926. In 1927, however, like the Kiambu LNC, the Central Kavirondo LNC passed a resolution recommending that marriage registration be voluntary.[16] Clearly, the councils did not support or implement marriage registration.

Indeed, for all the energy expended and resolutions passed, by March 1939, 'not one soul had appeared to register a birth, a marriage or a land transaction' in Fort Hall District.[17] The PC there indicated that the situation was equally bad in Kiambu, where only eight registrations had been made. The community was generally 'apathetic' about registration, he said. In some instances, there seemed to be total ignorance about the process. A case in point involved an individual's attempt to register a birth in Fort Hall in which Livingstone, the LNC clerk entrusted with the task, said he knew nothing about certificates or registers. Councillors expressed the hope that if the registration books were left with the *Kiama* [Elders' Council] clerks, people would register. The government's failure to recognize local customary power structures thus seemed to undermine anticipated reforms.

In some cases, districts seemed to be emulating each other in their resistance to transforming the marriage institution. For example, in December 1945, the Meru LNC was informed that the registration of 'pagan' marriages in Kiambu and Fort Hall had virtually failed. With this information, the Council considered it unnecessary to introduce a marriage registration resolution in Meru district.[18] As we shall see, the shifts that the registration process anticipated were not easy to bring about.

Monogamy

Possibly the most radical aspect of the proposed registration of marriages was the provision for the conversion of a polygamous marriage to a monogamous one via 'its registration as such'. A major concern among colonial renovators of African marriages was the perceived need to popularize monogamy, which they 'regarded as a higher state than polygamy'. For that reason, it was considered necessary for the government not just to provide legislation that would allow for the civil registration of marriages contracted under native law and custom, but also to convert them into monogamous unions.[19] This did not imply that all such marriages were already polygamous. Some were, and some were not.

However, monogamous marriages contracted under customary law were potentially polygamous. Therefore one goal of the civil registration was to eliminate that possibility.

The performance of such conversions would take place before a registrar in charge of the registration of civil marriages. It would take place at the request of the parties who, although already married under the native law and custom, wished to have a monogamous union. This obviously meant that some of the men would have to divest themselves of all but one of their wives. The proposal did not address the question of the inherent social dislocation of women, children, and kinship marriage alliances that such divestment would entail. It was one thing to expect the man to continue to provide for the deserted women and children. It was quite another to construct and normalize such a process almost overnight.

The civil registration of monogamous marriages had different ramifications for different people. Women who were returned to their parents could not be termed divorced under the customary law. However, in the case of a customary divorce, the man could keep the children and forfeit his dowry. One can therefore speculate that most men entering into statutory marriages also would keep their children, so that overnight a woman might lose her position as mother, wife, and daughter-in-law. We can also assume that in the 1920s, mostly young and possibly middle-aged couples might be persuaded to rework their marital situation in this drastic fashion. There might consequently be young children and teenagers who would be separated from their mothers. At the same time, the chosen woman would be faced with managing a large, ready-made family without the support network of co-wives. There were also problems posed for Christian women who lived in polygamous household and as a result did not enjoy full membership in churches. Should they decide to leave their marriages, they would be seen to conform to church teaching while forcing their kin to return dowry to the deserted husband. [20]

Aware that they were considered partisan in their teachings against polygamy, the missionaries were determined to support the promotion of merely civil marriages as a means to attain their goal of monogamy among their followers. In their enthusiasm to rework the lives of professed converts, missionaries focused on nuclear families, claiming that the major threats against them were the clans and polygamy. If these were eliminated, they claimed, women might be emancipated.[21] The Church Missionary Society (CMS) prevailed upon those of its adherents who were not yet Christians to marry according to the Civil Marriage Law of the colony. However, the DC for Embu found this middle ground problematic. In essence, mission followers were caught between two systems, Christian and indigenous, and forced toward a third alternative, Europeanized civil marriage – viewed as less than satisfactory by both those systems.

In one such situation in 1938, the DC refused to oblige a marriage request and instead sent the man back with a letter to the CMS Mission at Embu explaining the intricacies of the civil registration of marriage. The DC stated:

> Such a marriage is merely a civil contract without any religious background. It is a marriage according to European custom and quite foreign to native ideas. I feel that it is extremely difficult if not impossible for me to explain to the man and much more to the young girl the implication of such a marriage and the difficulties involved should they desire to dissolve it. In my view, native Christians should be married in church or by Native Law and Custom, and should not resort to the arid civil form of marriage, which is entirely alien to them.[22]

In addition to this clash of cultural values, the transition from cultural and ethnic constructions of marriage to civil and statutory formats created a situation that might result in very protracted litigation, as well – precisely what the programme for the registration of marriages was intended to avoid.

The customary moral economy, cultural values, and laws and practices also retained their own attractions, and this was particularly the case with respect to polygamy. At the Church of Scotland Mission in Meru, 1943 was said to be a particularly difficult year because of what was euphemistically labeled 'sad backslidings' – references to a return to polygamy. For example, a leading evangelist and one of the oldest teachers at the Chogoria Mission had taken a second wife. Both were said to be 'very unhappy', and the head of the mission, Dr. Irvine, sarcastically observed that missionaries thanked God for the unhappiness of the two, since 'It was only when the prodigal tasted the husks that he arose and went to his father'.[23] To explain the situation, Dr. Irvine stated that 'to the African the Christian code of purity before marriage and of faithfulness to one wife is particularly difficult.'[24] That was the universal moral condemnation dealt on whole communities by many missions

Dr. Irvine also detected a socio-cultural rationale whose ramifications were largely economic. 'Polygamy does not arise from falling in love as we know it. Polygamy means bigger harvests, bigger villages, more children, more prosperity and importance in community. These things are dearer to the African heart than what we should call comforts.'[25] Polygamy facilitated increased production, the accumulation of wealth and therefore boosted the social status of men. This portrait did not augur well for African women who embraced Christianity, and with it, monogamy. Like all missionaries, Dr Irvine did not investigate the possible predicament of second wives should their husbands return to mission ways.

That polygamous men were able to contract customary marriages, going through all the necessary rituals, after their 'Christianization' is an indication of the scepticism with which non-Christians held church marriages.[26] The legal provisions and moral demands of church weddings did not seem to create any moral dilemma in the realm of customary marriages. The juxtaposition of customary and Christian marriages within a single household illustrates the fluidity of the marriage institution. For a colonial state that was hoping to streamline, delineate, rationalize, and 'civilize' the institution of marriage, this was a major setback.

In response to the return to polygamy, by 1943, the Meru Methodist Mission had abandoned its support for the registration of marriages by the colonial administration and 'substitute[d] a purely religious ceremony at which both parties took mutual vows of monogamy, this ceremony supplementing the civil marriage which had already taken place according to Meru Custom and Law'. [27] However, even under such a 'mixed' marriage, if the man broke his vow of monogamy by taking a second wife, the members of the LNC stated that the first wife had 'the enforceable right to obtain a divorce according to Meru Law and Custom'.[28] For the Methodist Mission and the LNC, the construction and dissolution of this category of marriages represented major shifts in the conceptualization of both marriage and divorce. Customary Law was employed to allow for a divorce where a clansman who also subscribed to the Methodist doctrine of monogamy had become a polygamist, thus in effect entrusting the enforcement of monogamy to customary law.[29]

Registration and Women's Consent

Initially, to implement the registration programme, the Attorney General's chambers drafted a very simple and skeletal schedule titled 'Form A', in which the notice would be given by the male spouse. The form was addressed to the Registrar of Native Marriages in the respective District and read thus:

> Notice of conversion of marriage by native law into legally binding marriage:
> To the Registrar of Native Marriages for the – District of Kenya.
>
> I hereby give notice that I, the undersigned, and the other party hereby named, being married to each other by native law or custom intend within three months from the date hereof to convert that marriage into a marriage by which we shall be legally bound to each other as man and wife so long as both shall live.[30]

Other information to be filled on the form included the name of the man, his occupation or rank, age, and dwelling place. Consent, if any, and by whom given was to be documented. Lastly, the applicant, his prospective bride, and a witness were to sign and date the form.

In a later and more refined format, the government required that a girl's consent be obtained at the time of giving notice of marriage, before the marriage ceremony, and that such consent be reflected in the notice. This elaboration provided for the bride's signature or thumbprint, and the indication of her age.[31] Both the bride and the bridegroom were also supposed to get the consent of their parents or guardians. This would be indicated by the latter's signature or thumbprint. 'In the event of the consent of guardians being refused, the applicants were requested to state whether the Provincial Commissioner consents.'[32] The Provincial Commissioner also had to sign the form. The notice had to be displayed where the bride resided.

The need to ascertain the girl's consent was indicative of the official belief that forced marriages were rampant. It is true that a long litany of complaints from missionaries, colonial administrators, and a small, but increasing number of concerned Africans, both men and women, had claimed that although forced marriages were not the rule, they were widespread enough to warrant official attention. In these complaints, there appeared to be a blurring and blending of two manifestations of how marriages could be seen as 'forced'. These took two forms: a ritualized enactment of a new wife's reluctance to leave her kin, which was part of amicable marriage customs and which was perfectly legitimate, or the use of actual physical force against an unwilling bride. In explaining the possible source of misunderstanding, Stanley, a member of the Nyeri LNC, observed: 'It was impossible to decide what a girl really wanted because according to Kikuyu custom it was improper for a girl to appear to go willingly to her husband. She must pretend to be reluctant otherwise her conduct would be considered shameless. She must be carried off.'[33] The *meko*, where the bridegroom's relatives among the Luo seized the bride and dragged the girl to her marital home, was a central part of these marriage customs, and was not forced marriage at all.[34]

In his anthropolitical treatise on the Kikuyu, Jomo Kenyatta insisted on the distinction:

> A Gikuyu wedding is a thing which baffles many outsiders and terrifies many Europeans who may have an opportunity of witnessing the events. This wedding drama misleads foreign onlookers, who do not understand the Gikuyu custom, into thinking that the girls are being forced to marry, and even that they are treated as chattels … the [wedding] day is fixed and kept secret from the girl – thus adding a dramatic touch to the proceedings. On the wedding day the boy's female relatives set out to watch the girl's movements.... On finding her they return with her, carrying her shoulder-high. This is a moment of real theatrical acting. The girl struggles and refuses to go with them, protesting loudly and even seeming to shed tears, while the women giggle joyously and cheer her with songs and dances.[35]

Kenyatta emphasized the fact that a prospective couple had ample opportunity to meet and decide whether they wished to get married.[36]

The seizure did not come as a complete surprise to the girl and could be anticipated after the payment of most of the dowry. Although the father of the girl might give the go-ahead, among the Luo, according to Simeon H. Ominde, it was expected that the girl's brothers would 'put up a fight not in order to detain the girl, but to test the courage of the people taking her. This is also done to test the value attached to her as a future wife in her husband's community.'[37] Ominde does acknowledge the bride's genuine reluctance to leave her natal home on the day of *meko*. 'This unwillingness, accompanied by violent outbursts of emotion, is partly caused by the break with her family and familiar environment that marriage involves. Sometimes the emotional outbursts reach undue proportion, rendering the woman a thorough misfit in her new home. Screaming is common even among those who are secretly pleased with the situation.'[38] *Meko* obviously elicited discrepant reactions:

> [T]hough some of the women may be sincerely upset, a large number of them look back on the incident with great satisfaction and confess that they screamed because it was customary to do so. This is made even clearer by their reactions when they are later present at similar incidents. Amidst great laughter they say comforting words to the girl being dragged, assuring her that she will meet with excellent treatment.[39]

For some girls, the application of actual physical force was not mere theatrics, and the girls' screams were not made in jest. At times, girls opposed to their arranged marriages put up one last resistance before being transferred to their marital homes. As Milcah Wanjiru observed, 'Since she did not wish to get married, there would be struggles and screaming before the woman was carried into marriage.... For those married off by force, there was no peace since it was not something they wanted.'[40] These wives sometimes ran away, went to mission stations, fled into other marriages within and beyond their areas of origin, or moved to urban centres. There were also some communities that had strategies that gave girls and newly married women the opportunity to change their mind.[41]

With the establishment of colonial rule, resentment of all aspects of the practice became manifest. The woman's signature on the marriage registration form was added as proof that she was a willing partner to an imminent marriage. It gave her the opportunity to make a decision, and helped her plan her own wedding. Earlier official responses to the question of women's consent in marriage were conflicted. For example, while a high court judge ruled that any customary marriage without the bride's consent was invalid, the practice of family choice of spouses was widespread and rendered the judges decision derisory.[42] For example, Peristiany states that among the Kipsigis, family choice of spouse would override all prior liaisons formed by either party. However, if a young man was determined to marry a particular girl, he could tie the *segutiet* grass bracelet on the girl as soon as she emerged from initiation, thus preempting the possibility of her marriage to anyone else. This action was immediately followed by elopement and subsequent attempts by the man to make amends. A ritual apology and commencement of accumulation of dowry livestock were considered to be steps in the right direction. Since the *segutiet* was a once in a lifetime ritual for a woman, it served as a very strong weapon to counter parental interference in the choice of marital partners.

The requirement that a prospective bride should sign a consent form was double-edged. It signified the inscription of the woman's voice and view on an impeding marriage ceremony, but was an assent to colonial intrusion into an intimate and private aspect of her life. This necessarily made her an accessory to the official usurpation of family and kinsmen's authority in matters pertaining to marriage – a matter that troubled some members of the LNCs a great deal. This emanated from the 1939 Native Marriage and Divorce Bill, according to which a marriage could be contracted between the spouses, officiated by a registrar and witnessed by two people. That the Registrar and a minimum of two witnesses in a government building constituted a public arena belittled the communal and hence public production of customary marriages. The life cycle of customary marriage, including all the rituals and persons involved in betrothal, payment of dowry, and the sustaining of the marriage, were replaced by individuals who were accountable not to their kinsmen, but to the colonial government. Presiding over subsequent aspects of civil marriage would be government officials and functionaries who could not be witnesses to the organic aspects of the marriage in indigenous cultures.

Theoretically, the provision requiring the consent of the woman could be employed to challenge an arranged or forced and unwanted marriage. The effectiveness of the legislation would to some extent depend on the authorities' ability to enforce it. And as it stood, the registration format did not include punitive provisions for the breach of any of its components. The most it could do was to provide a template of cold facts that might be useful at a later time in case of disputes. There was no guarantee that a family might not prevail on a prospective bride to sign the notice of marriage against her will.

At a time when women were applying other more arduous methods to challenge unwanted marriages, it might be hoped that the registration process would provide one official and legitimate tool in their favour. In areas where the marriages had to be registered within the first three months, the provision might ensure that a woman did not have long to wait to make her disposition known. If she had been forced into a marriage under customary practices, she could inform the authorities by refusing to sign the notice of marriage, but that would depend on the couple's agreement to undertake the registration. This was an unlikely event in the case of an arranged marriage unless more coercion was used in forcing the woman to sign the consent clause in the registration form. The bridegroom also might be opposed to registration. The introduction of legislation that enabled women to report coercion *before* marriage took place might have been a more useful tool. At any rate, the spaces that the registration of marriages seemed to open up for women to assert their agency sometimes proved illusory.

Although the consent clause gave women some leverage in marriage, it also created certain limitations. As we have seen, regardless of her age, a woman still needed the consent of her parents or guardian before she could get married. In those cases where the parents were adamant about an impending marriage, a colonial administrator or a missionary would have to take the position of guardian and give his consent, allowing the marriage to take place, thus again displacing traditional kinship roles with the authority of the colonial administration. Although the proxy guardian would be salvaging a situation in which a girl's choice of a spouse did not meet the approval of her parents, unlike the groom, she still needed the authority of a third party before she could contract a marriage. In this respect, she was treated as a minor. While rural elders might have felt marginalized as colonial authorities patted themselves on their backs, for the woman, it is doubtful that her signature or thumbprint on the registration form transformed her position within the marital and kinship power structure. The reifying act of signing names, or imprinting of thumbs, invariably completed the colonial process of erasing the moral legitimacy of customary marriages without necessarily doing anything to affect all the other existing beliefs and practices surrounding the institution of marriage.

In some cases, confusion arose from the fact that the registration of these 'new' marriages took place at different institutions. Ultimately, the process represented different layers of meaning regarding legal significance and social relevance. While mission marriages represented a specific personal transition in a couple's life, the civil ceremony acquired an ambiguous character in the public mind. By 1939, this discrepancy was common knowledge, prompting the president of the Fort Hall LNC to assert that marriage registers held at missions had legal validity, while birth, baptismal, and bride-price registrations did not. He suggested that 'births and bride-price transactions be registered at the tribunals as well as at the missions.' [43] The process might give a wife legal recourse should the marriage become sour.

If a couple was already married under customary law and decided to contract the civil marriage, a contradiction regarding the official perception of native marriages and the whole customary code emerged. This contradiction was evident in the two most important clauses which were read out to the intending couple, at once recognizing their prior state of marriage under customary law and in the same breath denying the legal standing of the same. Either directly, or through an interpreter, the superintendent would say: 'Do I understand that you, A. B. and you C. D. have heretofore been married to each other by native law or custom, and that you come here for the purpose of binding yourselves legally to each other as man and wife so long as both of you shall live?' If the parties answered in the affirmative, the superintendent would drop a bombshell that nullified the only union the bride and the bridegroom had known. He informed them that by giving notice of the conversion of their marriage into a 'legally binding marriage', they were not just calling into question the legality and the status of their customary marriage, but, more broadly, surrendering the legitimacy of customary law itself.

> Whereas you, A.B, and you C.D, profess that you have heretofore been married to each other by native law or custom and whereas that marriage does not bind you by law to each other as man and wife so long as both of you shall live and whereas you desire to bind yourselves legally each to the other as man and wife so long as both of you shall live: know ye that by the public taking of each other as man and wife so long as both of you shall live, in my presence and in the presence of the persons now here, and by the subsequent attestation thereof by signing your names to that effect, you become legally bound to each other as husband and wife so long as both of you shall live although no other rite of a civil or religious nature shall take place and that hereafter your marriage cannot be dissolved during your lifetime, except by a valid judgement of divorce.[44]

He also informed the couple of the provisions of the ordinance which made it illegal for either party to contract another marriage while their marriage to each other was undissolved. In such an eventuality, the offending party would be guilty of bigamy, a punishable crime.[45]

This provision, and with it the effort to transform marriages solely into the sort sanctioned and regulated by the colonial authorities, did not have the intended effect. The legitimacy of customary law and the practices it sanctioned was not so easily abrogated. As early as 1928, Africans were getting convicted of 'contracting marriage by Native Law when already married under the 1902 Ordinance'. In Nyanza, three 'natives' had been so convicted under section 51 chapter 167 of the laws of Kenya. While the three were accused of bigamy in following the customary marriage process including the payment of bridewealth, they must have been under the impression that they were entering into legitimate polygamous unions. Assuming that it was 'first' wives who reported the 'misconduct' to the mission, women were thus active in the remaking of their marriages. The Nyanza DC under whose jurisdiction the three lived was unsure about what the legal position of the three offenders would be after their release. He enquired of the PC, 'If they return to live with their wives, can they be prosecuted again or is the matter a *res judicula*?'[46] Clearly the DC anticipated more such cases.

The registration of marriages did not so much displace customary marriage as occur alongside it. Thus, Archdeacon Owen of the Church Missionary Society 'inundated the administration with cases of bigamy, i.e. baptised and married converts who had taken a second wife by native law and custom'. The administration agreed on a uniform fine of 40 shillings for this infraction. Offenders were said to break the law with impunity. Having paid the fine, there was nothing to prevent the offender from continuing to live with his newly wed wife in open wedlock. After a short period of time, 40 shillings became popularly known as simply the price of a licence to take a second wife, and many actually presented the sum for such a license.[47]

Customary marriage practices endured even among the so-called 'progressive', mission-educated proto-elite. There, the need to establish social alliances with like families at times had the taste of earlier arranged marriages. There was a trend among the emergent African lower middle class to forge alliances, which at times were based on 'orchestrated' unions. Muthoni Likimani (nee Gachanja), for example, the daughter of one of the earliest ordained pastors, a man who was a very progressive farmer and businessman in Central Province, was considered marriageable at the end of her intermediate school education in the late 1940s. The man her parents had chosen, or rather, the man the whole society had chosen, was a most eligible bachelor, one among the first crop of graduates from Makerere, the only University College in Eastern and Central Africa in the 1940s and 1950s. Equally important was the fact that the suitor was the son of a local elder who was himself a member of the emergent local leaders, a member of the Fort Hall Native Council 'and a very progressive farmer.... He was also a preacher and a teacher, [and another of] his sons eventually became a chief, chief Mathara.'[48] The two families were mission protégés and were close. The suitor's father, James Munano, in 1933 had expressed his socially progressive objection to the betrothal of immature girls.[49] What was at stake, however, was a marriage to be desired and arranged, if possible.

It is a sign of the changes wrought by colonial opposition to 'forced marriages', that despite the payment of dowry and the publishing of banns, Muthoni refused to marry the chosen man, a defiance previously unimaginable. She would not succumb to parental and societal pressure to get married, and she set her sights instead on higher education. She recounted her extremely unconventional behaviour:

> I will tell you something. I was supposed to get married after completing intermediate school. Dowry was paid for me, but I refused to get married. If you enquire at Kahuhia [Muthoni's hometown], even if I walked naked in Kahuhia, nobody would reprimand me ... [they would ask] is she not the one whose wedding banns were announced and she refused to get married? I refused [to get married] completely.[50]

Neither Muthoni's family nor her suitor's was an average rural household. Among the majority of peasant families, however, pressure for girls to marry men handpicked by their families remained a common occurrence. The same applied to a smaller degree to men. As we have seen, the prime motive for these alliances was represented as efforts to *kumatia ndugu*, strengthen friendship between two families, especially between the patriarchs; economic considerations loomed large in choosing prospective sons and daughters-in law.[51]

Nevertheless, the rejection of family-chosen spouses and insistence on making one's choice was becoming more widespread,[52] and some who succumbed to family pressure did not do so peacefully. Beth Njambi portrayed a scenario in which a girl who was determined to avoid an arranged marriage would continue active resistance even after the marriage process was at an advanced stage:

> You were unhappy and you did not wish to get married to that man. After the dowry livestock had spent the night at your home, early next morning you would get a stick and drive the livestock away. You knew your parents' livestock and you could tell that this particular herd had been brought.... You would drive them to the man's homestead. The young man would realize that he had been rejected.[53]

However, as Beth observed it was difficult for either a woman or a man to wriggle out of an arranged marriage if the families were friends. In such a situation, a girl found it difficult to defy her father. Nevertheless, precisely because customary and legislated marriage practices now were operating in parallel, some young couples could avoid the process of subsuming individual preferences to family or community interests.

In some cases families were caught unawares as their young daughters exposed the ridiculous nature of some of the marriage arrangements. A woman who as a single girl was opposed to her family's wishes that she should marry a rather elderly gentleman gave a most poignant example. Not wishing to disobey her parents blatantly, she put her elderly suitor to what she considered to be the ultimate test. Giving him a sewing needle and a thread, she challenged him to thread the needle. Try as he would, the elder was unable to do so. The girl did not need to labour the point. Fortunately, her family gave up their attempt to marry her off to the elder.[54]

A dissenting daughter's brothers could make her predicament more difficult, however. In other words, as well as being potential beneficiaries of bridewealth, brothers also wielded patriarchal authority and could intervene, sometimes too much:

> There would be a lot of trouble. Her brothers would beat her and seek to know why she was behaving so. They would ask her what her intended destination was [i.e. where she wanted to get married].... [They would tell her] 'if you do not want the dowry from so and so, go on and bring us the dowry that you prefer. But if we don't like him, we shall not eat [accept] the dowry.'[55]

It was often difficult to receive support from even a mother or female sibling. While coaxing her stepsister to persuade their father not to marry her off to an undesirable older man, Hannah Wariara Kahanya would not confront her father on her sister's behalf. 'My sister would ask me to plead on her behalf. I told her I would not do it since if and when my father decided to marry me off, I would have to face the music alone.'[56] Hannah's sister did not dare seek her mother's support in her predicament, either, since the girl's father would beat her mother and send her away. Eventually, Hannah herself rejected a suitor chosen for her.

In this world of opportunities created by parallel practices, nostalgic representations of unfragmented but unrealistic male-dominated pasts abound. In Hamisi Makapia Wanga's portrayal of the past, 'Women did not choose [their spouses]. It is today that women choose their husbands but today they never receive bridewealth in return. We demanded to have a hand in the choice because we determined bridewealth.'[57]

Ironically, despite their opposition to forced marriages, missions themselves were not immune from accusations of forcing both young men and women to marry spouses not of their own choice. From the indigenous point of view, they could be seen as practising what they preached against. S. N. Bogonko captures this violation of socio-cultural sensibilities:

> Missionaries interfered with the individual choice of a life partner ... and affianced unwilling partners.... Mission school readers and catechumens were under pressure that they were to marry other readers or catechumens, and the so-called pagans were to be left to other pagans. Some who went to Nyabururu and Nyanchwa [mission stations] were forced to get life partners from their counterparts of the opposite sex. Hence, and as would be expected, the question of personal choice did not arise. The consequence was forced marriages under Christiandom: marriages, which also quickly broke asunder for lack of bases.[58]

The mission effort to restructure marriage and create Christian communities resulted in exchanges of cultural practices regarding marriage in both directions. For example, Eliud Amatike noted that although 'there was a great deal of Christianization of courtship', and although 'the traditional wedding ceremony called *andere* actually died and Christian weddings took root…some local customs were assimilated in Christian weddings. The girls could collect their friends to escort them on the day of the wedding. They accompanied her carrying gourds. They would stop at the gate where they demanded to be paid something before proceeding into the homestead.'[59] In the end, the parallel tracks of colonial and customary marriage influenced each other reciprocally in unanticipated ways.

Marriage, Sex and Immature Girls

The question of the marriage of immature girls played a part in concerns about women's consent and the age of majority. A meeting of Native Catholic Union on 30 September 1926 raised the issues, especially the question of the marriage of immature girls to old men.[60] Most likely the old men had many wives already. In Nyanza, the District Commissioners were urged to raise with the LNCs the prohibition of a father from marrying off his daughter 'until she has reached the age of 14 or 15'.[61] A large cloud hung over the definition of 'maturity'. Various groups, both indigenous and official, supported a purely biological measure of preparedness for marriage: the onset of menstruation. In this view, maturity was not a matter of chronological age, which might reflect the level of a girl's social development and hence her readiness for marriage and procreation. Rather, it was seen as a matter of her biological readiness for procreation. There were, however, dissenting voices. For this group, the onset of menstruation was a purely physiological function that did not necessarily entail social preparedness for marriage. From either point of view, the issue provides glimpses of the mental geographies of various groups of people regarding the sexuality of African girls and women.

The correlation of maturity and therefore of marriageability with a girl's physical ability to conceive and procreate was also a widespread belief among colonial administrators. Dr. Ross was a government employee who was also a vociferous critic of the government. He was quick to note that it would be difficult to place an age limit with regard to girls' marriage, stating that many native girls were mature at the age of twelve or even less, referring to the onset of the menstrual cycle. Hence, if a girl's suitability for marriage was determined 'by taking into account her physical development as well as her approximate age', then there was every likelihood that a girl's childhood could be brought to an abrupt end if she were physically larger than her age-mates and her periods had set in earlier than normal.[62]

Although certain LNCs were in the forefront of advocating drastic reforms to curb the practice, they held no consensus about the age at which girls were considered mature enough for marriage. The Fort Hall LNC considered the practice of marrying immature girls an old one, but 'only resorted to in times of dire need'.[63] In Nyanza in 1927, one LNC proposed the alteration of the Indian Penal Code section 375 so that in the case of Africans, 'sexual intercourse by a man with his wife [became] rape if the wife [was] under 15 years of age.'[64] The PC was aware of the difficulties involved in the introduction of such a law for one district alone and for Africans only. It seemed more expedient to pursue the introduction of a law that would apply to all races – Africans, Europeans, and Indians – in the whole country. This points to the initial assumption of sexual promiscuity among Africans that motivated the proposal in the first place.

As we have seen in other aspects of the institution, during the colonial period, marriage was interrogated to the limit. In the case of the marriage of immature girls, the discourse called for verification of whether these marriages were followed by actual consummation on a basis widespread enough to warrant special legislation. The Nyanza PC set his field 'boys', the DCs, on a fact-finding mission. Personally, the PC said, he had no problems with child marriage, since he believed this had a legal basis in English law. As he said, 'I would point out that as far as I have been able to discover even under English law a man may marry a child of 12 and it is certainly allowed among the Indians.'[65] If the bride was officially characterized as a child and yet the union was considered legitimate, it is improbable that such child marriages were legally taking place in Britain. The English law referred to, or rather the practice, must have been applicable in colonies only. But child marriages in India had raised a lot of opposition, especially among missionary societies.

The PC's enquiries regarding the marriage of immature girls elicited an avalanche of different responses. It is in these that the most striking assumptions about the sexual activity of African girls and women are to be found. The DC for Kakamega, for example, framed the legal age of marriage on the basis of claims of widespread sexual activity among children. He stated, 'I do not consider that any harm is done, however young a girl may be provided she has attained maturity, whether the age be 12 or 15. The trouble in my opinion is not the marriage of girls about the age of 15 but the illicit intercourse which goes on about this age with the knowledge of the parent'.[66] This administrator was not alone in considering juvenile sexuality more harmful than child marriage. In Nandi country, the DC painted a disturbing picture: 'The trouble is the consummation without marriage which takes place, although not invariably, from 10 years upwards, it being almost impossible to get evidence to support a conviction for rape.'[67]

Maturity and Marriage

With such assumptions about the sexual activity of African women at work in structuring colonial attitudes toward the marriage of immature girls, and with a variety of assumptions and customs prevalent among indigenous

Africans, it is difficult to assess the actual extent of the practice. There are indications that physiological maturity did not result in immediate marriage. Aggrey Ham Wanzetse, a Wanga, observed that 'once they [girls] reached the age of twelve, they were engaged to a man. By the age of eighteen they were married off.'[68] Thirteen or fourteen was held to be the average age at which girls married in Nandi. The local DC did not find this objectionable in the light of 'the early maturity age of native girls'. In general, however, marriage in the early teens seems to have been more common in Nyanza Province than in any other part of the colony. It was also from Nyanza that the loudest objections to the practice emanated. It is not clear whether all the incidents referred to were forced marriages.

In his response to the PC's fact-finding mission, one of the staunchest critics of the practice, the missionary E. A. Beavon, stated that the Kisii 'allowed' girls over twelve years to marry. As far as some sections of the community were concerned, it would be impossible to forbid men who had married girls under fifteen from having intercourse with their wives.[69] For this group, the introduction of resolutions would be 'useless'. Nevertheless, Beavon observed that the practice of teenage marriage consummation was widespread enough in Kisii country to warrant special legislation to stop it. In contrast, he believed the practice was not so widespread among the Luo, Abagusii's northern neighbours, among whom polygamy was on the decrease. He attributed the drastic fall in teenage marriage consummation in Luo country to 'the dissemination of Christian principles'. For Beavon, teenage marriage was an evil not easy to eradicate, but needing to be tempered from every direction. Where Christian men were to be found in the LNC and the chief's *barazas*, outschools, and mission stations, he believed, the practice would eventually disappear.[70]

Beavon obviously equated the spread of Christianity with the eradication of practices considered inimical to the faith. By 1927, the influence of mission work, even in its most successful areas must have been limited to a small proportion of the population. In outlying areas where mission influence was nonexistent, even in Luo territory, the marriage of immature girls was said to be extensive. In a more conciliatory spirit, H. W. Innis from the Church Missionary Society mission at Ogada suggested that rather than make the marriage of girls under fifteen an offence, energy should be expended on criminalizing the marriage of girls who had not reached the age of puberty. It did not matter if such a marriage was contracted under civil, native and customary, or Christian auspices. Such marriages of prepubescent girls, he believed, should be treated as rape.[71] O. C. Keller of the Nyang'ori Mission asserted that among the Tiriki, parents encouraged girls to 'cohabit with their male companions from the time that they [were] about ten years of age'. [72] The cohabitation ostensibly took place in community sleeping huts. For Keller and other concerned parties, such publicly sanctioned sex, which tied the girls down to particular men, was better than 'having new companions every few weeks'.[73] Tiriki parents were also said to 'force [girls] to live with husbands against their wishes and not only husbands, but also other male friends of the family'.[74]

What some missionaries, 'progressive' Africans, and colonial administrators characterized as premature sexualisation of the African girl, however, was but one facet of the lives of women. There were diverse ways in which girls were prepared for marriage. Menstruation was but one marker of a woman's eligibility; among the Kikuyu, for example, it was not permissible for a girl who had not begun menstruating to get married.[75] Milcah Wanjiru emphasized: There was something that indicated that she was ready to marry.... For a start, a Kikuyu would have his daughter circumcised. Then it would be known that she had matured once she started menstruating. This was a mature girl ... and her breasts would be examined and it would be confirmed that she was mature'.[76]

Menstruation was an obvious marker among the Luyia, too. Among the Wanga (one among many Luyia subgroups), 'Whenever a girl started getting her monthly periods, in Kiwanga they said *okhukula eshialo*, that one was ready for marriage.'[77] The Banyole, another subgroup of the Luyia of Western Kenya, used the menarche to determine a girl's physical maturity and hence her marriageability. Thus, 'when she began experiencing her monthly periods and her breasts had fully developed', a girl was considered to have graduated to an 'age' of maturity.[78] This seemed to have been a practice that was widespread among diverse ethnic groups. Writing in the early 1950s, Ominde noted, 'Although the betrothal of a [Luo] girl could take place as early as ten, the social attitude was, and still is that girls should not be handed over to their husbands before attaining maturity.'[79]

There were social, as well as biological aspects to the ways in which young women were ushered into marriage. They were also prepared for their new relationship and given support in it, both before and after their marriage. A new bride was not simply confronted immediately with all the social responsibilities associated with marriage. There is extensive ethnographic material that indicates that brides, especially young brides, were initially the wards of their mothers-in-law if the husband did not have other wives. In a polygamous home, the young bride initially lived with the eldest wife, referring to her as 'mother'.[80] While under her wings, the older woman would teach the bride the basics of becoming and being a wife.

There is evidence to prove that in some societies this training went on after the onset of menstruation. For example, among the Luo, in cases where a girl was handed over to her husband before 'maturity', 'the girl was obliged to live in the home of some older woman until the advent of menstruation. It is still believed that premature marriage results in great weakness of the girl.'[81]

Pawned Child Brides and Child Pledging

Sometimes girl children found themselves in marriages that did not afford them this kind of premarital training. They might be born into and grow within marital arrangements largely out of their control whereby part of the dowry had been paid during the girl's infancy, obviously without her knowledge. Additional dowry would be paid periodically as the girl grew, and at 'maturity', she might be forced to marry the payer. In 1936, members of the Nyeri LNC argued that forced marriages emanating from such arrangements were the exception to the rule in their area. Hence, the LNC argued, 'It was not considered according to custom to coerce a girl physically [to marry], if she entirely refused to marry the man, the dowry was returned by the girl's father, or if he could not repay it, by the man who eventually married her.'[82]

As we have seen, during times of famine, families might pledge or 'pawn' young girls to more fortunate families in return for food and other resources, including livestock. The girls, too, would receive sustenance even as they continued to grow in their 'adoptive' families. It was hoped that at some more fortunate time, the girls would be redeemed. In the meantime, among the Kisii, the head of the adoptive household had 'the privilege of cohabiting with these girls as if they were his own wives'.[83] In some cases, the head of the adoptive family might develop a liking for the girl, wishing to marry her. While the man might proceed to formalize his marital intentions, there is every probability that the girl-child might not be keen on such a union. Given her circumstances, however, it is unlikely that her objection would be taken seriously. In this case, the girl's consent would be lacking, and parent complicity was implicit.

In some cases, parents of pawned girls might fail in their efforts to redeem their daughters. This was observed among the Kipsigis. Here, *kabwatereret*, the betrothal of infant girls to grown men, happened at times of duress, especially famine. The betrothal ceremony would also be accompanied by the advance payment of bridewealth. 'Until the day of initiation the girl would live with her parents.' After initiation and 'coming out', marriage ceremonies would begin. However, 'if at this moment the parents have changed their mind, they can return the cattle given by the bridegroom to them and ask him to anoint the girl, so as to set her free. But he can refuse to do so and take his case to the elders.'[84] It is possible that in some cases, the parents of the girl would lose the litigation. The situation would be more tragic if the girl did not wish to get married to the man.

When making the original marriage arrangements for pledged or pawned brides, the families involved anticipated the consent of the grown girl. However, over the fifteen years or so before the girl was considered mature, a lot could happen to family fortunes making it difficult for the father to refund the dowry if the girl objected to the imminent marriage. This would increase the probability that the family would prevail on the girl to accept marriage to the long-term suitor. The pledging might be between cordial families for whom a projected marriage might be construed as a way to strengthen the friendship. In such cases, economic hardship on the part of the family of the girl might not be a factor in the establishment of the alliance. The child would be the bond and means to the redistributing of social capital between the two families.

As was the case with other aspects of the effort to legislate marriage, efforts to put an end to child pledging had uneven results. In certain sections of the country, terse legislation against child pledging was adopted. Thus, in 1929, the Nyeri LNC deliberated on the issue and decided that in initiating payment of dowry for a minor, a prospective suitor was guilty of a crime punishable by fine or imprisonment. The girl's father might also be liable for a fine.[85] The 1929 resolution was more definitive in its recognition of the eventuality that the girl for whom dowry had been paid might leave her husband and marry somebody else. The resolution provided that the abandoned man could not claim the dowry he had paid since this was a faulty move on his part in the first place.

> *Na ikiwa yule mke baadaye aolewe pengine ule mtu wa kwanza hawezi kudai mbuzi alizolipa kwa maana ni makosa yake.* [86]
>
> If that woman later marries [someone else] the first man cannot claim the goats he paid because it was his mistake

The South Nyeri LNC quickly confirmed the above resolution on the 13th and 14th of September 1929. It also adopted the resolution [Minute 60 of 1929] 'as the guiding principle in all the Tribunal cases throughout the Kikuyu province at the combined meeting of Kiambu, Fort Hall and South Nyeri LNC's held at Nyeri [on] 14 November 1929 and presided over by the Senior Commissioner'.[87] When the problem of forcible marriage of girls was again raised in Nyeri in 1937, the president of the LNC was desirous that the 1929 resolution should be re-examined with the aim to establish whether it was adequate. If found wanting, the President anticipated the passing of another resolution 'so as to help the Kikuyu girls to escape future forced marriages if any'.[88]

Conversely, however, the Murang'a LNC perceived no conflict in the betrothal of immature girls and in 1933 stated that the custom of child pledging was an old one and was resorted to only at times of dire need. Also, the councillors said, 'it was now permissible to ask for advances only after the girl [had] been circumcised and after she had been consulted.'[89] However, the council saw the need to restrict the custom. James Munano, who in a letter to the council had expressed concern over the payment of dowry for girls before they reached maturity, believed that the practice 'led to many unhappy marriages'.[90] In Meru in 1948, the LNC decided that chiefs and parents were responsible for guarding against the danger of early marriages and that long engagements 'as had always taken place formerly should be reintroduced'.[91] This, the council believed, would help alleviate the problem. A girl would be sufficiently mature to decide whether she wished to get married to her fiancé. Additionally, the long engagement would ensure that girls were at an appropriate age at the time of marriage.

The intricate web of events regarding any one aspect of marriage was endless. Any resolution or legislation perforce failed to address a whole range of other related, yet distinct problems. For example, Native Tribunals were faced with the task of having to prosecute young men accused of marrying girls who were 'engaged' to other men. While this was intended to address an entirely different issue, it nevertheless affected cases where children had been pledged or pawned, because a marriage alliance that started with an infant might be broken once the girl matured and chose to marry a different man. After an initial marriage to the paid-up man, the married woman might choose to abandon her husband for a man of her own choice. Rather than sue his prospective father-in-law, the suitor might identify the young man who married his betrothed as the culprit. This resulted in protracted rounds of acrimony, litigation, and seemingly endless deliberations by a host of authorities as they tried to decide what sanction to apply.[92] In the meantime, the use of the term 'engagement' by colonial officials in reference to girl-child betrothal had the unintended effect of bestowing respectability on the process.

Widowhood, Leviratic Marriage and Women's Agency

One of the principal issues which colonial authorities tried to legislate involved the status of married women after their husbands had died. Indigenous societies did not anticipate dealing with households that were not under male leadership.[93] The loss of a spouse resulted in more vividly striking changes for women than men. Except in cases of mental and extreme physical incapacity, adult men were never placed under the guardianship of others. A widow, however, became a ward of her marital family, a position of dependence that might rapidly escalate to dependence upon males much younger than herself, including her own grown male children. This kind of guardianship was a gender-based institution to which women were subjected both in their youth and their adult life. As a ward of the marital family, various factors, including the widow's rank within a polygamous marital situation and the hierarchy of possible inheritors, determined the fate of a widow. If her sons were minors, a woman was usually inherited by her deceased husband's brother, who in a leviratic marriage assumed the role of surrogate husband and thus 'automatically [became] her natural guardian'.

Colonial administrators and missionaries were opposed to both leviratic marriage and the use of coercion in effecting a widow's guardianship, considering the former to be forced marriages.[94] According to the East Africa Marriage Ordinance of 1902, Christian widows were considered to have attained the status of legal majority, and the Senior Commissioner for Kisumu observed in 1927 that such widows were free to marry whom they pleased. Under colonial law, they were considered to be of full age and could not be forced to marry anybody against their will, which would be 'repugnant to justice and morality and can be prevented'.[95] In this matter, the church and colonial administration were in agreement. And the Native Christian Marriage and Divorce Ordinance of 1931 provided that a woman:

> shall be deemed to have attained her majority on widowhood and shall not be bound to cohabit with the brother or any other relative of her deceased or any other person or to be at the disposal of such a brother or other relative or other person but she shall have the same right to support for herself and her children of such marriage from such brother or other relative as she would have had if she had not been married as aforesaid.[96]

In trying to legislate against leviratic marriage and the wardship of widows, neither the church nor the government, found it odd that a grown woman would remain a legal minor till her husband died. On this issue, official, church, and indigenous patriarchies were in agreement.

For individuals who believed in the wisdom of custom and who were faced with the responsibility of executing it, official or mission efforts to redefine the predicament of widowed women could create conflicted situations. Such people had to do what was expected of them, but what that entailed under the aegis of the colonial administration according to the customs under which they has been raised could be very different.

Early in 1946, for example, Mr. George Ogilo, a Kenyan Luo who was a Grade III Local Civil Service Clerk with the Provincial Administration in Tanganyika, applied for twenty-five days' leave to come to Kenya, stating:

> My late father was a Senior Chief and also a polygamist. I am his elder son; and according to our [Luo] customs his wives *must* be re-married on the first anniversary of his death which will be the 30th June 1946. Being the elder son I must be present otherwise they cannot be remarried till 30th June, 1947, which will put them in an awkward position particularly when taking into consideration the loss, which they have already sustained owing to my father's sudden death.[97]

Ogilo was definitely convinced that life would be difficult for the widows unless the remarriage ritual was performed soon. Their social status and functionality was in jeopardy.

Ogilo's 'mothers' do not seem to have been married under statutory marriage ordinances. None of the above provided for polygamous situations. If his father had at some stage undertaken or converted any of his marriages into a monogamous union, he had definitely reverted to polygamy, as some people did. As widows in a polygamous situation, the women's lives were bound to an intricate set of social conventions that could make daily life difficult, if broken. Even for widows ostensibly freed from the customary treatment of widows under the East African Marriage Ordinance 1902, the intervention of local male elders was vital for the acceptable functioning of a widow's household. As Mary Wanjiru observed, 'For all the deliberations of her homestead, [a woman] had to look for local elders.... Many elders would come to deliberate on the issue thoroughly. No woman would be summoned to deliberate on the issue. No. It was men's prerogative [men's word].'[98] In the execution of daily deliberations of a household, the need to interact, negotiate, and consult with an intricate kinship network necessitated acknowledging and incorporating established cultural conventions and sensibilities.

The Kikuyu, like other Kenyan communities, perceived leviratic marriages or wife inheritance as a way of securing the future of the deceased man's family. If a widow had neither brothers-in-law nor mature male children, she might be allowed to represent the interests of her household in the context of the wider patriliny until her eldest son was considered old enough to undertake such responsibilities.[99] The same was applicable among the Kikuyu:

> She could not attend the deliberations of the elders' council. But, she would participate in family and clan councils. Those she would attend. When her children mature, she will choose one of the children who is older, a male child and tell him, 'from now on you will be going to your older father [father's older brother], to your younger father [father's younger brother], when they have something to discuss...' From that point on, even if the mother [widow] attends the meeting, she will only listen. The son will listen to the deliberations ... if he is an intelligent person, he will keep the words.[100]

But in the broad scheme of things, conventional wisdom represented wife inheritance as social security for the wife and children of a deceased kinsman. Whoever was chosen to inherit a widow was also entrusted with the task of 'building for her and burying her when she died'.[101] These words were a metaphor for the total transfer of the widow to the care of another man. It excluded any agency on her part.

Widows thus could be considered economic burdens, just as marriageable young girls who could bring dowries could be considered economic resources. As a result, leviratic marriage became increasingly tenuous. With regard to the Meru, on whom he wrote most prolifically, the colonial administrator H. E. Lambert noted that 'the only thing that the heir inherits is the responsibility. He cannot inherit the widow's person against her will. But he must provide for her and her children and faithfully administer his brother's estate for their benefit, not his.'[102] Gerhard Lindblom asserts that among the Kamba, in-laws did not always inherit widows. Rather, the widows could be married off to non-kinsmen. Some of these men might not even be Kamba; at times they were Kikuyu.[103] That these women might be married off cheaply points to a community's anxiety to pass on the responsibility for a widow to another. Where families were poor, widows, young brides, and divorced women might be mistreated to such an extent that they would flee their marital homes and resort to prostitution.[104]

At times, the in-laws appropriated all manner of assets from the widow's household.[105] This was the predicament of Miriam Wambui Kanyanja's family. Because she was an only child, and a female child at that, in the absence of a prospective male heir, when her father died, Miriam's father's stepbrother had no qualms about using some of the property for his own dowry. He had the moral support of his father, who argued that 'since Kanyanja's wife has failed to give birth to another child you will be the first one to marry [pay dowry] with the property.'[106] Thus, when he died, 'my father left sugar cane, banana plants ... these were used to pay dowry for his step-brother.' Miriam's mother 'also kept goats ... she was very hard working. My father's stepbrothers would sell the goats.... And we did not get the money.'[107]

In Miriam's opinion, her mother had been reduced to the state of *ndungata*, an individual totally dependent on another: 'She became a *slave*. We would cultivate. We depended on agricultural produce which we would sell in order to purchase cloth wrapper since that was the contemporary attire ... we did not depend on the livestock that we were herding because whenever he [her father's stepbrother] sold the livestock he did not give us the money ... [we only got money] if we sold produce.'[108]

Despite such incursions on the property of the widow, a dead man's brother could not inherit the property of the dead man if the latter had left male children behind. The widow would act as custodian until the male children were old enough to inherit the property. Then they would ' take care of the property as well as their mother'.[109] While the children were young and the property was in the widow's hands, her in-laws kept a watchful eye as to how she utilized it. According to Mzee Elijah, the widow had little or no control over substantial property such as livestock within her household:

> Her [late] husband's brothers would be on the sidelines watching whether she was squandering the property or taking good care of it. They watched to see if she sold [some of the property] for frivolous reasons, or transferred the property without consulting them. She must consult them, and they must come and consult with each other.
>
> 'We will take these cattle to such and such a place, to somebody she knows, since there is no grass here,' [a brother-in-law would advise.] If it becomes necessary to sell any of the cattle she will inform her brothers-in-law about her financial need and her inability to solve the problem unless he gave her permission to sell some livestock. The brother would agree to either sell the animal on her behalf, or accompany her to sell the animal. If she wished to make a legitimate purchase they would consent to make the sale and ensure she bought the intended item ... but if she goes to sell the animal on her own, she might be planning to run away.... [For this reason] they would stop her from making the sale.
>
> [However], garden produce is women's food. When she goes to the market does she not need soap, does she not need sugar? Even if her husband was alive, he cannot oversee what a woman is going to sell in the market with regard to garden produce.... She cuts and sells bananas, I don't stop her . . she takes and sells millet, I don't ask her, at times she exchanges this for that ... that is women's food. We men do not bother about that. What we watch is goats, sheep, cattle, but not small stuff like chicken, maize, and millet. [110]

In summing up the nature of women's transactions including the sale of bananas, maize, and potatoes, Rajab Ngashira said, 'That was money to buy salt. But real business was absent.'[111] In other words, women did not commit substantial family assets in their trading activities.

Even some educated widows found themselves playing the old roles after their husbands had died. Referring to her father-in-law, Beth Njambi remarked: 'This one's father had a lot of property.... It is only recently that such property is being entrusted to women because of children who will divide the property among them. Otherwise one would not have access to his property.' Her father-in-law's property 'would never be registered in a woman's name' while he was alive.[112] Beth asserted that even in situations where women were employed, they were reluctant to buy property, since the men in the family would appropriate it.

Custody of Children

Under the Native Christian Marriage and Divorce Act, a widow became the guardian of the children of the marriage until the children turned sixteen or married. She was considered 'competent to dispose of such children in marriage, but in such event the customary bride price shall on demand be paid to such person as is entitled thereto by native law and custom'.[113] This might be the closest male kin of the deceased man. The legislation thus combined colonial and customary practices, simultaneously granting to, and withholding agency from widowed women with marriageable daughters. But the effort to impose colonial marriage legislation on top of the continued adherence to customary law and practices meant that the interpretation of custody issues and the resultant outcome depended on what legal code was applied, statutory or customary. Two cases that were reassessed by the Supreme Court in 1929 serve to illustrate the problem. In particular, they serve to inform us about women's strategies for asserting agency in marital issues using the provisions of customary and colonial law as interpreted in colonial courts to expand their options in choosing the partners they would marry.

In 1929 Ngeso Arap Leseret, a Maasai, had sought to recover the custody of his deceased brother's widow, seven children, and fifty-three head of cattle from Ibrahim, a Nubian.[114] Ngeso claimed that his brother Kemilil had died 'in the days before the government' in a foray with the Kitosh. As part of the spoils, his widow had been awarded seven heads of cattle. Kemilil left behind a son, Ndewa, and four other children. It is safe to say that Ndewa must have stepped in as the custodian of his deceased father's household, including property, children, and wife. The widow must have engaged in some liaisons, because she bore three other children after her husband's death. Ndewa, the son, then died and left two children. The defendant, Ibrahim, alleged that Ndewa had placed the cattle and the children under his care in custody for Ndewa's brother and son, claiming that he had no other living relatives, that is, no grown male relatives who could assume the custodial role at his demise.

Ngeso, the plaintiff, was basing his request for custody of children and property of the deceased on the basis of Maasai customary practice, and this point was not lost to the widow. She flatly contradicted the story told by Kemilil's brother, denying that the deceased had been her husband or that he was a Maasai. She thus denied the validity of all the possible premises on which the plaintiff might justify his claims. For the widow, a marital tie and the obligations and sanctions it entailed among the Maasai were very circumscribing. Even as she denied her alleged marriage to Kemilil, it could only enhance her case to add that the deceased was not Maasai. In denying her alleged marriage to Kemilil, the woman necessarily denied the state of widowhood. As we have seen, widowhood under the aegis of customary marriage practices might jeopardize the woman's future.

Although the Chief Justice was of the opinion that the woman was lying, and although he held that 'according to Maasai custom, the plaintiff as brother of the deceased, is entitled to the custody of the children and cattle',[115] his ruling did not grant Ngeso custody of the woman.[116] The woman thus had managed to retain her domestic arrangements. It is possible that the woman was married to Ibrahim. This separation of family members was 'uncustomary', except in cases where the widow had remarried outside her deceased husband's family. Although she lost custody of her children and her family property, she was at least spared forceful removal from her preferred domicile and seems to have successfully used the adjudication of customary law in a colonial court to achieve that end.

It was equally possible, however, for a colonial judge to decide that 'questions of guardianship are determined according to English law', not customary law.[117] In the case of Hamisi bin Ali who sought to get custody of his niece Fatuma, his brother's daughter, from her mother 'on the grounds that her mother was a prostitute, leading a bad life and may teach the child bad ways',[118] the judge declared that 'upon the death of the father the mother has a common law right to the custody of a child of tender years as natural guardian, unless she has forfeited it by misconduct.'[119] The judge found no evidence to suggest that Mariamu was a common prostitute. Neither was there any evidence of 'ill treatment, any unkindness or any ill-teaching of the child … or [that] she is living an evil or immoral life'. Instead, he applied the British common-law tradition to recognize the respectability of the woman's marital choice, and he sustained her right to keep the child.

The juxtaposition of these cases exemplifies ways in which, with the advent of colonial rule, efforts to legislate marriage and the subsequent attempts to interpret the rights of women under the sometimes parallel and often conflicting regimes of customary and colonial law opened opportunities for women to pursue alternative paths. The inconsistencies and lacunae created by the complex overlay of customary and colonial values and practices could not be counted on always to offer such opportunities or to permit their successful use. Nevertheless, when they appeared, there is evidence that women took advantage of them.

Nullification of a Christian Marriage: Orality and Textuality Revisited

A case was recorded of a call for the nullification of a marriage because a woman could not meet her conjugal responsibilities. Luka Akoch, a mission adherent married one Mushiri on August 11th, 1919 at the CMS Maseno in Nyanza. In 1926, Luka approached the office of the Senior Commissioner seeking to 'institute a case for nullity' because his wife was not developed. For the suit to succeed, medical evidence was considered absolutely necessary. The Commissioner's office advised Reverend E.A. Pleydell of CMS Maseno to arrange for the wife to be examined by a medical doctor who would provide a certificate indicating that 'the woman, owing to malformation or other reasons, was unable to fulfill her part of the contract.'[120]

The medical and marriage certificates were vital documentary evidence in court. Additionally, the doctor would be expected to give evidence before the Supreme Court at Kisumu. Ostensibly Luka had made one prior unsuccessful attempt to present his case to the judge. He was said not to have 'a particle of evidence' during this previous occasion.

Documentation and not verbal testimony represented the legal and moral shifts that the couple had undertaken. The lessons were learned gradually and were punctuated with false starts. Luka's decision to seek nullification as opposed to divorce implies that the marriage had not been consummated. The case evokes various lines of investigation. For a start, what was the nature of Mushiri's malformation? More significantly, was it something conventional local knowledge of body anatomy would have identified as ground for unmarriageability? If Mushiri did not know this medical factor, what was the nature of anatomical and sexual knowledge in the community in general? Why had Luka waited for about seven years before seeking nullification?

Colonial inscriptions on such modern couples created different legal procedures. New institutions and individuals were entrusted with creating, overseeing, and when necessary, dismantling such marriages. The provision of biomedical information along with the presentation of their marriage license in a court of law would help dissolve Luka's marriage.

Conclusion

Colonial social engineering did not always acknowledge indigenous sensibilities. It is possible that changes in the economic basis of households pointed toward the devolution of polygamy. Whichever strategy was applied, some of the women in polygamous marriages stood to lose their marital and social status. What the government was groping for was a legal context to effect the changes.

The East African Marriage Ordinance under which such marriages would be contracted provided seemingly idyllic solutions to a host of marital problems. At the heart of the matter was the argument that the Ordinance would provide legal basis for retribution. Thus, if a wife deserted, the husband could apply for restitution of conjugal rights, and in the case of adultery, he could claim damages. That this did not differ from the situation under customary law brings to the fore the irony of colonial codification and transformation of definitions. Amidst massive misgivings, some colonial administrators were willing to recognize native law and custom within the reserve as practised by Africans among themselves. Not so the church. Membership to the church required the abandonment of certain aspects of customary marriage practices, and the transformation of others. Unlike marriage according to native law and custom, the constituted statutory law of the land recognized Christian marriage. This law was not recognized or operative among the majority of the population in the colony.

There was widespread skepticism about Africans embracing the 'legal marriages' in large enough numbers to make any visible difference. The alternative, i.e. the test of time, was met with even greater skepticism. Civilization, it was believed, would take a long time to change the mentality of Africans. Some of the officials were resigned to leaving the matter to the test of time. It was hoped that ultimately, with the spread of civilization, many more people would come under 'the ordinary law', i.e. statutory law. This transition would be a positive thing for the African woman too because she would escape the 'retrogressive customs' of the natives and would no longer be suppressed. The ultimate goal was to allow her to 'come of age and have an individual existence'.[121] To a large extent the emancipation of women was closely tied to the spread of civilization, which was crudely translated as the implantation of British statutory laws and social institutions. In the meantime, as long as native law and custom prevailed in the larger part of the country, when it came to determining the legal status of women, the administration would be fraught with difficulty and contradictions.

Notes

1. Sir Robert Hamilton C.J. in ruling of Rex v. Amkeyo, (7E.A.L.R.14), 1917, quoted in Arthur Phillips (ed.), *Survey of African Marriage and Family Life* (London, 1953), xi–xii.
2. South Africa provided a useful precedent in the formulation of native policy. For example, this was evident in the evolution of agricultural labour policy with regard to the White Highlands. See R. M. A. van Zwanenberg, *Colonial Capitalism and Labour in Kenya* (Kampala, 1975). In South Africa provincial governments had broached the question of native marriages except in Natal. The codification of customary law was a *fait accompli* by the turn of the century. Sections of the Natal Code of Native Law dealt with the question of the emancipation of women. In the rest of South Africa, 'marriages in accordance with native law and custom [were] not valid'. See KNA: AG 4/2791

CNC to acting Provincial Commissioner, 22 March 1920.

3. The remaking of marriage in colonial Kenya raised eyebrows in the most unlikely quarters. Section 8 of the Native Christian Marriage and Divorce Ordinance, 1931 provided for the appointment of church ministers as Registrars of marriages. In the Salvation Army, some of the ministers were women. In 1933, the Attorney General feared that there was concern that 'the celebration of a marriage by a woman would to the native mind convey little or nothing'. KNA: AG 4/2793 AG to Colonial Secretary, 27 February 1933. One suspects that this 'native mind' was male, since authority and legitimacy were conceptualized in male terms.

   The CNC, who did not know that some Salvation Army women were ministers 'within the meaning of the Principal Ordinance', did not up to this point consider these to be ministers of a recognized church. He suggested that if the government refrained from appointing these women from being registrars that might provide one solution to the problem. If the governor had no option but to appoint such women as registrars upon application, and if Africans followers of the Salvation Army preferred or consented to being married by the same, then the government could assume that no harm had been done to the Africans. The twists and turns to the process of reconfiguring African marriages knew no bounds.
4. KNA: AG 4/2790 Registration of Heathen Marriages: Proposed Legislation, Resident Commissioner Naivasha to Officer-in-Charge of Maasai Reserve, Narok, 8 March 1922.
5. In order to adopt the recommendation for the registration of marriages, each Local Native Council needed the governor's approval. For example, in September 1927 the secretariat in Nairobi reported that the governor, on the advice of councils, had approved the resolutions passed by Central Kavirondo, Teita, and Kitui LNCs. KNA: PC/NZA.3/28/4/1 Native Marriages and Divorces: The Secretariat Nairobi to CNC, Registration of Native Marriages, 24 September 1927. Further south among the Luo-Abasuba a resolution for voluntary registration of marriages had been passed and forwarded to the CNC by November 14, 1928. KNA: PC/NZA.3/28/4/1 Native Marriages and Dowries, LNC Meetings, South Kavirondo (Luo-Abasuba), 27–28 September 1928. By 1927, the Kiambu Local Native Council had resolved that all pagan marriages would be registered voluntarily. KNA: PC/CP 4/1/1 Kikuyu Province Annual Reports 1927, 27. As early as November 1925 the scheme for the registration of marriages had been explained and accepted by a large majority of members of Fort Hall Local Native Council. KNA: PC/CP/2/1/5 LNC Meetings, Fort Hall District, 18–19 November 1925. The motion was carried 20 to 3.
6. KNA:AG 4/2790 Crown Counsel H.W.B. Blackwell to CNC, 3 April 1922.
7. KNA: AG 4/2790 Officer-In-charge of Maasai Reserve to Honourable CNC, 13 March 1922.
8. Bogonko, 'Christianism and Africanism', 18.
9. The LNC president's attempt to assuage this anxiety only revealed the extent of government intervention. He explained, 'The registration does not refer to Christian marriages. Once the amount of *Mahari* (dowry-bridewealth) paid is written down, there can be no dispute in future. The bride and bridegroom would have to attend and the bride's father and three witnesses and if the woman ran away subsequently the entry on the register would be cancelled.' KNA: PC/CP/2/1/5 LNC Meetings, Fort Hall District, 27 May 1927. The assurance that in any eventuality dowry paid would be safeguarded should have created a stampede of men rushing to register or contract civil marriages. As we have seen, the question of dowry was more complicated than the president made it out to be.
10. KNA: PC/CP/2/1/5 LNC Meetings, Fort Hall District, 27 May 1927.
11. KNA: PC/RVP.6A/14/16 The Native Marriage and Divorce Ordinance, 1939. A bill drafted by Chief Registrar of Natives, sent to all Provincial Commissioners for Comment, 9 February 1940, 8.
12. KNA: PC/CP/2/1/5 LNC Meetings, Fort Hall District, 27 May 1927.
13. KNA: PC/CP/2/1/5 LNC Meetings, Fort Hall District, 17 June 1936, Registration of Marriages. In January 1936, the president of the council had explained to the

councillors the benefits that would ensue if all native marriages [including Pagan, Mohammedan, and Christian marriages] and brideprice were registered. The councillors expressed unanimous support for the compulsory registration of marriages and dowry. A fee of two shillings payable by the husband would be charged for the service. This would cover the cost of registers and salaries of clerks. KNA: PC/CP/2/1/5 LNC Meetings, Fort Hall District, 7–8 January 1936..

14. KNA: PC/CP/2/1/5 LNC Meetings, Fort Hall District, 27 May 1927.
15. KNA: PC/CENT/2/2/1/4 LNC Meetings, Kyambu District, 26 September 1927. In Kiambu, the governor's approval of the registration of marriages resulted in the decision in March 1928 to purchase registers, initially to be kept by a clerk in the DC's office until the workload increased. Then registration might be moved to locational centres. The headmen were to be notified once the registers were installed at the DC's office. Then they could inform the people within their jurisdiction. KNA: PC/CENT/2/1/4 LNC Meetings, Kyambu District, 5 March 1928. In North Kavirondo, it was decided that the only practical way was to have locational registers kept by chiefs and clerks (possibly Native Tribunal Court clerks). A two shillings fee (one shilling each to the clerk and chief) would be charged. KNA: PC/NZA.3/28/4/1 Native Marriages and Divorces: DC Kakamega, North Kavirondo to Senior Commissioner, Registration of Native Marriages, 25 June 1927.
16. No fee would be charged for the registration except for a one-shilling fee for a certified extract. Upon the annulment of the marriage, the party and witnesses were to inform the administration. KNA: PC/NZA.3/28/4/1 DC Central Kavirondo to Senior Commissioner Nyanza, 21 April 1927.
17. KNA: PC/CENTRAL/2/1/8 LNC Meetings, Fort Hall District, 7–8 March 1939.
18. KNA: PC/CENT/2/1/9 LNC Meetings, Meru, 18–20 December 1945.
19. KNA: AG 4/2793 Some Notes on the Need for the Provision for the Civil Registration of Marriages Contracted According to Native Law and Custom as Monogamous Unions. nd.
20. Kershaw, *Mau Mau from Below*, 190; E. N. Wanyoike, *An African Pastor* (Nairobi, 1974), 42.
21. Mary F. Holding, 'Christian Impact on Meru Institutions', Rhodes House Mss. Afr. r. 191, 64.
22. KNA: AG 4/2793 Some Notes on the Need for the Provision for the Civil Registration of Marriages Contracted According to Native Law and Custom as Monogamous Unions.
23. KNA: PC/CENTRAL/2/1/11 Irvine Papers, Church of Scotland Mission, Chogoria, 1943 Annual Report, 1
24. *Ibid.*
25. *Ibid.*, 1–2.
26. For Christians who committed bigamy, there was the additional problem regarding the dowry paid for the second wife. The DC for Central Kavirondo wondered what the legal position of such men would be after their release from prison. He wondered whether they '[had] a valid claim for the refund of *mahari*, dowry'. KNA: PC/NZA.3/28/4/1 Native Marriages and Dowries, DC Central Kavirondo to PC Nyanza, 6 January 1928. There were other possible developments for those Christian men who reverted to 'paganism' by marrying another wife while still married under the East African Marriage Ordinance. Some leaders believed that if in such cases the first wife left and the man could not get his brideprice back, this would serve as a warning to others contemplating such action. In the Catholic Church, such a syncretic practice resulted in expulsion. Christian marriages cannot have been doing well. KNA: PC/CENT/2/1/4 LNC Meetings, Kyambu District, 21 November 1925. Polygamy and Christianity were strange bedfellows.
27. KNA: PC/CENT/2/1/9 LNC Meetings, Meru, 2 March 1943.
28. *Ibid.*
29. Ibid. Should the divorced woman choose to remarry, her first husband would have no right over the children of the second marriage. Although silent on the issue, it would appear that the divorced man kept the children of their marriage. Such children and the

dowry that was paid for their mother were the subject of enquiry by LNCs. See, for example, KNA: PC/CENT/2/1/9 LNC Meetings, Meru, 18–20 December 1945. In other contexts, a more generalized explanation of the 'ownership' of progeny was adopted. 'by native law the title to children descends in perpetuity [to, and through the male lineage]'. KNA: DC/NYI/3/10 Native Affairs: Return of Akamba Women from Kenya 1921–23, DC Embu to Senior Commissioner Nyeri, 18 November 1921.

30. KNA: AG 4/2792 Schedule Form A.
31. Once the marriage had taken place, either under the Marriage Ordinance, the Native Christian Marriage Ordinance, or under Native Law and Custom, the registration certificate required, among others, the signature of the bride. A caveat noted that the document would not be registered by the clerk 'until the signature or thumb mark of the bridegroom and bride have been set to the document in his presence and the presence of witnesses'. KNA: PC/RVP.6A/14/16 Schedule III Form B, Registration of Marriage.
32. KNA: PC/RVP.6A/14/16 Schedule I Form A Notice of Marriage.
33. KNA: PC/CENT/2/1/6 LNC Special Meetings, Nyeri, 21–22 October 1936.
34. Simeon H. Ominde, *The Luo Girl from Infancy to Marriage* (London, 1952), 48.
35. Kenyatta, *Facing Mount Kenya*, 164–5; Robert A. LeVine and Barbara B. LeVine, *Nyansongo: A Gusii Community in Kenya*, New York: Academic Press, 1966, 54.
36. Kenyatta, *Facing Mount Kenya*, 165–7; Davison, *Voices From Mutira*, 70–1, 99, 124–5.
37. Ominde, *The Luo Girl*, 48.
38. *Ibid.*
39. *Ibid.*
40. Milkah Wanjiru, oral interview, Nairobi, November 1996.
41. Phillip U. Mayer, 'Privileged Obstruction of Marriage Rites Among the Gusii', *Africa*, 20 (1950), 115–19; Peristiany, *The Social Institutions*, 83–4; Kenyatta, *Facing Mount Kenya*, 171–2; Satish Chandra Saberwal, 'Social Control and Cultural Flexibility Among the Embu of Kenya, (CA. 1900)', PhD dissertation, Cornell University, 1966, 39.
42. KNA: AG 4/2791 Status of Native Women, R. W. Lambert, Assistant DC Kaloleni to PC Mombasa, February 1919.
43. KNA: PC/CENT/2/1/8 LNC Meetings, Fort Hall District, 25 July 1939.
44. KNA: PC/RVP.6A/14/16 The Native Marriage and Divorce Ordinance, 1939. A bill drafted by Chief Registrar of Natives, 8.
45. *Ibid.*, 9.
46. KNA: PC/NZA.3/28/4/1 DC Central Kavirondo to PC Nyanza, 6 January 1928.
47. K. L. Hunter, 'Memoirs of Life as an Administrative Officer in Kenya, 1919–1950', unpublished manuscript, 1942, Rhodes House Mss Afr. S. 1942.
48. Muthoni Likimani, oral interview, Nairobi, 22 December 1993.
49. KNA: PC/CP/2/1/5 LNC Meetings, Fort Hall District, Payment of Advances on Dowry of Girls Before They Reached Maturity, 12–13 July 1933.
50. Muthoni Likimani, oral interview, Nairobi, 22 December 1993.
51. Serah Wambui Mukabi, oral interview, Limuru, 20 July 1993; Beth Njambi, oral interview, Limuru, 14 July 1993.
52. Josephine Gathoni, oral interview, Nairobi, November 1996.
53. Beth Njambi, oral interview, Limuru, 14 July 1993.
54. *Ibid.*
55. *Ibid.*
56. Hannah Wariara, oral interview, Limuru, 27 August 1993. Girls' reluctance to marry older suitors was evident elsewhere. See for example, Peristiany, *The Social Institutions*, 83–4.
57. Hamisi Makapia Wanga, oral interview, Ebumanyi, Mumias, 21 January 1997.
58. Bogonko, 'Christianism and Africanism', 18; S. N. Bogonko, 'Catholicism and Protestantism in the social and political development of Kenya', unpublished paper read at the Eastern African Historical Conference, Naivasha, Kenya, 1981.
59. Eliud Amatike Oluchina, oral interview, Ebukambuli, Kakamega, February 1997.
60. While the question of women's consent occupied the minds of top administrators, the Attorney General was quick to observe that the criminalisation of fathers entering into

marriage contracts for their underage daughters was *ultra vires*. This meant that the councils were not empowered to make resolutions over matters of such gravity. KNA: PC/NZA.3/28/4/1 DC Central Kavirondo to Senior Commissioner Nyanza, Marrying of Immature Girls, 5 August 1927. Councils had no authority to make the actions of fathers in this regard punishable. This put LNC's in a tight spot since from time to time concerns about the practice were brought before them.

61. KNA: PC/NZA.3/28/4/1 Senior Commissioner Nyanza to DC's Nyanza (except Kisumu-Londiani), 2 October 1926.
62. KNA: PC/NZA.3/28/4/1 J. A. Ross, Medical Officer-In-Charge North Kavirondo and Nandi Reserves to DC Kakamega, Marriage of Immature Girls, 5 May 1927.
63. KNA: PC/CP/2/1/5 LNC Meetings, Fort Hall District, 12–13 July 1933.
64. KNA: PC/NZA.3/2/1 PC Kisumu to DCs Nyanza Reserve, Marriage of Immature Girls, 11 November 1927.
65. *Ibid.*
66. KNA: PC/NZA.3/28/4/1 DC Kakamega, North Kavirondo to PC Nyanza, Marriage of Immature Girls, 14 November 1927.
67. KNA: PC/NZA.3/28/4/1 DC Kapsabet to PC Nyanza, Marriage of Immature girls, 18 November 1927.
68. Aggrey Ham Wanzetse, oral interview, Wanga, Kakamega, 24 January 1997.
69. KNA: PC/NZA.3/28/4/1 E. A. Beavon, Missionary in Charge, Kamagambo Mission, Kisii, to PC Nyanza, 24 November 1927.
70. KNA: PC/NZA.3/28/4/1 E. A. Beavon, Kamagambo Mission, Kisii to PC Nyanza, 24 November 1927. That a local colonial administrator came up with a different reading of the situation in Kisii, however, is instructive. According to the acting DC, S. O. V. Hodge, the Kisii community appreciated fully the evils of both underage marriages and the consummation of the same. Here, public opinion was bringing such pressure to bear as to make the introduction of special legislation superfluous. Had Hodge been duped into believing that positive change was taking place, or was it that Beavon was overzealous and too judgmental of the Abagusii people?
71. KNA: PC/NZA.3/28/4/1 H. W. Innis, Ogada Mission Station, Nyahera, Kisumu, to Senior Commissioner Nyanza, 27 December 1927.
72. KNA: PC/NZA.3/28/4/1 O. C. Keller, Nyangori Mission, Kisumu, to Senior Commissioner Nyanza, 3 January 1928.
73. *Ibid.*
74. *Ibid.*
75. Liza Nyambura Mwangi, oral interview, November 1996.
76. Monicah Wanjiru, oral interview, November 1996.
77. Rajab Ngashira, oral interview, Ebumanyi, Mumias Location, 22 January 1997.
78. Mrs. Keran Akoto, oral interview, Mbale, Kakamega, 22 February 1997.
79. Ominde, *The Luo Girl*, 40.
80. For example, see the case of Karuana. Although not underage when she was married, having been fetched by, and spent the first night of her wedded life at Wamutira's (the first wife's) house, she referred to Wamutira as her mother. See Davison, *Voices from Mutira*, 81.
81. Ominde, *The Luo Girl*, 40.
82. KNA: PC/CENT/2/1/6 LNC Special Meetings, Nyeri, Forced Marriage of Girls, 21–22 October 1936.
83. KNA: PC/NZA.3/28/4/1 O. C. Keller, Nyangori Mission, Kisumu, to Senior Commissioner Nyanza Province, 3 January 1928. Although writing about the Luyia people in general, Keller specifically referred to the Tiriki sub-group with regard to this practice. There is evidence, however, of similar arrangements in other ethnic groups. See, for example, Peristiany, *The Social Institutions*, 64–5. For child betrothal among the Kamba see, Gerhard Lindblom, *The Akamba in British East Africa* (Uppsala, 1920), 78.
84. Peristiany, *The Social Institutions*, 65.
85. Mtu akianza kutoa mali kuoa ndito naye haja fikirilia [sic] umri were [sic] kuweza mume.... Mtu akifanya hivi aweza kutoshwa fine ao [sic] kufungwa, na mwenye kupokea mali hii pia aweza kutoshwa.

If a person begins to pay bridewealth for a girl who is not old enough to manage a husband.... A person who does this could be fined or imprisoned. The recipient of such bridewealth too could be fined. LNC Meeting, Karatina, 3 September 1929 cited in KNA: PC/CENT/2/1/6 LNC Special Meetings, Nyeri, 20–22 July 1937.

86. *Ibid.*
87. *Ibid.*
88. *Ibid.*
89. KNA: PC/CP/2/1/5 LNC Meetings, Fort Hall District, 12–13 July 1933.
90. KNA: PC/CP/2/1/5 LNC Meetings, Fort Hall District, Payment of Advances on Dowry of Girls Before They Reached Maturity, 12–13 July 1933.
91. KNA: PC/CENT/2/1/9 LNC Meetings, Meru, 6–8 November 1948.
92. The chairman of the Kyambu council was quick to note that the parents of girls were often to blame 'for taking the marriage price of their daughters before they had come of age'. KNA: PC/CENT/2/1/4 LNC Minutes, Kyambu District, Native Tribunals:The Prosecution of Young Men for Marrying Girls Who are Engaged to Other Men, 12–14 January 1933. At a later stage the region was referred to as Kiambu. He urged the members of the LNC to put a stop to that practice.
93. In a work that revolves around the tribulations of widowhood regarding such issues as migrant husbands, financial needs, the raising and marrying off of daughters, property rights, and litigation for diverse reasons, Kenda Mutongi has discussed circumstances under which widows might seek the help of a variety of men. See Kenda Beatrice Mutongi, 'Generations of Grief and Grievances: A History of Widows and Widowhood in Maragoli, Western Kenya, 1900 to the Present', Ph. D dissertation, University of Virginia, 1996.
94. Cagnolo, *The Akikuyu*, 289–93; L. S. B. Leakey, *The Southern Kikuyu Before 1903*, I (New York, 1977), 12.
95. KNA: PC/NZA.3/28/4/1 Native Marriages and Divorces, Senior Commissioner Kisumu to DC Central Kavirondo, Re: Christian Widows, 29 July 1927.
96. KNA: AG 4/2792 An Ordinance to Provide for the Marriage of Native Christians and for the Dissolution of Such Marriages, or The Native Christian Marriage and Divorce Ordinance, 1931. See also, KNA: PC/RVP.6A./14/16 The Native Marriage and Divorce Ordinance, 1939, a bill drafted by Chief Registrar of Natives, 16. In a drawn out and complex legal saga relating to contestation over the burial of S. M. Otieno in 1987, the juxtaposition of customary and British legal provisions put to question the rights of widows in civil marriages. The former carried the day. See Patricia Stamp, 'Burying Otieno: the politics of gender and ethnicity in Kenya', *Signs*, 16, 4 (1991), 808–45; Cohen and Odhiambo, *Burying SM*; Wambui Waiyaki Otieno, *Mau Mau's Daughter: A Life History* (Boulder, CO, 1998).
97. KNA: PC/NZA/2/1/183 acting Chief Secretary, the Secretariat, Dar-es-Salaam to Chief Secretary, Kenya, 11 February 1946.
98. Mary Wanjiru [Nyina wa Cibira], oral interview, Limuru, 14 July 1993.
99. This was certainly the practice among the Kamba. If a woman did not have brothers-in-law, and did not have mature sons, in her role as temporary head of household, she would join the men of the clan as they deliberated over various issues. Mzee Elijah Mbeketha, oral interview, Tala, Machakos, 30 July 1993. It was inconceivable for a widow to undertake certain transactions on her own: 'if she was a good woman, she would not give instructions for the sale of livestock, land, or the marriage of her daughter [without consulting her in-laws].' Mzee Elijah Mbeketha, *ibid.*
100. Beth Njambi, oral interview, Limuru, 14 July 1993.
101. *Ibid.*
102. KNA: PC/CENTRAL/2/1/11 Part III Meru – Disintegration and Reintegration in the Meru Tribe, H. E. Lambert, 9 January 1940, 26–7.
103. Lindblom, *The Akamba*, 82ff.
104. White, *The Comforts of Home*, 84.
105. Even before widowhood, a woman's personal property was very limited. ' Her role was to care for livestock brought to her by her husband. The goats would be placed in the pen ... she would supply them with sweet-potato vines ... if she was still bearing

children, the fattened *ngoima* might be slaughtered for her after she gave birth.... She could not have her own goat [livestock] because she did not own a homestead'. The acquisition of personal property by women was said to be a later development attributed to education. Beth Njambi, oral interview, Limuru, 14 July 1993. We have indicated the complexity of this in chapter two. The situation was different with regard to African prostitutes in colonial Nairobi. Empirical research points to an earlier and different process of accumulation of personal property. Luise White has illustrated the link between the process of prostitution in colonial Nairobi and the acquisition of real estate by these early entrepreneurs. White, *The Comforts of Home*, 45–6, 123, 218–19. See also Oboler, *Women, Power and Economic Change*, 172, for Nandi prostitutes who returned to the rural areas from various urban centres before 1950 and purchased land and livestock, becoming independent heads of households. While educated women adopted a Western materialist lifestyle, they did not, during our period of study, rush to accumulate property on an individual basis. They did, however, marry into a *petite bourgeoisie* that accumulated land, adopted progressive agricultural practices, and expanded production, owned transportation, retail and wholesale businesses, and in general adopted a culture of conspicuous consumption. While living a relatively different lifestyle that allowed them greater social latitude, in general, they did not attain an equal, let alone majority hold over the family property unless, and until they were widowed. Even then, this was a highly conflictual situation, contested by a whole range of people.

106. Miriam Wambui Kanyanja, oral interview, Nairobi, 29 July 1993.
107. *Ibid.*
108. *Ibid.*
109. Mzee Elijah Mbeketha, oral interview, Tala, Machakos, 30 July 1993.
110. *Ibid.*
111. Rajab Ngashira, oral interview, Ebumanyi, Mumias, 22 January 1997.
112. Beth Njambi, oral interview, Limuru, 14 July 1993.
113. KNA: AG 4/2792 An Ordinance to Provide for the Marriage of Native Christians and for the Dissolution of Such Marriages, or The Native Christian Marriage and Divorce Ordinance, 1931. See also, KNA: PC/RVP.6A./14/16 The Native Marriage and Divorce Ordinance, 1939, a bill drafted by Chief Registrar of Natives, 16.
114. Colony and Protectorate of Kenya, The Supreme Court, Law Reports of Kenya, Vol. XII, 1929–1930, Ngeso arap Leseret v. Ibrahim, C.C. 42/1929, 50.
115. *Ibid.*
116. *Ibid.*
117. Colony and Protectorate of Kenya, The Supreme Court, Law Reports of Kenya, Vol. XII, 1929–1930, Hamisi bin Ali v. Mariamu Binti Ali, C.C 44/1929, 51. See Halsbury, Vol. 17, Section 255, 108.
118. Colony and Protectorate of Kenya, The Supreme Court, Law Reports of Kenya, Vol. XII, 1929–1930, Ngeso arap Leseret v. Ibrahim, C.C. 42/1929, 50.
119. *Ibid.*
120. KNA: PC/NZA.3/28/4/1 Native Marriages and Divorces, Senior Commissioner Nyanza to Rev. E.A. Pleydell, CMS Maseno, 30 June 1926.
121. KNA: AG 4/2791 Status of Native Women, John Ainsworth, Chief Native Commissioner to acting Attorney General, Provincial Commissioner, 22 March 1920.

Six

The Medicalization & Regulation of Maternity[1]

> My attachment [servant] was a funny looking, wizened little chap bearing the incongruous name of Kilimanjia, which means the hill road. Since names indicate some circumstance connected with birth, I suppose he must have been born on a road in the hills. You see, birth is not the elaborate business it is with us civilized folk. A few minutes by the wayside, perhaps, then up and away with a wee little mite tucked in a leather pouch on the back. That is all.[2]
> Willis R. Hotchkiss, Missionary, 1937.

On the December 20, 1931 at a special meeting of the Nyeri Local Native Council, Chiefs Japhet Githaiga and Johana Ngugi recommended that the council should not make any financial contribution to the Lady Grigg Maternity and Child Welfare Hospital and Training Centre at Pumwani in Nairobi. The council took this decision after two of their members visited the hospital.

> [T]he reason was that the women most assisted by the home were Kikuyu women who had run away from their own husbands in the Kikuyu reserve and joined up with detribalized natives in Nairobi and lived with them. When they [members of the council] visited the home they found several Kikuyu women there who would not give their father's or brother's name: they said they were Nairobi people and it was obvious they had run away from their husbands in the reserve.[3]

The two chiefs were convinced that the council should not help 'such women'. As it turned out, all the other members of the council were also opposed to the idea of making any grant to assist the Pumwani Home.

The idea of the errant woman, so common in other debates, became part of the discourse about ethnic identity, modernity, and the access of indigenous women to Western medicine in colonial Kenya. Earlier, towards the end of 1930, the Chief Native Commissioner had asked the Murang'a LNC to vote a contribution towards the same facility, which included a maternity hospital and a training centre for African nurses. It soon became evident that, in the minds of these councillors, the Nairobi institution was associated with all the vices that supposedly befell women once they ventured into the big city. Such women were said to be fallen, immoral beings who had nothing positive to contribute to their rural areas. Hence, the council was averse to investing in an institution that would benefit unrespectable women. According to Macharia Kinungi, 'If women go to Nairobi they get into bad ways'.[4]

When the members of the Murang'a LNC decided to visit the institution 'in order to obtain a better idea of prevailing conditions and to explain their difficulties and misgivings',[5] they ended up making a favorable report. Although the hospital was a long way from Fort Hall, they observed that 'there were plenty of people from Fort Hall and women should feel at home there.'[6] Even though some of the councillors lobbied for the building of a local maternity hall, the LNC unanimously decided to contribute 500 shillings to the Pumwani Maternity Home in1931.

By 1935, the motivation behind their decision was clear. A large number of the patient population at the Pumwani Maternity Hospital was indeed Kikuyu resident in Nairobi. Councillor Joseph Wanjie indicated that it had even become the practice of certain Kikuyu living in Fort Hall 'to take their wives there, all the way [to] Nairobi' to deliver babies. This was a distance of about one hundred miles. More importantly, the councillors were beginning to look at Pumwani as a possible source of trained personnel to work in the Fort Hall District. Overall, the home was said to be 'doing a good job', a far cry from the verdict five years earlier.

These LNC responses to the issue of maternity care in an urban centre distant from their own jurisdiction obviously show to what extent the spatial mobility of Kenyan women was affecting efforts by native authorities to make policy regarding maternity, a central aspect of women's lives. Stereotypes of urbanised, detribalised women competed with traditional concerns for the welfare of an ethnic group's expectant mothers and their children as women in new places found new ways to assume the role of motherhood.

This was not just an issue for the Local Native Councils. The question of maternal health care put women under the surveillance and gaze of a whole range of interested parties. For missionaries and colonial administrators, Western medicine was the panacea for birthing, for infant and maternal health care, and for training indigenous professionals in these areas.[7] These concerns consequently were embedded in processes of colonial and missionary legitimation, the refashioning of conceptualizations of pregnancy, motherhood, womanhood, work, citizenship, and social order. Mission and government hospitals became centres of cross-cultural contacts. Here, maternity and domesticity unfolded in a context of gendered colonizing.

For a long time, indigenous males dominated the maternity debate during the colonial period. They did so not only as members of the Local Native Councils, which funded the construction of maternities, but also as health workers, mediators with colonial authorities, surveyors of the moral domain, and ultimately, as the financiers of their wives' maternity bills.

With the advent of the colonial administration and the subsequent medicalization of birth, men's role as mediators between women and the colonisers became a source of power and authority. Where it was within their powers, rural patriarchs deliberated on the distribution of maternity services and disseminated medical and other information in a manner that came close to determining which women could access these services. Patriarchs were concerned with perpetuating ethnic identities by asserting their authority over not only marriage, but also procreation; not only motherhood, but pre-initiation pregnancies and abortions. In this endeavour, it was possible for them to see women in distant urban areas as peripheral, as the Nyeri LNC did, but it was also possible to see them as kin for whom they were responsible, like the Murang'a LNC. And of course, 'civilizing' maternity by medicalizing it was a project that held the attention of colonial administrators.

Although damning observations were made about women's kinlessness, marital infidelity, unsanctioned marital unions, detribalisation, and general unruliness as the LNCs deliberated on the propriety of funding urban maternity homes, at the same time, other readings of Kenyan womanhood were inscribed in other maternity issues. The allegory of maternity, of giving birth to the future out of the continuity of the past, like other aspects of the colonial social situation that appropriated women's bodies as signifiers of large social issues, involved a lot of unfinished societal business. Changes were simultaneously being introduced, contested, negotiated, and assimilated to existing practices. Pregnant patients, their bodies clothed or unclothed, pregnant under acceptable or unacceptable circumstances, served as barometers of the transformations that society was undergoing.

Both general Western medicine and maternity care were introduced in Kenya by various missionary societies. The provision of medical services in the rural areas was at times slowed by disagreements between mission groups and colonial authorities regarding who should control the service.[8] Among the earliest hospitals and dispensaries were those established by the Church Missionary Society including Weithaga Dispensary in 1903, Maseno and Kaloleni Hospitals in 1908; the Friends (Quakers) hospital at Kaimosi in 1903; the Church of Scotland Mission hospitals established at Kikuyu in 1908, Tumutumu in 1910, and Chogoria in 1922; the African Inland mission dispensary at Machakos in 1922; the Methodists at Maua Hospital in 1929, and in Nyeri the Consolata Catholic Mission's Mathari hospital in 1940. A part of the missionary triple package [including schools, churches and hospitals] the medical project had a faltering start and generated protracted debates.[9]

Prenatal Care

Medical specialists sought the intervention of LNC members in their efforts to persuade local populations to patronize hospitals for maternity care. This included conforming to stipulated schedules concerning the 'minimum period of labour before women were brought to hospital for treatment', according to the Fort Hall Medical Officer (MO) in 1930. Some expectant women had been delaying at home for up to four days while in labour, 'which gave the medical officer very little chance of bringing about a successful result and endangered the life of both mother and child'.[10] While initial concern revolved around the period immediately before childbirth, medical practitioners also endeavoured to introduce local women to the benefits of prenatal care. For example, in March 1937, the MO for Meru advised 'that pregnant women be encouraged to come to hospital to be examined as soon as they knew they are pregnant. If they [did] this, many later difficulties may be avoided.'[11] By November of 1937, the Medical Officer had to appeal again to the members of the LNC, whom he asked to 'encourage women to come to hospital for pre-natal advice'. [12] Despite these efforts, the antenatal clinic did not become operative until 1949. Once started, 'ante-natal advice and general gaenocological [sic] treatment would be given on Mondays and Thursdays from 2 to 4 p.m.'.[13]

Modern medicine's attempt to regulate absolute timetables for birthing proved difficult. Although in 1939 a Dr. Preston implored the Murang'a LNC members to impress on women who had previous difficult child births the importance of getting to a hospital well before the expected date of delivery,[14] and although he stressed that had many women been brought in earlier, they 'would have been alive to-day',[15] in Meru, as elsewhere, this advice did not yield positive results, at least not immediately. Four months after the initial dissemination of the advice, 'very few women had attended [prenatal clinics]'.[16] To some extent, their ability to attend clinic depended on whether they lived 'within reasonable distance of the hospital'.[17]

It was impractical to expect a perfectly healthy pregnant woman to go to hospital to await the birth of her baby. In any case, even with modern medicine, the unpredictability of timing births was a well-known factor. More importantly, pregnancy was part of, and not separate from a whole range of other social processes. To isolate it, and by inference the woman, was unusual. Pregnancy, childbirth, and postnatal care inhabited a continuous social rhythm. This is not to overlook a whole range of local observances revolving around these three processes;[18] rather, it is to question the attempt to impose a different construction of maternity that entailed what seemed to be an irrational break with past rhythms and practices. As with other colonial changes, this aspect of modern medicine sought to restructure maternity in its temporal and spatial aspects.

The issue had further complexities. In some cases, pregnant women went instead to nearby mission hospitals, and only if their situation became worse were they moved on to larger and better-equipped district hospitals. Such was the situation in Murang'a District, where women might start by going to Githumu Mission Hospital and were only later referred to Murang'a District Hospital. This, however, might be too late to save the woman's life or that of her unborn child.

What is more, by claiming perfect results for maternity cases that conformed to the Medical Department's stipulations, the MO misrepresented the efficacy of Western medicine. When deaths inevitably occurred during hospitalized pregnancies, people became afraid to go to any hospital, as they were associated with death. In essence, unpredictable fatalities put both the smaller local hospitals and modern medicine in general in bad repute.

Bureaucratic bottlenecks, together with the inequitable distribution of qualified medical staff, did not always produce the desired results. With this in mind, in 1940 the MO for Murang'a observed that 'it is far better to bring them [the expectant women] direct to Fort Hall because the cases will get better and quicker treatment, as quite a number of the cases from Githumu arrive at Fort Hall too far advanced to enable us to deal with them satisfactorily.'[19] In some instances, a visit to either hospital might not have been the most practical solution, owing either to the great distance to the hospital or to the prevailing belief that maternity is a natural condition that does not call for hospitalization. Sometimes a family was not able to establish the degree of potential danger posed by the medical condition. Whatever the case, it was impractical to expect a perfectly healthy pregnant woman to go to hospital to await the birth of her baby.

The medicalization of pregnancy provides us with an indicator that registered peoples' responses not only to modern medicine, but to other social changes, too. Those who embraced Christianity and literacy were most likely to seek medical help at childbirth. Equally important, a family's socio-economic status helped determine how it responded to Western medicine. Poverty certainly kept some expectant women from seeking medical help. This was not lost to providers of Western medicine. Hence, in Meru, Dr. Gerald of the Maua Mission Hospital came up with the idea that if the Council made a five-shilling grant for each maternity case coming to the hospital, this would 'encourage the women to come in, [since] if the council made this grant the women would not be charged anything'.[20]

The president of the Council, who was also the District Commissioner, did not find the idea appealing. He knew that civilization could be a slow and burdensome process, and that it did not come free. In his eyes, modern medicine was a commodity that had to be purchased. Therefore, only women from wealthy families could benefit from this form of modernization. The president retorted that 'in all parts of the world those who could do so had to pay for their medical services', and he suggested that 'that money was better spent on putting up hospital buildings than on grants for individuals'.[21] His assessment, rather than the doctor's proposal, proved to be the more realistic. Socio-economic differentiation was increasingly becoming evident in Kenya by the late 1930s.[22]

Although the colonial administration was interested in imposing Western practices on the culture of childbirth, it was not particularly willing to pay the amount listed on that price tag. Despite recurrent admonitions about fatalities resulting from women's failure to go to hospitals at all, or in a timely manner, the government did not wholly promote or underwrite medical care, especially in rural areas.[23] Sometimes, for example, men who had travelled and lived in centres of 'progress' and desired the same for their home areas, initiated the demand for the provision of maternity wards or hospitals back home. With their newly-acquired skills, including literacy and ideas about the workings of the colonial machinery, they intervened on behalf of their rural kin. They were not often successful. Despite the flurry of activity maintained by the medical personnel in colonial Kenya, changes were very slow, both in their introduction and adoption.

In 1944, when Nahashon Gudo and J. Edward Opuko from Nyanza Province petitioned L. J. Beecher of the CMS Mission to intervene with the colonial administration for a maternity hospital for East Kano Reserve, the PC who replied for the administration noted that Kano lay relatively close to Kisumu Hospital and Maternity Centre 'and there were more distant areas, which would, I feel certain, receive prior considerations'.[24] Gudo and Opuko then informed Beecher that Awasi was twenty-five miles from Kisumu, while Ahero was fifteen miles away, and West Kano was said to have an estimated population of about twenty-five thousand, while East Kano had about twenty-four thousand and 'so merited its own maternity [ward]'.[25] Adopting what they perceived to be the official strategy for apportioning welfare and development services, Opuko and Gudo came up with population figures for their regions four years before Kenya's first official census. Figures, statistics, and documentation were central to colonial administration and Gudo and Opuko used these 'scientific' tools of the colonial state to try to wrestle medical services from the government for their natal homes. It didn't work, however. The PC simply told them to take the matter up with the appropriate LNCs, to which the dissemination of medical information was entrusted and which mediated between the community and new medical ideas.[26]

Maternity services for the majority of women continued to be inadequate. Prenatal clinics were meant simply to weed out the normal from abnormal pregnancies with the idea of controlling congestion at the terribly inadequate maternity services. In the case of Nyeri, 'those who were not likely to have difficulties [w]ould be kept out [of the hospital] to leave room for those who needed attention'.[27] In its wisdom, the Meru LNC council resolved in 1937 that expectant mothers should not exceed two days of labour before seeking medical help.[28] Clearly the prevailing sensibilities fell short of modern medical practice. In Nyeri in 1942, not every woman who chose to have a hospital birth could do so. There was insufficient room at Nyeri and Tumutumu Hospitals, one government-funded and the other mission-funded, respectively. By 1946, the shortage of maternity wards and of room in existing wards, plus the lack or shortage of trained midwives, led the Nyeri African District Council to recommend that 'accommodation in Hospital Maternity Blocks should be reserved for complicated cases and for first babies [only]'.[29] In general, the construction of maternity wards, or the setting aside of wards for maternity cases competed with the provision of wards for general medical patients. It is in this context that in 1937 the Medical Officer in Meru quipped, 'Up to now, no maternity cases had been turned away, and there have been no ill-effects from the children being born in the sick wards.'[30] As we shall see, this did not go down well with the local communities.

Cleanliness, a virtue that the colonial government, missionaries, and foreign medical personnel had identified as lacking among Africans, was equally absent among prospective and new mothers in maternities. An antiseptic environment did not seem easy to achieve in some of these centres of modern medicine. At Murang'a Hospital, patients complained of inability to take baths as often as they would like to. For maternity patients, efforts made by the hospital to ease the situation were insufficient. Other than the general shortage of water in the hospital as a whole, the maternity faced an additional problem. Although 'there [was] a bathroom attached to the maternity block … the trouble is that all the water has to be carted in one water cart [sic] to the hospital and this is kept constantly on the go from 7.0[0] am to 4.0[0] pm.' Western medicine was portrayed as scientific, clean, and rational, but it frequently failed to live up to this representation in its treatment of the pregnancies of African women. The maternity ward did not always safeguard the hygiene of its patients.

Institutionalizing Maternity

Competition for meager resources increasingly pitted maternity cases against all other medical cases, and hospital against hospital. Consequently, it was not unusual to have hospitals that did not have maternity units. In 1934, members of Nyeri LNC complained that the thirty-three-bed hospital in Nyeri was much too small and did not provide other much-needed services. More importantly, however, 'What was most wanted was a maternity ward where women in child birth could be kept separate.'[31] Institutionalizing maternity, treating it as a separate medical condition to be overseen by specialized medical personnel, rather than as an integral part of everyday life, was a slow process.

The Meru Hospital as a whole remained without a separate ward for female patients till 1935, when this was established 'under the supervision of a female dresser'.[32] Up to this point, men and women were admitted in the same wards. Even after a separate women's ward was established, however, pregnant women detested being put in the same wards as sick people. As late as the end of 1936 the Director of Medical Services opposed the idea of constructing a maternity ward separate from the other wards in the hospital in Meru on financial grounds. The Medical Officer in Meru was hopeful that the director would be persuaded once he was informed that the Meru LNC intended to fund the project.[33] By the end of 1937, the question of erecting a maternity hospital was far from being resolved, even though Councillor M'Angaine supported it because: 'it was bad for children to be born in an ordinary ward, amongst sick people'.[34]

Conventional wisdom among Africans had always called for a physical separation between the sick and the expectant because expectant women and newly delivered mothers and their children ran the risk of being infected with diseases when they were admitted in the general wards. Initial efforts to medicalize maternity in the absence of separate facilities for birthing thus only served to discourage the hospitalization of expectant women.

The situation was no better in the general wards. Because of room shortages, infants might be admitted in hospital without their mothers. Such children might sleep with women who were not their mothers. It was reported that at times these children might fall out of bed. In Meru hospital, the overnight overseer at the hospital denied these claims. However, in 1948 a request was put for a separate children's room with children's cots. The cots would be for children under three years of age. At the time 'only children being breastfed were being admitted with their mothers.'[35]

Efforts to institutionalize modern medicine thus rearranged social conventions and thwarted other customary expectations concerning maternity care, as well. Could it happen that a woman was admitted in the same ward as her father-in-law and occupied a bed next to his? Might a woman give birth while admitted in the same ward as her father-in-law? There was no end to the multiplicity of possible social infractions. Finally, in 1945, a maternity ward was built at Meru Hospital. That this ward was placed under the supervision of a female dresser was itself a milestone, a recognition that the institutionalization of Western medical practices for women had to take into account indigenous sensibilities. However, male dressers attended to births, a practice that was contrary to custom. Mr. Samson Njoroge, who was among the first Africans to train as a dresser at Kikuyu Hospital in 1908, was also among the first male midwives. 'He soon found himself regarded as an outcast. This was because he had touched dead bodies, contrary to the accepted way of life. He had also learnt to conduct deliveries and as such he could not be allowed to mix with other people.'[36]

The novelty of African male midwifery was tolerated only until women could take their place. Sara Sarai, who trained as a midwife before 1950, did not allow men to witness deliveries. Still agitated about the situation, Sara observed that wherever she practised, ' No man would dare come near during delivery. I was fierce, *uuuuuu*![37] As one of the first midwives trained in Western medicine, Sara was a novelty in her world. Referred to as 'doctor' at Mbiri, where she practised, Sara continued to work with white male doctors and auxiliary African female staff at Murang'a. Recognizing their medical expertise, Sara was not opposed to the participation of male European doctors in birthing. It was the spectacle of indigenous males that irked Sara and others like her. In this respect, she was both a catalyst for change and a defender of custom, restoring birthing to the female domain. In Sara's and the community's understanding, the European male doctors were not categorized as men. They were purveyors of Western medicine, specialists who were not bound by social or ritual restrictions: they could cross gender lines. Like Sara the 'doctor', they constituted a new stratum of society, one that was not constrained by custom. This effort to represent male European doctors in a genderless mode is odd for an institution that was so charged with gendered constructions. Although the incursion of native men into traditionally female roles under the aegis of Western medicine was frowned upon, men dominated in the administration of maternity care, a hegemony that was not limited to the financial control of resources. Indigenous authority structures at the family level did not readily allow the usurpation of their powers by the practitioners of modern medicine, and women would not be given a free hand in accessing Western medicine. The institutionalization of maternity, to the extent that it was successful, did not overthrow traditional gender roles. This interfered with the provision of maternity care.

For example, a husband's permission was required before a woman could be operated upon. In 1947, however, it was reported at a Meru LNC meeting that the CNC had found it necessary to invoke the discretionary power of the doctor to operate on a willing woman 'in certain cases without [the] husband's consent'. While the Meru LNC was in agreement with and adopted the view of the CNC, protocol demanded that the point be submitted to the government. Until it had made a decision, the prevailing practice with regard to the operation of women would remain in force. When traditional gender roles and the dictates of modern medicine clashed, in the long run, the authority of traditional gender roles won. In Nyeri, at the beginning of 1948, the LNC 'agreed that in each and every case the husband, or if he was not available, his brother, should be consulted'.[38]

During the 1947 deliberations, a Dr. Sandford had 'instanced a recent case where the refusal of a husband to allow an operation on his wife resulted in her being rendered permanently sterile.'[39] Proof of fertility, and its perpetuation was vital for a wife's social acceptance and legitimation in a marriage and within a marital lineage. Sterility would mean that she could not participate in the perpetuation of her husband's kinship group. In as much as Western medicine promised to facilitate this very primary reproductive role of women, the doctors might have hoped to get unreserved support from the male councillors who mediated Western medicine in their localities, but it was not always the case.

The hospitals themselves were not particularly hospitable to pregnant indigenous women. The representatives of Western medicine urged women to get into hospitals before they went into labour, and in cases where women did not know their expected date of delivery, they might go to hospitals earlier than necessary and wait out the birth of their children. During this interim period, the women complained, 'they did not get food that they liked and as their homes were a long way off their families were unable to supplement the hospital rations'.[40] No details are available about hospital food, but it can be expected that they supplied a rationalized diet that was considered to be nutritionally appropriate in terms of Western medicine. Indigenous tradition and custom, however, dictated specific food guidelines for pregnant women. Among the Luo, for example, 'the restrictions aim[ed] mainly at minimizing the chances of the child being too big, thus rendering it easier for the mother to give birth.'[41] For this reason, bananas, which were considered fattening, were eliminated from the diet, besides other sugary items. The poor reputation of modern maternity wards, with their unappealing diets, was spread by former hospital inmates, undermining efforts to persuade women to attend for care. Elsewhere, at Maua Methodist mission hospital no food was provided for maternity patients, a factor that caused concern among Council members. While requesting that food be provided, the council 'was willing to make a grant if necessary additional to the present grant'.[42] The matter necessitated consultation between the council president and Dr. Stanley Bell of the hospital.

Whether the women were talking about regular foods or special cravings is unclear. Food is cultural. These pregnant women felt alienated and frustrated by hospital food; the regimented cuisine at these centres of modern medicine clearly left a lot to be desired. Amidst a general increase of rations for other patients 'other than that of those in Maternity Block' and pending investigations about the rations, the Nyeri Medical Officer requested supplementary estimates of Shs. 3,500 in 1948 for feeding of patients in the maternity block.[43] Once more, cultural difference and medical absurdity were evident. While it was common for expectant women in certain communities to observe dietary sanctions, we have no evidence of total denial of food in those communities. The measures at Maua and Nyeri hospitals were irrational and potentially medically harmful.

Maternity, Motherhood, and Cultural (Ex)change: Clothing and Difference

In a variety of ways, maternity wards served as sites at which women confronted and negotiated the encounter between traditional culture and modernity in colonial Kenya. In addition to the conflicts and problems we already have explored, the issues raised at these sites included the Christianization of maternity, the imposition of Western notions of propriety and decency of dress, and the participation of women in practices with widespread cultural significance – including infanticide and abortion.

In precolonial Kenya, childbirth was part of a wider social-cultural construction among all native societies. Adherence to the Christian faith was expected to stop continued belief in and practice of local rituals and observations deemed backward, irrational, and heathen, including those surrounding childbirth. Christian dogma was used to discredit local constructions of pregnancy, birthing, stillbirths, and infant mortality. Attributions of paganism, superstition, and unhygienic practices were used to discourage traditional birthing, while Western medicine and maternity were praised for bringing civilization, health, progress, and even spiritual uplift. The author of the 1948 *Chogoria Mission Hospital Annual Report* demonstrated ways in which missions helped eliminate these beliefs:

> The spirit is irradiating the most ordinary people. In the maternity ward a mother had lost her first baby but instead of disappointment and the fear of defilement by death that is so often there as a hangover from paganism she was full of triumph that the Lord had done what was best and that he made no mistakes.... [One year later,] [t]here she was, the same woman, but this time a newborn mite was murmuring away in the cot beside her.[44]

Part of the missionary cure for the 'hangover from paganism', involved re-dressing pregnant indigenous women. While clothing was and is personal, a mark of one's identity, it also binds people in social relationships. Issues involving clothes thus serve as one measure of community changes in colonial Kenya. Clothes map physical and ideological migrations and encounters.[45] The fashion of maternity dresses at Murang'a, for example, did not meet colonial notions of decency, and the indecent exposure of women's bodies was another colonial violation of social order. In 1940, the Fort Hall LNC observed that the clothes '[left] nothing to the imagination'[46] and resolved to budget for 'more flowing garments' in the next supplementary estimate. Controversy over maternity clothes took a different form in Meru hospitals. In 1948 the president of the LNC observed that 'one of the complaints apparently was that women were dressed in man's [sic] shorts and shirts.'[47] The Medical Officer explained that at times there was an insufficient number of dresses, making it necessary to dress women in men's outfits, and he promised to try to get more dresses. It is not beyond reason to assume that this cross-dressing so infuriated both male and female patients that they might have concluded that it was a colonial prank. At any rate, it is amusing to imagine the debates that the situation might have generated regarding European gender ideology and the question of cross-dressing. By the mid-1940s, however, Kenyans had restructured their sense of clothing style to such an extent as to cover up most of their bodies.[48]

Just as some expectant women's efforts to access modern medicine entailed the wearing of men's clothing, the general transition by women from traditional costumes to imported cloth caused dismay in the community. The complaint from the Fort Hall LNC mirrors the tensions and transitions between culture, Christianity and modernity. In 1933 chief Kimani wa Thuo had observed that:

> It was becoming a prevailing custom for non-Christian women, especially young girls to wear white *shukas* [an unstitched piece of cloth] instead of skins which was the time,[sic] honoured dress of women. He considered that the *shuka* as presently worn was not decent and asked for the opinion of the council.[49]

Christian girls wore 'European' clothes, but even these were problematic since they did not come below the knee. It was Kimani's hope that these women would drop the hemlines of their clothes to the appropriate length. The president was noncommittal in his response to this dress code issue. He was of the opinion that the matter could be dealt with 'by the chiefs in conjunction with the relatives of the women who did not wear dress in keeping with the wishes of the people.'[50] Exaggerated accounts of women's dressing possibly reflected the pervasive rate of change and the extent to which the trend differed from conventional European pattern.

Administrators' accounts about female clothing were juxtaposed with observations of other material culture denoting changing notions of domesticity. From separate kitchens which were becoming common once it was known that these were not taxed as huts, to enamel mugs, plates, *sufurias*, and cheap boxes for keeping clothes, the DC South Kavirondo created a long catalogue of such acquisitions by 1927.

Even courtship changed as it became, in some ways, predicated on the new consumption patterns of the women:

> Maidens have now taken to demanding clothes for[sic-from] their admirers in return for services rendered. They take the form of a single piece of garment and are frequently displayed into *dukas* [shops] on dummy figures. Unfortunately hats and coloured glasses, instead of being merely a decoration, shortly become absolute necessities.[51]

Women were said to goad their husbands into waged labour to raise money for the purchase of consumer goods, especially clothes. That dependence on males did not always augur well for some women. A husband might turn up with any manner of dress; some of their choices were most offensive and a source of perpetual pain and displeasure on the part of the woman. Bought in the absence of the woman and to the man's taste and or financial situation, a whole range of things might be wrong with the attire including the size, material, or style. Sometimes all three attributes were deemed wrong. As Beth Njambi observed, this situation mirrored the myriad ways in which that dress signified the subjugated predicament of women in the rural areas:

> Sometimes you would be given a single *gakuo* [dress defined in its diminutive form] like this one. It would be brought to you, you would never go to the shop and enquire of the Asian [shop owner] as to the price of the dress [you had no choice]. The dress would be thrown to you [by the husband and he would say], 'there is a dress'.... Today as we speak, nobody can bring you a dress and tell you 'there is a dress'.... Not even Kigo's father [informant's husband] can bring a dress and throw it to me saying 'there is a dress'. He can only say ' try that dress and see if it fits you.' In those days ... you might be brought a dress that had no plan [an ill-fitting dress] ... a khaki dress that will continually hassle you; it has nothing, khaki! Do you know khaki? It is what is now used to make school uniforms. It [khaki] used to be referred to as prison attire. It was very rough and your hands would bleed as you tried to wash it. In a year or two that might be the only dress he brings.[52]

In general, however, there was a great demand for European clothes of every variety. As the DC for Kavirondo had noted in his 1927 report, 'Fine clothes are used merely for show and are sometimes hired out to friends.'[53] In the light of the above debates, it is clear that Western clothes elicited all manner of responses. The community too subjected clothes provided for pregnant women at hospitals to the same critical gaze. They were ill-fitting specimens of modernity, which also offended the social sensibilities of the community. In many ways, they were clothes without a plan.

Increasingly, however, the female body was no longer for everybody's eyes. Hospitals, on the other hand, did not always respect this change in African sensibilities. In Meru, there was concern about the privacy of children and females being inoculated against a variety of diseases. In 1936, a member of the Meru LNC, Philipo, appealed to the Medical Officer requesting that 'women be inoculated in some private place instead of in public as at present'.[54] By 1948 the situation remained far from satisfactory and the council found itself reiterating the suggestions that the inoculation of women be done inside the outpatient building.[55]

Infanticide

While the efforts to impose notions of decency on women in maternity wards had its light moments, the full extent to which maternity wards served as negotiating sites for culture and modernity was evident in controversies that arose over more serious issues – infanticide and abortion. These conflicts emanated from a belief among the Kipsigis and the Meru that conception before initiation is contemptible and ought to be regarded as a crime. It was feared that sex prior to circumcision and hence premarital pregnancy evoked supernatural powers and overwhelming evil. The preservation of social order thus required the intervention of the community. It was also believed that children born in such situations 'would be weaklings', both physically and mentally, as well as ritually impure. Girls who conceived prior to initiation were not only considered ritually unclean, but were said to become barren after giving birth.

Girls who conceived before circumcision were humiliated and ostracized, and it was said not only that 'they usually end up by turning prostitutes and leaving the [Kipsigis] country altogether', but that 'when they are rich they return here and introduce into the blood of the tribe the virus of syphilis, from which it has been comparatively free until recently, according to local medical observation.'[56] The pathologization of these women created a desire in some quarters to annihilate their progeny, both physically and from the collective memory.

To prevent this social, ritual, and potentially physical blemish on the community, such girls would be rushed to initiation as soon as their pregnancy was discovered. Then the child was suffocated with mud during birth: 'Immediately the child's head appear[ed], the old woman who [was] assisting the girl cram[med] its mouth and nose with mud, so that it may not utter a single cry.'[57] The Kipsigis LNC minutes of 6 October 1926 indicate that where it was feared that a girl intended to keep a baby conceived under the above circumstances, old women [birth attendants, midwives] killed the baby in the girl's womb. This inflicted excruciating pain on the girl and the foetus. According to J. G. Peristiany, if the child died at birth, the girl would be spared disgrace. A ritual sacrifice by the girl's father would remove all uncleanliness, and she could 'behave like a normal person' again.[58]

In the precolonial world of the Kipsigis, if such a child were allowed to survive, the mother could never marry as long as it lived. This remained the case for some time during the colonial period. Young women who were able to prevent their children from being killed in these circumstances suffered in other ways. To the degree that efforts to prevent infanticide were successful, they propagated a different form of pain and loss. For most of their adult life, women's identity, especially their social status, was defined within the institution of marriage. This was the frame on which the complex tapestry of a woman's life as a wife, daughter-in-law, sister-in-law, co-wife, mother, grandmother, producer, and reproducer among other roles was woven. Her agency as an adult in society was dependent upon these various sets of relationships. In general, her status as a daughter became insignificant as she grew older. A woman who did not get married thus was condemned to social stasis. While an unmarried woman could attain some of the above positions by virtue of being a member of a lineage, she did not have the leverage to execute some of the responsibilities or enjoy some of the privileges, which came at different times of a woman's life cycle. Measures that enabled a mother to decide to keep a baby which society had condemned to death thus entailed social death for the woman. Children who escaped suffocation faced an even worse lot, for they still might be killed in a number of ways including strangulation, exposure, or mere neglect.

Infanticide was by no means a general practice when it became an issue for the colonial administrators. When the colonial government requested administrators in the areas adjoining Kipsigis territory to find out what the situation was, the Officer-in-Charge of Maasai reported that the practice of killing infants born to uncircumcised girls was unknown among the Maasai.[59] Among the Nandi, infanticide had also almost died out. In summarizing the field report from the DC for Nandi, the PC for the Rift Valley did not see any need for any special legislation to deal with the issue. The same was true for Elgeyo, where infanticide was 'not a matter of great importance'.[60] However, the Kipsigis were not the only ethnic group for whom conception and motherhood before initiation were abhorrent. Among the Meru, such girls were disgraced and the resultant progeny perceived as social outcasts who were a danger to the kinship and wider community. Because clitoridectomy was a prenuptial rite among the Meru, girls would become sexually mature, and at times sexually active, a sure recipe for pre-excision pregnancy. Lynn Thomas has shown how among the Meru, pre-initiation pregnancies were dealt with by abortions.[61]

In order to prevent this cruel practice, colonial officials advocated and sought to enforce excision before puberty.[62] During the mid-1930s, the heyday of anti-abortionist deliberations in Meru, efforts to counter abortion with prepubescent clitoridectomy antagonized those opposed to any form of excision and thus elided the two issues. Consequently, when post pubescent excision became a punishable crime under the Native Tribunals Ordinance,[63] girls were initiated into a 'nuptial' mode much earlier.

Not satisfied that civic responsibility would ensure adherence to the Local Native Council requirement for prepubescent clitoridectomy, Meru local authorities organized sporadic mass initiations from the middle of the 1930s to the beginning of the 1950s. The surprise element in these forced excisions earned them the name *kigwarie,* 'the one which was unexpected'.[64] While some girls resorted to flight, some parents bribed the *kigwarie* perpetrators in order to avoid the subjection of their daughters to this unconventional rite. As in the case of pre-initiation pregnancies and abortions among the Meru, efforts to institute 'enlightened' practices for motherhood and childbirth not only transformed women's sexuality into contested territory but also resulted in unforeseen negative consequences.

Among the Kipsigis, where infanticide occurred and where the missionaries and the colonial administration consequently turned their attention, women's sexuality was doubly contested. As with the Meru, the issue of infanticide was linked to the issue of clitoridectomy and thus in the preservation of ethnic identity, a nexus of contested issues we have already explored. Clitoridectomy was a prerequisite for marriage, pregnancy, and thus for motherhood.

Although Kipsigis customary practices provided for the termination of pre-initiation pregnancies, it was obviously doubly traumatizing to the girls who fell victim of the practice to allow the pregnancy to come to full term and then kill the newborn baby. It is not surprising that girls who conceived before initiation were quick to seek refuge at mission maternity hospitals and wards, once these were established in their localities. Uncircumcised women could keep their babies there. By taking advantage of the ability to escape to these new spaces in order to save their infants, the women were thus necessarily questioning conventional wisdom and societal construction of maternity, citizenship, and sexuality.

There was not much room in either the conventional attitudes upholding infanticide, where it occurred, or in the supposedly enlightened and medicalized attitudes toward pregnancy and birth espoused by the colonial administrators to contest these issues. LNC discussions in 1930, 1931, 1935, 1936, 1938, 1939, 1940, and 1942 registered 'increasing general condemnation of the practice', but not sufficient will to abolish it. As late as 1942, the Kipsigis LNC was still trying unsuccessfully to make the mission solution to the problem of infanticide official by hospitalizing the mother, ensuring that the baby would be born safely, then putting the baby up for adoption. As part of the regulatory structure, the parents or guardians of Kipsigis girls participating in this restructured solution were to ensure that the girls did not abscond from the programme. The girls were expected to stay in the mission hospital with their infants for a period of six months. The idea was to let the baby benefit from breast-feeding while at the same time allowing the mother and child to bond. During this period, the girl might choose to keep the baby. If not, the baby would have benefited psychologically from the mother's proximity, and, the mother would have had time to make adequate arrangement for the adoption of the child.[65] This legislation on motherhood and maternal bond was a new frontier in colonial Kenya. While it was a less drastic solution to the problem than the traditional set-up, it still introduced a major shift in the formulations of motherhood in the context of the infanticide controversy.

In many ways, the LNC was ahead of its time on the question of adoption. The Council was aware that 'if a referendum [on adoption] was taken, [it] would be lost by a great majority'. The missions, which offered to keep the children, were said to 'unwittingly bring in a new evil in the neighbourhood'. Despite that, the appeal of this strategy from the Kipsigis point of view was that it would keep the children from automatic absorption into the lineage. Whether the adoption of such children would be forbidden among the Kipsigis was not addressed in the LNC deliberations, but it can be assumed that the LNC anticipated that no Kipsigis would reintroduce these 'blemished ' children into the social fabric of the community: they constituted social capital that the LNC was willing to discard. This way, ritually unclean motherhood would not pollute the ethnicity. In this context, the mission station was looked upon as constituting a different people, although it was located in Kipsigis land. As in the case of the Meru families who did not circumcise their daughters, or Meru men who married uncircumcised girls and were considered detribalized *Misheni,* it was all right for children born to uncircumcised Kipsigis girls to stay at Litein Mission. They were not Kipsigis: they were something else.

Although F. D. Hislop, the DC in the affected Kipsigis area, felt obliged to support the LNC's adoption proposal in order 'to bring enlightenment' to 'the African Middle Ages of night, cruelty, [and] superstition', setting them on 'the path of civilization',[66] this solution proved unacceptable to both the principal groups with final authority over the matter. Those who considered both the girl and her baby to be polluted believed that the condition called for drastic action – infanticide – if the social purity of the wider community was to be maintained. The colonial administration, despite the ideological paternalism evident in Hislop's remark, was willing to cave in to popular opinion.[67] This outcome was indicative of the predicament of women on the frontier. They could find themselves between a rock and a hard place, their ability to have a say in their own reproductive activities ignored by both those who upheld native customs and by the colonial administrators as it made compromises in crafting public policy.

The marriageability of such women was at stake since even after they were circumcised they were still considered unclean. No self-respecting

Kipsigis man would marry such a girl. On the other hand, if a girl became pregnant before marriage but after circumcision, there was no long-term disgrace involved and after the necessary rites her child was considered an asset in her father's lineage. It is for this reason that the suggestion of the circumcision of girls before puberty was touted as a possible remedy to the problem.

Although in general the men responsible did not marry girls who became pregnant before circumcision, by 1942, there were reports of one such marriage in the recent past in Kipsigis land. In another case, a man who was responsible for impregnating an uncircumcised girl had married her and had accepted her baby, and the three were said to be living happily. So in small ways, opinion about this custom was beginning to change. Because infanticide involved deciding who was qualified to inhabit the Kipsigis nation, killing of children born under 'impure' circumstances still perpetuated the myth of ethnic purity.

In the West, infanticide was ultimately represented as a social crime. As a remedy, foundling hospitals were established where unwed mothers could have their children and adoptions arranged. Such cases were less intricate in that only the unmarried state of the woman was in question. In supporting the three maternity wards in Kipsigis land, the LNC was said to be emulating the foundling hospitals, which had come into existence in Europe in the Middle Ages. This action subverted conventional notions of sexual morality and self-perpetuation. That the activities of the council were described in metaphors of civilization and enlightenment illustrates the pervasiveness of colonial paternalism.

What seemed paradoxical to the colonial officials and even to local people opposed to infanticide was the collaboration and indeed the prominence of women in the process. But, as this study has shown repeatedly, women did not constitute a homogeneous group. They adopted divergent positions over various issues. While the authorities believed that nearly all women supported the practice, it is safe to assume that it was older women who were more likely to support old customs in larger numbers. In their role as matriarchs and midwives, older women were in a perfect position to enforce conformity with the sanctions that followed sex and pregnancy prior to circumcision, and to thwart efforts from whichever quarter seeking to change the status quo. Dubbed 'the final conservatives', these women were represented as an impediment to civilization.[68] Under other circumstances, colonial officials represented these women positively as the custodians of tradition in a rapidly changing colonial context. However, infanticide fitted uncomfortably into the category of traditions that colonial officials liked to think they were upholding. It survived in the realm of the unspoken, the unacknowledged, and the erasable.

By contrast, those women – often younger women – who sought to access a variety of spaces recently made available, including formal education, waged employment, and urban centres, challenged indigenous patriarchs who preferred that women and girls remain in the rural areas as much as possible. In the infanticide controversy, girls seized the mission maternity opportunity, in particular, to minimize the potential repercussions of their predicament.

Challenges to the practice of infanticide grew as the process of colonization altered the social and cultural landscape that Kenyan women inhabited. As a culturally constructed practice, infanticide required acceptance of a specific cosmological worldview. That and the socio-ritual fabric it entailed were beginning to be abandoned as a small, albeit increasing segment of the Kipsigis community began to question the rationale for infanticide. The mission became a site for renegotiating the predicament of mother and child caught in this controversy.

In 1926, for example, senior chiefs, elders, and headmen in the Kipsigis LNC who were keen on stopping infanticide submitted a memorandum which suggested that:

1. The old women who killed these children should suffer the death penalty.
2. That persons cognizant of the offence should be fined shs.200/=, also a father or mother who permitted it should be fined shs.200/= unless reported.
3. That any girls in this condition should be taken to Litein Africa Inland Mission.
4. That the young man responsible for the girl's condition should provide for the child with cow milk.
5. [That] the girl's father was to provide food for her [while she was at the mission].
6. When the child has reached the age of six months, the girl can choose to return to her home or stay at the mission, but the child will remain in the mission.[69]

While the mother could return to her community after a prescribed time, to the social death that was her fate, the child was permanently banished to a mission life or to adoption, a life away from 'society'. To gain even limited acceptance into her community, the woman had to relinquish her right to motherhood.

Infanticide proved difficult to eradicate, and even this reworking of the way to deal with pregnant uncircumcised girls was not acceptable to some sections of the Kipsigis community. The 1926 Kipsigis LNC was divided fifteen to fifteen for and against this proposed solution, and in such an impasse, the anti-infanticide members cut their losses.[70] The council agreed that 'the best remedy was the early circumcision of girls, until such time as there was a more general wish to do away with the custom [of infanticide].' For a community in which the circumcision of girls represented the attainment of adulthood and coming of age, such a shift in the timing of circumcision would entail a major restructuring of the meaning of the ritual and profoundly alter the construction of womanhood. On the other hand, even the adoption of the revised time of circumcision would not erase the community's practice of defining females by the refashioning of their bodies and maintaining surveillance over their sexuality. Other solutions suggested for ensuring that uncircumcised girls did not get pregnant also had inherent problems. It was possible to marry off girls immediately after the period of seclusion that followed circumcision. However, since at this stage the girls were still relatively young, marriage would exacerbate the problem of child marriage.

Ultimately, the Kipsigis LNC decided to vote funds for two missions, Litein and Tenwek, to 'maintain special maternity wards for uncircumcised pregnant girls, providing a safe haven'. In addition, the funds would pay for four special *askari*, policemen, entrusted with the task of collecting and reporting to chiefs information about pregnant uncircumcised girls in the four divisions. Maternity thus had been transformed into an officially supervised process, not a matter of cultural surveillance. Effort would be made to help the girls get into any one of these maternity wards. This financial commitment started in 1934, and the council continued both to honor and increase its cash contribution. By 1942, the LNC hoped to obtain legal power to enforce the mission intervention strategy described above.

Preventing infanticide by official supervision of pregnant uncircumcised women, however, proved difficult. Infanticide continued, and attempts to prosecute perpetrators of infanticide during 1926, 1927, 1928, and 1935 proved unsuccessful due to lack of evidence and the general high mortality rate from normal births. This made it difficult for the authorities to prove foul play in suspected cases. Part of the frustration in trying to stop infanticide emanated from the fact that birthing was largely a private affair, and there was suspicion that the crime would continue to be practised in secret.

British Precedents

A large number of the changes were tailored on British precedents. In Britain the Affiliation Order ensured the financial input of men responsible for fathering children but not marrying the women. The Kipsigis LNC sought to introduce a similar maintenance fee. The men would pay shs.100/= per year toward the infant's upbringing. Since the child would spend its infancy in a mission maternity pending adoption, the money would be transferred 'in toto' to the mission hospitals on a prorated basis depending on the number of children each maternity was handling. The council would pick up any deficit arising from default and extend a basic grant to the hospitals.

For a council that was half-hearted in its commitment to the abolition of infanticide, it is interesting to note the extent to which it was willing to divest itself of its limited resources in an effort to salvage some dignity through its solution to the problem.

The contestation, transformation and ultimate annihilation of old customs resulted in a reformulation of some familiar notions of motherhood, which now could be brought to an abrupt end, not due to the death of the infant, but due to what was tantamount to a forced removal of the baby. In this respect, formal adoption became an alternative to mother parenting, and an abundance of willing foster-parents appeared. It was important to the prospective foster parents that the adoption paperwork was done correctly to ensure that it could not be revoked in the future. Despite that, the minority LNC members opposed to infanticide believed that it was 'completely repugnant to justice and morality and is essentially at variance with the law of the colony.'[71] The missions were in agreement with the proposals put forward by the council and hoped that the resolution would find favor with His Excellency the Governor. For a young mother, giving consent to her child's adoption was no doubt an agonizing decision. Still, compared to the possibility of infanticide, it was a major reprieve. The community had no positive comments about the fate of women whose children had suffered infanticide. Colonialism had created new spaces which provided safe havens for these women who continued to be considered unclean and unnatural. They were said to flee to urban centres where they became prostitutes. In leaving the rural areas, the women, like their children, would represent social capital lost to the region; more importantly, their movement ensured the moral cleansing of the land, an important process for the ethical well being of the country. Maternity did not only replenish populations; it could contaminate them. The banishment of such mothers was seen as one solution. The space they evidently occupied, that of prostitution, became associated with problematic children. A rapid connection developed between the social ostracization of such migrated women and their pathologization.

Prostitutes, Ethnicity and Motherhood

It was argued that when they [the infanticide controversy women] eventually returned to their homes as rich madams from their urban sojourn, they also 'introduce[d] into the blood of the tribe the virus of syphilis, from which it [the tribe] has been comparatively free until recently', according to local medical observations.[72] As if in a last ditch effort to destroy the 'tribe', the women returned as vectors of a contagious venereal disease that would destroy the health of the community. In their imagined form, the women attained epidemic proportions evidenced by the character aspersions such women were subjected to. Coming full circle, the women's sexuality was represented as a dangerous tool that destroyed the ritual, moral and medical health of their homeland. This representation ignored the phenomenon of male migrants and returning veterans of World Wars I and II, some of who were proven to have contacted venereal diseases at their places of work and introduced these to the rural areas.

While Kipsigis LNC did not belabour the issue of the polluting nature of returning prostitutes created by the infanticide ordeal, there were ample discussions regarding other types of prostitutes in the country. The age-long link between town and prostitution was a constant in rural discourses about this problem. Top among the undesirable urban towns was Nairobi, the colony's capital. It was readily associated with low life, lack of normative purity and evasion of sanctioned civic duties and responsibilities. It is important to explore further the concern of rural [male] leadership with the issue of prostitution in order to underscore the gender asymmetry in notions of social pollution and maternity associated with errant female sexuality. Thus, in discussing the predicament of Kikuyu people living in Nairobi, several members of the Fort Hall LNC believed that ' Nairobi was a cesspool of loafers, harlots and tax evaders.' The chiefs were willing to provide the District Commissioner in Nairobi with information 'regarding Kikuyu tax evaders whose names and whereabouts the chiefs could indicate'.[73] Rural legislators advocated the prohibition of African women from going to Nairobi to sell produce, where they risked disease and low morals. This was said to be the unanimous conviction of the population in the rural area. Here, 'there were strong feelings among all sections in the Reserve in favor of such a measure.'[74] In an uncharacteristic response, the chairman of the council indicated that the control of women was a domestic affair 'and that it would be useless to put such a resolution for his Excellency's approval; Headmen and Elders should use their personal influence to prevent undesirable tendencies among women, but legislation was incapable of controlling women's morality.'[75]

Although prostitution was often represented in metaphors of disease, contamination, and infection, venereal diseases were not limited to prostitutes. In 1926 the Fort Hall Native Council resolved that ' [I]t shall be an offence for any person to conceal the fact that he or she is suffering from venereal disease.'[76] The health of the community pre-empted an individual's claim to medical privacy.

Sometimes the rural-urban divide became blurred when prostitutes operated from townships that served as district headquarters for the surrounding rural areas. LNC deliberated on issues affecting both these urban centres and the rural environs. In 1930 Job Muchuchu of the Fort Hall LNC suggested that prostitutes be evicted from Fort Hall town 'and made to return to their homes as in his opinion they did immense harm and were a bad example for young women and girls who came into the townships for their shopping.' The fact that if evicted these women would return to more populous and supposedly less 'contaminated' areas as represented by the councillors created a no win situation. The only workable solution would be to minimize damage. As another councillor, Joseph Mungu observed, 'their influence might be even worse in the villages than in townships.'[77] That the majority of councillors disagreed with the latter suggestion is interesting. Representations of the rural area as a pristine environment susceptible to contamination by women returning from towns are pervasive. It does seem probable that there was a general belief that rural areas did not present fertile ground for prostitution and that in good time the prostitutes would reform. The hope was that rural moral sensibility and sense of social order would set them straight.

The task of enforcing the eviction of prostitutes from Fort Hall town to the reserve was left to the president of the council, the District Commissioner.

Fear about the danger that would befall reserves if prostitutes were cleared out of townships continued to haunt rural councillors. In 1943 the Nyeri District African Council deliberated on ways to combat the menace and concluded that prostitutes 'should be segregated in places set apart in towns, and, once entered, never allowed to return to entice other girls to follow their example'.[78] In this context it is important to point out that according to Peristiany, women caught up in the infanticide controversy experienced temporary physical banishment: '[A]t the day of parturition, the girl is taken outside into the bush, and far from all human habitation, so that she may not soil them by the proximity of her blood.'[79] Prostitution continued to be represented as a contagious disease warranting the isolation of the carrier. A decade after Fort Hall councillors expressed their hope that prostitutes relocated from towns to rural areas would be reformed by the good life therein; the Nyeri councillors did not want anything to do with those of their kinswomen who had resorted to prostitution in towns. They wanted them isolated away from the rural area.

Prostitution, however, was sometimes right next door. In this case, Karatina, a budding township was located right in the middle of the Nyeri reserve. It was one thing to restrict prostitutes to some distant town. It was different to have them in one's backyard. The colony had dozens of such townships. Houses in Karatina used for prostitution were portrayed as a moral and architectural blight. In 1943 the councillors approved the following resolution empowering the Headman to demand demolition of such premises:

> If any building erected within two miles of a trading centre or recognized market is, in the opinion of Headman, being used as a brothel, lodging house, eating house, or is being rented or sub-let by the owner, or the building is being occupied by a native not normally resident within his jurisdiction, he may order the owner or occupier to remove the house within fourteen days. Such an order will be given when the Headman has received permission in writing of the DC to do so and the DC will only grant the order if he is satisfied that the continuance of the building *is likely to prejudice the health and well-being of the natives residing within the Headman's jurisdiction.*[80]

The president of the Council drafted this resolution. Before its presentation, the councillors had requested the introduction of a law, triable by Native Tribunals empowering chiefs 'to order the vacation of any house, which in his opinion was being used, for an immoral or disorderly purpose'. Quite obviously the president had more stringent recommendations, with which the councillors were in total agreement.

Even in custody, prostitutes were regarded as a blight to the prison population. The concern to quarantine prostitutes was common. Sometimes charging them with vagrancy and imposing a custodial sentence upon failure to pay fines achieved this. During one such scheme in Kisumu, the prostitute received medical attention while in prison, and in isolation. As each was declared free from venereal infection, she would be released and deported to her village with the admonition 'never again to show her face in Kisumu'.[81] This effort to localize the scourge by not sending infected prostitutes to the village created additional problems in Kisumu. Some of the warders and convicts had already contracted the disease.

Councillors in Nyeri were particularly concerned about the mixing in custody of young females who were first-time offenders with prostitutes from Nanyuki and elsewhere. The breach of sexual mores seemed to evoke stronger social sanction than any other crime. The young detainees were represented as innocent, pure, reproductive potential, the prostitutes as older, hardened offenders who needed to be isolated from other detainees. Prostitutes were not generally associated with procreation. As we shall see, this was a false premise, which also put their motherhood to question.

The councillors suggested the physical removal of the prostitutes 'out of the environs of the native location'.[82] The line between order and disorder had to be drawn. In May 1945 the council suggested that the prostitutes be moved to an Agricultural Department Farm where they would perform manual labour. It seemed they could not be punished enough. Later, still concerned about the mixing of 'minor' offenders with prostitutes, and believing that 'the two categories' should be 'segregated', the council suggested that prostitutes be held in jail and the other offenders in a detention camp. The onus was on Tribunal elders at Mathira 'to give special consideration to this problem when convicting females'.[83]

Prostitutes continued to return to the Reserve, often under court order. In the case of Nyeri they mostly came back from Nanyuki, a military post for British soldiers about fifty miles to the North of Nyeri. Once in the rural areas, the prostitutes opted to build their own houses rather live with their parents. It was asserted that these women 'carried on their trade' from their new abodes ' attracting other girls to join them and demoralizing the local youth'.[84] In all likelihood these women were able to purchase or lease land in the vicinity of the market square where they put up their houses. This investment was characteristic of the penetration of capital and the increasing wave of individualism in rural areas. This latter factor also afforded the women agency in determining various aspects of their lives. Luise White has argued that prostitutes in Nairobi established their own independent households and lineages. Motherhood was not alien to prostitutes.

In the rural areas their geographical proximity to community leaders made prostitutes subject to greater surveillance. Their immoral past might have been easier to overlook if it did not impact on the future of the community. These women were said to often have children who were fatherless and who were 'unable by custom to inherit any land, became a landless, rootless, urban class, prone to crime and vice'.[85] Prostitution did not preclude maternity. Unlike children of unwed mothers who in previous times were absorbed into their maternal grandfather's clan, children of prostitutes were criminalized along with their mothers. As with the infanticide controversy, the children were considered dangerous to the well-being of the community. As a social disorder, prostitutes were deemed to tear the moral and social fabric of the community. Rather than jeopardize the welfare of the group, the councillors wished for the chief 'to have the power to demolish existing houses [belonging to prostitutes] and prohibit the building of new ones.'[86] Both mothers and children were banished. Motherhood, that touchstone of womanhood could be a very troubled state for those labeled prostitutes.

By February 1946 the Nyeri African District Council had unanimously passed a Standing Resolution granting the chief the power to evict the owner or occupiers and demolish any dwelling structure, or other premises ' being used (a) for the purpose of a brothel or house of ill-fame; (b) for any other purpose which is prejudicial to the morality or the public peace'. Failure to comply with the chief's order was a punishable crime.[87] The presence, progeny and memory of these women would be smoked out of the Reserves. They had failed to measure up to the societal images of daughters, wives, mothers, and kin. The demolition of their houses would be symbolic of their banishment and the condemnation of the ideas they represented. Meru District was less forthright in its resolution. In similar circumstances as those found in Nyeri, the headman in Meru was empowered to 'order the owner of such dwelling, structure or other premises to take such action as such headman may consider necessary for preventing the use thereof for any such purpose'.[88]

In Nyeri, there was added anxiety about 'problems likely to be raised by prostitutes returning from the towns' after the Second World War. These prostitutes would seek to establish dwelling places in the villages. Afraid that these 'fallen' women would have a bad influence on the rural communities, the councillors advised 'strict control be exercised by chiefs over the erection of houses by such women'.[89] The reserves constituted imagined communities in which immoral women were not wanted. When they were allowed in, they were placed in a glass bowl for close surveillance.

So far, we have noted how various communities in their concern to preserve what they perceived as ethnic purity sanctioned women's sexuality, maternity, and motherhood. In this context, the communities identified many dangers lurking in public places. In Nyeri the councillors were wary of Indians who 'had been seen at Ruringu market on Saturdays and Sundays attempting to seduce African girls and women'.[90] Liaisons between local women and the Indians, who were most likely shopkeepers from Nyeri town, might result in unwanted offspring. The president of the council promised to take up the matter with the Local Indian Association.

Foster Motherhood

If the lives and maternity of uninitiated girls and prostitutes endangered the purity of their rural neighbourhood and put their motherhood to question, another development introduced a different dimension to motherhood.

In 1947, Chief Nkiria enquired whether the Native Civil Hospital, Chogoria Mission and Maua Mission Hospital could 'be asked to accept and nurture sucking infants whose mothers died in childbirth'.[91] The response of the members of the council was that the father of the infant could look for a foster mother or look after the child himself 'rather than have hospital beds otherwise needed for genuine hospital cases taken up'. For the father to have looked beyond the extended family in his search for maternal help was either indicative of a breakdown in family social networks which customarily would have provided such a service, or it was a question of imposing on the emerging maternal services of the hospital. There was always the possibility that the bereaved fathers were hoping to extend and use the services of an institution that claimed to revolutionize the maternal process.

On the other hand, the suggestion that the fathers take care of the children themselves was an even more radical reconceptualization of early infant nurturing, a suggestion of gender inversion. Previously a foster mother might have been located within the extended family network. By 1947, however, this would have been more difficult as changing socio-economic circumstances engendered individualism and atomization of family ties. It is perhaps in this vein that people at Chuka disagreed with the assertion that a bereaved father could always find a foster mother for his infant. Chief Petero suggested that the question regarding the provision of a home for motherless children should 'be submitted to the finance committee for the inclusion of the estimates'.[92] How long these children would be with either foster mothers or in homes for the motherless was not discussed. The general process of redefining and renegotiating maternal domestic responsibilities with some external authority was indicative of rapid social changes. The mothering of infants, like maternity was becoming a publicly supervised and negotiated process.

The Professionalization and Feminization of Maternity Personnel

Part of the process of medicalizing maternity entailed the restructuring of midwifery. Indigenous colonial functionaries were aware of the dire shortage of birthing nurses trained in Western medicine. In Nyeri, the African District Council therefore suggested the official recognition and reinstatement of traditional midwives. For a start, they anticipated the establishment of 'a service of certified village midwives at centres giving ante- and post-natal supervision as well as attending to delivery in the mothers' own homes'.[93] This would be under the aegis of the LNC, which would initially finance it without charge to the local population. In order to give more credence to the proposal and the project, it was suggested that a list of traditional midwives living at home should be compiled and the medical department asked to interview all possible candidates.

It must have been common knowledge to the council that the bulk of these midwives were responsible for the majority of births, which took place away from hospitals. Despite official reservations regarding their efficacy, the colonial administration hoped that more and more village midwives would be employed by LNCs. The Othaya Division in Nyeri had only five such employees by 1949. In general, the midwives received positive appraisals. At the same time, by accepting official engagement under the LNC, the midwives rendered themselves subject to official surveillance and to the sanctions that went with it. This enhanced further male intervention in maternity in colonial Kenya. Unlike other medical personnel, whose work would be evaluated by medical professionals, the village midwives were subject to the appraisal of local untrained male colonial functionaries such as chiefs and headmen. Quite obviously, this was not the most efficient approach to the transformation of maternity services. At best, the system was open to abuse. At worst, it reflected the rudimentary nature of the process of 'professionalization' of maternity services. For reasons that we can only speculate about, the above proposal was not very successful. Traditional midwives did not accept colonial employment in any large numbers, but that is not to say that they did not continue to practise their trade.

Patients, female medical workers, and the community at large increasingly expressed the need for incorporating African women into the medical profession. This need was especially great with regard to maternal health and childcare. In time, as women got more education and began to venture into professional training, nursing came a good second after teaching as a career choice. The association of nursing with nurturing and other maternal concerns seemed to create natural, albeit lower-status positions for women. At the same time, society responded to the increasing pressure for training women, especially in the maternity section of Western medicine. The desire for female intervention in midwifery was also elicited by local repulsion at the presence of male birth attendants.[94] Women's entry into other branches of medicine remained minimal, however. David Wakalo, who trained as a clinical officer from 1946 to 1949, captured the situation: 'During my days [at the Medical Training Centre] we had only one girl, Violet Wandua. She was a brave girl.'[95]

Government hospitals gave whatever rudimentary training they could to female employees of the hospital.[96] They were few. By 1936, female employees numbered 139. Of these, only 87 could read and write Swahili. Those who were in training were at the level of nursing orderlies.[97] As discussed earlier, until 1935, training at the Medical Training Depot was largely for men; at the introduction of hospitals, even the purely female domain of birthing was entrusted to men.

As in the case of formal education, it was mission groups that were in the forefront of providing training facilities for women in the medical field. They played the dual role of providing medical services to the community at large while training personnel. Recruitment was highly sectarian. In some cases, even the provision of medical services depended on the patient's denominational affiliation. In such a climate, the deployment of trained staff was partisan. It was not unusual for some to remain unemployed in the midst of dire shortage, as they waited for an opening in hospitals within their mission group.

The training of African women in the medical profession in many ways mirrors the secondary nature of girls' education in colonial Kenya. Parents, missionaries, and government officials considered the education of girls a minor investment compared with that of boys. As a result the education of girls tended to focus on 'domestic' skills. The domestication of women's education became a joint project of diverse agencies. Emphasis on nutrition, cookery, housewifery, laundry, sewing, and knitting largely encompassed the extent of women's education beyond literacy.[98] Therefore, one of the principal factors hampering women's entry into the medical profession for a long time was the paucity of sufficiently well-educated girls.

In 1933, the Kyambu LNC announced that there were vacancies for two 'probationers' at the African Maternity Hospital and Training Centre at Pumwani. Members were requested to submit the names of two 'suitable female candidates'.[99] The first two girls sent to Pumwani hospital for midwifery training had been considered unsuitable, possibly because they were not academically up to the challenge. The next batch was put on probation. In 1939, the Nyeri County Council suggested the selection of four suitable girls, one from each district, for training at Pumwani in Nairobi. Not wanting to risk a repeat of the first disaster, the Medical Officer preferred that the candidates undergo preliminary training at Murang'a Hospital as they awaited vacancies.[100] As early as 1934, it had been stated that work at Pumwani was conducted in Swahili, hence girls to be trained therein needed a good knowledge of the language.[101] A close watch was kept both on the trainees and the qualified staff. In 1940, two midwives in the Fort Hall hospitals were discharged for 'culpable negligence'. Their discharge was considered unavoidable 'to prevent further similar occurrences'.[102]

When women did eventually begin to enter the profession in the 1930s, they were initially trained as auxiliary staff helping male nurses and clinical assistants. The first cohort of female medical workers were trained and employed, not always in that order, in mission stations. In the wards, these women dressed wounds, waited upon the male staffers in their professional activities, and did general cleaning.

Bureaucratic inertia compounded the shortage of suitably educated women by limiting the resources necessary for women to enter the medical profession. For example, in November 1938, the Meru LNC enquired about the training of girls as midwives in Meru Hospital. The president of the council responded that midwifery training 'needed educated girls; the training was long, and it was not at present feasible'.[103] Although he did not elaborate on other problems associated with the request, in the first place, there was then no maternity ward at Meru Hospital. Neither was there a nursing sister posted at the hospital. The Medical Officer considered these two resources necessary for training to commence. Although he would request the LNC to vote for funds to build a maternity ward, initially, the Meru would have to make do with a Kikuyu trained midwife who would be instrumental in the training of Meru girls as midwives. The Medical Officer was reminded that the council had already voted for the construction of the maternity ward. Phillipo, a member of the council, wondered why the project was being held up, to which the president replied that there was no accommodation for a nursing sister at Meru. These kinds of bureaucratic entanglements were to a large extent avoided in mission hospitals where a mission's centralized administration was in charge of planning, training, providing infrastructure, and hiring and firing all personnel.

Another problem dogged the entry of women into the professions, as well. Kinsmen closely controlled their movement from their natal or marital homes. Quite often, employment necessitated physical relocation. In Murang'a, Maurice Gatithi of the LNC reiterated in 1941 what had become common practice. Referring to girls who were employed as nurses at Fort Hall Hospital, Gatithi said: 'girls should not be employed without the consent in writing of their father or guardian'.[104] In 1941 in Murang'a, as was the case in many other places in colonial Kenya, women's agency, the ability to chose education, careers, employment, or marital partners for themselves was still tenuous. Clearly, the debates of the 1920s and 1930s revolving around the status of native women, the age at which they acquired legal majority, and their ability to contract on their own had not abated in the 1940s. By 1944, there was still a massive shortage of nurses in the rural areas. The government asserted that the appeal from the Nyeri community for more African nurses in the reserves where they would reach more patients coincided with the government's future policy. Even at this late date, however, the request was viewed as unrealistic due to 'lack of proper training facilities'.[105]

Until 1950, the training of African female enrolled nurses and dressers was not systematic. Government training institutions were also few. The period 1950–1951 was a watershed in terms of girls' formal education and medical training. The establishment of what came to be the Alliance Girls' High School at Kikuyu was matched by the first major bulk admission of African girls for medical training. This was the first time the Department of Health had 'undertaken the training of educated girls as nurses on any considerable scale'.[106] Thus, in 1951, fourteen African girls were admitted to the Medical Training School in Nairobi, a low figure that still reflected the low standard of girl's education and lack of accommodation for girls at the various training centers.

In some cases women entered into the nursing profession through fortuitous routes. Dr. Irvine of the Chogoria Mission Hospital in Meru told of one such story. Miriam had entered the mission hospital in 1932 with partially paralyzed legs due to spinal tuberculosis. She stayed in the hospital for some years, during which time, as well as receiving medical care, she became a Christian. She entered medical service in 1943. Because of her medical history, she was unlikely to marry, which according to Dr. Irvine was 'a devastating prospect to any African girl'. Miriam was said to have 'sublimated her natural instinct to the service of African motherhood' and was the hospital's 'complete standby in [the hospital's] maternity work'.[107] Miriam's cheerfulness and capability were held responsible for the dramatic rise of maternity admissions at the hospital, which stood at 75 in 1944 and rose to 161 in 1945.

Women's entry into waged labour and the travel that it entailed, did not sit well with the majority of African men, and some women, especially in the older generation. This was the case with women's entry into the medical professions as well. It was difficult to stem the association of education, training, and subsequent employment of girls with prostitution because all entailed travel away from home. Crossing the spatial, gender and ideological boundaries of a community was a hurdle that most women and girls had to confront.

In most instances, families were responsible for bringing an early end to girls' education. The pursuit of post primary education was a highly contentious issue across generational, gender, and moral constituencies. Commenting on her desire for medical training, Keran Akoto observed:

> Parents used to refuse. I even wanted to go for a nursing course in Mombasa in 1944 but my parents refused. Maragoli culture made people not to encourage girls' education because the fear was that an educated girl would be spoilt, become a prostitute, hence not get married. This would deny them the chance of getting dowry.... Parents preferred girls joining teaching and not nursing because the latter would make a girl work far away from home.[108]

A girl's life was bound in a wide network of competing moral economies. Attendance of school did not free the girl from a variety of social responsibilities, including getting married when her parents thought it was time to do so. As women became exposed to new experiences, society adjusted its sense of the social role of women. Women were not expected to surpass prospective suitors in formal education. Likewise, once married, husbands might extend their control of women's lives in the new spaces recently available for women.

Among both the Kipsigis and the Meru, the underlying motive in the restructuring of the timeframe and modalities of clitoridectomy was the desire to control unsanctioned pregnancy and motherhood. In a flagrant effort to reinforce 'customary' constructions of motherhood, indigenous colonial retainers adopted strong-arm tactics to coerce whole communities into complying with a reworked ritual that incorporated intrusive male gazes. In a scene reminiscent of those enacted by colonial functionaries who examined female initiates to ensure that they had not been subjected to the major operation, a Meru chief was seen 'bending to look [at the initiate]' to verify that she had not been excised twice.[109] The resultant public surveillance of maternity and womanhood by male employees of the colonial state went well beyond the circumvention of social conventions.

Notes

1 An earlier version of this chapter was published in Atieno Odhiambo (ed.), *African Historians and African Voices.* See Kanogo, ' The Medicalization of Maternity in Colonial Kenya' 75–113.
2. Willis R. Hotchkiss, *Then and Now in Kenya Colony: Forty Adventurous Years in East Africa* (London, 1937), 28. Mr. Hotchkiss was an African Inland Mission missionary among the Kipsigis from 1905 to 1935. He also served on the Advisory Council of the Native Land Trust Board in charge of African Reserves.
3. KNA: PC/CENT/2/1/6 LNC Special Meetings, Nyeri, 20 December 1931.
4. KNA: PC/CP/2/1/5 LNC Meetings, Fort Hall, 23-24 October 1930. In an attempt to persuade the councillors regarding the appropriateness of the contribution, the President assured the councillors that 'the authorities at the Hospital [would] look after [trainee nurses] properly and we must choose the right kind of women.'
5. *Ibid.*
6. *Ibid.*
7. Both general Western medicine and maternity services were introduced in Kenya by various missionary societies from the first decade of the twentieth century. The provision of medical services in the rural areas was at times slowed by disagreements between mission groups and colonial authorities regarding who should control the service. See Ahlberg, *Women, Sexuality and the Changing Social Order*; Ann Beck, *A History of the British Medical Administration of East Africa, 1900–1950* (Cambridge, 1970). George Oduor Ndege, *Health, State and Society in Kenya* (Rochester, 2001). For the training of doctors see John Iliffe, *East African Doctors: A History of the Modern Profession* (Cambridge, 1998).
8. Ahlberg, *Women, Sexuality and the Changing Social Order*; Beck, *Medical Administration.*
9. Simon Ndirangu, *A History of Nursing in Kenya* (Nairobi, 1982).
10. KNA: PC/CP/2/1/5 LNC Meetings, Fort Hall District, 18 February 1930.
11. KNA: PC/CENT/2/1/7 LNC Meetings, Meru, 17 March 1937.
12. KNA: PC/CENT/2/1/7 LNC Meetings, Meru, 25–27 November 1937.
13. KNA: PC/CENT/2/1/9 LNC Meetings, Meru, 7–9 March 1949.
14. KNA: PC/CENT/2/1/8 LNC Meetings, Fort Hall District, 21 November 1939
15. KNA: PC/CENT/2/1/7 LNC Meetings, Meru, 25 July 1935.
16. KNA: PC/CENT/2/1/7 LNC Meetings, Meru, November 1935.
17. KNA: PC/CENT/2/1/7 Medical Officer, Prenatal Advice to Pregnant Women, Meru LNC Meetings, July 26, 1935.
18. See for example, Ominde, *The Luo Girl*, 1952, and Davison, *Voices From Mutira*, 73, 74, 125–6,150–5,159.
19. KNA: PC/CENT/2/1/8 LNC Meetings, Fort Hall District, 19–20 November 1940.
20 KNA: PC/CENT/2/1/9 LNC Meetings, Meru, Application by Dr. Gerard for a Grant for Maternity Cases, Minute 4, 1939.
21. *Ibid.*
22. See for example, Hugh Fearn, *An African Economy: A Study of the Economic Development of the Nyanza Province of Kenya, 1903–1953* (London 1961); Kitching, *Class and Economic Change in Kenya*; Tignor, *The Colonial Transformation of Kenya.*
23. Ndege, *Health, State and Society.*
24. KNA: PC/NZA/2/1/169 PC Nyanza to Mr. Beecher, 22 May 1944 cc to Messrs. Naashon Gudo and J. E. Opuko.
25. KNA: PC/NYANZA/2/1/169 Naashon Gudo and J. E. Opuko to L. S. Beecher, 29 February 1944.
26. It was the councillors' duty to 'make it more widely understood that expectant mothers should go to be examined....in good time beforehand so that those who were found likely to have difficulty could be told when to come to hospital for the actual child birth.' KNA: PC/CENT/2/1/10 Minutes of Nyeri Annual District Council, 1 December 1942.
27. *Ibid.*
28. KNA:PC/CENT/2/1/7 LNC meeting, Meru, 17 March, 1937.

29. KNA: PC/CENT/2/1/10 Minutes of Nyeri African District Council, 12 August 1946.
30. KNA: PC/CENT/2/1/7 LNC Meetings, Meru, 25-27 November 1937.
31. KNA: PC/CENT/2/1/6 LNC Special Meetings, Nyeri, 8 August 1934.
32. KNA: PC/CENT/2/1/7 LNC Meetings, Meru, November 1935. The equivalent of an auxiliary nurse, a dresser performed the nonprofessional services including cleaning and feeding patients, dressing their wounds, and making beds.
33. KNA: PC/CENT/2/1/7 LNC Meetings, Meru, 30 November 1936.
34. KNA: PC/CENT/2/1/7 LNC Meetings, Meru, 25–27 November 1937.
35. KNA: PC/CENT/2/1/9 LNC Meetings, Meru, 6–8 November 1948.
36. Ndirangu, 21. Ndirangu's brief book remains the most comprehensive account of the systemic development of the nursing profession.
37. An exclamation underscoring the seriousness of the matter. Sara Sarai, oral interview, Kinoo, Kiambu, December 1993.
38. KNA: PC/CENT/1/2/10 Minutes of Nyeri African District Council, 16–19 February 1948.
39. KNA: PC/CENT/2/1/9 LNC Meetings, Meru, 10 December 1947.
40. KNA: PC/CENT/2/1/8 LNC Meetings, Fort Hall District, 19-20 November 1940.
41. See Ominde, *The Luo Girl* (London, 1952), 57.
42. KNA: PC/CENT/2/1/9 LNC Meetings, Meru, 11–13 March 1947.
43. KNA: PC CENT/2/1/10 Minutes of Nyeri African District Council, 9–12 August 1948.
44. KNA: PC/CENT/ 2/1/11 Church of Scotland Mission, Chogoria, 1948, 2.
45. For example, see Hildi Hendrickson (ed.), *Clothing and Difference: Embodied Identities in Colonial and Post-Colonial Africa* (Durham, 1996); Cohen & Atieno Odhiambo, *Siaya* (1989).
46. KNA: PC/CENT/2/1/8 LNC Meetings, Fort Hall District, 19-20 November 1940.
47. KNA: PC/CENT/2/1/9 LNC Meetings, Meru, 6-8 November 1948. An interesting inversion of clothing was reported regarding an incident during the first decade of the twentieth century. In preparation for a royal visit to Port Florence as Kisumu was then known, a yard each of Amerikani cotton cloth was given to local Africans 'in order to cloak their normal nakedness'. Turning out in large numbers to welcome their royal guest, it was observed that 'Some draped the strip of cloth around their head like a turban; others fashioned it into a bow below the knee; still others tied it around the neck or arms. None thought of hiding their naked bodies where most desirable'. See Foran, *A Cuckoo in Kenya*, 263.
48. KNA: PC/NZA.3/3/1/9 DC Kakamega (North Kavirondo) to PC Nyanza, Changes in Native Life and Customs, 20 December 1927.
49. KNA: PC/CP/2/1/5 LNC Meetings, Fort Hall District, 20-21 April 1933.
50. *Ibid.*
51. KNA: PC/NZA.3/3/1/9 DC South Kavirondo to PC Nyanza, Kisii, 31 December 1927.
52. Beth Njambi, oral interview, Limuru, 14 July 1993.
53. KNA: PC/NZA.3/3/19 DC Kavirondo to PC Nyanza, Kisii, 31 December 1927.
54. See KNA: PC/CENT/2/1/7 LNC Meetings, Meru, 30 November 1936 and KNA: PC/CENT/2/1/7 LNC Meetings, Meru, 8 June 1937.
55. See KNA: PC/CENT/2/1/9 LNC Meetings, Meru, 6–8 November 1948. One imagines women lined out in the open exposing themselves for injections.
56. KNA: PC/NZA/2/1/142 Infanticide. Memorandum in Support of Kipsigis Local Native Council Resolution No. 8 of 1942: The Present Position Regarding Infanticide Among the Kipsigis by F.D. Hislop, DC 1942. The parallel situation in Victorian England was the pregnancy of an unmarried girl from a respectable family. She was 'frequently disowned and driven from home, ultimately swelling the ranks of prostitutes in the great cities'.
57. Peristiany, *The Social Institutions* (1939), 53. The following discussion is based on a summary of the proceedings of Kipsigis Local Native Council meetings over a twenty-year period on the question of Infanticide. This summary is in the form of a document entitled 'Memorandum in Support of the Kipsigis Local Native Council Resolution No.

8 of 1942: The Present Position Regarding Infanticide Among the Kipsigis' written in 1942 by F.D. Hislop, the area District Commissioner. See KNA: PC/NZA/2/1/142 Infanticide. Infanticide was also said to take place among the Tiriki in those cases where the mother of the baby did not know its father. See KNA: PC/NZA.3/28/4/1 O.C. Keller, Nyang'ori Mission, Kisumu to Senior Commissioner Nyanza Province, 3 January 1928.

58. Peristiany, *The Social Institutions*, 54.
59. KNA: PC/NZA/2/1/142 Infanticide, Officer-In-Charge, Maasai, Narok to Chief Secretary, 5 January 1943.
60. KNA: PC/NZA/2/1/142 Infanticide, PC RVP to Honourable Chief Secretary, 23 January 1943.
61. Lynn Thomas, 'Imperial Concerns and "Women's Affairs": State Efforts to Regulate Clitoridectomy and Eradicate Abortion in Meru, Kenya, c. 1910–1950', *Journal of African History*, 39 (1998), 128. Early colonial reports of abortions of this type indicated the connivance of pregnant girls and their paramours. A 1920 report gave an explicit description of how the abortion was secured. It was 'induced by means of kneading of the abdomen and the force used is so considerable that death [of the pregnant girl] sometimes ensures'. KNA: PC/CP/9/1 A. C. Chamier, 'Some notes on Meru tribal organization and customs', 13 February 1920, quoted in Thomas, 'Imperial Concerns', 123. Infanticide was a last resort. Thomas, 'Imperial Concerns', 128.
62. *Ibid.*, 121. The following summary of the abortion debate among the Meru is based on the above article.
63. *Ibid.*, 137.
64. *Ibid.*, 139.
65. KNA:PC/NZA/2/1/142 Infanticide. Memorandum in Support of Kipsigis Local Native Council Resolution No. 8 of 1942.
66. *Ibid.*
67. The Attorney General considered the resolution of the Kipsigis LNC to be outside the powers conferred by the Native Authority Ordinance of 1937. Adoption was already governed by the Adoption of Children Ordinance of 1933, and the Chief Secretary ruled that the resolution could not be laid before the Governor in Council for approval. However, if the resolution had enough support by the provincial administration, legislation might be drafted and applied to any particular tribe. In the same way that customary practice censured women's sexuality and claims to motherhood, the administration thus was willing to implement a process that would deny the involved women the right to motherhood.
68. KNA: PC/NZA/2/1/142 Infanticide, PC RVP to Honourable Chief Secretary, 23 January 1943.
69. KNA: PC/NZA/2/1/142 Infanticide, LNC Meeting, Kipsigis, Minutes on Infanticide, 6 October 1926. See also Hotchkiss, *Then and Now*, 103.
70. Regarding the infanticide controversy, there was a clear difference of opinion between LNC members of the ruling *Kimnyigei* age group and the members of the *Nyongi* age grade, which would be the immediate successor after *Kimnyigei*. The older *Kimnyigei* supported the custom while the younger *Nyongi* members were opposed to it. The administration was hopeful that once members of the *Nyongi* age group came to power infanticide would be eradicated.
71. KNA: PC/NZA/2/1/142 Infanticide, 'Memorandum in Support of Kipsigis Local Native Council Resolution No. 8 of 1942: The Present Position Regarding Infanticide Among the Kipsigis' by F.D. Hislop, DC, 1942.
72. Peristiany, *The Social Institutions*, 54, quoted in KNA: PC/NZA/2/1/142 Infanticide, 'Memorandum in Support of Kipsigis Local Native Council Resolution No. 8 of 1942: The Present Position Regarding Infanticide Among the Kipsigis' by F.D. Hislop, DC, 1942. At the height of the clitoridectomy crisis Kikuyu couples where the wife was uncircumcised were denied normal kinship services after the wife had given birth. Nobody 'would cook for them.' See Sandgren, *Christianity and the Kikuyu*, 181.
73. KNA: PC/CP/2/1/5 LNC Meetings, Fort Hall, 17-20 July 1934. For a comprehensive analysis of prostitution in an urban centre see White, *The Comforts of Home.*

74. KNA: PC/CENT/2/1/4 LNC Minutes, Kyambu District, 22-23 November 1928.
75. *Ibid.*
76. KNA: PC/CP/2/1/5 LNC Meetings, Fort Hall District, 20-22 March 1926.
77. KNA: PC/CP/2/1/5 LNC Meetings, Fort Hall District, 18 February 1930.
78. KNA: PC/CENT/2/1/10 Minutes of Nyeri African District Council: Unauthorized Village Prostitutes Near Karatina, 1 September 1943.
79. Peristiany, *The Social Institutions*, 53.
80. KNA: PC/CENT/2/1/10 Minutes of Nyeri African District Council: Unauthorized Village Prostitutes Near Karatina, 1 September 1943. Emphasis added.
81. Foran, *A Cuckoo in Kenya*, 218.
82. KNA: PC/CENT/2/1/10 Minutes of Nyeri African District Council, 17 May 1945.
83. KNA: PC/CENT/2/1/10 Minutes of Nyeri African District Council, Female Prisoners, 13 May 1946.
84. KNA: PC/CENT/2/1/10 Minutes of Nyeri African District Council, Houses of Ill-fate in Native Reserves, 1 March 1945.
85. *Ibid.* The elders were most likely worried that the demobilized soldiers would have infected such women. The women might also make sufficient money from the soldiers to warrant their efforts to resettle themselves in the rural areas.
86. *Ibid.*
87. KNA: PC/CENT/2/1/10 Minutes of Nyeri African District Council, 11 February 1946.
88. KNA: PC/CENT/2/1/9 LNC Meetings, Meru, 25 July 1945.
89. KNA: PC/CENT/2/1/10 Minutes of African Native District Council, 16 August 1945.
90. KNA: PC/CENT/2/1/10 Minutes of Nyeri African District Council, Control of Women in Nyeri Township, 10-13 November 1947.
91. KNA: PC/CENT/2/1/9 LNC Meetings, Meru, Care of Motherless Infants, 23-26 September 1947.
92. KNA: PC/CENT/2/1/9 LNC Meetings, Meru, Care of Motherless Child, 10 December 1947.
93. KNA:PC/CENT/2/1/10 Minutes of Nyeri African District Council, August 12, 1946.
94. Sara Sarai, oral interview, Kinoo, December 1993.
95. David Wakalo, oral interview, Dembwa, Taita, January 1997.
96. The East African Women's League, a welfare organization composed of European women, resolved in 1923 to urge the Chief Native Commissioner to initiate medical training for African women at the Native Civil Hospital in Nairobi: Ndirangu, *A History of Nursing in Kenya*, 41. The EAWL was founded in 1917 and continues to operate in a multi-racial setting.
97. *Ibid.*, 42.
98. For example, see Kanogo, 'Mission impact on women in colonial Kenya', in Bowie, Kirkwood & Ardener (eds), *Women and Missions*, 165–86.
99. KNA:PC/CENT/2/1/4 LNC Minutes, Kyambu District, 2-4 March, 1933.
100. KNA: PC/CENT/2/1/10 Minutes of Nyeri African District Council, 23 August 1939.
101. KNA: PC/CP/2/1/5 LNC Meetings, Fort Hall District, 22-23 March 1934.
102. KNA:PC/CENT/2/1/8 LNC Meetings Fort Hall District, 23-24 July, 1940.
103. KNA:PC/CENT/2/1/9 Meru LNC Meetings, November 22, 1938.
104. KNA: PC/CENT/2/1/8 LNC Meetings, Fort Hall District, 20–21 November 1941. While the minutes of the above entry do not give the circumstances that precipitated the statement, archival and oral data are replete with information on male control of female movement.
105. KNA:PC/CENT/2/1/10 Minutes of Nyeri African District Council, July 13, 1944.
106. Ndirangu, *History of Nursing*, 68.
107 KNA:PC/CENT/2/1/11 Church of Scotland Mission, Chogoria, Annual Report, 1946,7.
108. Keran Akoto, oral interview, Keveye, Kakamega, 26 February 1997.
109. Thomas, 'Imperial Concerns', 143. Older women opposed to LNC interference with the rite might subject girls who had undergone the *kigwarie* excision to secondary surgery.

Seven

Girls are Frogs[1]

Girls, Missions & Education

> The question of female education is in its infancy in East Africa. It presents even more difficult problems than the education of boys.... A certain amount of opposition must be expected from the tribes to any attempt made to educate their womenfolk. We were given an illuminating example of the attitude of the tribal chiefs and older women towards the education of their girls at Kapsabet. There a Nandi chief threatened that there would be violence done if the native girls at a local mission station were, as he termed it, withheld from their parents, prevented from submitting to the circumcision rite, and so spoilt for marriage with the young men, thus causing their parents to lose the dowry which would have been given to them in return for the girls in marriage.[2]
> Report of the East African Commission.
> Cmd. 2387, 1925.

> Within two days of my entry into the mission, my ears [upper and lower lobes] had been sewn up.[3]
> Serah Mukabi, 20 July 1993

> I was abducted in the morning on our way from the chapel to the dining hall.[4]
> Sara Sarai , November 1993

> '[W]hen we went to school at Kaimosi our parents requested the missionaries to provide grinding stones and *jembes*, hoes, for their daughters to use in school so that they did not become lazy.[5]
> Keran Akoto, Kakamega, 25 February, 1997

> If you went to school, what home would you return to? Or if you went to church, what home would you go back to?[6]
> Mary Wanjiru, Limuru, 14 July, 2001

Even by the 1950s, the education of African female nurses was still sparse. Women who sought medical training faced a protracted process that was mediated by institutions, authorities, and individuals across gender, culture, race, and class lines. Whether young women pursued the educational opportunities opened up by the medicalization of maternity, or whether they took advantage of those offered by the missions and colonial authorities, they faced loneliness, the upheaval of relationships, and an inevitable series of 'border crossings' in identity, gender perceptions and social relations. As wards of multiple patrons who mediated different aspects of their lives, girls found it difficult to navigate the different layers of vested interests. The missionary agenda was just one among many in the molding of the lives of girls. To study the education of girls in colonial Kenya is to explore a mosaic of cultural and gender constructions, negotiations, and contestations.

Grace Nyanduga

In its Western form, and as introduced to Kenya, education called for the suspension of all other social, cultural, and economic activities. It removed a woman from society and strained society's efforts to accommodate or reintegrate that woman once she had completed her studies. Nothing illustrates this more strikingly than the effort of Grace Ogot, *née* Nyanduga, to progress in her chosen field.

Grace, or 'Sister Joseph', as she was commonly addressed, had qualified as the first Kenyan Registered Nurse and Midwife at Mulago Hospital, in Kampala. In 1950, she returned to Kenya to practice nursing and tutoring at Maseno Hospital. Up to that point, Grace had been among a select few for whom the less travelled road of formal education had family support. However, things took a sudden turn once Grace was offered a scholarship to pursue advanced nursing overseas in 1955.

The intensity of emotions and the confluence of family, clan, neighbourhood, religious, and medical interventions that unfolded within less than twelve hours as Grace sought permission from her family to go to Britain, illustrates the predicament that even women who had a measure of family approval, had to confront in colonial Kenya. What happened took place at her natal home in Asembo Bay, at a place called Rakombe, in the vicinity of Lake Victoria, the largest freshwater lake in the world. As she and her kinsman, Joel Ojal, approached her home, the sight of the lake and the seagulls seemed to represent security, then, more than ever before. Now, she was going to ask her parents for permission to go to a distant country, from which she would not always be able to contact her parents when she needed them.

After social niceties, Grace did not waste any time in breaking the news. 'I whispered to my father that I had been sent a [scholarship] from Uganda. They wanted me to go abroad, to read nursing and be away for three years.' Although Grace's father had been in the forefront of support for formal education, especially girls' education, she was nervous. This was an unusual request. 'Ah,' her father said. 'How shall we tell your mother?' Her mother, when told about the scholarship, 'could not take it', Grace recalled. Her parents were at a loss. They could not make meaningful sense of the situation. Although Grace had arrived at her home late in the afternoon, events unfolded in such quick succession that by nightfall, uncles and aunts had been summoned to help solve the problem. As her father had said, 'This is something I cannot take on my own.' As it turned out, it would soon involve the wider village beyond Grace's extended family.

People were called from all directions. Runners were sent to summon all manner of relatives considered indispensable for the big decision. And so they came, men and women. Suddenly Grace looked and felt strange. Everything was strange. 'I could have cried', she said. Amid the gathering crowd, she felt very lonely. It would be a very long night. The gathering group had never heard of an African girl going abroad. Her own mother abandoned cooking and 'just sat'. Even after her mother's friends had cooked, nobody ate the food.

When all her uncles and their wives were gathered, Grace was asked to tell them what had happened. Their response brought to the fore widespread community concerns about the effect of women's education on vital cultural practices. Their response was terse.

> All this time you have always wanted to go. You have wanted to go. When will you go to your husband's house?… You are always putting pressure on us. You went to Butere, we allowed you. To Ng'iya, we allowed you. You went to Mengo, we allowed you. And now again you want to go. And you want to go to the white man's country [from] where people never come back. And where no [African] woman has gone.[7]

After attending local schools, Grace had attended Ng'iya Girls School, her first mission boarding school away from home, at a time when her mother was ill, prompting her father to offer to do some domestic chores so that Grace could remain at school. From age twelve to fifteen, Grace would have been at her most useful in and around the household, but she was not available. Her subsequent term away for intermediate education at Butere Girls Secondary School from 1946 to 1948 then occupied what the community might have considered to be the prime of her youth, sixteen to eighteen years. From about age sixteen, a girl was considered ready for marriage.

But Grace was not ready for marriage. She was preparing to enroll as a private candidate for the Kenya Junior Secondary school examination. There was no school for girls offering this examination in Kenya. Hence, enrolling as a private candidate, Grace was struggling against the educational reality of the colony. She studied for the examination for two years, 1949 and 1950, and then went out of the country to the neighboring colony, Uganda, to train as a nurse. From Mengo Nursing Training College, she had qualified as a Registered Nurse and Registered Midwife, U.R.N. and U.R.M., respectively. She had then come back to Kenya and had worked for a few years when she got a Church Missionary Society scholarship in early 1955 to go to Britain for advanced studies in nursing.

This is the offer that members of her extended family were discussing.

Having postponed marriage thus far, Grace observed that she had been ridiculed and called all sorts of names as her age mates got married at the ages of sixteen, seventeen, and eighteen. 'And by the time I was twenty, I knew the chances were dwindling.' What Grace did not know was that the wider community had been watching her academic progress beyond elementary school with reservations. Her father might have approved her going to Butere for intermediate school and to Mengo Kampala for nurse training, but in the mind of the members of the community, she was marriageable all this time, and time was running out with each transition that she made to these institutions of higher education.

Her travels to all these places were symbolic of her increasing cultural migration and her evident alienation from the social rhythms of her kinsmen. It seemed obvious that to contemplate going to Britain was absurd. Marriage and motherhood were the basic characteristics of womanhood. Her only link with these institutions, however, was through her profession. Because she was birthing mothers, the majority of whom were married, Grace was not totally removed from these icons of respectability. However, she was not a wife or a mother. This was what her kinsmen were trying to impress on her. In the society's moral economy, marriage could not be postponed indefinitely. Three years was too long to wait. They wanted her to stay and get married. The only travel that would appease the community was travel related to marriage.

Fortunately, in Grace's words, 'something happened which saved us'. Each time Grace visited her home, she did not forget to carry her black medicine box from Maseno Hospital. She had brought it this time, too. During her regular holidays to the village, she attended to the sick who sought her expertise. She was particularly keen on midwifery. Many nights, the villagers would call on her to deliver babies. Used to save other peoples lives, this time, the kit would save Grace from an intricate social predicament.

In the middle of the night, as the scholarship talks continued, there was a knock at the door. A group of people holding a lantern had come to seek the services of Grace. A woman had been in labour for six hours, and the group feared the worst. It was a case of breech delivery in which the baby was trying to come out legs first. Local birth attendants had failed to correct the situation. In the late afternoon, a car had been seen heading in the direction of Grace's home, and they suspected Grace was visiting her parents. She always came in a car, although she did not own one. This time, her kinsman Joel Ojal had driven her home.

Quickly, Grace got her black box, threw a blanket over herself, and together with a female relative, walked with the group that had come to seek her help to the homestead, which was about forty minutes away. When she got there, 'it was like a funeral. Everybody was sitting around and the women [believed] the [patient] was dead.'[8] Immediately, Grace made sure that both mother and baby were still alive. Within an hour, Grace had manipulated the foetus into the correct position and had helped the woman deliver successfully. She had everything that she needed for home delivery, including fresh sheets for the new mother. She stayed with the mother for a short while, making sure that both she and the baby were fine. A hot drink was prepared for the mother, who was very dehydrated.

Having helped the family out of their crisis, Grace asked them all to walk back with her, because she had a crisis of her own at home.

> Now that I had solved their [medical problem], and they were friends of my father, they had better come home and convince the other uncles who were holding on to my father not to let me go. So we walked back. We arrived home at three [in the morning]. They were still sitting. And so they said Grace had saved the baby and the mother. 'And we know Grace has a problem here. And we just came to tell you, let her go. Just let Grace go. She saved the baby, and she saved the mother. If she [had not come] for this important [meeting] the mother and the baby would have died. So we have come here to tell you to let her go'.[9]

For Grace, the gift of a healthy baby and mother under such difficult conditions confirmed that God wanted her to go to Britain. As thanksgiving prayers were being offered for the safe delivery, Grace had prayed privately that her family's heart might be softened and that they might allow her to go to Britain. Amid all the agonizing and the discussions on practical matters, intercessory prayer remained important. The scholarship crisis thus juxtaposed cultural, professional, and religious issues. At the end of the intervention by the party of the new mother, it was decided that all present should pray together.

The patriarch of the household, Grace's paternal grandfather, finally communicated the decision that broke the ice. Grace considered him a conservative. He had never addressed her by Christian name. Doing so would have robbed him of his granddaughter, as he knew her. Very grudgingly, her grandfather said, 'Let Akinyi go.' He had obtained the approval of Grace's father and her mother. Apart from those who were present throughout, other members of the extended family were not immediately happy about this decision. 'They were furious. But when they ... were told that the community had said yes, grudgingly they agreed.' It had taken external community intervention, and a last-minute affirmation of the usefulness of her nursing and midwifery training to convince her immediate and extended family and the community to let Grace go for further education. In a symbolic manner, porridge prepared after the consent was shared by all who a few hours earlier had declined dinner. Communion over food indicated that all was well.

A hierarchy of social responsibility and accountability was operative in the course of the negotiations. On receiving the scholarship news, Joseph Nyanduga's first confidante had been his wife. That, however, was for informational purposes only. He had to consult the next rung of authority vital for his family's maintenance of social order in the community. The first group of relatives that was summoned for consultation included paternal uncles and aunts; the maternal relatives were informed only after the decision that had been taken. The relatives, both maternal and paternal, could not override the wishes of the larger community. Unilateral, individual decisions would have unpleasant social consequences; people like Grace remained attached to the community in diverse ways.

Grace was of the opinion that if the decision had been entirely dependent upon her parents, they would have consented at the very beginning. As Christians, Grace's parents must have encountered opposition from the community on various issues. In embracing their new faith, the family undertook cultural, moral, and in some cases physical migrations, but these were never complete. Although some of the choices they made were dictated by the teachings of the church, there were limits on how far the family could go against community expectations. In their middle age, her parents felt less independent of the community. They felt that the issue at hand had such long-term implications that they could not make the decision independent of the extended family. Neither could they risk antagonizing the community. Grace's mother was particularly careful about this fact. 'Mother always [dealt] with the community and she knew that if anything happened to my father, and father dies, she [would] always remain with the community whereas if she was rebellious [against] the community, she would have nowhere to [go].'

In May 1955, Grace left for Britain. Grace was the first Kenyan State Certified Midwife to be trained in England. She graduated in 1956 and proceeded to obtain a Diploma in Methods of Teaching at St. Thomas Hospital, England, in 1957. Her services as a Staff Nurse and Tutor at Maseno Hospital, to which she returned, were eagerly awaited.

Personal histories such as that of Grace Nyanduga illustrate all the complexities that resulted from the entry of Kenyan girls into schools. As such, they serve as roadmaps of the extremely contested terrain of formal education. The quest for formal learning was a process that juxtaposed modernity and tradition and that often made for strange bedfellows under the constant gaze of divergent constituencies. What follows is not a history of the structural development of Western education for girls in Kenya; rather, it the story of the ways in which the growth of mission stations and schools created new spaces beyond the control of indigenous authorities and of how colonial social engineering and the administrative infrastructure facilitated women's migrations to these spaces. Seeking knowledge engendered intricate negotiations and transformations in the personal, cultural, and social lives of female students and their families.

Mission Schools

Up to the middle of the 1930s, Christian missions had a monopoly on the provision of formal Western education in colonial Kenya.[10] Entry into mission schools called for extensive ingenuity and resilience on the part of female students. As sites for the negotiation of diverse cultural practices, missions and mission schools antagonized local populations at the same time as they entrenched their wards into new ways of being.

Missions endeavoured to produce moderately literate girls steeped in Christian ideals and suitable as wives for Christian men. The girls were introduced to educational syllabi designed to cultivate their domestic skills for their roles as wives and mothers. Unlike Grace Nyanduga, the majority of mission girls had less than five years of schooling, and few completed intermediate level, which would add up to approximately eight years of formal instruction. In the great scheme of things, missions anticipated that the majority of women would not pursue careers. Even when some did, missions hoped that this would be for about two to three years only before marriage. In the missions, as well as in villages such as Grace's, women were not expected to combine marriage and careers.

Kiambu District was in all probability the most progressive region in Kenya regarding the provision of girls' education.[11] When T. F. C Bewes, a British missionary, arrived in Kenya in March 1934, 'the Kabete Girls Boarding School was being run on the lines of a Refuge for girls, from all districts, wishing to begin school.'[12] The Church Missionary Society (CMS) was responsible for its establishment and management. Bewes was affiliated with that mission and also became its Secretary.[13] On his arrival, there were ninety-six girls at the refuge.[14] For these and other girls, going to school was still a precarious undertaking. The majority of them had fled to the mission stations in the face of fierce opposition from their families. The Church of Scotland Mission had established one of the earliest refuges for girls in 1909 at Thogoto.

The mission envisioned the girls' dormitory 'mainly as a protection against unwelcome marriages to heathen husbands, mostly polygamist'. In addition to affording this protection, it envisioned the girls' dormitory as a place 'to prepare wives for our mission boys who as time went on were getting more and more beyond the status of the raw native [girl]'.[15] Indeed, providing suitable Christian wives was considered to be a more immediate need than providing sanctuary at most Protestant missions. In 1936, at the newly established girls' boarding school in Meru, 'a number of betrothed girls were trained for periods ranging from six months to two years. The purpose of such training was not academic but practical'.[16] For all enrolled, practical hygiene, general housewifery, and baby care were taught. Some, like Grace, also sought formal education. But the girls themselves went to mission schools for a variety of reasons.

One of the girls who fled to Thogoto, Serah Mukabi (discussed in Chapter 4) grew up in a family whose head was so opposed to the education of women that, she recalled, 'my mother would tell me that I would get killed [by my father] if I went to school'.[17] At about the time that Serah was steeling herself to defy him and seek an education, her father had introduced her to a prospective suitor. As we have seen, Serah had earlier witnessed the forced marriage of a sister, and as a result, she had promised herself that she would never comply with such an arrangement.

It was not possible for a girl to make direct entry into mission stations, however. She was required to 'live with a Christian [family] during which time one's character would be appraised to determine whether she would stay [or not]'. In Serah's case, there was a Christian elder named Kibue who maintained a safe house for runaway girls who desired to enter the mission without the approval of their families.

Serah's uncles, who sympathised with her aspirations, undertook the precarious task of delivering her to Kibui in Thogoto in preparation for her entering Thogoto Mission. The procedure involved an initial visit to the mission station to express the intent to join the school. From this point on, a quick succession of events signified the many ways in which the candidate's life would be transformed. The new mission girls would discard of Kikuyu attire in exchange for mission uniforms. The beginning of a totally novel and alienating regime would follow this. Girls who went to mission schools were under greater pressure to abandon a whole range of rituals and practices immediately they set foot in the mission. In Keran Akoto's experience, the forbidden practices were associated with specific places, people, and moralities. For example, Christians were forbidden to 'worship at *misambwa* shrines, [participate in] sacrifices for childbirth, [join] such traditional dances performed at men's drinking places at Lunyerere, and they were to wear modern clothes instead of banana stem [*vivoya*] clothes, avoid the making of tribal marks on their faces [*madimu* or *tsimogero*] and on their bellies [*tsisate*]'. The forbidden things 'would retard us from development'.[18] The initial stay at the mission would be followed by a more protracted seclusion at the safe house once the 'external' remaking of the candidate had been accomplished.

Yet flight to the mission station was also looked upon as a liberating experience. 'Education is what liberated a woman. Once women began to appreciate the *cama* [sweetness], of education, a girl, regardless of what she looked like, even if she had *ndogonye,* leg jingles, she would remove and throw them away. *Hui*, she would be off to Thogoto [Mission].'[19] Sara Sarai, who also fled to Thogoto, expressed the same sentiments thus: 'Once you went to her place, that was it. You would be given refuge [hidden] and once room was found for you [in the mission], few girls went back home. Why would you? You would change clothing, get employed, be introduced to sewing, reading and writing. At this point, one was a real *muthomi* [student/convert]. One would learn, aiming to go to the Alliance High School.'[20]

The lure of the Gospel message, especially as captured in Christian hymns, also had significant effect on the candidates. The following song made an indelible impression on Sara on her first encounter with mission adherents.

> Good News
> Has reached our land
> This is good news
> About our savior.[21]

Sara Sarai cried as she sang it to this writer. She said she also cried when she first heard the song.[22] 'After this song … I did not fear the hyenas along the route to Thogoto'.

While opening their doors to any runaways interested in formal education, missions also appealed for government intervention in an attempt to persuade communities to allow their daughters to go to school. However, while some individual colonial retainers might be particularly zealous about ensuring that parents sent their female children to school, there was no public official policy towards these actions. Nevertheless, there was a general conviction both among missionary and colonial officials that the education of women should be part of the civilizing mission. It was within this broad understanding that the 1925 East African Commission said, 'ultimately the social progress of the natives of Africa depends on bringing forward the women as well as the men'.[23]

The education of girls thus was closely linked to official and missionary notions of social eugenics, not just the cultivation of domesticity. There was a basic belief that 'the standard of living of the community [was to be] dictated largely by the standard adopted by the women'.[24] Consequently, the cultivation of women's domestic and moral qualities was considered central to the educational endeavour.[25] Young girls would be converted into Christian wives and mothers. In 1937, Bewes spoke for many when he stated that such a transformation would be attained through instruction in 'practical Christianity and practical knowledge of Homecraft'.[26] This way, the girls could 'face life from the deepest, as well as the utterly practical point of view'.[27] Education would create the 'awakening of the mental life' of educated women. 'Homecraft' subjects included 'Child Welfare', 'Cooking', 'Nutrition', and 'Housewifery'. 'Sewing', although included, was not considered to be of the same value as the other subjects with regard to the stated goal of 'raising the standard of living in the villages'.[28]

Although the missionaries and colonial administrators thus hoped to make women into exemplary figures for the promulgation of 'civilization' in the home, church, and wider community, they did not expect such women to possess a formal education, any more than did the members of the indigenous communities who wanted to know when Grace would get married. A gendered domestic education would provide minimal literacy, at best. Age was critical for the process of producing these demure paragons. After fourteen years, girls would be too old for the anticipated transformation. The 'outlook' and 'subconscious reactions' of older girls, Bewes feared, would hold back the new recruits.[29] The process of remaking African women therefore required young malleable minds that were not too set in the ways of their communities.

Becoming 'Something Else': The Social Death of Mission Girls

There was a lot of skepticism among local communities about the missionizing and educational projects. For example, S. N. Bogonko observed that 'the Abagusii looked at mission education as a long term investment, if it was that at all, which in the end might not profit anyone and as a tool which was alienating Gusii youth from the traditions of their progenitors.'[30] This portrayal of a monolithically negative response to education among the Gusii people belies the variegated reception of mission education. In general, different missions affected the social fabric in different ways. Catholic missions were far less restrictive of the practice of a whole range of cultural activities. In Agnes Wairimu Hinga's experience, 'The Catholic priest … came to seek an understanding with the Kikuyu, he did not impose too many regulations [restrictions].'[31] However, the general response in different parts of the country at the beginning of missionary presence was negative.

The majority of elders hated the prospect of their daughters going to schools because such girls abandoned traditional ways. This made them 'something else'.[32] In many ways, such girls were no longer members of their own ethnic groups and did not participate in other corporate activities of the community. In certain respects, these girls had undergone social death. Elders feared that girls who went to school might *kugweto*, get bewitched, by whites. Parents were also annoyed because 'by going to the mission a girl became *muthungu*, a white person'.[33] Some 'feared that white people would run away with their daughters'.[34] Keran Akoto, who was born in 1927, said that the reason why her own mother did not go to school was because her grandparents were afraid that Keran's mother 'would get lost and get married to Europeans' if she was sent to school.[35]

At stake was the basic question of group identity and social cohesion. There was a sense in which the elders believed they were losing their children to Western education and Christianity. Agnes Wairimu Hinga observed that this sense of loss was exacerbated by the fact that elders loved children *tari muguongo*, as if they were ivory.[36] Apart from the physical isolation of girls who joined mission stations without their parents' permission, 'many of the elders would say that when a child went to school, that child was dead'.[37] In Mary Muthoni Njogu's village, this place of death, the site of the transformation, was the school at Tumutumu Mission near Nyeri Town. Part of the loss related to the removal of vital labour power, since, as we have seen with Grace Nyanduga, students attending boarding schools away from home were not available to perform daily chores at their homes. It also was not unusual for communities to claim that upon return from mission schools, educated girls 'regarded themselves as superior to their neighbors and often looked upon their parents as misguided primitives'.[38]

The social death of a girl who ran away to the mission station was evident in many ways. Formal education constituted an alternative organizing category that sought to restructure the totality of an individual's life: it threatened generational allegiance and peer solidarity. The girls were no longer present in the daily life of the community to receive the broad spectrum of indigenous knowledge. The protracted process of instruction among the Kikuyu was replicated in all ethnic groups, albeit in different settings.[39] Among the Luo of Nyanza Province, girls were traditionally instructed by the *pim*, an old woman, in the *siwindhe*, a girls' dormitory within a household. As David Cohen and Atieno Odhiambo have noted,

> It was within the *siwindhe* that much of the critical social intelligence of the Luo world was imparted by the *pim* to those with little experience or knowledge of it. Children learnt about the people, the groups, and the settlements around them. They learnt a geography of succour and a geography of danger. They learnt about sexuality, about marriage, and about childbirth. And from her wide-ranging social knowledge the *pim* was able to supply information that both broadened and delimited the fields of possible and optimal marriages for her charges.... They learnt about health, illness, misfortune, and death. They learnt about interest, opportunity, and obligation, factors that would both open up and restrict their lives. As the *pim* nurtured and instructed her charges, linking them with the adult world, the experience she brought from outside the enclosure neighbourhood and from outside the patri-group provided the young with information extending far beyond the patrilineage and gave them the elements of an intimate understanding of a complex and physically remote social universe.[40]

Apart from this wide-ranging instruction, the *pim* also undertook very specific instruction focusing on girlhood and womanhood.

> The *pim* instructed the girls concerning their sexuality. *Pim* taught the girls to be tolerant of their future spouses and in-laws during domestic problems. She taught them about responsibilities of the adult woman and she taught them about the respect due husbands in marriage. *Pim* instructed the girls to refrain from sexual relations outside marriage. A successful union was perceived as being marked from the very beginning when a young woman was found to be a virgin, '*en kode ringre*'. The girls were taught never to eat at a boyfriend's house. Secret visitations, *wuowo*, with boyfriends were undertaken at night and girls were instructed to be back before dawn. Such visitations were only known to *pim* and the girls of the *siwindhe*, not to the parents. They were instructed not to visit their boyfriends during menstruation, *dhi boke*. *Pim* taught the girls to offer persistent boyfriends an experience of lovemaking, but without penetration, through the skilful use of the thighs while making love.[41]

Having missed out on all or part of this socialization process, how could mission girls expect to be part of the corporate consciousness of their peers? Not just the indigenous communities, but now missions and a variety of government institutions mediated culture, ideology, notions of social order, girlhood, womanhood, cleanliness, sexuality, and a host of other customs and practices. Caught between two contesting worldviews and not fully steeped in the indigenous cultural life, mission girls found themselves being wooed, and at times being coerced, into a new, and in most cases massively different social milieu. The conflict between the different knowledges and the attempt by missionaries to arrogate a superior position for the Western, Christian culture exacerbated the situation.

The very identity of mission girls was at stake. Gender, kinship, and ethnic identities succumbed to the rapid adoption of mission ideas and imageries of womanhood. This was evident in observations made by former mission women over a variety of issues:

> They [the missions] started by introducing formal and health education. In the first place they concentrated on teaching against female circumcision [clitoridectomy]. Circumcised women experienced a lot of difficulties at childbirth....The missions opposed female circumcision, piercing of ears, *kwehwo,* removal of two lower teeth.
>
> [The lives of girls and women] changed tremendously because when the missions came, they were the first to establish how a woman should have clean clothes and more importantly how a girl should dress. They are the ones who introduced ideas about cleanliness. And they were the first to teach women such things as *miikarire* [lifestyle], childcare, and cookery.[42]

As we have seen in Chapter Three, part of the opposition to missionary efforts to eliminate clitoridectomy among the Kikuyu took the form of the *Muthirigu* song. Serah Mukabi noted the parallel existence of a *Marobo* song among ' the educated mission followers who were not considered Kikuyu. They did not embrace Kikuyu customs'.[43]

In a way that would have been gratifying to mission ears, Mary Muthoni Njogu referred to indigenous practices targeted by missions as *mathina*, 'problems'. The domestic scene of the educated and missionized was dramatically recast in contrast to that of the uneducated. There was an unmistakable assumption of the superiority of Western education in the preparation of girls and women for the lifelong marital journey. The lived experiences of educated women reconstituted conceptualizations of certain aspects of domesticity: 'Those uneducated ones had little knowledge about organizing a home. At school we learnt domestic science, laundry, and cookery. This exposed us to cleanliness and good cooking habits. Because of this, parents observed that we were smart and took care of their houses, household utensils and even we used to wash their clothes and iron them. They also looked smarter.'[44]

The role of the *pim* thus was usurped by *bibi*, the white female missioner in charge of mission girls. She would personally supervise the external transformation of new wards while collaborating in the long-term resocialization of the girls. The mission station, the refuge, *mambere,* became the new *siwindhe.*

Opposing the Education of Girls

In addition to the social death that resulted from missionary efforts to transform the girls they were seeking to educate, there were other reasons why a particular family or the wider community might oppose the education of girls. School was seen to interfere with the temporal calendar of girls' social rhythm, especially marriage. Education delayed access to the anticipated dowry, something to which fathers of girls did not take kindly at all.[45] Many elders believed that investing in a girl's education was a waste of resources on the part of her natal family because a girl would get married and transfer her labour and any earnings from employment to her husband's family. 'It was a problem because a girl's father believed he was educating a wife for another man. This he saw as a loss.'[46] Younger sisters of these students would be particularly upset because the delay of their sister's marriage would affect their own. One did not get married before one's older sister had done so. As we have seen in the case of Grace Nyanduga, girls were expected to marry as soon as they were considered ready, about fifteen years of age, and at about eighteen, neighbours and peers believed schoolgirls were getting too old to get married.[47] Many girls did not have parents, families, and communities as understanding as Grace Nyanduga did. Prisca Ayuku's father thought that at fourteen she was 'big enough' to get married and should not be contemplating going to school. It took an adamant brother who supported Prisca's wish and paid her school fees to convince her father to let her go to school.[48] Her sister, Grace Alukwe, was less fortunate. By the time she had qualified to go to high school, a suitor had paid her dowry, and, as Prisca said, 'father forced her to get married'.[49]

As we have seen, when mission girls contemplated marriage, missionaries wanted their students to marry other mission protégés, and they condemned as drunkards, smokers, and participants in local dances and death rituals any outsiders who presented themselves as suitors. Missions maintained close surveillance over their protégés, both within and outside the missions. In mission dormitories, women who had been attached to the mission for a considerable time were appointed to chaperon the younger girls.[50]

The most common reason for refusing to send girls to mission schools, however, as Rajab Ngashira explains it, was that 'in the 1930s and 1940s old people feared that educated women would take to *obutseche,* prostitution. They believed this strongly'.[51] Perceived as physically weak, women were also represented as highly impressionable and liable to immoral activities. Families and communities were particularly wary of new places, which spawned new ideas and lifestyles. Mary Wanjiru observed that it was commonly said, 'every white person brought prostitution in the land.'[52]

Education thus was represented as a pollutant, and this pollution was seen to affect a wide range of cultural practices and beliefs. Mary Wanjiru's father, Kang'ethe Kihika, considered himself a pure Kikuyu, someone who was opposed to formal education, the Christian religion, and Western attire. For Kang'ethe, 'If you were educated, and dressed in cloth not treated with ochre, you were a prime prostitute.'[53]

In some cases, the school uniform symbolized this alienating characteristic of education. In Monicah Wandura's experience, the patriarch in her family preferred to temper this influence by getting his children to change into *cuka*, the unstitched cloth, as soon as they came back from school. This way, *mutugo wa gigikuyu*, Kikuyu culture, would not disappear. Clothes made a difference. Monicah could go to school, but, as soon as she got back home, she had to blend and fit in with the norm, the acceptable, the Kikuyu.

Kang'ethe's disdain for missions and their intrusion into his community and into his household was initially played out in a very explicit manner. He forbade those of his children who had gone to the mission from ever returning to his homestead. For two years, two of his daughters who had fled to the Church of Scotland Mission at Thogoto did not come home. The psychological torture endured by the siblings, their mothers, and other relations of the two girls was exacerbated by the constant complaints of the patriarch. This was said to be responsible for outbreak of lesions on one of the two 'errant' daughters, Njeri. The infection was so bad that an operation was deemed necessary.

Cultural artifacts associated with missions and with colonialism in general also made schools unpopular. Thus, some parents refused to send their daughters to school because it was rumoured that in school, 'the students drank water from human skulls'. Most likely referring to enamel or chinaware, the perception evoked death and evil. There was also a general belief that educated girls were badly behaved.[54] Confronted with beliefs such as these, many girls preferred not to go to school. Having to choose between cultural practices and formal education, the majority of girls chose the former.[55] Embracing education entailed denouncing large components of one's cultural life. Regarding the majority of girls who did not go to school, Wycliffe Etindi mused, 'We just felt it was normal for them.'[56] Born in 1922, Hamis Makapia Wanga had fourteen siblings, eight brothers and six sisters. Makapia noted that:

> Of the women, none went to school. They could not be taken to school by our parents. Also, they could not ask to be taken to school. Old men refused; they did not like it. It is only people like those of our family whose fathers were *muliangos* [clan leaders] that went to school. And only boys were taken to school. The Wanga believed that an educated girl easily became a prostitute. They never allowed girls to be educated. Only boys were allowed.[57]

Indigenous cultures simply did not provide space for the education of females. Simon Lizanga Sabwa, who is among the first generation of highly educated Africans, reflected upon the gender disparity in education: 'I am not sure if the colonial government caused this. It was a tradition that men thought that they were more superior to women.'[58] Juliah Ojiambo recalls that 'to our community, a girl [was] nothing. There is no way any normal man would invest in a girl.... You know in our tradition girls were called frogs....'[59]

Unlike a man, whose fixed home was his natal home, a woman's home was wherever her husband was. She did not seem to belong to any one place. She transferred her productive and reproductive labour permanently from her natal to her marital home and simply belonged to and with whichever husband she was married to at the time. Thus, unless her marriage failed and she had to return to her natal home for a short duration or permanently, she seemed to be hopping around from one place to another – like a frog. As Hamis Makapia Wanga explained regarding the cultural perception of educating women,

> Before I went to the war [Second World War], I had seven children. Among them were three girls. Only one went to school. It was a waste of time to take them to school. Our culture did not allow it. It's only when I worked in the police force that I realized the need to take them to school. It became important to know how to write a letter. During our days, it was not important. During the war, African women were not employed. Only white women went to war. It taught me that educating women is important. That is why I educated my last daughter.[60]

As a result of contact with other cultures, which treated girls differently, Makapia changed his mind regarding the education of his daughters, and within a generation, thanks to such cultural exchanges, attitudes to girls' education began to change. Unlike Etindi, Rajab Ngashira, who was born in 1921 and was father of ten daughters and eight sons, took all his daughters to school, but without much success. 'I took my first daughter to school in 1950 but she did not pass. [I] again took another who got pregnant in standard seven. Another one went up to class eight but did not make it.... In my family, sons are more committed to education and have passed examinations. I do not think that my daughters are inhibited from education by anything. It is just bad luck.'[61] Sometimes girls *could* not go, however, because there simply were no girls' schools in their neighbourhood. When Eliud Amatika Oluchina went to school in 1927 at the age of thirteen, his female age mates did not because 'there were no schools for girls those days.'[62]

Going to School

A variety of factors accounted for a girl's ability to get formal education. In general, boys accessed formal education at a much earlier period and in far larger numbers than girls. Hence, in some areas, the initial entry of girls into schools was closely related to the desires of such mission 'boys' to marry mission-prepared girls. Reporting on the first tentative beginnings of girls' education in Meru, Mary Holding observed that these 'were made at the request of some of the young men who had been pupils at the boys' school'. With the brides already identified for the young men by the latter's parents, the young men wished to 'have wives who had some knowledge of hygiene. So they asked if their wives could be taken in at the mission and given a little training.'[63] As we have seen, the domestication of women at missions was to spill into school curriculum where subjects 'more suited to the needs of girls' would be introduced. It was a short step to having 'the school leaving examination adapted so that girls were able to study Domestic Science for their certificate.'[64]

Girls whose fathers were educated or had mission connections, or both, were more likely to be sent to school than those whose parents were uneducated and had no mission affiliation. Amos Omurambi, an elder in the CMS church, even used force to get people to send their children to school.[65] Within her ethnic group, Keran Akoto observed that 'Maragoli who did not go to church never wanted their children, both boys and girls, to go to school. For parents who went to church, their daughters went to school. The girls whose parents refused them to go to school felt that they had been let down. They wished that they learnt how to read and write and speak English.'[66] Clearly, children did not always see eye to eye with their parents. Susana Aseka, who was born 1927, was the daughter of a mission employee. Her father had had six years of formal education and worked as a tutor and pastor at the Kima Church of God Mission. Her entry to school was predictable: 'I went to school in 1938 in standard one. During those days, the European took us and we stayed at Kima. They only took girls whose fathers knew at least something, say a pastor or a believer, because girls were not allowed to go to school.... Whoever came for me was one of the missionaries who were looking for children to be taken to school.'[67]

As their influence spread, there was a wider constituency of possible students from which missions could choose. In showing preference for those already connected with missions, missionaries necessarily eliminated some girls and avoided a lot of acrimony from non-Christian families. Like Susana, Selina Nyona's father had 'passed through' a mission 'where the importance of writing letters and speaking English was emphasized by Leech [a missionary] and Mulama [a colonial chief]'.[68] Along with all her siblings, Selina, who was born in May 1935, was sent to school.

Relatives had ample opportunities to interfere with and in some cases destroy a girl's chances for formal education. As we have seen in the case of Grace Nyanduga, the fear of harbouring a culturally alienated clanswoman who might be an embarrassment to the clan created vigilant relatives. Indigenous cultural beliefs could bring embarrassment and unwanted surveillance to the family of an educated girl in a host of ways. Prisca Ayuku grew up at her maternal grandparents' home and later with her stepfather in a setting where girls were not very keen on formal education and those who were in school were not doing well. Prisca, who was doing quite well, was accused of stealing luck from her host village. Although very stubborn, she was forced to remove her six lower front teeth despite the fact members of her family in Butsotso no longer participated in this rite.[69] For Prisca, access to education was mediated by unwanted ritual practices and accusations from immediate kinsmen. It was difficult for a young girl to resist the prevailing social sensibilities of her domicile, especially if she was in the vulnerable status of a stepchild, as was Prisca.

On the other hand, a determined father, or girl for that matter, could ignore or withstand the pressure from kinsmen. Even then, the educational process had so many dimensions that it was common for relatives to object to one thing or the other, even when they were not opposed to the general idea of the girl's education. This was the case for Keran Akoto:

> There was no opposition to [education] since my father was a church leader and he saw the use of education for me. But my uncles did not like me going to boarding school since they felt I would be lazy and therefore would not be married. Some of my brothers went to school. One of my sisters went to school at Mbale but she misbehaved by removing her teeth against the wishes of my father. For this reason her studies were discontinued. In most cases it was boys who went to school and just a few girls.[70]

In this act, Keran's sister defied both the mission and her father by claiming a traditional practice as her birthright. For doing so, she was removed from the environment she was defying and cast back into the traditional environment that gave her the means to rebel. Such were the negotiations that were possible in the lives of girls sent to missions for education that did not always result in clear-cut choices. At times girls straddled the traditional and the modern, an uncomfortable predicament.

While parents' affiliation with missions was an excellent indicator of a girl's chances of being sent to school, the individual family had to contend with wider social pressure, as Grace Nyanduga discovered. Isaak Were Osundwa, a retired teacher born in 1930, educated all his children, including six daughters and three sons. 'Many people did not want me to educate girls. They said that I was wasting time. They thought that way because they said that these [girls] are people who would after all get married. My experience was that … daughters don't care what they have; they give you the money they have. But sons are very careful with their money.'[71]

According to Rajab Ngaohira, 'a daughter took more care of parents than a son. The little she got was shared with parents. But a son gave out but not as much as a daughter.' Thus, while educating daughters was deemed to be more expensive than sending boys to school, once they started working, daughters were more useful to their natal homes than their male siblings. More often than not, it took the completion of a girl's education and her employment for skeptical members of a community to appreciate the benefits of educating girls. Once women were trained for a profession that the community was beginning to respect, attitudes to formal education began to change. In Marciana Munyendo's case, when 'people heard that I had gone to Mukumu to train as a teacher, they were surprised. Some even emulated my father [by educating their own daughters].'[72]

For some women, the opportunity to acquire formal education came rather late. Mary Muthoni Njogu, born in 1937, said that her mother went to school after marriage. 'She would go to the garden and later go to school.'[73] Her mother's younger siblings probably had a better opportunity to go to school. One of Mary's maternal aunts possibly went to school at a younger age, since she became sufficiently educated to take up a teaching job. Even though the first generation of teachers was not highly educated, it would have been very difficult for a woman to start school after marriage and to sustain the feat long enough to qualify for a teaching career.

It was easier for Agnes Wairimu Hinga to go to school because her widowed mother was 'like the men of today',[74] making the major decisions in her household. Agnes's mother decided to become a Christian and to send her children to school. Agnes believes that had her father been alive, she might not have been able to go to school. He would most likely have responded like the majority of his peers who were opposed to the education of girls. Hence, the authority figure in a household was very significant in determining the educational opportunities of girls. However, this did not follow a predictable pattern.

What actually went on when girls were at school could vary considerably. Despite the common talk about free education for the early mission girls, many had to pay for it in kind by performing domestic chores for the missionaries, and cultivating gardens, 'putting manure on cabbage', among other tasks.[75] During the initial period, tasks performed would be substituted for school fees. At a later period, there would be a direct correlation between the work done and the money earned: the girls would be given school fees for work done.[76] There were other students like Sara Sarai who did not have to pay fees, those 'who had come from a primitive milieu to light', as the missionaries put it.[77]

Farming was a large component of mission life. Fears that girls who went to live on mission stations would become lazy and alienated from the rigour of subsistence agriculture were mistaken. Indeed, there were complaints that mission protégées were grossly overworked; they provided free, and at times forced labour on mission stations. In reality, according to Sara Sarai, they grew their own food, any surplus was sold, and the proceeds invested in the running of the mission.

Each student had her own plot. Sara was as proud of hers, and some of her colleagues were jealous of it. Early one morning, an unprovoked attack by a fellow student escalated to a physical confrontation. 'She came to my bedside in the morning and asked [me] why I, the farmer, was late to my garden. Initially I thought this was a compliment. However, she followed the statement with a sharp slap. She was older than me. I think she belonged to the *Ciringi* age group. *Hi, hi, hi!* She underestimated me! I beat her up so badly everybody was surprised. All this happened within the mission.'

In their efforts to establish peer hierarchies, mission girls did not hesitate to resort to violence. Mission schools were not for the timid. There were scores to be settled and pecking orders to be acknowledged. Commenting on life among students in dormitories at Chogoria in Meru in 1935, Dr. Geoffrey Irvine noted that 'The girls seem[ed] to find each other's company generally much less tolerable than do boys, who have a gift of living happily together.'[78]

In the classroom itself, Agnes Wairimu Hinga recalled that there was not a single African teacher when she went to school, at least not in her area. 'Father [the Catholic priest] came as a visitor. He did a lot of work, struggling to build [the mission], trying to teach the Kikuyu, who did not understand what he was saying' due to the language barrier.[79] Most of the instruction that was offered during this early period was religious. According to Agnes, she and her contemporaries kept repeating the same text over and over. Having spent eight years in school, Agnes, a very ardent student, felt that she had not learnt much. This was because 'Father [the Catholic priest] "*ni gutuhithira uugi*" [hid/rationed knowledge], since he was the only source of formal education.[80]

This belief that the missions were rationing or hoarding Western forms of knowledge was quite widespread. Education was extended to Africans in judicious doses. Commenting on her mother's education, Muthoni Likimani observed: 'at the beginning education was equivalent to learning how to read the Bible. You would be taught how to read the Bible properly, and to write letters, so that you could write to your husband. They were not taught mathematics.'[81]

Summarizing her father's education, Selina Nyona also indicated the close relationship between formal education and religious instruction. 'He went to school in 1920. Learning went up to the third year when one was confirmed as a Christian and as one who knew how to read and write.'[82] Literacy was tied to church matters. After three years of religious and educational instruction, a candidate was considered qualified for confirmation, the equivalent of graduation.

What went on in the classroom was also affected by other factors. In Agnes's school, the shortage of teachers at times resulted in the combining of students from up to four classes that were at different levels of education. Eventually, when the teachers arrived from Kabaa Mission, more mainstream kinds of education, including hygiene, were introduced. Agnes did not recall any separation of boys and girls for instruction. Neither were there uniforms, although students did wear Western clothing to school.

Although boarding school was not compulsory, some of Agnes's contemporaries did become boarders at Riara Mission. The girl boarders were referred to as *airitu a watho*, 'girls under authority'. The priest was personally responsible for locking them in the dormitory in the evening and letting them out in the morning. This physical restriction, symbolic of the missions' attempt to pry their wards from corrupting influences outside, was occasionally looked upon as a positive thing. Comparing mission and government schools, Liza Nyambura observed that 'in mission schools people were well looked after. Girls would not be allowed to do undesirable things; they were closely protected, *kumenyererwo muno*.'[83]

Change and Continuity

Women's access to education and their experiences at school and afterward changed in some ways in the 1940s and 1950s in the wake of the earlier efforts that women had made. As we have seen in the case of Grace Nyanduga, even by the middle of the twentieth century, the cultural status of women's education was very much in doubt. Cultural inertia contended with the dynamics of change, and the former very often prevailed. The experiences of Juliah Ojiambo and Eddah Gachukiah illustrate this interplay of change and continuity.

One aspect was that some girls were entering school much better prepared – yet many were not. In 1942, when Juliah Ojiambo went to Sigalame Primary School, a mission school that her father had helped establish, Juliah, like others with literate parents, had a head start. She could write and read before entering school. At this time, there were no nursery schools, which at a later stage prepared children for school. Her father offered this preparation privately. When Eddah Gachukiah went to school in the same year in a different part of the country, her mother and an aunt, both of who were literate, also had prepared her for school, and her father supported her desire to pursue an education.[84] Yet the cultural isolation that education could bring already had made itself felt.

It was still the case that very few families in Eddah's neighbourhood sent female children to school. During her primary education, she remembers only four such families, 'so you are talking about very few girls in fact, very few girls in the system'.[85] In addition, most of Eddah's female classmates were grown girls. 'The girls that were going to school were adults. It was almost like an adult class, really because you know there were girls ... many of them would get married after one year, or two.'[86] Eddah belonged to the Mbari ya Kihara clan, renowned for its conservative, 'traditional' outlook that held that 'even boys did not go to school'.[87] Her parents were also very staunch Christians whose only way of maintaining their different lifestyle was to stay apart from the rest of their neighbours. 'Clearly, we were not part of that community.'[88] When she was still a little girl and was tempted to join her peers during a trip to the river for a quick swim, Eddah was punished. The exposure of one's nakedness during those swimming escapades was not considered an honourable thing for the children of Christians. The novelist James Ngugi wa Thiongo represented this fission in the title of his novel, *The River Between*,[89] which relates how the introduction of Christianity and its adherents' break with tradition tore families apart.

After four years in the school, in 1950, both Eddah and Juliah were ready for the first national examination, the Common Entrance Examination. Only the select few who passed this examination would be admitted into the limited places in intermediate schools. Because of that, and the fact that many of the female students were quite mature by the time they got to the fourth grade, further education could only take the form of vocational training for most girls. In Juliah's case, the examination was scheduled to take place at Butere Girls Intermediate School, a distance of about forty miles. Candidates, of whom few were girls, came from all over the district. Some from her neighbourhood were her own 'close' cousins, who themselves came from Christian families.

During the last year before the Common Entrance Examination [CEE, taken after four years of elementary school], Eddah had moved to a school at Kiambaa, since this was the only school in the neighbourhood with an examination class. Her home was eight to ten miles away – a distance she had to walk twice every day. It was a day mixed school, with forty students from the surrounding area admitted to the senior class. At the end of the first term, a preliminary examination test was administered; twenty of the forty students were eliminated, including all the girls except Eddah: 'So I was left in a class all by myself … so for one whole year I was all alone in that [class].'[90] The gender imbalance created a great sense of isolation for Eddah, a situation made worse by the fact that the majority of her male classmates were much older than she was. Additionally, Eddah was surprised at how often the response to her superior performance in school elicited the response 'if only she was a boy'.[91] She was perceived as a misgendered talent.

Further educational opportunities for women were very limited. At the end of one year, a girl might be a CEE candidate. At the beginning of the following year, she might be a teacher in her old school. She would be 'converted into a teacher almost overnight'.[92] Thus, Liza Nyambura became an untrained teacher after five years of formal education. Born in 1933, and having a father who had had three years of formal education, Liza, her sisters, and her brothers were all sent to school.[93] Some of her contemporaries in different parts of the country likewise would have proceeded to vocational training in nursing or teaching after the CEE. Liza chose to be a teacher because 'teaching was characterized by upright behaviour,'[94] and because she believed that her level of education was insufficient for any other kind of job. Juliah and Eddah, on the other hand, were in a cohort of female students determined to explore a road less travelled by girls – that of intermediate education.

For Juliah the transition from primary to intermediate school was quite smooth. Not so for Eddah. Although she had passed the national examination, there were other hurdles ahead. Her possible admission to the girls' intermediate school at Kikuyu, *Mambere*, was thwarted by the structural setup of the school. In addition to attending class, students were expected to do their own laundry, clean their dormitories, and grow their own food, among other tasks. This was the same Church of Scotland Mission school that Sara Sarai had attended in the late 1930s. [95] A decade and a half later, in 1946, the girls were still expected to grow their own food. When Eddah was taken to the school for an admissions interview, the headmistress rejected her because of her age and size, declaring: 'She cannot manage the chores at the school, she is too young.'

Eddah was forced to cross the denominational divide and got admission into a Catholic school at Loreto, Limuru. Her father was 'furious' about the religious shift involved. Protestants perceived the Catholic Church as very lax. It did not stop its adherents from drinking or from circumcising their daughters. To Eddah's father, these were fundamental issues. He therefore took the earliest opportunity to remove his daughter from the Catholic school. Eddah thus transferred from Loreto Limuru to a Protestant school at Kabete. It was here that she sat her Kenya African Primary

Examination, K.A.P.E. In 1950, Juliah too sat for the K.A.P.E. not knowing what would become of her with regard to higher education because this examination was the terminus for the majority of girls.

In 1950, five and a half decades since the beginning of British rule, there was not a single high school for African girls in Kenya. A small group of Kenyan girls had been admitted to the Alliance Boys High School in 1947. As well as these, a few more girls went to high school in Uganda, a neighbouring British colony. Thus for the majority of girls, the Kenya African Primary Examination, the K.A.P.E, was the end of their academic road regardless of how well they had performed.

Going Home: Eating Chicken

The cultural effect of education on communities and their traditional values and practices was most evident when women with mission education returned home. We have already seen in the case of Grace Nyanduga that even under the most favourable circumstances of parental support, the relationship between a girl who had left home to pursue an education and those who remained at home could be very complicated. This was especially true when she returned, either for a visit or permanently. Going home meant bringing with her the forces that were changing Kenyan society, whether they were welcome or not. Crossing previously impermeable barriers and journeying both physically and culturally to previously unknown places meant not only that women who returned to their places of origin were themselves changed, but that they became part of the dynamics of change in their families and communities, as well.

Returning as 'something else', returning changed and as an agent of change, could be dangerous. For example, after two years at Thogoto Mission School, Serah Mukabi decided it was time to visit her home. Her father's hostility to her education had continued unabated, and she was concerned that she had put her mother, who had supported it, through too much suffering. Whatever the cost to Serah herself, she felt she must put this suffering to an end. She believed that she would definitely receive severe beating from her father, but it was a consequence she was ready to face. Serah's determination to visit her family encouraged four other girls whom she had inspired to come to Thogoto, including two of her sisters, to venture as much. 'We will go and die together',[96] the sisters concluded, arranging to make the visit during the Christmas break.

It was important to Serah that the visit take place publicly, that she did not sneak back home. She was clear on two things: she would not get married, and she would go right back to the mission after the visit. Under the circumstances, it is understandable that she would want to alert as many people in her new milieu as possible about the impending visit. She and her friends informed the mission and the church about their plans. The school and the church in turn asked the girls to convey their greetings to their families, assuming all would be well.

Serah's return was anything but a normal visit of a boarding-school girl to her family. A man of considerable means and a befitting social stature, her father, Kang'ethe Kihika, was an opinion-setter who had made it very clear that he was opposed to the mission intrusion in his area. While other people in his circle might defer to him, three of his daughters had taken him on in what amounted to a public duel of wits. Serah captured her homecoming thus:

> Our home was at Mathere facing the direction of Nakuru town. My father's homestead was on a hill. We alighted from the train. When we alighted, people who saw us and heard that we were going home to Kang'ethe wa Kihika's homestead … the famous and widely known person, they were very surprised to hear that that was where we were going. The people said, 'We do not know to which home you will go.' 'Why?' Serah asked. 'We will go there and face death if necessary.'

So Serah and her sisters proceeded to go to their homestead, much to the consternation of the neighbours and despite these cautionary remarks.

It was not so much the threat of physical violence, but the social death that a mission education could bring that was uppermost in the minds of everyone. As luck would have it, the first person the girls encountered on entering the homestead was their paternal grandmother, *cucu*.[97] Serah's father was an only child. As soon as their grandmother saw them, she started crying. She could not believe her eyes. 'We have been thinking that you died,' *cucu* said.

Anxious moments elapsed as, from the safety of their grandmother's house, Serah and her sisters awaited the arrival of their father. Even as she prepared food for her grandchildren, *cucu* was anxious as to when her son would appear. Everybody was anxious. The fact that the girls' first meal after two or three years of absence was prepared at their grandmother's house was significant. In the whole large homestead, only the house of the paternal matriarch was safe. Only she could face and possibly calm the rage anticipated from Serah's father. The girls soon emerged as pawns in the intricate process of mediating social change in their household. Such drama must have been replayed in numerous other homes.

When Kang'ethe arrived, he was drunk, but not too drunk to appreciate the gravity of what was happening in his homestead. The news of his daughters' return was broken to him by his mother. Using the most endearing address, she said 'Let me tell you son of Njeri [referring to herself], my children who have been dead all this while are back. Wambui [Serah] and all the other children are here.' The grandmother's claim of progeny in a patriarchal society might have represented an inversion of convention. On the other hand, the two, Kang'ethe and his mother, had a special rapport.

In a graduated sequence of threats, Kang'ethe first threatened to beat the girls. The grandmother retorted that Kang'ethe would have to beat her first, and kill her, before he could touch 'her' children. *Cucu* played all her maternal cards. She reminded Kang'ethe that motherhood had not been particularly kind to her. Children were not to be taken for granted. They were precious. For that reason, she would not allow Kang'ethe to beat the children. She went on for some time admonishing her son.

The girls, however, were quite apprehensive, believing that despite the intervention of their grandmother, their father would beat them. Their only recourse was to remain at their grandmother's house as long as their father was raging. They spent that first night at *cucu*'s, escaping the initial wrath of Kang'ethe. The next morning, however, Kang'ethe changed tactics in his attack of the mission's encroachment into his household.

Their father insisted that the girls get rid of their Western mission dresses and lashed out at Serah's sewn ears. For those two reasons, he demanded that the girls leave the homestead. The mission's external refashioning of its wards set them apart, not only from their peers, but from their father, too. Kang'ethe did not want to harbour or be identified with daughters who identified with a foreign and different social structure. He was a true Kikuyu, and so would all the members of his household be. Perhaps it was possible to force them into their old selves by making them abandon the ways in which the mission had refashioned their external appearance.

For all his anger, however, Kang'ethe did not carry out his threats. He had great fear of and respect for his mother and did not take her recriminations lightly. She had used very strong language and had put her own life on the line in her effort to protect her granddaughters. Her challenge to Kang'ethe to beat her or kill her was taboo. Kang'ethe had no recourse but to back down; he withdrew into his hut, and did not talk to anybody for a week. He would not visit his mother. Still afraid that their father might beat them, the girls continued to stay at their grandmother's place, but they did have contact with their respective mothers. A cloud of uncertainty descended upon the homestead, because nobody knew what the outcome would be.

After a week, Kang'ethe was ready to take control of the situation. He summoned the girls to his private hut, the *thingira*. They would not willingly take themselves to their father's hut for a beating – they preferred to run away. They told their grandmother so and she acted as go-between. She would not hear of the girls running away, and assured them that she had already spoken to her son and that he did not intend to beat them. To calm them down, she spoke to her son again, and he said: 'Tell them I will not beat them. If I had intended to beat them I would have done it when they first arrived.'[98] Beyond the tension and heat of the moment, things could be settled in a better way.

In the end, things worked out differently from what either Serah or her father had anticipated. Serah changed her plans for her future, but Kang'ethe also changed his sense of who he was and what his family had become. Serah's defiance of her father's wishes with regard to formal education and mission activities had astonished him. He was not used to anybody within his household challenging him. It was as if in his own daughter he had found his match, despite gender and age differences. Even if it meant being thrown out of her natal home, Serah had made it clear that she intended to go back to school, and was resolute about continuing her education, especially now, since 'Jesus would help'. She had vowed to God to pursue formal education, and she would keep the promise. As it turned out, however, she would not keep it by returning to the mission. She and her father reached an accommodation.

Once the girls had entered his house, Kang'ethe got up, walked out, and asked the girls to follow him. He headed for the large family farm. At an appropriate place, he started striding in a deliberate manner demarcating individual plots for each of the girls. The plan was for each girl to cultivate her plot and to finance her education from the proceeds. Serah was the first to respond to the challenge. 'Yes, if you give me land I will cultivate. I will not go away.... I will educate myself.' Doubtful of Serah's ability to execute both tasks competently, her father asked her whether she would manage to cultivate and go to school at the same time. Serah's answer was in the affirmative. So the girls were allotted land which they would cultivate, selling the proceeds to finance their education. From that point on, Kang'ethe did not forbid any of his daughters to go to school. In fact, he surpassed all expectation: 'I have opened the door for your education. From today, there will not reside a single uneducated child in this homestead. Seeing that you [Serah] left my homestead and went to school, I will never offer another sacrifice.'[100]

In his attempt to ensure the growth of his children into pure Kikuyu, Kang'ethe had conformed to all the required rituals and sacrifices, ensuring that his daughters underwent all rites of passage. In going to the mission, Serah, and her sisters had renounced their Kikuyuness. Kang'ethe did not intend to stand in their way. There would be no more Kikuyu rituals in the family, except in their reconstructed form – reconstructed by Kang'ethe. As Serah put it, ' Kikuyu rituals came to a complete stop [at our home] from that day'. This possibly referred to clitoridectomy and the piercing of ears.

The girls proved to be very successful at their farming venture. Growing all manner of vegetables, they catered for the local indigenous market and Asians at the local township market. The girls planted cabbage, potatoes, onions, and peas. Serah remembers that she also grew carrots, a foreign vegetable that was not eaten in her home, yet was cherished by her 'European' clients. If it took raising carrots to go to school, Serah was going to do it.[100] Instead of going back to the boarding school at the mission station in Thogoto, the girls went to a neighbourhood school at Kanyekine. Serah had more educational skills than her sisters and friends. For this reason, her stay at the Kanyekine School was short-lived. She soon graduated to Githuyo School.

Serah was still dissatisfied because her younger brother, Peter, was not going to school, yet. While a student at Githuyo, Serah arranged to have him admitted at Kanyekine. Obviously, this entailed the payment of fees, which Serah had to factor into her cultivation plans, but it was an extra burden she was willing to take. Although her father could afford to educate Peter, he never offered to do it, nor did Serah ask for any financial help from her father. 'He would not sell his livestock to pay school fees.' Peter's mother, however, did pitch in, since some of the produce from her garden was sold and the proceeds used to supplement Serah's income from her own plot. Since Serah also worked on her mother's land, quite obviously her contribution towards Peter's education was major. As well as paying her own and her brother's school fees, she was also able to buy clothes for herself and to contribute to the household's consumer items. However, as her experience had shown her, things did not always work out that neatly in the Kang'ethe homestead.

This latest of Serah's educational initiatives was bound to create more problems. Like other uncircumcised boys in the family, Peter had looked after the large family herds. In a polygamous family, all the boys would come together to tend the flock. Peter's absence did not go down well with his father, and his brothers and their mothers probably resented him. His own mother was strongly reprimanded for letting her son abandon family livestock in order to go to school. In allowing Serah and her sisters to get back to school, Kang'ethe had sworn that there would never be uneducated children in his homestead. Why then, was he upset when Peter went to school?

Clearly, Serah was still a strong-willed daughter whose actions continued to antagonize Kang'ethe, among other people. In her own flight, Serah had fanned her father's opposition to missionaries, but in taking Peter to school, she had interfered with the labour needs of the family, encroaching on the wealth basis of the homestead. Serah, a girl, had crossed the gender divide and, in a way, had usurped the leadership position within the family, redeploying family labour at will. She was an open challenge to her father and a source of trouble for her mother.

In the end, Serah did not attain as high an education as her brother did. Settling for elementary education, she decided to concentrate on educating her brother. Peter was a good student and proceeded to graduate from high school, a rewarding investment for Serah. Upon completion of school, Peter was employed at the local Bata Shoe Company. In the end, none of her other brothers went to school. In an indirect way, Serah attributed her limited education to lack of money. It is possible that at some stage she had to make a choice between her own and her brother's education. Girls like Grace Nyanduga, girls for whom money was no problem, or who came from homes where fathers appreciated education, could go on to Kahuhia Medical Training School where they would train to be 'doctors', that is, nurses and midwives. In her case, Serah's educational plans were 'confused by my love for my brother'.[101] She craved to continue in school even as she educated Peter. Ultimately, it became necessary for her to sacrifice her own hopes for further education.

Although after her return from Thogoto Mission Serah had fallen into the same routine as everybody else in the homestead,[102] for twelve years after circumcision, she did not get married. This was an unusually long time. While her peers were surprised, they were also critical and downright nasty about Serah's delay of marriage. They would openly say that as a result of her advance in years, she would never give birth. Serah's response was characteristic of her singleness of mind: 'We did not mind being despised, or being continually slandered.'[103] According to Serah, however, uneducated boys feared girls who had gone to school. There is ample evidence indicating that they, like the majority of the community, continued to have a low opinion of mission protégées.

Although Serah Mukabi's return home from the mission school became permanent, her mission education nevertheless transformed both her life and the lives of those with whom she now continued to live. The transformations wrought by returning mission-educated girls could be even more radical, more extensive, and indeed more subversive than the case of Serah Mukabi suggests. They also could elicit even more extreme responses than those exhibited by Kang'ethe.

While Sara Sarai was at Njoro, her Rift Valley home, and before her return to the mission, for example, she combined preaching about the imminent second coming of Christ with the creation of an underground network that conveyed willing girls to the mission at Thogoto. Her missionizing meetings were well attended by girls from the surrounding farms. 'My task henceforth was to record their names for onward transmission to Thogoto.'[104] Sara would facilitate the girls' flight from their homes, and more importantly, she would give them introductory notes to the mission.

This missionizing task took its toll on her family. On several occasions, Sara abandoned her family livestock as she pursued her preaching or recruitment tasks. Wild animals devoured many of the livestock, and as Sarah reminisced about these issues, she observed that she could never compensate her father sufficiently. He no longer knew how to communicate with Sarah, whom he believed had become insane in her quest for education. The fact that her father considered her a good daughter and could not explain her aberrant behavior made the situation more confounding. He wondered whether she was bewitched. He soon came up with one last attempt to exorcise from Sara what appeared to be a fixation with the mission.

As a last resort, Sara was taken to a *mundu mugo*, a medicine man, who it was hoped would establish the nature of her problem and cure it. Sara remembers the administration of 'medicine' through incisions made on her body. Sara's father took her many times to the soothsayer, each time hoping that the latter would cure his daughter's condition. Abandoning his livestock, Sara's father ultimately took her for divination at Elementeita, a distance of about thirty miles South East of Njoro. At this point, she was considered 'a nonperson'.

Among other things, her family offered sacrifices in an attempt to rid Sara of any evil spirits deemed responsible for her weird behaviour. This also entailed an attempt to appease and entreat God to save the situation. But neither the application of the indigenous brand of moral intervention nor physical force was enough to constrain Sara. She returned to the mission and completed her elementary education. Subsequently she trained as a midwife and was the first African-trained midwife to be posted at Mbiri Native African Hospital at Murang'a.[105]

Not all of the changes that mission-educated girls brought home with them were so radical, but some were actually more far-reaching. They could transform the character of everyday life – for example, what people ate and who was allowed to eat it. The spread of what once would have been regarded as culinary impropriety was one result of the expansion of girls' education.

Food can be a cultural and social map of any community. For example, among the Luyia, there were widely accepted food sanctions and taboos, some constructed along gender lines. The missionaries who introduced Christianity not only tried to alter the diets of its adherents, but also dismissed the food taboos as baseless superstition. With regard to food taboos that affected women, the added argument that these were meant to rob women of vital nutrition attracted the attention of mission families. In Juliah Ojiambo's home, women and girls ate all the foods denied women by custom, including chicken, eggs and some wild game.

The rationale for the delineation of culinary practices and taboos becomes obscure with time. The observance of the practices, however, goes on. What passes for conventional knowledge becomes binding, yet difficult to explain.[106] Like Magdalene Musundi, Isaak Were Osundwa could not remember why women were not allowed to eat chicken. 'These were rules that we found at birth. As you know, chicken is sweeter than meat. I think it was just men's plan.... What eventually made women eat chicken was Christianity.... Once they got converted testimonies were exchanged which encouraged them to start eating chicken.'[107]

The dissemination of alternative and subversive knowledge and experience through new church networks reworked the dietary and gender sensibilities of newly evangelized and educated communities. For the educated who returned home, conviction in their new dietary practices was reinforced by the acquisition of new nutritional knowledge. Marciana Munyendo, a retired teacher observed:

> I am the only one in our home who ate chicken. My elder sister never ate it. I learnt to eat it while I was in boarding [school] at Mumias. There we were told that poultry has bodybuilding nutrients. When we went back home, we used to eat chicken as the villagers laughed at us. They sung songs that indicated that poultry was reserved for boys.... Neither were we allowed to eat rabbits. To me this was meant to keep the respect in those days. I started eating chicken when I was very young. I am the only one who ate chicken with my father.[108]

Like Marciana, Magdalene Musundi also first ate chicken at school. Her neighbours 'really wondered how women could eat chicken. They laughed at us'.[109] In the Ng'iya area of Kisumu Ezekiel Apindi, who joined missionaries in 1905, was closely associated with the establishment of girls' education in the region. He rose up the ladder of mission hierarchy to the position of canon. His advocacy of poultry and eggs in women's diet encouraged transgression, soon captured in their joyful song:

> My hen, my hen will know me. The chick will enter my throat.
> And my daughter will eat with me. Apindi the husband of husbands
> Is the only one in our village.[110]

Eating chicken, among other items and practices, served as a basis for the construction and reconstruction of gender, honour, and respect in different communities. The observance of the old practices reinforced gender delineation, maintained social order, and ensured honour and respect for the individual members of the family, as well as the corporate family and community bodies. A man whose wife and/or daughter ate chicken with or without his consent brought dishonour to the family. In this respect, the honour of men depended on the observance of the acceptable food codes by women.

Education brought a permanent shift in the dietary practices of some women. The gap between the conventional and the new wisdom about 'eating chicken' enforced a reworking of gender, honour, and respect as constructed in the affected communities. As surveyors of moral integrity and weavers of social order, husbands and their communities faced challenge from mission-educated women.

In the transgressions of norms of social order by a public and ritualized crossing of boundaries involved in quotidian acts such as 'eating chicken', the confluence of spatial, temporal, gender, and public performance added immediacy to the transgressions.

> It [eating chicken] started in our home. When my father was pastor, he called Barnabas Akwale's wife, Rael, then Milka, Mariam Mukuyua and my mother. They slaughtered a cock and they ate it. Everybody was surprised and given that it [the homestead] was along the way, everybody that passed spit saliva in surprise. The school-going girls followed up eating chicken. People did not like it. My father wanted to change the habit because they had been taught at school that all these things could be eaten [by both sexes]. All those who participated did so with their husbands.[111]

Mission adherents believed that the effect of missionary training permeated the whole culinary scene. It was not restricted to particular foods. As Isaak Were Osundwa stated, 'Even in the kitchens, there emerged a difference. While the uneducated [women] used traditional ash salt and milk butter for cooking, the educated bought [refined] salt and cooking fat.'[112]

Such changes, great and small, from a father's sense of his family's ethnic identity to overthrowing prohibitions on who ate what, gradually began to accumulate in ways that transformed the behaviour and values of families whose children had received education – mission education – in particular. Communities within existing communities began to emerge, away from mission stations, but linking the homes of mission adherents and mission students, and defined by their adherence to different practices and rituals. Mission children and their families increasingly grew up in communities of their own, including non-family members who came to join them.

The milieu in which Juliah Ojiambo grew up was one such emerging community. Juliah's home, like other homes of mission adherents, was a center of social change. It was a venue for many types of transitions, personal and communal. As Juliah grew up, she witnessed various rituals of Christianity and formal education in her extended paternal and maternal families, including church weddings, baptisms, conversions, and professional career training. As Juliah said, 'They picked it up and went for it'.[113] Although she was referring to formal education, it was the effects of formal education that lay at the center of the social change that families like hers were effecting.

Juliah's homestead was a daily hive of activity from the large number of non-family members who either lived there or sought the services of Juliah's mother. As Juliah observed, ' [My mother] was a first class evangelist … that woman had learnt the highest communication technology in her own way, she was a lawyer, she was a teacher, she was a communication expert, and she knew how to woo people in her own language.'[114] She was deeply involved in the affairs of the community.

Juliah's mother had emerged as a community leader, a situation that in the 1920s and 1930s was quite unique. She did not receive the open support of the community, however. A lot of the situations in which she intervened were very sensitive. For example, a large proportion of her encounters revolved around matters of domestic conflict. She was particularly averse to domestic violence. She would 'never see a woman suffering' without intervening. For her actions,

> She was abused, and she would never stop.... She built a real big *banda* [shed] in our home, so we lived in a kind of dormitory because she went collecting all these women she found being beaten, or being forced into marriage. She would take [those] girls and give them refuge in our home. If she finds a widow being battered by the in-laws, she would bring [her]. She [Juliah's mother] was a nurse-cum social worker-cum everything. She would clean the wounds, bandage them, nurse them until they are well and then [lead] them [to] the church community and teach them how to read, and convert them, and baptize them, and eventually teach them to look for a Christian man and marry. You know, that kind of thing.[115]

The attainment of formal education increased the isolation of such emerging communities from the traditional communities around them. Magdaline Musundi, who went to school from the mid-1940s to 1956, when she completed her teacher training, remembers this separation:

> From school our parents did not allow us to socialize with the uneducated ones. Our parents feared that uneducated girls who thought about local dances and marriage would influence us. Teachers had instructed us to be careful with ourselves so that we too may become teachers or nurses like them.... We never used to sit and play with [uneducated] girls. They called us *Abasungu*, Europeans. In fact because of our example, many people started going to school as parents took their daughters to school.[116]

This did not mean that the children had lonely lives. A common day might bring up to twenty outsiders for various reasons. Many of those who spent the night at the home were not family members. It was one crowded place: 'When we went to sleep it was like a dormitory and we just spread mats and we all slept in this open hall.'[117] In many ways, Juliah's home was very much like Muthoni Likimani's, which also hosted a variety of mission adherents, among others. 'Communicants would fill our home on the eve of Holy Communion. This was because during those days Holy Communion was only celebrated at the main "mother" church. So they would come from Iyego and elsewhere very early in the morning. Some of them spent the previous night at my home.'[118] Other visitors, pursuing an education, 'not wanting to be late for their examination, and in order to pick their examination numbers in advance ... would be sent by their parents to our home to spend the eve of the examination at our house. We would make an outside enclosure where they would sleep. We would sleep on the ground. At times they would be told to sleep in the granary. My mother would cook in a huge pot.'[119] Education thus created new communal spaces in the midst of existing indigenous communities.

Women, Education and Work

We have focused largely on education at mission stations and on the physical and cultural migration of women to the sites of change. Only the smallest minority of students at higher levels of education went to boarding schools, however. The rest had to balance an unyielding schedule of domestic responsibilities against their academic pursuits, as Serah Mukabi eventually had to do. Education and work competed for these girls' undivided attention. Selina Nyona's experience was typical.

> We used to go to school far away. We went all the way to Butere because the school at Matioli was not a C.M.S. school. We cooked in the morning and we went to school at 8:00 A.M. We never took lunch and parents could not give us money for lunch. We left school at 4.00 P.M. Back home girls would find grains made ready and supper prepared. We thereafter started grinding [millet, sorghum] until 9.00 P.M. At 10.00 P.M. we would then sleep. For garden work, we did it in the morning before going to school. We never studied at home. Normally we arrived home and found a lot of work left. We only read at school. Books would only be found at school. There were no books at home.... In fact, because of these arrangements we lost a lot of knowledge.[120]

Food preparation took a large part of the work routine in all homesteads. This was because of the rudimentary nature of the technology in use. Grinding grains for the production of flour loomed large in the domestic chores of most homesteads. It was definitely important to the schoolgirls. The same was true of the whole agricultural process, including digging, weeding, harvesting, shelling, threshing, and winnowing. All these, except digging, were done manually. In a few homes, the plough was used for opening up the land. While this was a faster and more efficient technique, it also expanded women's labour time, since all the land so opened was subsequently worked manually.[121] Schoolgirls had to participate in these expanded chores. 'We all went to the *shamba*, garden, and did the grinding together. There was no difference. Grinding flour was difficult because we used stones. In fact I saw a grinding mill for the first time after I married here in Mumias', Magdalene Musundi said.[122] These tasks established the girls in the ways of their communities, and more importantly, validated their identities, verifying their preparedness for the productive aspect of marriage.

The pressure from this double work was greater for the more educated girls. There was greater fear in the community that the further such girls climbed the educational ladder, the more alienated from their communities' ways they would become. To avoid that, they would have to engage in some astute bargaining and scheduling. Ham Aggrey Wanzetse was of the opinion that academic work was not affected by the heavy domestic demands: 'These girls would also come back and do the work of grinding at night. So the mother only cooked the next day. Also going to school and coming back was not like today. They came back at 3.00 P.M.'[123] In general, as already noted, studying at home away from the school was almost impossible anyway, since students were not allowed to take their schoolbooks home. Magdaline Musundi remarked that 'when we were about to do our examinations, that is when we were allowed to come home with books. We asked for permission to study but we never had enough time to study because no sooner had one started studying than she was given another task to accomplish.'[124]

For Prisca Ayuku, who from a very early age lived with her grandparents, household tasks were almost overwhelming. 'I used to wake up very early in the morning, go for water [from the river, two to three trips], after which I would go to the *shamba*, garden. Cutting fodder for cattle was my responsibility [because] my grandmother had nobody else to do that job for her. [After that] I went to school and in the evening I had to grind *wimbi*, millet, and *mtama*, sorghum, in order to get flour for our food.'[125] This routine continued until 1950, when Prisca went to Butere Girls' Boarding School.

However, the pressure of domestic duties was not always the end of the road for some girls. As mentioned earlier in this chapter, Mary Muthoni Njogu's mother had gone to school as a married woman.[126] Other married women adopted various strategies that baffled their contemporaries and drew contempt from some family members. Mama Deborah started school in 1944 and stayed in mission education until the end of 1948. Although she passed the Common Entrance Examination, her place in the next grade was ostensibly given to a pastor's daughter, so she dropped out of school and subsequently got married in 1952. Upon her husband's death in 1956, and already with two children, Deborah immediately went back to school, where she stayed for two more years.

Still 'married'[127] in the same homestead, Deborah took her two young children to school and 'left them at the office' during classes. While the wider community believed she was insane, her in-laws were more elaborate on the nature of social infractions committed by Deborah: 'They said I was wasting time [in school]and [that] there was no need for me to go back to school instead of cultivating, taking care of the children, and the homestead. They said *mimi natangatanga*, I was loitering.'[128] A brilliant student, Deborah had the full support of her teachers. Most importantly, her father continued to pay her fees for as long as he was able to do so. Furthering her quest for 'development' by participating in Maendeleo ya Wanawake [Women's Progress] meetings, Deborah also worked as a ticket 'master' at Homa Bay market for some time, beginning in 1966. She proceeded to be a union representative of market people till 1976, when she opted for self-employment. A mission protégée, Deborah continues to practise traditional medicine, a skill she learnt from her father. The ways in which women who had a thirst for education could successfully pursue it were many and varied, despite the very excessive demands of women's work.

Not Pursuing Higher Education

The pursuit of higher education and professional training in the late 1940s and throughout the 1950s was a relatively new development. Both entailed greater alienation from peers and the community. Compared to personal hurdles, it was even more difficult for the girls to surmount structural problems that hampered higher education and training for women. These included a glaring dearth of high schools and training facilities for girls and women, official reluctance to provide these facilities, and a general lack of community support.

There was no high school for girls in Kenya before 1950. In that year, a handful of girls were admitted at the Alliance Boys High School. However, 'Carey Francis [the headmaster, Alliance Boys' High School] would not admit more than three girls [in any one given year]. Even [admitting] three was a crime, mixing [boys] with girls. [Those admitted included] Margaret Kenyatta, Grace Wagema, and Joan Waithaka [née Gitau].'[129]

For those lucky enough to undergo professional training, advancement within the field was difficult. By 1948, for example, Rachel Warigia had taught as a T.3[130] teacher for five years, having passed her Lower Primary Training course in 1943 at Kahuhia Normal School. Earlier, in 1941, she had passed her Primary Certificate Examination at CMS Kabete. Having accomplished more than her female contemporaries, Rachel set her sight on higher education. In an entry dated October 1948, a colonial official from the Education Department observed that there was no objection to Rachel writing her application examination [for admission to Makerere College]. The officer added 'I hope she will not be admitted to Makerere

College unless her papers indicate that she is likely to complete the adult course, successfully in the normal two years.'[131] Rachel would be trying for the most advanced opportunity without the advantage of T.2 training, or a high school education. This was the next level of professional teacher training for women, which was not introduced until January 1950. Bureaucratic Catch 22s could always be thrown up by administrators sceptical of women's education.

Sometimes, communities even attributed to missions the partial responsibility for the early termination of girls' education and for their failure to go to secondary school. Rajab Ngashira, who worked at Mumias Mission boarding school from 1950 to 1966, got this impression from his observations of female teachers at the school. By 1950, an increasing number of female teachers here, including Wanga women, came from Ngashira's home area. Ngashira observed that: 'these women were educated during the days when *muliangos*, lineage heads, forced them. But at the missions, students rarely went to secondary school.'[132]

For some, the simple need to maintain some level of stability in a changing world where men were pursuing wage labour in distant places and frequently absent, served as an incentive for women not to pursue education for themselves. Such women chose to maintain a home for their family in rural areas while their husbands worked in the cities. Rural areas represented a sense of order, familiarity, continuity, and stability. For Magdaline Musundi, leaving home disrupted the whole homestead.

> In our days, if my husband worked away from home, I would opt to remain at home to do my work. I would remain to cultivate crops, rear a cow, and generally keep the home clean. I also stayed with my husband in Kericho, Mombasa, and Taita. But when I came back the home was poorly maintained. In those days we never liked staying out for those reasons. We liked it if our husbands came back on retirement and found an organized and good home.[133]

Even educated women who could have accompanied their husbands to work in urban areas either chose or were under pressure to work in rural areas. Women also were not expected to surpass prospective suitors in formal education, and successful suitors were often unhappy when their prospective wives attempted to do so. As Keran Akoto remembers:

> Marriage interfered with my plans since I wanted to continue with my education, get good training and a job. But because my parents were interested in getting cows [dowry], they spoilt my plans. ... they refused since they wanted me to get married. I got annoyed but since I was under their care I had nothing to do but to oblige. I had [also] wanted to join secondary school and even if possible pursue much higher education. I had developed interest in joining Alliance High School so that I could get a better job.... Again, when I got married in 1947, my husband refused to allow me to go [for the nursing training] He wanted me to do a job that would keep me around the home.[134]

As we have seen in most cases, it was parents that had the most immediate effect of the future of a girl's educational hopes, and parents were most frequently responsible for bringing an early end to girls' education. To justify preventing a girl from pursuing an education, parents would cite all the negative characterisations of educated women that we have seen were endemic in Kenyan culture. Keran Akoto's account of the reasons parents gave for preventing her further education is a virtual compendium of the attitudes toward physically and culturally mobile women that we have been examining.

> They feared that I would become a girl of bad morals. Boys also never wanted girls whom they were classmates with to get higher marks than them. They sometimes beat up such a girl. This dampened the morale of the girls.[135]

Changes in attitudes toward education – indeed, toward women's agency in general – thus came slowly and unevenly to the indigenous cultures of Kenya. For those who saw change as opportunity, resistance to it could seem inexplicable. Although it is widely attested that parents compromised the education of girls for purposes of marrying them off, this nevertheless bewildered some daughters when it happened. Selina Nyona, for example, did not understand why her father married her off in the middle of her educational career. She still wonders about it. In the context of her transformed world, the world of the educated, Selina considered herself to have been too young to marry. Asked why her father married her off when he did, Selina responded: 'I don't know. I still remember and wonder about it. He thought that that was my only chance [to get married]. I had nothing to tell my parents.... But when I left school my teachers complained bitterly because I was very good in English and other subjects like music. Even today there is a teacher who still complains bitterly. What really pushed my father was bridewealth.'[136] At times, the juxtaposition of the old and the new left both the elders and the youth at a loss.

The opportunity for further training was offered to a small number of girls from different parts of Kenya. Muthoni referred to all these girls as 'university material'. Miss Janisch, the Department of Education Officer in charge of girls' education in the late 1940s had the unenviable task of ensuring equitable gender representation in training. The crop of girls who were ready for high school continued to question the rationale for their exclusion. As Muthoni and her classmate Patricia Oloo, whom Muthoni described as 'fantastic and brilliant', tried to deal with their predicament, they would ask, 'how can they cut us [off] like that?'[137] Muthoni described herself and her friend Patricia as 'radicals'. Emphasizing her friend's general defiant demeanor when they were students at the Teacher Training College, Muthoni mimicked the way Patricia would stand akimbo whenever things were not right.

Muthoni was not admitted to the Alliance Boys' High School. For her the only alternative was to travel to the neighbouring colony of Uganda where she would attend the much coveted and elitist Gayaza Girls High School. Mission adherents' construction of the 'good' girl or woman demanded a measure of self-effacement and blind acquiescence that Muthoni did not conform to. Her defiance of these social restrictions consolidated the local opinion of her as a rebel. At Kahuhia, where Muthoni did her intermediate studies in the mid-1940s, socialization between the two sexes was kept to a minimum. They were not even allowed to 'greet' each other as they criss-crossed on the school compound. Muthoni's gregarious quality that had her socializing freely with young men in her community was to cost her the chance to go to high school. The community argued, and her family agreed, that it would not be prudent to allow such an extroverted girl as Muthoni to attend high school in such a distant location.

Muthoni, who came from Kahuhia in Central Province, had to settle for a teacher-training course, along with other pioneer female elites including Phoebe Asiyo from Nyanza Province, Ruth Habwe from Western Kenya, and Hope Mwang'ombe from the Coast Province. They were admitted to a new government Teachers' Training College, which had initial temporary accommodation at the site of the present day Mary Leakey High School at Kabete, just outside Nairobi.

The gender and moral dimensions in the above case were pervasive throughout the period from the 1930s to the 1950s. Some aspects of the specifics of Muthoni's experience serve to illustrate the nature of the mundane issues that helped to determine the direction of a woman's public and private careers. The level of gender separation imposed by missions and missionized families was considered ridiculous by some of the mission girls. The control of women's mobility was closely associated with the basic concern to control their sexuality. Often this included efforts to limit social contact between the sexes.

In providing education in the late 1940s, the government had failed to balance the gender distribution of institutions of higher learning, especially high schools. Even as girls settled for low-level professional training, qualified boys could chose between Mang'u, Kagumo, Alliance and Maseno high schools. Muthoni attained a high school diploma at a later period, when as a married woman she studied as a private candidate through a correspondence programme.

The early 1950s were characterized by tremendous changes in women's education. For some girls, a new development in government policy saved the day. By 1950, it was decided to establish the first high school for African girls at Kikuyu in Central Province. This became the African Girls High School, later the Alliance Girls High School. Eight girls representing different parts of Kenya were admitted as the first class. It was important for the government to balance the country's ethnic mix. The girls were picked on merit; they were the best of the best. The eight girls were Eddah Gachukiah, Winifred Wanyoike, Loice Waruhiu, Charity (?surname), Margaret Alivitza Martins Kibisu, Serah Migiza Lukalo, Grace Odhiambo, and Juliah Ojiambo.

Initially it was not clear whether the girls at Alliance would pursue a four-year high school course, or whether that would be reduced to two years. Symbolically, the girls' school did not have any permanent buildings. A temporary structure, the school also did not provide adequate facilities for the girls. The girls believed their future was in their own hands. If some of them did not survive the rigorous educational instruction, they would drop off and 'the remainder would go to Alliance [Boys School]. We were living from day to day and carrying on [learning] in our classrooms, and where we didn't have facilities, we'd go across to the boys' school.'[138]

Going over to the boys' school had symbolic significance for the female students. The girls had to match the performance of the boys if their school was to stand the test of time. Additionally, Alliance Boys' High School was 'the' school in colonial Kenya. Juliah captured this implied struggle thus: 'We knew what the boys were doing.' This, one would add, was thanks to the inadequate facilities at the girls' school. Would the girls make good of the adversity?

By 1950 no African girl had sat for the school certificate examination [high school diploma] whereas 61 boys had done so. At independence in 1963, '1292 boys took the examination. [T]he corresponding figure for girls ws [sic] only 199 (six times less).'[139] The ratio was even lower at the Nairobi University College. In 1965, it stood at one woman to 40 men.[140] Both Eddah and Julia went on to gain doctoral degrees – unusual feats. As Eddah reminisced, before his death her father had asked her 'do you know you can become so educated, you could one day be called Doctor Nelson.... And my family remembers that, so when I graduated [getting her Ph.D. in 1981] they said, "now you have laid [your father's] ghost to rest".'[141]

Notes

1. This unflattering phrase was in reference to the 'migratory' nature of women, moving from their natal to marital homes. In cases of multiple marriages, then such movement would be repeated.
2. Report of the East African Commission presented by the Secretary of State for Colonies to British Parliament by command of His Majesty, April 1925, London: His Majesty's Stationery Office, 1925, Cmd. 2387, 52, 176–77. Members of the commission included the chairman Hon. W. Ormsby-Gore MP (Conservative Party), Major A.G. Church D.S.O MP (London), Mr. F.C. Linfield J.P. MP (Liberal), and Mr. J.A. Calder the Colonial Office Secretary.
3. Serah Mukabi, oral interview, Limuru, 20 July 1993.
4. Sara Sarai, oral interview, November 1993.
5. Keran Akoto, oral interview, Keveye, Kakamega, 26 February 1997.
6. Mary Wanjiru (Nyina wa Cibira), oral interview, Limuru, 14 July 1993.
7. Grace Ogot, oral interview, Nairobi, 24 July, 19994. Between 1942-1945 Grace was a student at Ng'iya Girls School. From 1946-1948 she was away at Butere Girls' School

for her intermediate education. From 1948-1950 she was in Uganda training as a Registered Nurse and Midwife. All these were boarding institutions that took her away from her home.

8. *Ibid.*
9. *Ibid.*
10. An even smaller number went to Independent schools emanating from the clitoridectomy controversy of 1929 to the mid-1930s. Squatters on settler plantations in the White Highlands established few schools. See Rosberg & Nottingham, *The Myth of 'Mau Mau'*, 125–31,134–5; Kanogo, *Squatters*, 84–91.
11. See Nyambura J. Njoroge, *Kiama Kia Ngo: An African Christian Feminist Ethic of Resistance and Transformation* (Legon, Ghana, 2000), 13–17.
12. KNA: CMS/382 T. F. C. Bewes to Mr. Smith 25 May 1937. Letter was to be forwarded to the latter by Miss A.M. Bourne of CMS Girls' Boarding School, Kabete.
13. For a summary of Bewes' activities and experiences in Kenya, see T. F. C. Bewes, *Kikuyu Conflict: Mau Mau and the Christian Witness* (London, 1953). The Church Missionary Society had its headquarters in London, England.
14. Within three years of Bewes' arrival, the CMS, with the help of the government and some supportive Africans, had transformed the refuge into a boarding school for girls. To be admitted the girls had to be over fourteen years of age, have come from Kiambu District, and have reached standard three in the elementary school. However, by 1937, the number of pupils had been reduced from ninety-six to fifty. Fourteen of the latter group had entered the school within the past eighteen months. The remaining thirty-six had come in as refugees and had reached standards two, three, and four by 1937. Of the thirty-six, '6 had gone into work of various kinds, 3 [had] become teachers, 3 [had] married, and 6 [had] left for different reasons, bringing the total down to 32'. This included eighteen girls from the refuge period and fourteen from the newer group. The dearth of female students and the low level of education attained by girls about forty years after the establishment of British rule in Kenya underscores the intricacies of African girlhood and womanhood.
15. KNA: Education Department Annual Report, 1928, 68.
16. Zablon, 'A History of the Methodist Church in Kenya, 175.
17. Serah Wambui Mukabi, oral interview, Limuru, 20 July 1993. Sometimes a girl was coaxed to attend school by a friend. Muthoni observed 'My mother was dragged to the mission by my father.' At the time Muthoni's mother was a young unmarried girl. Muthoni Likimani, oral interview, Nairobi, 22 December 1993.
18. To make the bodily marks, people used a plant locally known as *ekekove*, razor blades, and juices from a plant known as *ekisungurwa*. Keran Akoto, oral interview, Kakamega, 26 February 1997.
19. Beth Njambi, oral interview, Limuru, 14 July 1993. Sometimes other factors lured prospective students into mission stations. As Muthoni Likimani said, 'My father told me that as a young man he used to hang around the Kahuhia Mission, grazing his family livestock as well as listening to piano music coming from the mission. It was the music that attracted him to the mission. He deserted his home to join the mission. Canon Gachanja took his early theological training at St. Emmanuel's Divinity School at Freretown, Mombasa. Muthoni Likimani, oral interview, Nairobi, 22 December 1993. See also Cynthia Hoehler-Fatton, *Women of Fire and Spirit: History, Faith, and Gender in Roho Religion in Western Kenya* (New York, 1996), 27.
20. Sara Sarai, oral interview, Kinoo, December 1993.
21. *Ibid.* The Gikuyu words are:
    Uhoro wa gukena,
    Niukite guku gwitu
    Uhoro mwega ni uyu
    Wa muhonokia witu
22. *Ibid.*
23. Report of the East African Commission Presented by the Secretary of State for Colonies to British Parliament, and by Command of His Majesty, April 1925. London: His Majesty's Stationery, 1925, CMD2387, 52.

24. KNA: CMS1/136/Folio 53 Education Department General Circulars and Correspondence: Memorandum On the Education of Girls in Kenya Colony prepared by the Girls' Education Committee of the Christian Council of Kenya.
25. The notion of *tumaendeleo*, 'smatterings of "progress"', as the objective of women's education becomes easier to define in the light of the 1950, when the colonial government introduced a whole range of programs directed at the domestication of African women. Cookery, baking, laundry, sewing, knitting, and mothercraft refocused women's energy at the height of the liberation struggle. This project was put in place under the Maendeleo ya Wanawake movement. See Ruth Nasimiyu, 'The History of Maendeleo ya Wanawake Movement in Kenya, 1952-1975', in Khasiani & Njiro, *The Women's Movement in Kenya*, 87-110.
26. KNA: CMS 1/382.
27. KNA: CMS/382 T. F. C. Bewes to Mr. Smith 25 May 1937.
28. KNA: CMS1/136/Folio53 Education Department General Circulars and Correspondence: Memorandum on the Education of African Girls in Kenya Colony prepared by the Girls' Education Committee of the Christian Council of Kenya.
29. KNA: CMS/382 T. F. C. Bewes to Mr. Smith 25 May 1937.
30. Bogonko, 'Christianism and Africanism', 15.
31. Agnes Wairimu Hinga, oral interview, Ndumberi, Kiambu, 18 July 1993.
32. *Ibid.*
33. Mary Wanjiru [Nyina wa Cibira], oral interview, Limuru, 14 July 1993.
34. Isaak Were Osundwa, oral interview, Lubinu, Kakamega, 23 January 1997.
35. Keran Akoto, oral interview, Keveye, Kakamega, 26 February 1997.
36. Agnes Wairimu Hinga, oral interview, Ndumberi, Limuru, 18 July 1993.
37. Mary Muthoni Njogu, oral interview, Nairobi, November, 1996.
38. M. H. Kovar, 'The Kikuyu Independent School Movement', 99.
39. Older women among the Kikuyu were engaged in the education, counseling, and discipline of female children and women. While grandmothers were the most common instructors, there were other specialists including circumcisers. The older woman would give the girls *uhoro wa kumaguorithia uria mwana wa muiritu atagiriire gwika*, revelation regarding what girls should not do. Beth Njambi, oral interview, Limuru, 14 July 1993.
40. Cohen & Atieno Odhiambo, *Siaya*, 92–3.
41. *Ibid.*, 93. For a similar practice among the Kikuyu, see Kenyatta, *Facing Mount Kenya*, 155–60.
42. Mary Muthoni Njogu, oral interview, Nairobi, November, 1996.
43. Serah Mukabi, oral interview, Limuru, 20 July 1993. In an interesting twist, Serah Mukabi asserts that mission adherents in her area did not consider themselves Kikuyu. This would affirm the belief among the Meru that mission adherents who denounced clitoridectomy had engaged in a process of self-detribalisation. See Chapter Three.
44. Magdaline Musundi, oral interview, Kakamega, 25 January 1997.
45. Beth Njambi, oral interview, Limuru, 14 July 1993.
46. Susana Aseka, oral interview, Ebukambuli, Kakamega, February 1997.
47. Rose Otoolo, oral interview, Nairobi, 17 July 1993.
48. Prisca Ayuku, oral interview, Ebulakayi, Kakamega, 12 January 1997.
49. *Ibid.*
50. Rose Otoolo, oral interview, Nairobi, 17 July 1993.
51. Rajab Ngashira, oral interview, Ebumanyi, Mumias, 22 January 1997. See also Mzee Elijah Mbeketha, oral interview, Tala, Machakos, 30 July 1993; Mary Wanjiru (Nyina wa Cibira), oral interview, Limuru, 14 July 1993; Liza Nyambura Mwangi, oral interview, Nairobi, November 1996.
52. Mary Wanjiru [Nyina wa Cibira], oral interview, Limuru, 14 July 1993.
53. *Ibid.*
54. Liza Nyambura Mwangi, oral interview, Nairobi, November 1996.
55. *Ibid.*
56. Wycliffe Etindi, oral interview, Ebulakayi, Kakamega, 11 January 1997.
57. Hamis Makapia Wanga, oral interview, Ebumayi, Mumias, 21 January 1997.
58. Simon Lizanga Sabwa, oral interview, Keveye, Kakamega, 26 February 1997.

59. Juliah Ojiambo, oral interview, Nairobi, 14 July 1994.
60. Hamis Makapia Wanga, oral interview, Ebumanyi, Mumias, 21 January 1997.
61. Rajab Ngashira, oral interview, Ebumanyi, Mumias, 22 January 1997.
62. Eliud Amatika Oluchina, oral interview, Ebukambuli, Kakamega, February 1997.
63. Holding, 'The Education of a Bantu Tribe', 48.
64. *Ibid.*, 51.
65. Keran Akoto, oral interview, Keveye, Kakamega, 26 February 1997.
66. *Ibid.*
67. Susana Aseka, oral interview, Ebukambuli, Kakamega, February 1997.
68. Selina Nyona, oral interview, Bukura, 22 January 1997. Her father, Thomas Kuchushi, had become a Christian in 1920 and had married Selina's mother in church at Butere in 1923. Prior to the marriage he attained three years of formal education, between 1920 and 1923.
69. Prisca Ayuku, oral interview, Ebulakayi, Kakamega, 21 January 1997. As well as the claim that the removal of the lower teeth made it easier to feed an individual should they become seriously ill, this was a rite of passage that signaled transition from childhood to adulthood.
70. Keran Akoto, oral interview, Kakamega, 26 February 1997. The removal of teeth was a ritual practice among some Luyia groups. It might entail the symmetrical extraction of an even number of all or some of the lower incisors. At a practical level, the gap might prove handy for feeding a sick person, especially if they suffered from lockjaw.
71. Isaac Were Osundwa, oral interview, Lubinu, Kakamega, 23 January, 1997.
72. Marciana Munyendo, oral interview, Kakamega, 23 January 1997.
73. Mary Muthoni Njogu, oral interview, Nairobi, November 1996.
74. Agnes Wairimu Hinga, oral interview, Ndumberi, Kiambu, 18 July 1993.
75. Rose Otoolo, oral interview, Nairobi, 17 July 1993.
76. *Ibid.*
77. Sara Sarai, oral interview, Kinoo, Kiambu, December 1993.
78. KNA: PC/CENTRAL/2/1/11 Dr. Geoffrey C. Irvine, Church of Scotland Mission, Chogoria, Annual Report, 1935, 9.
79. Agnes Wairimu Hinga, oral interview, Ndumberi, Kiambu, 18 July 1993.
80. *Ibid.*
81. Muthoni Likimani, oral interview, Nairobi, 22 December 1993.
82. Selina Nyona, oral interview, Bukura, 22 January 1997.
83. Liza Nyambura Mwangi, oral interview, Nairobi, November 1996.
84. Eddah's mother died when she was six years old. Although her father soon married a lady who was Eddah's teacher, Eddah's fondest recollections are of her father's deep concern for his children's welfare. Her father worked in Nairobi, but went to the village to see his children every weekend. The third of five children, Eddah was not exactly a child, yet she remembers her father's concern for her. 'My father bathed me every Saturday when he came home.' She was not a baby to be bathed by whoever was taking care of the other children. On the other hand, she was not old enough to do a good job of it herself. Her father ensured that she had at least one proper bath per week. As well as showing great concern for the ablutions of his children, he also 'looked through our books.... He was very particular about how many ticks you got right, how many wrongs [sic] you got and so you had something to look forward [to] every Saturday. If you performed well [at school] you are going to show off. He was full of what [one] could become.' Eddah Gachukiah, oral interview, Nairobi, 2 August 1994.
85. *Ibid.*
86. *Ibid.*
87. *Ibid.*
88. *Ibid.*
89. James Ngugi wa Thiong'o, *The River Between* (London, 1965).
90. Eddah Gachukiah, oral interview, Nairobi, 2 August 1994.
91. *Ibid.*
92. *Ibid.*
93. Liza Nyambura Mwangi, oral interview, Nairobi, November 1996. By the time she went

into teaching her mother was widowed. She used some of her income from her teaching job to help educate her siblings. However, she taught for two years only.

94. *Ibid.*
95. Eddah Gachukiah, oral interview, Nairobi, 2 August 1994.
96. Serah Wambui Mukabi, oral interview, Limuru, 20 July 1993.
97. *Cucu* is kikuyu for grandmother.
98. Serah Wambui Mukabi, oral interview, Limuru, 20 July 1993.
99. *Ibid.*
100. Market gardening in Kiambu is said to have thrived especially during the Second World War. This would coincide with Serah's initiative. See Robertson, *Trouble Showed the Way*, 105.
101. Serah Wambui Mukabi, oral interview, Limuru, 20 July 1993.
102. Mary Wanjiru [Nyina wa Cibira], oral interview, Limuru, 14 July 1993.
103. Serah Wambui Mukabi, oral interview, Limuru, 20 July 1993.
104. Sarah Sarai, oral interview, Kinoo, Kiambu, December 1993.
105 Murang'a was also referred to as Fort Hall during the colonial period.
106. Magdaline Musundi, oral interview, Kakamega, 25 January 1997.
107. Isaak Were Osundwa, oral interview, Lubinu, Kakamega, 23 January 1997.
108. Marciana Munyendo, oral interview, Kakamega, 23 January 1997.
109. Magdalene Musundi, oral interview, Kakamega, 25 January 1997.
110. Peter Albert Indaru, *Man with the Lion Heart: Biography of Canon Ezekiel Apindi* (Achimota, Ghana: Africa Christian Press, 1974), 35. See also Cohen & Odhiambo, *Siaya*, 95–6.
111. Aggrey Ham Wanzetse, oral interview, Wanga, Kakamega, 24 January 1997.
112 Isaak Were Osundwa, oral interview, Lubinu, Kakamega, 23 January 1997.
113. Juliah Ojiambo, oral interview, Nairobi, 14 July 1994
114. *Ibid.*
115. *Ibid.*
116. Magdaline Musundi, oral interview, Kakamega, 25 January 1997.
117. Juliah Ojiambo, oral interview, Nairobi, 14 July 1994.
118. Muthoni Likimani, oral interview, Nairobi, 22 December 1993.
119. *Ibid.*
120. Selina Nyona, oral interview, Bukura, 22 January 1997.
121. See for example, Kitching, *Class and Economic Change in Kenya*, 54
122. Magdalene Musundi, oral interview, Kakamega, 25 January 1997.
123. Aggrey Ham Wanzetse, oral interview, Wanga, Kakamega, 24 January 1997.
124. Magdaline Musundi, oral interview, Kakamega, 25 January 1997.
125. Prisca Ayuku, oral interview, Ebulakayi, Kakamega, 12 January 1997.
126. Mary Muthoni Njogu, oral interview, Nairobi, November 1996. It is most likely that her mother undertook the unusual feat of combining marriage with formal education during the early years of her marriage in the late 1920s or early 1930s. Mary came from a polygamous family of twenty-one children, including fifteen girls and six boys. Her mother was the first wife, and her stepmother was married after Mary was born. Her father, who had very little education, was employed as a forest guard.
127. Upon widowhood, Deborah entered into a leviratic relationship with one of her brothers-in-law and had six children with him. Mama Deborah, oral interview, Nairobi, 12 February 1997.
128. *Ibid.*
129. Muthoni Likimani, oral interview, Nairobi, 22 December 1993. Margaret Kenyatta, the daughter of Kenya's first president went on to become the first female mayor of Nairobi, the capital city in the post independence period.
130. This was one of the lowest ranks of trained teachers.
131. This was dated October 1948. There is every likelihood that Janisch had written it. KNA: CMS 1/136 Education Department, General Circulars and Correspondence, M. Janisch for Acting Director of Education to Principals of all African Junior Secondary Schools and Education Secretaries of all Missions.
132. Rajab Ngashira, oral interview, Ebumanyi, Mumias, 22 January 1997.
133. Magdaline Musundi, oral interview, Kakamega, 25 January 1997.

134. Keran Akoto, oral interview, Keveye, Kakamega, 26 February 1997. See Stichter, 'Women and the Labour Force in Kenya', 45–64; and Stichter, *Migrant Labour in Kenya.* Despite her disappointment about not being able to go to secondary school, Keran was able to go the Jeanes School, in Kabete, where she trained in Homecraft for six months. She then 'taught *Maendeleo Ya Wanawake* to women in Bugina, Kegodi, and Keveye from 1947 to 1960'. She also had learnt the skills of nursery school teaching while at the Jeanes School and subsequently taught in nursery schools. Between Homecraft and nursery school teaching, Keran served in numerous rural centres including Keveye, Kegode, Kegodi, and Bugina. She was an employee of the Locational Council. 'In 1948 my salary was twenty five shillings per month.' Keran Akoto, oral interview, Keveye, Kakamega, 26 February 1997.
135. *Ibid.*
136. Selina Nyona, oral interview, Bukura, 22 January 1997.
137. Muthoni Likimani, oral interview, Nairobi, 22 December 1993.
138. Juliah Ojiambo, oral interview, Nairobi, 14 July 1994.
139. Teresia Mbari Hinga, *The Role of Religious Networks in the Provision of Education to Women in Africa: Kenyan Case* (Nairobi, 1995), 10.
140. Celina Oloo and Virginia Cone, *Kenya Women Look Ahead* (Nairobi, 1965), 35.
141. *Ibid.* The use of Christian names instead of surnames was a common practice demanded by missions and centres of Western education.

Conclusion

Indigenous and official surveillance of female sexuality, clitoridectomy, premarital sex and pregnancy, formal education, bride wealth and marriage in an effort to regulate women's lives produced a mosaic of experiences for women. Domesticity, motherhood, reproductive rights/politics, and maternal health constitute crucial themes in the colonial history of women in Kenya. This study has attempted to historicize women's experiences (some of them of a private nature) as revealed in official debates and oral evidence. The study has reinterpreted women's experience of the colonial encounter by depicting the complex, varied, and for some, partially liberating impact. The diversity in women's experiences and responses complicates our comprehension of African womanhood in colonial Kenya, as it does of governance.

This study has also reinterpreted colonial governance by portraying its uncertainties and, at times, diverse and contradictory policies; additionally, it has explored indigenous participation in colonial policy formulation through negotiating, collaborating, and, at times, vehement disagreements with other key architects of the colonial state. Amongst Africans, colonial appointees including such authorities as Local Native Councils, Native Tribunals and local chiefs were confronted by a local patriarchy supported by other anticolonial groups, including both young and older women. Like their colonial counterparts, African authorities were not always united, or in support of colonial policies on women. As rural dismay for women's entry into newly created colonial spaces increased, women and their bodies became sites of public, political, and personal struggles. The regulation and restriction of women elicited endless discussions, and some legislation. It also engendered resistance from women. As well as providing an opportunity to foreground gender in analyzing the colonial period, it is hoped this volume has provided a greater understanding of the colonial process, including some insight into the limitations of the colonial state.

The practice of colonial rule in Kenya was marked by competing visions of the future. At the beginning, colonial administrators toyed with the idea of a territory based on an Indian plantation economy, the America of the Indian; there was also a possibility that the region might be developed as an African peasant economy, or a Jewish settlement. Even after Sir Charles Eliot had decided against the Indian, Jewish and African options, and embarked on an aggressive campaign to lure a white settler community, that did not eliminate the African and Indian options. Two decades later in the early 1920s, the adoption of the dual policy acknowledged the importance of African peasant agricultural production in the economy of the country. While the role of Asians in the agricultural sector of the economy was minimal, their role in the commercial sector remained paramount. The Indians also played a key role in the manufacturing sector. The African and Indian dreams lived on.

Not an impartial arbiter, the colonial government pursued a settler-centric policy bent on buttressing the plantation sector at all costs, and certainly at the expense of the African and Asian communities. In particular, this partisan practice impacted land, labor, communication infrastructure, finance, subsidy, and extension services, which favored the settler sector. Throughout the colonial period, many debates, conflicts and negotiations raged around the economic policy in the land. Hence, the exercise of power in colonial Kenya converged around a host of issues including land, labour, agriculture, settlers, governance, and other matters pertaining to race.

If colonizing the land was a contested process, colonizing women drew together the largest number of relentless power brokers. Thus, central as the economic well-being of a country was, the greatest contestations took place in the social and cultural spheres. Here, an intensive, protracted, and very intricate contestation developed as indigenous, colonial, missionary, and imperial forces sought to implement their visions of the future. These makers of the emergent colonial state were concerned to create a society whose female population passed through key life stages in an acceptable fashion. Leading lives that were marked by continuity and change, women were a central focus of colonial administration.

Societal anxieties about the impact of colonialism on the female population were rife. Colonial administrators and indigenous authorities vested women with tremendous importance as the barometer of societal well being. Colonial efforts to regulate the social and biological lives of women troubled local communities. The crafting of the African woman, like the social engineering of the general population, produced mixed reactions from both the colonized and the colonizers.

The fluidity of the colonial situation created a broad spectrum of responses including enthusiastic embracing of colonial processes on the one hand, and vehement rejection on the other. There were those in between who straddled across old and new ideas and practices. This amalgam of nervous existences among the colonized was also evident in the practice of governance. While some of those in power struggled to safeguard culture, others espoused the adoption of novel practices bound to disturb the cultural landscape. The new forces included the Christian religion, formal education, new legal spaces, waged labour, and the abandonment of basic institutions such as clitoridectomy and bridewealth, among others. This study has examined the intertwined efforts of colonial, missionary and indigenous authorities to define and control various institutions that regulated womanhood. More importantly, it has surveyed the dithering African response to the colonial process, a condition that was replicated amongst the power brokers.

One of the most pronounced impacts of colonialism was the process of social differentiation. For women, this resulted in the further fragmentation of women as a social category. Earlier categories and hierarchies based on age, marital status, motherhood, specialist skills like midwifery or herbal knowledge among others were at times supplanted, or complicated by new categories including educated mission girls and women, the uncircumcised, prostitute, landlady, urban trader and entrepreneur, or the professional – nurse, teacher, or secretary. For the employed and propertied, there developed changes in the methods of ascribing socio-economic status to women. The varieties of women's experiences and activities expanded women's visibility even as it pushed them into the closer surveillance of colonial state and indigenous patriarchs. Amongst all the emergent categories, the urban woman was the most vilified and regulated.[1]

By incorporating situations of historical continuum, dissonance, and ambiguity, this text has tried to trace the transformations of certain aspects of the lives of girls and women in colonial Kenya. It has recognized the forging of uneasy alliances between various official and unofficial groups that were determined to shape the lives of African girls and women. Women and girls became wards of a host of patrons who did not always see eye to eye regarding the roles and status of their wards within the colonial order. Neither did girls and women always conform to the designs of their patrons.

More often than not, travel and modernity were deemed responsible for women's unacceptable abandonment of 'traditional' obligations, roles and spaces. Amidst rapid changes, the invention of what were considered to be appropriate gender spaces, roles, and identities for women during the colonial period became an enormous and diverse project. Women were reformulated; they too sought to reformulate themselves. Different chapters have illustrated the complexity of women's initiatives and responses to change during the colonial period. In diverse situations women adopted negotiated solutions; sometimes they outrightly violated conventional norms, or they innovated novel solutions to intractable problems. Through oral interviews it was possible to capture the immediacy of some of these transformations.

The civilizing missions of colonial administrators and missionaries exacerbated gender relations. Missionaries believed that their task of inculcating drastic moral shifts and vocational skills necessitated the physical separation of initial novices. The missionaries envisioned situations where they would have to refashion the whole person. There was talk of:

> endeavouring to educate the rising generation of a pagan race by the process of stimulating their intelligence not only by imparting upon them instruction and enlightenment but by the persuasive inculcation of beliefs with the intent to teach them thereby to master their desires and impulses and to order their lives in a manner not only conducive to their eternal salvation but also more agreeable to civilized standards. [2]

For the missionaries, this project entailed the isolation of their protégés from 'polluted' environments. To raise their protégés above mere existence into a civilized world, the missionizing task incorporated notions of capitalism with regard to native labour. Technical or other manual training was deemed mandatory unless the natives were to remain 'hewers of wood and fetchers of water'. The period of apprenticeship, or 'statu pupilla' raised the question of wardship, which was especially problematic with regard to girls.[3]

While the government and missionaries looked upon themselves as guardians of such girls, the controversy this raised left missionaries in favour of volunteers rather than 'pupils bound by agreement'. This referred to the 1910 Masters and Servants Ordinance section 16–23, which bound apprentices for five years for any trade.[4] Neither the administration nor missions approved the parents' claim to the right to withdraw their children from schools and vocational institutions before they had completed their training. In practice, however, missions continued to harbour girls and women who did not have the permission of their families to join missions. The majority of these girls and women did not undergo any certifiable artisan or professional training.

Women and girls left their rural homes against parental and spousal authority for various reasons. Young girls ran to mission stations to avoid arranged marriages, to escape clitoridectomy, or to get formal education and religious instruction. Older married women might leave their matrimonial or parental homes in an attempt to leave a bad marriage, or to escape poverty, which might be partly a result of land shortage or landlessness. The individualization of land tenure and the commercialization of agricultural production also put divorced women in greater economic hardship. Changes in kinship obligation patterns, and the individualization of property ownership robbed women of a whole network of rights and obligations, which secured their livelihoods in the pre-colonial periods. Such women found it necessary to relocate from their natal or matrimonial homes in order to fend for themselves and their offspring.

Early missions established what they considered to be 'refuge homes' for such women. By giving refuge to girls and women who ran away from their homes, missions were targets of constant accusations of interfering with customary practices. Spaces beyond patriarchal/spousal control offered women the possibility of creating and joining new communities. The process of moving to the new spaces, and making sense of their new abodes was, however, a contested and closely controlled undertaking.

That issues pertaining to the welfare of women were deliberated upon, and decisions largely made in the absence of women to a large extent did not seem to bother those engaged in the deliberations. These silences are countered through oral interviews in an effort to restore and recognize the agency of women. Even in the general absence of overt women's voices in the archives, a study of the debates of the day have made it possible for us to map out the nature of women's social engagement with change and society. The intensive and extensive official and unofficial deliberations on issues relating to women are a clear indication of the vibrancy of the female population amidst repeated efforts to contain it during the colonial period.

Did African men expect colonial administrators to adhere to 'customary law' in arbitration over disputes that straddled between customary and not-so-customary practices? How effectively could statutory law be introduced in Kenya? Was evolutionary change the way to go, and if so, who was to set the pace? Was Ainsworth, the self-appointed proponent of women's emancipation discussed in chapter one too forward? What about women, what was their reading of what was happening around them? How did they seize and exercise their options? These are some of the concerns that have informed the directions that this book has taken.

This study has argued that gendered processes and colonial spaces increasingly attained all the qualities of frontiers and boundaries. These qualities became pivotal to the redefinition of African womanhood in the period 1900–1960 as women joined mission stations, unilaterally moved from natal and marital homes, sought formal education, and got employed. Travel, as an idiom of modernity, and modernity became problematic spaces around which gendered constructions of identities were undertaken. The criminalization of women's movement attained obsessional proportions during the first four decades of this century. These were seminal years for the evolution of colonial societies. Different communities of thought portrayed women who undertook independent travel away from sanctioned locations in the rural areas as uncontrollable (defiant of male authority), too independent, immoral, unmarriageable, lazy, and averse to manual labour, among several other undesirable images.

Some of the women who moved into urban areas became prostitutes. Luise White's work on prostitution in colonial Nairobi recasts the process in the context of colonial social engineering, urban housing constraints, and the provision of domestic and sexual services to a predominantly 'single' African population. White does not dwell on the moral issues that prostitution raised in rural colonial Kenya. This study's discourse on prostitutes, movement and identity goes a step further by examining societal notions of morality and ethnic purity. It also adds to the diverse notions of womanhood espoused in colonial Kenya.

The book has illustrated how the 1920s–1940s Local Native Councils' frequent discussions concerning the movement of girls and women were concerned with larger issues of ethnic integrity, citizenship, moral health, and gendered notions of respectability, honor and social order. Movement and immorality were closely linked, condemned and a variety of legislation passed in an attempt to contain the situation. More importantly, debates on colonial projects on gender reform did not seek women's views. This study has endeavoured to recover these views through oral interviews.

The colonial encounter brought the question of women's autonomy to the fore. Each of the seven chapters has examined some aspect of women's initiative and responses to specific circumscribing circumstances. Evidence points toward the adoption of diverse options and regional differentiation as girls and women navigated a complex social map. Ultimately, what emerges is not a linear narrative regarding any one issue, but a medley of paths, conflicts, contradictions, and negotiations that each situation elicited. For example, colonial officials were often caught between a rock and a hard place in their deliberations over matters pertaining to the status of women. In reality, administrators did not want to implement any legislation that might antagonize local elders. In the great scheme of direct rule, the administrators were heavily dependent upon the good will of the elders.

During the period under study, the African family was at the cross-roads. Some colonial administrators did not agree with some of the norms, practices or sanctions that the communities enforced for the maintenance of social order. There existed very divergent notions of right and wrong, justice and injustice, morality and repugnance, among others. That the administrator engaged in a selective and at times expedient support for contentious issues aggravated the local community. While the majority of elders believed they had the basic normative and customary law necessary to deal with ordinary daily domestic and other disorders, some of the elders were also inducted into a process that would reformulate some of the ground rules. The study has endeavoured to identify the various moralities that informed this most contested engagement. The pre-colonial sensibilities, which the elders espoused, did not always succeed in the unfamiliar colonial terrain. Sometimes new positions were adopted, or old ones reworked.

Elders tried to enlist the help of colonial officials to control African women and girls. In general, these two did not always see eye-to-eye with regard to the legal and social status of women; this quite obviously compounded an already intricate situation. However, that did not stop the evolution of extensive cooperation between colonial administrators, missionaries, and indigenous authorities in their multiple efforts, and partial successes in reworking the lives of women. There are cases of women and girls whose plans to move were thwarted by any one of the various agencies. In the oral interviews, these women reflect on their subsequent experiences in the context of aborted opportunities.

The autonomy of women was variously contested by different agencies. Women's initiatives and responses are incorporated the study. A common theme that runs through this text is the emergence of individualism among girls and women during the colonial period. This, however, was not a comfortable space: whether it was the mission girl who refused to undergo clitoridectomy, or the unexcised Kipsigis girl who gave birth in a mission hospital, both had to negotiate alternative social networks even as they adopted new identities. The same applied to the run-away wife, the mission student, the widow who had married under statutory law, and the mission woman whose father demanded exorbitant bride price. Seemingly 'liberating migrations' engendered other drawbacks. For the majority of these women, the social cost of 'relocating' could be extensive.

This book has attempted to examine some aspects of the mosaic of these defining moments. For the majority of women who underwent normative and spatial migrations, the process did not entail a complete severing of contact with their rural kinsmen and cultural sensibilities. The book characterizes the changes in the idiom of shifts, straddling, adoption of new religions affiliation, and acquisition of new skills and adoption of alternative legal strategies which might enable the women to manage their lives relatively better. In many situations it remained necessary for 'migrated' women to defer to moral economies they had ostensibly shifted from. These seeming contradictions, and the inherent conflicts illustrate the dynamics of the complexities of the colonial situation.

The text has also tried to illustrate how girls and women related to various authority figures in their day-to-day lives. Rather than transfer their total allegiance from one authority structure to another, evidence from different chapters represent women's multiple engagements with diverse structures. While they might find support from one outfit over a particular matter, it was not unusual for women to be opposed to other strategies espoused by the same group. In the same way as they questioned and rejected some indigenous sensibilities, they might express dismay against missions, Local Native Councils, maternity hospitals, missions, matriarchs, peers, and family members. On some level, therefore, it was a matted existence. The liberating breaks that changing circumstances might avail were tempered by a host of limitations emanating from colonial, indigenous, or mission quarters.

Ultimately, the book has illustrated the diverse ways in which women were shaped by the confluence of a host of new dynamics. It also depicts how girls and women redefined themselves. The reworking of women's lives occurred even as their interaction with the new dynamics became highly contested and closely controlled by indigenous men and women, colonial administrators and indigenous patriarchal authorities, and missionaries. It was in the clutter of colonial administration that African womanhood was forged. There was no sanitized linear progression in the life narratives of girls and women. Their stories were punctuated by twists and turns reflective of rapid changes in all spheres of life.

Notes

1. See for example, Kathleen Sheldon (ed.) *Courtyards, Markets, City Streets: Urban Women in Africa* (Boulder, CO, 1996).
2. KNA/PC/CP7/1/1: Native Customs and Law, PC Nyeri to DC Meru, 28/10/1919.
3. *Ibid.*
4. *Ibid.*

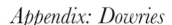

Appendix: Dowries

The data provided by the DCs reflected inter-regional variations in the prices of animals. It also included cautionary remarks about fluctuating prices depending on demand. Quite obviously other factors including drought, epidemics, and favourable climate or pasture affected the availability of livestock and its pricing thereof. Additionally, periods of agricultural prosperity reconfigured the geography of marriage sites for women. For example, the abundance of livestock among squatters not only inflated dowry, it also captured the attention of prospective brides who anticipated getting married in these centres of prosperity.[1]

In response to the official enquiry, five district commissioners provided the necessary information. In Kericho,[2] one of the most fertile and commercialized districts of the entire Nyanza province, the approximate prices of livestock in 1928 were as follows:

Cow	250 shillings
Heifer	160 shillings
Bull	100 shillings
Bullock	100 shillings
Sheep	12 shillings
Goat	15 shillings

In South Kavirondo,[3] in 1928, livestock seemed to be half as expensive as they were in Kericho.

Cow	130 shillings
Heifer	80 shillings
Bull	50 shillings
Bullock	70 shillings
Sheep	10 shillings
Goat	15 shillings

In Kakamega,[4] the most populous, highly commoditized and fertile area in the region, prices were not as high as Kericho, although they were higher than those in South Kavirondo.

Cow	120–150 shillings
Heifer	100 shillings
Bull	50–60 shillings
Bullock	120–130 shillings
Sheep	10–15 shillings
Goat	15–20 shillings

In some respects, Kapsabet District had the cheapest prices of some categories of livestock. Writing in 1929, G. W. B. Huntingford noted that although marriage price among the Nandi varied, it could be put at one bull, four cows, and five goats.[5] The price range at Kapsabet was:

Cow	60–100 shillings
Heifer	80–150 shillings
Bull	50–105 shillings
Bullock	80–110 shillings
Sheep	12–16 shillings
Goat	12–16 shillings

The second priciest place in Nyanza province was Central Kavirondo.[6] In early 1928, the prices were as follows:

Cow	160–180 shillings
Heifer	140–150 shillings
Bull	60–80 shillings
Bullock (Maasai)	150–200 shillings
Sheep	10–18 shillings
Goat	12–16 shillings

Greet Kershaw has compiled a table of approximate bridewealth in the period about 1835–1950 among the Kikuyu.[7] Together with a representation of minimum wages among workers in the White Highlands, these figures give some indication of the relative worth of dowry in relation to a suitor's income. Below are figures reflecting the number of goats given in bridewealth at different times.

Before Kirika[8]	minimum 25
After World War I	65–70
After Kirika	40–50
Before 1932	75
First World War	60–65
About 1940	90
Early 1920s	70
Before 1952	85

Minimum Wages per year in the Settled Areas were:[9]

Before 1932	shs 150/=
About 1939	shs 180/=
1945	shs 210/=
Before 1952	shs 240/=
1956	shs 300/=
1962	shs 600/=

Ocholla-Ayayo has engaged in a more detailed computation of cattle dissipation resulting from bridewealth and marriage transactions over a hundred-year period in two Luo communities.[10] The figures below are culled from his chart which includes figures of livestock slaughtered for dowry related rituals. These latter figures swell the total number of livestock expended in marriage to double what is reflected below. Together, these figures indicate a very intricate network of social relations and possible repercussions.

Interval	Fluctuation	Marriages	Dowry given
1860–1870	10–40	2,000	80,000
1871–1880	10–38	2,500	95,000
1881–1890	10–36	3,000	108,000
1891–1910	10–32	3,500	112,000
1911–1920	10–28	4,000	112,000
1921–1930	10–24	4,500	108,000
1931–1940	10–20	5,000	100,000
1941–1950	10–18	5,500	99,000
1951–1960	10–14	6,000	84,000

Simon Lizanga Sabwa, a Maragoli from Kakamega who got married in the late 1930s observed that 'There was no problem on the amount of dowry to be paid since it was standard ... everybody knew, for instance, that it was two cows and two goats, and so there was no question about it'.[11] The eight cows that a Kisii mission suitor had to pay in the late 1920s was a far cry from Sabwa's two cows and two goats a decade later in Kakamega.

It was not unusual for seemingly harmless actions to complicate a straightforward demand for refund of dowry. The giving of gifts to women by potential suitors was a common practice, but one whose consequences could be 'vexatious and undesirable'.[12]

> It frequently happen [s] now-a-days [sic] that a young man, after arranging with the father to marry his daughter and after paying the father a certain portion of the marriage price, would also give presents in the way of clothes, shillings, +c [sic: cash] without her father's knowledge. Something would then take place to prevent the marriage, and the young man would claim from the father not only the portion of marriage price which had

> been paid but also the value of presents received by the girl as well.... Tribunals (were) in the habit of supporting claims made for the value of small presents.... The fathers should not be held responsible for above unless 'they were interviewed and undertook responsibility at the time the present was given.'[13]

In this case, the LNC argued that fathers of such girls who received gifts from young men suffered injustice in having to refund the latter. The refund of dowry was a potentially enervating feat even without additional complications. Kiamas were to be instructed not to entertain claims for the return of gifts. In a bizarre twist of events, Kiamas could give the suit greater attention if it transpired that the 'gifts' in question were, in actual fact, a loan. In this case, the man 'must produce lots of evidence in support [of his allegation].'[14]

This last concern was reflected on the standard form, which constituted a voluntary register of bride price. The form required the provision of the following information: the location and district where the transaction took place, name and signature of the bridegroom, name of bride, name of bride's parent or guardian and their signature, marriage price agreed to be paid, countergifts (if any), signatures of three witnesses, the clerk, and the chief. The fee for this registration would be two shillings. Each of any subsequent entries made by consent of the parties would have to be attested by the signature or thumb marks of the parties to the transaction and three witnesses. A fee of one shilling would have to be made for each entry.[15] The bride was not expected to sign the form, although it was about brideprice paid and or pledged for her. In her stead, her parent (read father) or guardian (most certainly a male kin) had to sign the form. Unlike the bride, the bridegroom signed on his own behalf. In this troubled domain of marriage, women were still unable to enter into certain kinds of contracts in their own right. In certain respects, they continued to be held as legal minors. It is not a stretch of the imagination to assume that the witnesses to the contract were also male.

Notes

1. Kanogo, *Squatters*, 23; Leakey, *The Southern Kikuyu* 1: 172.
2. KNA: PC/NZA.3/28/4/1 DC Kericho to PC Nyanza, Marriage Price of Girls, 19 March 1928.
3. KNA: PC/NZA.3/28/4/1 DC South Nyanza to PC Nyanza, 20 March 1928.
4. KNA: PC/NZA.3/28/4/1 DC Kakamega, North Kavirondo to PC Nyanza, 20 March 1928.
5. Huntingford, 'The Tribes of Kenya', 53.
6. KNA: PC/NZA.3/28/4/1 DC Central Kavirondo, Kisumu to PC Nyanza, Marriage Price of Girls, 29 March 1928.
7. Kershaw, *Mau Mau from Below*, 286.
8. *Ibid.*, 36. Kershaw dates the Kirika riika, age set, between 1835–1840. Brideprice for the Embu at about 1900 is put at 1–3 cows, 4–15 goats, 2 bulls, one or two he-goats, and a

ram. See also Saberwal, 'Social control', 40.
9. Kershaw, *Mau Mau from Below*, 286.
10. Ocholla-Ayayo, 'Female migration and wealth dissipation', 29.
11. Simon Lizanga Sabwa, oral interview, Keveye, Kakamega, 26 February 1997.
12. KNA: PC/CP/2/1/5 LNC Meetings, Fort Hall District, 23/36 Suits for Return of Gifts, 7–8 January 1936.
13. KNA: PC/CP/2/1/5 LNC Meetings, Fort Hall District, 17–20 July 1934.
14. *Ibid.*
15. KNA: PC/RVP.6A/14/16 Schedule I: Voluntary Registration of Bride-price (1937).

Bibliography

Published Books

Abunzwa, Judith, *Women's Voices, Women's Power: Dialogues of Resistance from East Africa* (Peterborough, Ont., 1997).
Ahlberg, Beth Maina, *Women, Sexuality and the Changing Social Order: The Impact of Government Policies on Reproductive Behaviour in Kenya* (Philadelphia, 1991).
Anderson, David, M. and Killingray, David (eds), *Policing and Decolonisation: Politics, Nationalism and the Police, 1917-65* (Manchester, 1991).
Anderson, John. *The Struggle for the School* (Nairobi, 1970).
Atieno Odhiambo, E.S. (ed.), *African Historians and African Voices* (Basel, 2001).
Beck, Ann, *A History of the British Medicnl Administration of East Africa, 1900–1950* (Cambridge, 1970)
Berman, Bruce J., *Control and Crisis in Kenya: The Dialectic of Domination* (London, 1990).
—— & John Lonsdale, *Unhappy Vallley: Clan, Class and State in Kenya* (London, 1991).
—— *Unhappy Valley: Conflict in Kenya and Africa. Book 2, Violence and Ethnicity* (London, 1992).
Bewes, T. F. C., *Kikuyu Conflict: Mau Mau and the Christian Witness* (London, 1953).
Boyes, John, *King of the Wa-Kikuyu.* (London, 1968 [1911]).
Cagnolo, Fr. C., *The Akikuyu, their Customs, Traditions and Folklore* (Nyeri, 1933).
Callaway, H. *Gender, Culture, and Empire: European Women in Colonial Nigeria* (London, 1987).
Channock, Martin, *Law, Custom and Social Order: The Colonial Experience in Malawi and Zambia* (New York, 1985).
Clayton, A & D. Savage, *Government and Labour in Kenya, 1895–1963* (London, 1974).
Close, Etta, *A Woman Alone in Kenya, Uganda and the Belgian Congo* (Sydney, 1924).
Cohen, David William. & E. S. Atieno Odhiambo (eds), *Siaya: The Historical Anthropology of an African Landscape* (London, Nairobi, Athens OH, 1989).
—— *Burying SM: The Politics of Knowledge and the Sociology of Power* (Portsmouth, N.H, London, 1992).
Comaroff, Jean, *Body of Power, Spirit of Resistance* (Chicago, 1985).
Comaroff, John L., *The Meaning of Marriage Payments* (New York, 1980).
Cooper, Fredrick (ed.), *Struggle for the City: Migrant Labour, Capital, and the State in Urban Africa* (Beverly Hills, CA, 1983).
—— *On the African Waterfront: Urban Disorder and the Transformation of Work in Colonial Mombasa* (New Haven, CT, 1987).
Coquery-Vidrovitch, Catherine, *African Women: A Modern History* (Boulder, CO, 1997).
Cotran, Eugene, *Casebook on Kenya Customary Law* (Nairobi, 1987).
Davison, Jean & the Women of Mutira, *Voices from Mutira: The Lives of Rural Gikuyu Women*

(Boulder, CO, 1989).

Dinesen, Isak (Karen Blixen), *Out of Africa* (New York, 1987).

Eliot, C., *The East African Protectorate* (London, 1905).

Evans-Pritchard, E.E., *The Position of Women in Primitive Societies and Other Essays in Social Anthropology* (New York, 1965).

Fearn, Hugh, *An African Economy: A Study of the Economic Development of Nyanza Province of Kenya, 1903–1953* (London, 1956).

Fisher, Jean, *The Anatomy of Kikuyu Domesticity and Husbandry* (London, 1964).

Foran, W. Robert, *A Cuckoo in Kenya: The Reminiscences of a Pioneer Officer in British East Africa* (London, 1936).

Hakkansson, Thomas, *Bridewealth, Women and Land: Social Change Among the Gusii of Kenya* (Stockholm, 1988).

Hay, Margaret Jean & Sharon Stichter (eds.) *African Women South of the Sahara* (London, 1984).

Hendrickson, Hildi (ed.), *Clothing and Difference: Embodied Identities in Colonial and Post-Colonial Africa* (Durham, 1996).

Hinga, Teresia Mbari, *The Role of Religious Networks in the Provision of Education to Women in Africa: Kenyan Case* (Nairobi, 1995)

Hobley, Charles William, *Ethnology of the Akamba and Other East African Tribes* (Cambridge, 1910).

Hoehler-Fatton, Cynthia. *Women of Fire and Spirit: History, Faith and Gender in Roho Religion in Western Kenya* (Oxford, 1996).

Hollis, A.C., *The Nandi: Their Language and Folklore* (Oxford, 1909).

Hotchkiss, Willis R., *Then and Now in Kenya Colony: Forty Adventurous Years in East Africa* (London, 1937)

Humphrey, Norman. *The Liguru and the Land: Sociological Study of Some Agricultural Problems of North Kavirondo* (Nairobi, 1947).

Huxley, Elspeth, *The Mottled Lizard* (New York, 1962).

Jeater, Diana, *Marriage, Perversion and Power: The Construction of Moral Discourse in Southern Rhodesia, 1894–1930* (Oxford, 1993).

Iliffe, John, *East Africa Doctors: A History of the Modern Profession* (Cambridge, 1998).

Kanogo, Tabitha, *Squatters and the Roots of Mau Mau, 1905–1963* (London, Athens, OH, Nairobi, 1987).

Kenyatta, Jomo, *Facing Mount Kenya: The Tribal Life of the Gikuyu* (New York, 1965).

Kershaw, Greet, *Mau Mau from Below* (London, 1997).

Khasiani, Shanyisa (ed.), *Groundwork: Women as Environmental Managers* (Nairobi, 1992).

Khasiani, Shanyisa & E.I. Njeru (eds), *The Women's Movement in Kenya* (Nairobi, 1993).

Kitching, Gavin, *Class and Economic Change in Kenya: The Making of an African Petite-Bourgeoisie, 1905–1970* (New Haven, 1980).

Kituyi, Mukhisa, *Becoming Kenyans: Socio-economic Transformation of the Pastoral Maasai* (Nairobi, 1990).

Kratz, Corinne, A., *Affecting Performance: Meaning, Movement and Experience in Okiek Women's Initiation* (Washington, 1994).

Kyewalyanga, F.-X. S., *Marriage Customs in East Africa: with special reference to selected tribes of Kenya: Akamba, Bantu, Kavirondo, Gusii, Kipsigis, Luo, Nandi and Teita* (Freiburg, 1977).

Lambert, H.E., *Kikuyu Social and Political Institutions* (London, 1956).

Leakey, L.S.B., *The Southern Kikuyu Before 1903. Vols. I–III* (New York, 1977).

LeVine, Robert A. & Barbara B. LeVine, *Nyansongo: Gusii Community in Kenya* (New York, 1966).

Lightfoot-Klein, Hanny, *Prisoners of Rituals: An Odyssey into Female Genital Circumcision in Africa* (New York, 1989).

Lindblom, Gerhard, *The Akamba in British East Africa: An Ethnographical Monograph* (Uppsala, 1920).

Macpherson, Robert, *The Presbyterian Church in Kenya* (Nairobi, 1970).

Mboya, Paul, *Luo: Kitgi gi Timbegi* (Nairobi, 1967).

Meinerzhagen, Richard, *Kenyan Diary 1902–1906* (Edinburgh, 1957).

Middleton, John, *The Kikuyu and Akamba of Kenya. Ethnographic Survey of Africa: East Africa, Part 5* (London, 1953).

Miracle, Marvin, 'Economic Change Among the Kikuyu, 1895–1905.' IDS Working Paper No.158 (1974).
Mirza, Sarah & Margaret Strobel (eds), *Three Swahili Women: Life Histories From Mombasa, Kenya* (Bloomington, 1989).
Moore, Henrietta L., *Space, Text and Gender* (Cambridge, 1986).
Mungai, Evelyn, & Joy Awori (eds), *Kenya Women Reflections* (Nairobi, 1983).
Muriuki, Godfrey, *A History of the Kikuyu, 1500–1900* (Nairobi, 1974).
Ndege, George Oduor, *Health, State and Society in Kenya* (Rochester, NY, 2001).
Ndirangu, Simon, *A History of Nursing in Kenya* (Nairobi, 1982).
Ngugi wa Thiong'o, James, *The River Between* (London, 1965).
Njau, Rebecca & Gideon Mulaki (eds), *Kenya Women Heroes and their Mystical Power* (Nairobi, 1984).
Njoroge, Nyambura, J., *Kiama Kia Ngo: An African Christian Feminist Ethic of Resistance and Transformation* (Legon, Ghana, 2000).
Obbo, Christine, *African Women: Their Struggle for Economic Independence* (London, 1980).
Oboler, Regina Smith, *Women, Power, and Economic Change: The Nandi of Kenya* (Stanford CA, 1985).
Obura, Ann P., *Changing Images: Portrayal of Girls and Women in Kenyan Textbooks* (Nairobi, 1991).
Ochola-Ayayo, A. B. C., *Traditional Ideology and Ethics Among the Southern Luo* (Uppsala, 1976).
Ojwang, J.B. & J.N.K. Mugambi (eds), *The S.M. Otieno Case: Death and Burial in Modern Kenya* (Nairobi, 1989).
Oloo, Celina & Virginia Cone (eds), *Kenya Women Look Ahead* (Nairobi, 1965).
Ominde, Simeon, *The Luo Girl: From Infancy to Marriage* (Nairobi, 1950).
Orchardson, Ian, Q., *The Kipsigis* (Nairobi, 1961).
Otieno, Wambui Waiyaki, *Mau Mau's Daughter: A Life History* (Boulder CO, 1998).
Pala Okeyo Achola, Awori Thelma, & Krystal Abigail (eds), *The Participation of Women in Kenya Society* (Nairobi, 1978).
Parkin, David & David Nyamwaya (eds), *Transformations of African Marriage* (Manchester, 1987).
Parpart, Jane & Kathleen Staudt, *Women and the State in Africa* (Boulder CO, 1989).
Presley, Cora Ann, *Kikuyu Women, the Mau Mau Rebellion, and Social Change in Kenya* (Boulder CO, 1992).
Roberts, Richard & Kristin Mann (eds), *Law in Colonial Africa* (New York, 1991).
Robertson, Claire, *Trouble Showed the Way: Women, Men, and Trade in the Nairobi Area, 1890–1990* (Bloomington & Indianapolis, 1997).
—— and Iris Berger (eds), *Women and Class in Africa* (New York, 1986).
Rosberg Carl Jr & John Nottingham, *The Myth of 'Mau Mau': Nationalism in Kenya* (New York, 1966).
Sandgren, David P. *Christianity and the Kikuyu: Religious Division and Social Conflict.* (New York, 1989).
Sangree, Walter, H., *Age, Prayer and Politics in Tiriki, Kenya* (New York. 1966).
Scoresby, W. & K.P. Routledge, *With a Prehistoric People: The Akikuyu of British East Africa* (London, 1910).
Shaw, Carolyn Martin, *Colonial Inscriptions: Race, Sex and Class in Kenya* (Minneapolis, 1995).
Sheldon, Kathleen (ed.), *Courtyards, Markets, City Streets: Urban Women in Africa* (Boulder CO, 1996).
Spear, Thomas & Richard Waller (eds), *Being Maasai: Ethnicity and Identity in East Africa* (Athens OH, 1993).
Spencer, John, *The Kenyan African Union* (London, 1985).
Stichter, Sharon, *Migrant Labour in Kenya: Capitalism and African Response, 1895–1975* (London, 1982).
—— & Jane Parpart (eds), *Patriarchy and Class: African Women in the Home and Workforce* (Boulder CO, 1988).
Strayer, Robert W., *The Making of Mission Communities in East Africa: Anglicans and Africans in Colonial Kenya 1875–1935* (London, 1978).
Strobel, Margaret, *Muslim Women in Mombasa 1890–1975* (New Haven & London, 1979).
Tignor, Robert *The Colonial Transformation of Kenya: The Kamba, Kikuyu and Maasai from 1900 to*

1939 (Princeton, 1976).
Tinker, Irene (ed.), *Persistent Inequalities: Women and World Development* (New York, 1990).
van Zwanenberg, R.M.A., *Colonial Capitalism and Labour in Kenya* (Kampala, 1975).
wa-Githumo, Mwangi, *Land and Nationalism* (Washington DC, 1981).
Waciuma, Charity, *Daughter of Mumbi* (Nairobi, 1969).
Wagner, Gunter, *The Changing Family Among the Bantu Kavirondo* (London, 1939).
—— *The Bantu of Western Kenya: With Special Reference to the Vugusu and Logoli* Vols I and II (London, 1970).
Wanyoike, E.N., *An African Pastor* (Nairobi, 1974)
Welbourn, F.B., *East African Rebels: A Study of Some Independent Churches* (London, 1961)
Whisson, Michael G., *Change and Challenge: A Study of the Social and Economic Changes among the Kenya Luo* (Nairobi, 1964).
White, Luise, *The Comforts of Home: Prostitution in Colonial Nairobi* (Chicago, 1990).
Wilson, Gordon, *Luo Customary Law and Marriage Customs* (Nairobi, 1968).

Published Articles

Atieno Odhiambo, E. S., 'A portrait of Protestant missionaries in Kenya before 1939', in Atieno Odhiambo (ed.), *The Paradox of Collaboration and other Essays* (Nairobi, 1974).
—— E. S. Atieno Odhiambo, 'A world view for the Nilotes? The Luo concept of Piny,' in Atieno Odhiambo (ed.), *African Historians and African Voices* (Base, 2001), 57–68.
Bujra, Janet, 'Women 'entrepreneurs' of Early Nairobi', *Canadian Journal of African Studies* 9 (1975), 13–34.
Ciancanelli, Penelope, 'Exchange, reproduction and sex subordination among the Kikuyu of East Africa.' *Review of Radical Political Economy* 12 (1990), 25–36.
Clark, Carolyn M., 'Land and food, women and power, in nineteenth-century Kikuyu.' *Africa* 50 (1980), 357–70.
Clifford, James. 'Travelling Cultures', in Lawrence Grossberg, Cary Nelson & Paula Treichler (eds), *Cultural Studies* (New York, 1992) 96–112.
Davison, Jean. 'Who owns what? Land registration and tensions in gender relations of production in Kenya', in Davison (ed.), *Agriculture, Women and Land* (Boulder CO, 1988), 155–76.
Dawson, Marc, 'The 1920s anti-yaws campaigns and colonial medical policy in Kenya', *International Journal of African Historical Studies*, 3 (1987), 417–35.
Driberg, J.H., 'The status of women among the Nilotics and Nilo-Hamitics', *Africa*, 5 (1932) 404–21.
East African Law Report 134; Rex v. Palmer 1913, 2 K.B. 29.
Evans-Pritchard, E.E., 'Marriage customs of the Luo of Kenya,' *Africa* 20 (1950) 132–42.
Feldman, Rayah, 'Women's groups and women's subordination: an analysis of policies towards rural women in Kenya', *Review of African Political Economy*, 22–23 (1981), 67–77.
Guyer, Jane, 'Household and community in African studies', *African Studies Review*, 24 (1981) 87–137.
Hastings, Adrian, 'Were women a special case?' in Fiona Bowie, Deborah Kirkwood, & Shirley Ardener (eds), *Women and Missions: Past and Present, Anthropological and Historical Perceptions* (Providence & Oxford, 1993) 109–25.
Hay, Jean Margaret, 'Luo women and economic change during the colonial period', in Nancy J. Hafkin & Edna G. Bay (eds), *Women in Africa: Studies in Social and Economic Change* (Stanford, CA, 1976), 87–109.
—— 'Women as owners, occupants and managers of property in colonial Western Kenya', in J.M. Hay and Marcia Wright (eds), *African Women and the Law: Historical Perspectives* (Boston MA, 1982), 110–23.
Hobley, C.W., 'Kikuyu customs and beliefs. Thahu and its connection with circumcision rites', *Journal of of the Anthropological Institute*, 40 (1910), 428–52.
Holding, E. Mary, 'Women's institutions and the African church', *International Review of Missions*. 31 (1942) 290–300.
Huntingford G.W.B., 'The tribes of Kenya: some curious facts about the Nandi people', *The*

East African Standard, January 5, 1929, 53.
Judicial Department Annual Report 1926, Kenya.
Kanogo, Tabitha, 'Kikuyu women and the politics of protest', in Sharon Macdonald, Pat Holden & Shirley Ardener (eds), *Images of Women in Peace and War* (Oxford, 1987), 78–99.
—— 'Women and Environment in History', in Shanyisa Khasiani (ed.), *Groundwork: Women as Environmental Managers* (Nairobi, 1992), 7–18.
—— 'Colonialism and gender: depiction and control of African women', in Bianca Maria Carcangiu (ed.), Orientalia Karalitina, *Quaderni Dell' Instituto Di Studi Africani e Orientali*, 2 (1993), 85–100.
—— 'Mission impact on women in colonial Kenya', in Fiona Bowie, Deborah Kirkwood & Shirley Ardener (eds), *Women and Missions: Past and Present, Anthropological and Historical Perceptions (*Providence & Oxford, 1993), 165–86.
—— 'Women, patriarchy and production in Kenya', in Muigai wa Gachanja (ed.), *The Independent Review*, 1 (1997), 246–56.
—— 'The medicalization of maternity in colonial Kenya', in Atieno Odhiambo (ed.), *African Historians and African Voices* (Basel, 2001), 75–113.
Kenya Judicial Department Annual Reports, 1926, 1935, 1936, 1937, 1938.
Kershaw, Greet, 'The changing roles of men and women in the Kikuyu family by socio-economic strata', *Rural Africana*, 29 (1975–76), 173–94.
Kettel, Bonnie, 'The commoditization of women in Tugen (Kenya) social organization', in Iris Berger & Claire Robertson (eds), *Women and Class in Africa* (New York & London, 1986), 47–61.
King, Kenneth, 'A biography of Harry Thuku', in Kenneth King & Ahmed Salim (eds), *Kenya Historical Biographies* (Nairobi, 1971), 155–84.
Kinyanjui, Kabiru, 'Educational and formal employment opportunities for women in Kenya: some preliminary data', in Achola Pala, Thelma Awori & Abigail Krystal (eds), *The Participation of Women in Kenya Society* (Nairobi, 1978), 16–41.
Knowles, O. S., 'Some modern adaptations of customary law in the settlement of matrimonial disputes in the Luo, Kisii and Kuria tribes in South Nyanza', *Journal of African Administration*, 8 (1956), 11–15.
Leakey, L.S.B. 'The Kikuyu problem of the initiation of girls', *Journal of the Royal Anthropological Institute*, 61 (1931) 277–85.
Llewelyn-Davies, Melissa, 'Two contexts of solidarity among pastoral Maasai women', in *Women United, Women Divided: Cross-cultural Perspectives on Female Solidarity*, Patricia Caplan and Janet Bujra (eds), London: Tavistock, 1978.
Llewelyn-Davies, Melissa, 'Women, Warriors and Patriarchs,' in *Sexual Meanings*, S.Ortner & H. Whitehead (eds), (Cambridge, 1981), 330–8.
Lonsdale , John. 'When did the Gusii (or any other group) become a tribe?' *Kenya Historical Review*, 5, 1 (1977), 123–33.
—— 'The Moral Economy of Mau Mau', in Bruce Berman and John Lonsdale, *Unhappy Valley, Book Two* (London, 1992), 315–467.
Lovett, Margot, 'Gender relations, class formation, and the colonial state in Africa', in Jane Parpart & Kathleen Staudt (eds), *Women and the State in Africa (*Boulder CO, 1989), 23–46.
Mackenzie, Fiona, 'Local Initiatives and national policy: gender and agricultural change in Murang'a District, Kenya', *Canadian Journal of African Studies* 20, 3 (1986), 377–401.
—— 'Gender and land rights in Murang'a District, Kenya', *Journal of Peasant Studies*, 17 (July 1990) 609–43.
—— 'Without a woman there is no land: marriage and land rights in smallholder agriculture, Kenya', *Resources for Feminist Research* 19 (1990), 68–74.
Mayer, Phillip U., 'Privileged obstruction of marriage rites among the Gusii', *Africa*, 20 (1950), 115–19.
Mugo, Micere, 'The role of women in the struggle for freedom', in Achola Pala Okeyo, Thelma Awori & Abigail Krystal (eds), *The Participation of Women in Kenya Society* (Nairobi, 1978), 210–19.
Muigai, Githu, 'Women and property rights in Kenya', in Mary Adhiambo Mbeo & Oki Ooko-Ombaka (eds), *Women and Law in Kenya* (Nairobi, 1989), 113–22.
Nasimiyu, Ruth. 'The history of Maendeleo ya Wanawake movement in Kenya, 1952–1975',

in S.A. Khasiani and E.I.Njiro (eds), *The Women's Movement in Kenya* (Nairobi, 1993), 87–110.

Ndungu, Joseph B., 'Gituamba and the Kikuyu Independency in Church and School', in Brian G. McIntosh (ed.), *Ngano* (Nairobi, 1969), 131–68.

Nelson, Nici, '"Selling her kiosk": Kikuyu notions of sexuality and sex for sale in Mathare Valley, Kenya', in Patricia Caplan (ed.), *The Cultural Construction of Sexuality* (London, 1987), 217–39.

—— 'Women must help each other': the operation of personal networks among Busaa brewers in Mathare Valley, Nairobi', in Patricia Caplan & Jane Bujra (eds), *Women United, Divided* (Bloomington IN & London, 1979), 77–98.

Nobuhiro Nagashima, 'Aspects of change in bridewealth among the Iteso', in David Parkin & David Nyamwaya (eds), *Transformations of African Marriage* (Manchester, 1987), 183–97.

Ocholla-Oyayo, A. B. C., 'Marriage and cattle exchange among the Nilotic Luo', *Paideuma 25* 25 (1975), 193–193.

Pala Okeyo, Achola. 'Daughters of the lakes and rivers: colonization and the land rights of Luo women', in Mona Etienne & Eleanor Leacock (eds), *Women and Colonization: Anthropological Perspectives* (New York, 1980), 186–213.

—— 'Women's access to land and their roles in agriculture and decision making on the farm: experiences of the Joluo of Kenya', *Journal of Eastern African Research and Development* 13 (1983), 69–85.

Parkin, David, 'Kind bridewealth and hard cash: eventing a structure', in John Comaroff (ed.), *The Meaning of Marriage Payments* (London & New York, 1980), 197–220.

Pedersen, Susan, 'National bodies, unspeakable acts: the sexual politics of colonial policy-making', *Journal of Modern History*, 63 (1991), 647–80.

Potash, Betty, 'Marriage instability in a rural Luo community', *Africa* 48 (1978), 381–97

—— 'Wives of the grave: widows in a rural Luo community', in Betty Potash (ed.), *Widows in African Societies: Choices and Constraints* (Stanford, 1986), 45–65.

Ranger, Terence, 'The invention of tradition in colonial Africa', in Eric Hobsbawm & Terence Ranger (eds), *The Invention of Tradition* (Cambridge, 1983), 211–62.

—— 'The invention of tradition revisited: the case of colonial Africa', in Bianca Maria Carcangui (ed.), Orientalia Karalitina, *Quaderni Dell' Instituto Di Studi Africani e Orientali*, 2 (1993), 129–71.

Robertson, Claire, 'Trade, gender and poverty in the Nairobi area', in R.L. Blumberg & C.A. Rakowski (eds), *EnGendering Wealth and Well-Being* (Boulder CO, 1995), 65–87.

—— 'Transitions in Kenyan patriarchy: attempts to control women traders in the Nairobi area, 1920–1963', in K. Sheldon (ed.), *Courtyards, Markets, City Streets: Urban Women in Africa* (Boulder CO, 1996), 47–71.

Stamp, Patricia, 'Perceptions of change and economic strategy among Kikuyu women of Mitero, Kenya', *Rural Africana* 29 (1975–76) 19–44.

—— 'Burying Otieno: the politics of gender and ethnicity in Kenya,' *Signs* 16 (1991), 808–45.

—— 'Kikuyu women's self-help groups: towards an understanding of the relationship between sex-gender systems and modes of production in Africa', in Claire Robertson & Iris Berger (eds), *Women and Class in Africa* (New York, 1986), 25–46.

Stichter, Sharon, 'Women and the labour force in Kenya, 1895–1964', *Rural Africana* 29 (1975–76), 45–67.

—— 'Women and the family: the impact of capitalist development in Kenya', in M.D. Schatzberg (ed.), *The Political Economy of Kenya* (New York, 1987), 137–60.

Strayer, Robert W., 'Missions and African protest: a case study from Kenya 1895–1935', in Robert Strayer, Edward I. Steinhart, & Robert M. Maxon (eds), *Protest Movements in Colonial East Africa: Aspects of Early East African Response to European Rule* (Syracuse, NY, 1973).

Thomas, Lynn M., 'Imperial concerns and "women's affairs": state efforts to regulate clitoridectomy and eradicate abortion in Meru, Kenya, c.1910–1950' *Journal of African History* 39 (1998), 121–45.

—— '"Ngaitana (I will circumcise myself)": The gender and generational politics of the 1956 ban on clitoridectomy in Meru, Kenya', *Gender and History* 8 (1996), 338–63.

van Doren, J.W., 'African tradition and western common law: a study in contradiction' in J.

B. Ojwang & J. N. K. Mugambi (eds), *The S.M. Otieno Case: Death and Burial in Modern Kenya* (Nairobi, 1989), 127–32.

White, Luise, 'A colonial state and an African Petty bourgeoisie: prostitution, property, and class struggle in Nairobi, 1936–40', in Fredrick Cooper (ed.), *Struggle for the City: Migrant Labor, Capital, and the State in Urban Africa* (Beverly Hills CA, 1983) 167–94.

—— 'Separating the men from the boys: colonial constructions of gender, sexuality and terrorism in central Kenya, 1939–1959' *International Journal of African Historical Studies* 23 (1990), 1–25.

Whyte, Susan Reynolds, 'The widow's dream: sex and death in western Kenya', in Michael Jackson & Ivan Karp (eds), *Personhood and Agency: The Experience of Self and Other in African Cultures* (Washington, 1990), 95–114.

Wipper, Audrey, 'The Maendeleo ya Wanawake movement in colonial Kenya: the Canadian connection, Mau Mau, embroidery, and agriculture', *Rural Africana*, 29 (1975–76), 195–214.

—— 'Kikuyu women and the Harry Thuku riot: some uniformities of female militancy', *Africa* 58 (1989), 300–37.

Unpublished Dissertations & Papers

Ainsworth, John, 'Kenya Reminiscences', n.d., covering 1890–1900, Rhodes House Library.

Bogonko, S.N., 'Catholicism and Protestantism in the Social and Political Development of Kenya', conference paper, Eastern African Historical Conference, Naivasha, Kenya, 1981.

—— 'Christianism and Africanism at Crossroads in Kenya, 1909–1940.' Conference Paper, Kenya Historical Association, 1976.

Butterman, Judith M., 'Luo Social Formation: Karachuonyo and Kanyamkago, c. 1800-1945,' PhD Dissertation, Syracuse University, 1979.

Fisher, Jeanne, 'The Anatomy of Kikuyu Domesticity and Husbandry', London, 1953.

Hay, Margaret Jean, 'Economic Change in Luoland: Kowe, 1890–1945', PhD dissertation, University of Wisconsin, Madison, 1972.

Holding, Mary, 'The Education of a Bantu Tribe', Rhodes House, Oxford, Mss Afr. r. 117.

Hunter, K.L., 'Memoirs of Life as an Administrative Officer in Kenya, 1919–1950', Rhodes House, Mss Afr. S. 1942.

Jacobs, Alan, 'The Traditional Political Organization of the Pastoral Maasai,' D.Phil. Thesis, Oxford University, 1965.

Jalang'o-Ndeda, Mildred Adhiambo, 'The Impact of Male Labour Migration on Rural Women: A Case Study of Siaya District, 1894–1963,' PhD dissertation, Kenyatta University, 1991.

Kamuyu-wa-Kangethe, 'The Role of the Agikuyu Religion and Culture in the Development of the Karinga Religio-Political Movement, 1900–1950 With Particular Reference to the Agikuyu Concept of God and the Rite of Initiation', PhD Thesis, University of Nairobi, 1981.

Kelly, Hilarie Ann, 'From Gada to Islam: The Moral Authority of Gender Relations among the Pastoral Orma of Kenya', PhD dissertation, University of California, Los Angeles, 1992.

Kettel, Bonnie, 'Time is Money: The Social Consequences of Economic Change in Seretunin, Kenya', PhD dissertation, University of Illinois, Urbana, 1980.

Kinoti, Hannah, 'Aspects of Kikuyu Traditional Morality', PhD dissertation, University of Nairobi, 1983.

Kovar, M. H., 'The Independent Schools Movement: Interaction of Politics and Education in Kenya', PhD Thesis, University of California, Los Angeles, 1970

Mathu, George W., 'Gikuyu Marriage: Belief and Practices.' IDS Discussion Paper No. 17, 1971.

McVicar, K. G., 'Twilight in an East African Slum: Pumwani and the Evolution of African Settlement in Nairobi', PhD dissertation, University of California, Los Angeles, 1969.

Miracle, Marvin, 'Economic Change Among the Kikuyu, 1895–1905.' IDS Working Paper No.158, 1974.

Murray, Jocelyn, 'The Kikuyu Female Circumcision Controversy, With Special Reference to the Church Missionary Society's "Sphere of Influence"', PhD dissertation, University of California, Los Angeles, 1974.

Mutongi, Kenda Beatrice, 'Generations of Grief and Grievances: A History of Widows and Widowhood in Maragoli, Western Kenya, 1900 to the Present', PhD dissertation, University of Virginia, 1996.

Nthamburi, Zablon John, 'A History of the Methodist Church in Kenya, 1862–1967', PhD dissertation, University of California, School of Theology at Claremont, Berkeley, 1981.

Nthia, Njeru Enos Hudson, 'The Farming Herders: Irrigation, Reciprocity and Marriage Among the Turkana Pastoralists of North-Western Kenya', PhD dissertation, University of California, Santa Barbara, 1984.

Ocholla-Ayayo, A. B. C., 'Female Migration and Wealth Dissipation Among the Patrilineal Exogamous Communities in Kenya: With Special Reference to the Luo of Nyanza Province', paper presented at Nyanza Province Cultural Festival, Kisumu, Kenya, 19th–21st December, 1985.

Saberwal, Satish Chandra, 'Social Control and Cultural Flexibility among the Embu of Kenya (CA 1900)', PhD dissertation, Cornell University, 1966.

Thomas, Lynn M., 'Contestation, Construction and Reconstitution: Public Debates Over Marriage Law and Women's Status in Kenya, 1964–1979', M.A. Thesis, Johns Hopkins University, Baltimore, 1989.

Wambeu, D. N., 'Kikuyu Customary Marriage with Particular Reference to Elopement', LL.B Dissertation, University of Nairobi, 1979.

Waruiru, Christopher, 'The Female Initiation Controversy at C.S.M. Tumutumu, 1912-1937', B.A. Dissertation, University of Nairobi, 1971.

Unpublished Kenya National Archives

Provincial Commissioner Nyanza, Correspondence
Provincial Commissioner Central, Correspondence
Provincial Commissioner Rift Valley, Correspondence
Provincial Commissioner Northern Province, Correspondence
Attorney General's Office, Correspondenec re Status of Women
District Commissioners' Correspondence
Local Native Councils' Meetings
Department of Labour Report

Rhodes House, Oxford

Mary E. Holding, 'Christian Impact on Meru Institutions', Rhodes House Mss. Afr. r. 191

Mary E. Holding, 'The Education of a Bantu Tribe', unpublished manuscript, n.d., Rhodes House, Mss Afr. r. 117, 56, Kaaga Girls School Report, 1956.

K.L. Hunter, OBE, 'Memoirs of Life as an Administrative Officer in Kenya, 1919–1950', unpublished manuscript, Rhodes House Mss Afr. S. 1942.

Stanford University Law Library

East Africa Law Reports

Index

Abagusii, 205–6
Abaluyia, 65. *See also* Luyia
abortion, 176, 178, 195n61
adoption, 179, 182, 183
adultery, 35, 53–4, 65, 112
African Girls High School, 232
African Inland Mission, 99n16
African Marriage Ordinance, 150
age, 19, 20, 24, 25, 26–7, 32, 88, 91, 102n83, 143, 144–6, 161n60, 178, 181, 203
agency, 2, 8, 18, 29–30, 55, 74, 96, 105, 106, 113, 116, 118, 122, 139, 140, 152, 162n99, 231, 244–5. *See also* consent; individualism
Ainsworth, John, 17, 18, 20–1, 22–3, 25, 26, 27, 28, 31, 40n53
airitu a watho, 215
Akamba, 51, 65, 96
Akoch, Luka, 156
Akoto, Keran, 114, 192, 204, 206, 213, 212, 230-1
Ali, Hamisi bin, 155
Alliance Boys High School, 229, 233
Alliance Girls High School, 232–3
Alliance of Protestant Churches, 77
Alukwe, Grace, 209
Amatike, Eliud, 144
Aseka, Susan, 212
Ayuku, Prisca, 209, 212, 228

Baimbridge, Dr., 87
Banyole, 146
Barth, J. W., 107
Beavon, E. R., 109, 110, 111, 112, 124n30, 146
Beecher, L. J., 169
Bell, Stanley, 173
Berman, B., 13n3
Bowen, T. F. C., 203, 205
bigamy, 35, 141, 159n26
body, 74, 77, 88, 89
Bogonko, S. N., 143, 205–6
bribery, 117, 178
bride, 51–2, 53, 110, 136, 137, 138, 139, 147. *See also* marriage; wife
bridewealth: 3, 6, 9, 22, 23, 31,47, 50-1, 52, 53, 56, 64, 65, 82, 98, 104–5, 111, 114,119, 120, 121, 124n20, n30, 128n90, 141, 143, 148, 231, 241, 248, 249. *See also* dowry
British common law, 3
brothers, 52, 53, 54, 143

cash, 106, 117, 119–22, 127n89
Catholic Church, 76, 77–8, 99n16, 113, 206, 217
Central Province, 117
Channock, Martin, 9
childbirth, 51, 61, 86, 88, 89, 96, 133, 173–4, 207, 208. *See also* maternity/maternity care
children: and clitoridectomy, 83, 85–6, 87, 91–2, 96; and colonial authority, 70n72; and curative rape, 62; custody of, 53, 54–5, 69n52, 122, 134, 154–5, 159n29; disobedient, 18; guardian of, 65; illegitimate, 64; male, 150, 153; motherless, 188; pawning of, 44–50, 51, 148, 150; pledging of, 148–9, 150; of pre-initiation conception, 176–7, 181, 182; as property of father, 48; of

prostitutes, 186–7; rape of, 58–9; of widow, 150, 153. *See also* infanticide; marriage, age at
Chogoria Mission, 135, 214
Chogoria Mission Hospital, 191
Chogoria Mission Native Civil Hospital, 188
Christianity: and bigamy, 159n26; and clitoridectomy, 75, 76, 77, 78, 81, 84, 92; and clothing, 7, 174–5; and dowry, 109, 110, 111, 112, 113, 116, 122, 124n30; and education, 203–4, 206, 212, 215, 216; and leviratic marriage, 66; and marriage, 130, 131, 144, 157; and marriage age, 146; and maternity care, 168, 173; and mission schools, 203; and monogamy *vs.* polygamy, 134; and mothers, 205; and polygamy, 135; practices forbidden by, 204; and prostitution, 7; and wives, 205. *See also* missions; *specific sects*
Christian Marriage Ordinance, 109–10, 131
Chuka, 81, 82, 93, 188
Church Missionary Society, 134, 141, 146, 169, 203, 234n14
Church of Scotland Missions, 90, 94, 99n16, 135, 203, 210, 217
circumcision: *See* clitoridectomy
circumcisor, 86, 87, 88, 90, 94
civilization, 19, 20, 21, 23, 49, 85, 89–90, 111, 205, 241–2
Civil Marriage Law, 134
clan, 46, 53, 56, 81, 83, 106, 116, 212. *See also* community; family; kinship
cleanliness, 170, 208, 215
Clifford, James, 'Travelling Cultures," 8
clitoridectomy, definition, 73, 98n7; types of, 79; cultural significance of , 80; and ethnic identity, 80, 81, 83, 84; and social death, 74, 81; and ethnic fecundity; and marriageability, 83, 98; and motherhood, 86; and detribalization, 1, 81; and social status, 82; resistance to eradication of, 93, 97; and *muthirigu, 83*; and disinheritance; 83; mission opposition to, 77, 83, 84; girls' resistance to, 96; criminalization of, 77; condemned as barbaric mutilation 77; infant and maternal deaths and, 86; and eugenics, 87; male inspection of , 94-95; medicalization of, 87,88; modification of 87; and infants, 96; government position on, 91-3; banning of, 93; fines for, 93-4; politicization of 89-90, 97. *See also* initiation; *irua*
clothing, 7, 8, 174–6, 194n47, 204, 209–10, 215
Cohen, D. W., 207
colonial authority: and children, 70n72; and clitoridectomy, 81, 83, 84–90, 91–6, 97; and competing interests, 26–7; control by, 2; diversity under, 27; divorce under, 54–5; and dowry, 105–6, 113, 114, 115, 117, 118; and education, 205; and elders, 5–6, 244; and father's rights, 9; guardianship of, 242; and infanticide, 177, 180; and legal agency, 18; and legal systems, 25; and marriage, 16, 21–2, 29, 113, 129, 130–1, 136, 138–40, 154–5, 156–7; and maternity care, 166; noninterference by, 19; and rape cases, 56–60, 61, 62; settler policy of, 240; and sex, 63; and sexuality, 44; vision of future, 240; and women workers, 15–16
colonialism, 2–3, 7, 8, 9, 20; and child pledging, 148, 149, 150; and clitoridectomy, 74, 75, 76, 79, 82, 83, 84, 89; and dowry, 109; and gender, 17; and indigenous sensibility, 4–5; and marriage, 32, 131, 133, 140, 144, 145; and midwives, 189; and pawning, 45–9; social atomization under, 37; as socially disruptive, 18, 20; and widows, 150–1
community, 25–6, 30, 183, 202, 224–6; clitoridectomy as part of, 75–6, 78–80, 81, 82, 83, 89; and dowry, 120, 121; and education, 204, 206, 208, 212, 218, 228; and pawning, 45; and pregnancy, 167. *See also* kinship
consent, 7–8, 124n10, 191; to clitoridectomy, 75, 76, 81, 82, 83, 90, 91, 93, 96, 97, 102n83; for education, 198–200, 201–2, 203–4; form for, 136, 137, 138, 140; under Islamic law, 32; to marriage, 31, 32, 33, 47, 66, 123, 136–44, 138, 139; of parents, 148, 198–200, 201–2; and pawned girls, 148; to sex, 63; for surgery, 172. *See also* agency
Cooper, F., 13n9
culture, 7, 8, 74, 77, 79–80, 85, 87, 88, 91, 106, 167, 173, 204, 206, 207, 218, 221, 224–5, 231. *See also* civilization

daughters, 9, 82, 84, 110–11, 113–16, 213
Davison, Jean, 98n10
death, 52, 86, 87, 133
Deborah, 228–9
debt, 106, 116, 121
desertion: *See* marriage
detribalization, 81, 83, 130, 165, 179
dhi boke, 207
divorce, 31, 51–2, 53, 54–5, 65, 69n52,

70n58, 122–3, 132, 134, 136, 159n29
domesticity, 203, 205, 208, 211, 235n25
Downing, L. H., 16
dowry, 104–23, 159n26; cash for, 127n89; and child pledging, 148; and clitoridectomy, 82; and death of bride, 51; defined, 68n35, 104–5; and divorce, 51–2, 70n58, 122–3; and education, 209, 231; and elders, 109, 114, 117, 123, 124n30; and embezzlement, 121; extortion of, 110–11, 115, 116; and fathers, 50, 108, 112, 113, 114, 115, 118–19, 127n89; inflated, 110, 111, 127n89; and labour, 105, 108; limits on, 106–9, 116, 123, 124n30, 127nn79, 89; and marriage, 105, 106, 107, 112, 113, 114, 118, 138; and marriage desertion, 31, 69n45; and marriage registration, 117, 126n77, 130, 158n8; and missions, 16, 105, 109–13; and parents, 114; payment of, 50–1, 108, 112, 116; and prostitution, 114, 115; return of, 51–2, 53, 118, 122, 134, 148, 149; and suitor, 108, 109, 115–16, 120, 121; for unwed mother, 64–5; and widows, 32, 65, 122, 152–3, 154; and cash 119-122. *See also* bridewealth, property

East African Marriage Ordinance, 21, 23, 112–13, 129, 151, 157
East African Women's League, 101n52
East Kano Reserve, 169
economics/finances, 114–16, 118, 133, 152, 164–5, 168–9
economy, 3, 83, 119
education, 197–233; and agency, 231; and Church Missionary Society, 234n14; and civilization, 205; and clitoridectomy, 77, 78, 81, 84, 85, 92; and clothing, 7; and colonial authority, 205; and dowry, 209, 231; extent of, 215–17; and family, 192, 198–200, 201–2, 203–4, 206, 208–11, 212, 218–22; and gender, 190, 210, 211, 229, 232; higher, 229–33; and identity, 209–10; indigenous, 206–7, 210; intermediate, 216, 217; and marriage, 199, 200, 203, 208, 209, 211, 213–14, 222–3, 228–9; and marriage refusal, 142; and marriage registration, 131; medical, 189, 190, 192, 197–8, 199, 200, 217, 223–4; opposition to, 198–200, 201–2, 205–6, 208–11, 212–13, 216, 217, 218–22, 229–30, 231, 242; and parents, 198–200, 201–2, 203–4, 206, 212, 216, 217, 231, 242; permission for, 198–200, 201–2, 203–4; and *pim*, 207, 208; as pollutant, 209; practical *vs.* academic, 203; religious, 215; restricted, 192; and social mobility, 3; and society, 198, 206; superiority of Western, 208; traditional, 79, 204, 206, 207, 208; and work, 214, 221–2, 227–8
elders, 5–6, 9, 151, 206, 209; and clitoridectomy, 81, 82, 83, 84; and colonial authority, 244; divorce complaints to, 54; and dowry, 109, 114, 117, 123, 124n30; independence from, 108; and marriage, 28, 132, 139; and rape cases, 56–7; role in clitoridectomy, 79, 80
Elders Council, 97, 117, 133
Elgeyo, 79
Elgeyo Marakwet district, 92
Elijah, Mzee, 153
Eliot, Sir Charles, 240
elopement, 36, 37, 108
Embu, 73, 74, 75, 79, 81, 83, 84, 93, 97, 119
Embu Local Native Council, 85, 94, 96
enyangi, 50
ethnicity, 8, 48, 60, 61, 79, 80–4, 89, 97–8, 166, 206
Etindi, Wycliffe, 210
eugenics: and clitoridectomy, 85–6, 87, 89, 92; and education, 205
Europeans, 62, 82, 101n52, 171–2

family, 5, 18, 129, 132, 134; changes in, 218–23, 244; and clitoridectomy, 70, 81, 82; desertion of, 9; and dowry, 105, 112, 116, 120, 121; and education, 192, 198–200, 201–2, 203–4, 206, 208–11, 212, 218–22; in-law side of, 82, 147, 150, 152, 207; and marriage, 105, 106, 121, 141–3, 148; and widows, 150, 152. *See also* clan; community; kinship
famine, 44, 48, 49, 51, 66n12, 107, 116, 148, 150
farming, 214, 227–8
fathers, 9, 17–18, 31, 48, 51–2, 110–11, 122, 134, 142, 188, 191, 212, 213; and clitoridectomy, 82; and dowry, 50, 108, 112, 113, 114, 115, 118–19, 127n89; and education, 33, 212, 218, 219, 220, 221, 222; and marriage, 142, 161n60; permission of, 33, 198–200, 201–2, 203; and pre-initiation conception, 179–80 *See also* parents
food, 79, 172–3, 224–5, 227–8
Fort Hall, 56–7, 79, 90, 93, 95, 114, 165, 168, 185
Fort Hall hospitals, 190, 191
Fort Hall Local Native Council, 34, 94,

122, 126n77, 131–3, 145, 184
Fort Hall Medical Officer, 167
Fort Hall Native Council, 115, 184
Francis, Carey, 229
free unions, 66

Gachukiah, Eddah, 216–18
Gayaza Girls High School, 232
gender, 8, 17, 80, 85, 88, 171–2, 189, 190, 210, 211, 225, 229, 232
generations, conflict between, 34, 108, 109, 121, 206. *See also* elders; youth
Gerald, Dr., 168
Getundu, Paulo, 122
Githaiga, Japhet, Chief, 164
Gospel Misionary Society, 99n16
Gower, Ivon, 19
guardians, 21, 26, 31, 32, 33, 43, 55, 57, 65, 136, 139, 150, 154–5, 191, 242. *See also* ward/wardship
Gusii, 206

Hay, Margaret Jean, 43
high school: *See* education
Hinga, Agnes Wairimu, 75–7, 79, 80, 81–2, 84, 114, 206, 214–15
Hinga, T. M., 238n138
Hislop, F. D., 179
Holding, Mary, 211
home, 9, 29, 30, 210, 213
honour, 26, 55, 56, 57, 225
hospitals, 164–5, 167, 168, 169–71, 172–3, 180, 188, 190. *See also* medicine, Western
house, construction of, 28–9, 186, 187
household, 25–8, 118
Huntington, G. W., 114
husbands, 17–18, 21, 31, 48, 53, 65, 82, 116, 122, 139, 172, 210. *See also* marriage
hygiene: *See* cleanliness

icakamuyu, 52
identity, 4, 8, 18, 78–80, 81, 83, 84, 89, 97, 105, 166, 200, 206, 208, 209–10, 241. *See also* womanhood
Indian Evidence Act, 35
Indian Limitation Act, 107
Indian Majority Act, 27
Indian Penal Code, 36, 145
individualism, 4, 106, 108, 120–1, 128n101, 142, 188, 244–5. *See also* agency
infant, 91–2, 96. *See also* children
infanticide, 89, 176–82, 183, 185, 194n57, 195n70
inheritance, 52, 83, 129
initiation, 50–1, 63, 73–4, 75, 79, 80, 92, 96, 119, 138, 148, 176–82
Innis, H. W., 146
irua, 74, 79, 84–90. *See also* clitoridectomy
Irvine, Geoffrey C., 135, 214
Islam, 21, 22, 30–2, 36, 130
Islamic Marriage, Divorce, and Succession Ordinance, 36

Jalang'o-Ndeda, Mildred, 28
Janisch, Miss, 231
Jobson, E. W.C., 96

Kabaa Mission, 215
Kabete Girls Boarding School, 203
kabwatereret, 148
Kahanya, Hannah Wariara, 127n85, 143
Kahuhia Church of Scotland Mission, 90
Kakamega District Commissioner, 120, 145
Kakamega Local Native Council, 109
Kamba, 44, 45, 46, 50, 55, 64, 93, 97, 152, 162n99
Kang'ethe wa Kihika, 119, 209, 210, 218, 219, 220, 221, 222
Kanogo, Tabitha, 13n7, 13n13, 14n27, 40n43, 41n76, 103n104, 127n83, 193n1, 234n10
Kanyanja, Miriam Wambui, 152–3
Karatina, 185
Karuti, 45, 46, 47
Kavirondo: definition 74; as *Misheni*, 83; as ethnic and social death, 84; disinheritance of, 83; history of 98n6, 100n45
Keller, O. C., 146
Kenya Missionary Council, 24, 27
Kenya Order-in-Council 1921, 107
Kenyatta, Jomo, 137; *Facing Mount Kenya*, 79
Kershaw, Greet, 120, 248
Kerugoya Medical Officer, 87
kiama, 56, 57. *See also* elders
Kiambu, 79, 95, 106
Kiambu District Commissioner, 91
Kiambu Local Native Council, 33, 91, 97, 106, 115, 133
kigwarie, 178
Kikuyu, 46, 52, 57, 60, 97, 114–15, 118–19, 121, 152, 184, 206; and clitoridectomy, 73, 74, 75, 79, 81, 83, 87, 90
Kikuyu Central Association (KCA), 90, 91
Kikuyu Hospital, 171
Kikuyu Progressive Party (KPP), 89
kinship, 17–18, 46, 68n35, 113, 114, 118, 134, 139, 195n72. *See also* clan; community; family
Kinwangika, Mr., 15, 16
Kinyanjui, Chief, 97, 106

kipkondit, 66
Kipsigis, 50, 59, 66, 79, 138, 148, 177, 178–82, 192
Kipsigis Local Native Council, 178, 181, 182
Kirinyaga, 119
Kirinyaga District, 65
kirore, 76
Kisii, 50–1, 109, 110, 148
Kisumu, 185–6
Kitui, 61, 93
Kitui District Commissioner, 47, 48
Koinange, Chief, 106
Kratz, C., 67n10
kugweto, 206
kumatia ndugu, 142
kumenyererwo muno, 215
Kyambu, 107
Kyambu Local Native Council, 190

Lady Grigg Maternity and Child Welfare Hospital and Training Centre, 164, 165
Lambert, H. E., 28, 43, 119, 121, 152
Lambert, R. W., 30, 92
land, 42–3, 52, 82, 89. *See also* property
law, 5, 24, 26, 35–6, 37–8; on adultery, 112; and agency, 21; capacity under, 17; and child pledging, 149; on clitoridectomy, 84–5, 88, 91, 92, 93–4, 97, 101n68, 102n95, 103n106; customary, 20, 23, 38, 53, 106, 141; different systems of, 24–5, 141; divorce, 53, 54–5, 112–13; dowry, 105–6, 107, 108–9, 117, 124n10, 127n79, 81, 128n101, on legal majority, 150–1; marriage, 112, 129–57, 134, 141, 145, 149; and prostitution, 186, 187; on widows, 150–1. *See also specific statutes*
Leseret, Ngeso Arap, 154, 155
Likimani (nee Gachanja), Muthoni, 141, 142, 215, 231–2
Lindblom, Gerhard, 152
Litein Mission, 179, 182
litigation, 34, 35, 56, 57–9, 106, 107, 116, 117, 118, 123, 129, 132. *See also* law; Native Tribunals
livestock, 42–3, 106, 115, 116, 119, 122, 127n89, 148, 153. *See also* property
Local Native Councils, 3, 84, 85, 92–3, 94, 108–9, 124n30, 131, 138, 144–5, 166–7, 188. *See also specific councils*
Local Tribunals, 108
Lonsdale, John, 80
Luo, 28–9, 52, 74, 137, 145, 173, 206–7
Lushington, Mr., 15, 16
Luyia, 52, 146. *See also* Abaluyia
Maasai, 70n58, 122–3, 127n81, 154–5, 177
MacGregor, A. D. A, 27
Machakos District Commissioner, 49
Madoda, Malome, 36, 37
mambere, 208. *See also* missions
Mamure, Toya, 35
M'Angaine, Councillor, 170
Mann, K., 9
marriage: age at, 32, 143, 144–6, 161n60, 203; agency in, 139, 140; alliance from, 82, 105, 106, 121, 141–3, 148; bigamous, 35, 39n40, 141, 159n26; and child pledging, 148–9, 150; Christian, 130, 131, 144, 157; civil, 66, 132, 134, 139, 140–1; and clitoridectomy, 82, 83, 88; and colonial authority, 16, 21–2, 29, 113, 129, 130–1, 136, 138–40, 154–5, 156–7; consent to, 31, 32, 33, 47, 66, 123, 136–44, 138, 139; customary, 21, 22, 29, 35, 36, 129, 139, 140, 141; desertion of, 27–8, 29, 31, 37, 53, 69n45, 107, 118, 122, 132, 134, 138, 149; and dowry, 31, 69n45, 105, 106, 107, 112, 113, 114, 117, 118, 126n77, 130, 138, 158n8; and education, 199, 200, 203, 208, 209, 211, 213–14, 222–3, 228–9; forced, 16, 33, 56, 112, 136–7, 139, 143–4, 146–7, 148, 149, 150, 203, 209; and friendship, 148; and individualism, 128n101, 142; and Islam, 21, 22, 30–2, 36, 130; legislation concerning, 129–57, 149; leviratic, 65–6, 72n102, 122, 150–1, 152, monogamous, 129, 131, 133–6; polygamous, 21, 61, 65, 113, 133–6, 141, 150, 151, 156–7; and pre-initiation conception, 177, 179; registration of, 117, 126n77, 129, 130–3, 134, 135–6, 138–9, 158nn3, 9, 159n15, 160n31. *See also* divorce
Marriage Ordinance, 1902, 35, 36
Masters and Servants Ordinance, 242
maternity/maternity care, 168–92. *See also* mother
Maua Methodist mission hospital, 173
Maua Mission Hospital, 168, 188
Maurice, Gatithi, 191
Mbeketha, Mzee Elijah, 7, 8
Mbui, Kahuthwa, 45, 46, 68n14
Mbuthia, John, 95, 114
McKendrick, Mr., 16
Medical Training School, Nairobi, 191
medicine, Western, 60, 61, 71n78, 85–6, 87, 88, 92, 93, 96, 97, 165, 168, 193n7. *See also* education, medical; hospitals; nurses
meko, 137–8

Meope, Opiri, 57, 58
Meru, 34, 63, 97, 118, 119, 133, 152, 177–8, 179, 187, 203, 214; and clitoridectomy, 73, 74, 75, 79, 81, 83, 177, 178, 192
Meru Custom and Law, 136
Meru hospitals, 170, 173
Meru Local Native Council, 85, 97, 115, 121, 133, 149, 169, 172, 190–1
Meru Medical Officer, 167
Meru Methodist Mission, 135–6
Methodist Church, 77–8, 99n20
Michuki, Chief, 126n77
midwife, 171, 180, 188–9, 190, 198, 200–1, 223–4
migrancy, 7, 20, 25, 60, 61, 183, 230
Miji Kenda, 30, 31, 32
Miller, Dr., 90
Minority: legal, 24, 26–7, 139, 151. *See also* guardians; ward/wardship
Miriam, 191–2
Misheni, 75, 81, 82, 179
missions, 7, 8, 9, 32, 89, 131, 140, 146, 214; brides from, 110, 111, 113; and civilization, 241–2; and civil marriage, 134; and clitoridectomy, 74, 75, 76–8, 81, 82, 83, 84, 85, 91–2, 96, 97, 99n16, 208; and dowry, 16, 105, 109–13, 125n32; education at, 33, 202–5; and food, 224–5; and forced marriages, 143–4; and Kavirondo *misheni,* 100n45; as liberating, 204; and maternity care, 166, 167, 193n7; practices forbidden by, 206, 208; and pre-initiation conception, 178–9, 180–1; and prostitution, 114, 209; as refuge, 16, 24, 33, 203, 204, 242–3; as restrictive, 29, 204; and social death, 205–8; and suitors, 110, 111, 125n32, 203, 209, 211; surveillance by, 209; and work, 214, 221
mobility, 3, 9, 19, 20, 25, 29, 33–4, 44, 131, 184, 232, 243–4
modernity, 2, 19, 83, 131, 168, 241, 243
Mohammedan Marriage Ordinance, 130
Mombasa Provincial Commisioner, 29
morality, 7, 28, 29, 65, 78, 92, 135, 165, 180, 184, 186, 187
mothers: and arranged marriage, 143; Christian, 205; and clitoridectomy, 82, 84, 85–6, 87; and divorce, 53; foster, 187–8; identity from, 200; permission from, 198, 201, 202; pre-initiation conception by, 176, 177, 181, 183; prostitutes as, 186–7; unwed, 64, 180; and womanhood, 200. *See also* maternity/maternity care; parents; pregnancy; procreation/reproduction
motiiri, 75, 76
Muchuchu, Job, 184
Mukabi (nee Kang'ethe), Serah, 118–19, 203–4, 208, 218–23, 227
Mukene, 63
Mukuthi, 44, 45–6, 47, 48, 68n14
Mulama, 35
Munano, James, 149
Mungu, Joseph, 184
Munyendo, Marciana, 213
Murang'a, 167, 191
Murang'a Hospital, 190
Murang'a Local Native Council, 149, 164–5, 167
Muriranja, 95
muruithia, 75
Musundi, Magdalene, 226, 228, 230
Muthambi, 81
Muthirigu, 83
muthungu, 206
Mwakio Asani son of Mwanguku Criminal Appeal No. 63, 34–5
Mwimbi, 81, 82

Nahashon, Gudo, 169
Nairobi, 33, 34, 37–8, 62, 165, 184, 186, 191
Nandi, 49–50, 79, 83, 114, 145
Nanyuki, 186
Native Christian Marriage and Divorce Act, 154
Native Christian Marriage and Divorce Ordinance, 150–1, 158n3
Native Civil Hospital, Chogoria Mission, 188
Native Law and Custom, 21, 120, 131, 132
Native Marriage and Divorce Bill, 138–9
Native Marriages Registration Bill, 118
Native Tribunals, 3, 92, 93, 107, 117, 149–50, 185
Native Women's Ordinance, 26
Ndamayu, Chief, 115
Ndundas, C., 111
Ndung'u, Hezekiah, 33
Ngashira, Rajab, 153, 209, 211, 213, 230
Nginyi, Kamwete wa, 107
Ngugi, Johana, Chief, 164
Njama, Kimani wa, 94
Njambi, Beth, 142, 154
Njegga, 45, 46, 47, 48, 68n14
Njogu, Mary Muthoni, 206, 208, 213, 228
Njoroge, Samson, 171
North Kavirondo, 60, 119, 123
North Kavirondo Local Native Council, 109, 127n89, 133
nullification, of marriage, 156
nurses, 188, 189, 191–2, 217. *See also*

medicine, Western
Nyambura, Liza, 215, 217
Nyanduga, Grace Joseph (Grace Ogot), 198–202, 203, 206, 209, 212, 213, 215
Nyang'ori Mission, 109
Nyanza, 51, 52, 54–5, 144, 145
Nyeri, 45, 46, 79, 94, 169, 186, 187, 188
Nyeri African District Council, 122, 187
Nyeri County Council, 190
Nyeri District African Council, 185
Nyeri Hospital, 169
Nyeri Local Native Council, 115, 148, 149, 164, 188
Nyona, Selina, 212, 227, 231
Nzungu, Chief, 108

Odanga, Chief, 120
Odhiambo, Atieno, 98n6, 207, 162n96
Odong'o, Daudi, 35, 36
Ogada Church Missionary Society, 146
Ogaye, Leya, 36, 37
Ogilo, George, 151
Ojal, Joel, 198
Ojiambo, Juliah, 210, 216, 217, 218
Okiek, 79
Oloo, Patricia, 231
Oluchina, Eliud Amatika, 161n59, 211
Ominde, Simeon H., 137, 147
omukoko, 52
Omurambi, Amos, 212
Ongoro, Oguta, 109
Opuko, J. Edward, 169
Orma, 31
Osano, Opiri, 57–8
Osundwa, Isaac Were, 113, 213, 225
Otoolo, Rose, 113–14
Owen, Archdeacon, 141

pai-ke, 66
parents: and change to monogamous marriage, 134; and clitoridectomy, 91, 93; consent of, 136, 139, 148; daughter *vs.* son's care of, 213; and dowry, 113, 114, 120; and education, 198–200, 201–2, 203–4, 206, 212, 216, 217, 231, 242; and marriage registration, 130. *See also* fathers; mothers
pawning, of children, 44–50, 51, 148, 150
Pedersen, Susan, 80
peers, 79, 206, 207
Peristiany, J. G., 59–60, 65, 138, 177, 185, 194n57
permission: *See* consent
Petero, Chief, 188
pim, 207, 208
pledging of children (girls): *See* marriage
politics, 85, 89, 90
polygamy, 21, 61, 65, 113, 141, 147, 150, 151, 156–7. *See also* marriage
poverty, 50, 115
pregnancy, 55, 64, 91, 167, 168, 192. *See also* maternity/maternity care; mother; procreation/reproduction
prenatal care, 167, 169
procreation/reproduction, 80, 83, 86, 144, 186. *See also* maternity/maternity care; mother; pregnancy
property, 16, 24, 31, 32, 36, 42–3, 47, 48, 65, 66, 116, 152–3, 163n105. *See also* dowry; land; livestock
prostitution, 7, 33, 37–8, 114, 115, 152, 155, 165, 176, 183, 184, 185–6, 209, 243
Protestants/Protestantism, 76, 77, 81, 84, 99n16, 217
Pumwani Maternity Home, 164, 165
punishment, 55, 56, 57, 64, 65, 93–4, 101n68, 102n95, 103n106, 141

Ranger, Terence, 38, 13n8
rape, 55–9, 57, 59–62, 70n66, 145
Registration of Pagan Marriages Ordinance, 130
remarriage, 52, 54, 65, 66
Reuben, Chief, 122
Rex v. Amkeyo, 35
Rex v. Opiri Meope and Opiri Osano, 57–8
Rex v. Robin, 34, 35
Rex v. Toya son of Mamure, 34, 35
Riara Mission, 215
Rift Valley, 92
Rift Valley Provincial Commisioner, 177
Roberts, Richard, 9
Robertson, C., 13n12
Ross, Dr., 144
runaway, 6, 16, 45, 47. *See also* marriage, desertion of
rural population, 169, 175, 184, 186, 230

Sabwa, Simon Lizanga, 210
Salvation Army, 158n3
Sandford, Dr., 172
Sangai, Obedi, 3
Sandgren, D. P., 1, 125n58
Sarai, Sara, 171, 172, 204, 214, 217, 223
seduction, 34
sex, 62–6, 71n95, 80, 145
sexuality, 44, 55, 85, 89, 92, 207, 232
sexually transmitted diseases, 58–62, 176, 183
Sharia, 32
shenzies, 111

Sheridan, Joseph, 57, 58
shuka, 8
siwindhe, 207
social death/ostracism, 74, 81, 83, 177, 181, 183, 185, 205–8, 219
society, 2, 5, 82, 84, 198, 206. *See also* community
soothsayer, 223
South Nyeri, 93, 96, 120
South Nyeri Local Native Council, 127n89, 149
spinsterhood, 52, 56
suitor, 55, 56, 108, 109, 110, 111, 115–16, 120, 121, 125n32, 203, 209, 211. *See also* marriage
surveillance, 3, 34, 49, 94, 95, 129, 165, 181, 182, 189, 192, 209, 212
Swahili, 60

Taita, 96
teachers, 217, 230, 232
Teachers Training College, 232
Tenwek Mission, 182
Terik, 79
thaka, 63
theft, 48, 108
Thika Town, 34
Thion'go, Ngugi wa, *The River Between,* 216
Thogoto, 210
Thogoto mission, 118–19, 204
Thomas, Lynn, 177–8
Thuo, Kimani wa, 174–5
Tiriki, 66, 146–7
Tooth, Lawrence, 25
travel, 6–10, 184, 192, 241, 243–4
Tumutumu Hospital, 169
Tumutumu Mission, 206
Turkana, 50

urban population/centre, 7, 29, 36, 61, 118, 165, 184

wage-labor, employment, 19, 26, 108
Wakalo, David, 189
Wali, 38
Wambui, Mary, 83
Wandura, Monica Wanjiku, 8, 209, 210
Wanga, 52, 54, 146
Wanga, Hamis Makapia, 210, 211
Wanjie, Joseph, 165
Wanjiru, Mary, 8, 151, 209
Wanjiru, Milcah, 138, 147
Wanzetse, Ham Aggrey, 146, 228
ward/wardship, 4, 9, 17, 147, 150. *See also* guardians; minority
Warigia, Rachel, 229–30
Watu wa Mungu sect, 82
Weithaga Church of Scotland Mission, 90
White, Luise, 37, 186, 243
widows, 32, 65, 66, 122, 150–5, 162n99, 163n105
wife, 17, 18, 21, 31, 34, 35, 48, 82, 84, 116, 134, 172, 203, 205. *See also* bride; marriage; widow
wife inheritance: *See* marriage, leviratic
Wimbe, 93
womanhood, 17, 76, 79, 84, 97, 98, 200. *See also* identity
women: agency of, 17, 23, 25, 41n76, 42, 139, 140, 244–5; complex identity of, 18; guardians of, 21, 26, 43; and husband's home, 210; inheritance rights of, 129; and labour, 19, 26, 192; legal age of, 19, 20, 24, 25, 26–7, 139; legal status of, 5, 24, 25, 33, 34, 36, 150–1, 191; minority of, 24, 26–7, 139, 151; mobility of, 9, 25, 29, 33–4, 44, 232, 243–4; personal view of, 51, 55, 56; as property, 16, 23, 24, 36, 43, 47, 48, 116, 122; property of, 31, 32, 48; representations of, 9–10; and ritual uncleanliness, 61; and social connections, 83, 97–8; as source of vice and health, 59; subordination of, 17, 23, 43, 89, 90, 121; travel by, 6–10, 184, 192; voice in marriage, 131; wage of, 19, 26; as wards, 4, 17. *See also* daughter; maternity/maternity care; mother; widow; wife
work/labour, 7, 15–16, 19, 26, 28, 84, 105, 108, 116, 119, 192, 214, 221–2, 227–8
wuowo, 207

youth, 7, 96, 109, 115–16, 120, 121